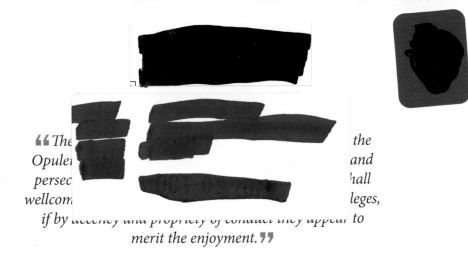

The ... **the**
Opule... **and**
persec... 'all
wellcom... leges,
if by decency and propriety of conduct they appear to merit the enjoyment. 🙶

– GEORGE WASHINGTON, letter to an association of
Irish American immigrants, 1783

❖

🙶 *It is said that the quality of recent immigration is undesirable. The time is quite within recent memory when the same thing was said of immigrants who, with their descendants, are now numbered among our best citizens.* 🙶

– GROVER CLEVELAND, veto message to
proposed literacy test to restrict immigration, 1897

❖

🙶 *I've spoken of the shining city all my political life, but I don't know if I ever quite communicated what I saw when I said it. But in my mind it was a tall, proud city built on rocks stronger than oceans, windswept, God-blessed, and teeming with people of all kinds living in harmony and peace; a city with free ports that hummed with commerce and creativity. And if there had to be city walls, the walls had doors and the doors were open to anyone with the will and the heart to get here.* 🙶

– RONALD REAGAN, farewell address, 1989

IMMIGRANT Struggles, IMMIGRANT Gifts

Edited by Diane Portnoy,
Barry Portnoy, and Charlie Riggs

For The Immigrant Learning Center, Inc.

CONTRIBUTORS

Wayne A. Cornelius

Nancy Foner

Anna Gressel-Bacharan

David W. Haines

Luciano J. Iorizzo

Alexander Kitroeff

Erika Lee

Deborah Dash Moore

David M. Reimers

William G. Ross

Robert M. Zecker

GMU PRESS

Immigrant Struggles, Immigrant Gifts
Edited by Diane Portnoy, Barry Portnoy, and Charlie Riggs
For The Immigrant Learning Center, Inc.

Essays by Wayne A. Cornelius, Nancy Foner, Anna Gressel-Bacharan,
David W. Haines, Luciano J. Iorizzo, Alexander Kitroeff, Erika Lee,
Deborah Dash Moore, David M. Reimers, William G. Ross,
and Robert M. Zecker

©2012, GMU Press
All rights reserved

Published by GMU Press
Fairfax, Virginia

Designed by Spectrum Creative, LLC
Fairfax, Virginia

Copyediting support by Aden Nichols
Little Fire Editorial Services

Library of Congress Control Number: 2012946711
ISBN 978-0-9818779-0-7

Printed and manufactured in the United States of America

First Printing

This book is dedicated to Simon and Sylvia Katz
(the parents of Diane Portnoy, founder and CEO
of The Immigrant Learning Center)
and to all immigrants to the United States,
past and future, whose courage, work ethic,
and ambitions for themselves and their children
will continue to create a better America.

———◈———

FOREWORD

THE IMMIGRANT LEARNING CENTER ("THE ILC"), located in Malden, Massachusetts, was founded in 1992 as a not-for-profit adult learning center to provide free, intensive English classes to immigrant and refugee adults. The mission is to give these people enough knowledge of English to lead productive lives in this country and to become successful workers, parents, and community members. The school opened with three teachers, sixty students, and a waiting list of eighty. Today, the school is fully enrolled with 400 students and a waiting list of 750. Since opening, over 7,000 immigrants from 109 countries have learned English. Most report that they have achieved their goals of finding jobs; starting businesses; entering training programs; going to colleges; becoming citizens; and successfully navigating our complex health, education, and economic systems. Their children are doing well in school, and most go to college.

I personally understand that learning English is one of the most important steps immigrants can take in creating new lives in this country. My parents were Polish Jews who survived the Holocaust but lost their entire families. A year after World War II ended, I was born in what was then East Germany. When I was three and a half, my family escaped from East to West Germany and then immigrated to America through Ellis Island. We were given three of the 415,000 visas the United States issued to displaced persons after the war. We crossed the Atlantic on a converted battleship with men on one side and women and children on the other. I was so sick that my mother and I were quarantined for over a week at the Ellis Island Hospital when we landed.

Shortly thereafter, we settled in Malden, Massachusetts, where my father got a job in a factory. We lived in a community made up entirely of immigrants, mostly Holocaust survivors who had lost spouses and children and who were now remarried and starting new lives. Their strength, bravery, resilience, hard work, and capacity for risk can only be admired. Most of my parents' friends, including my own parents, eventually opened their own businesses and created successful lives. All their children went to college and became professionals.

None of my family spoke English when we arrived. I went to public school and learned English quickly. However, for my parents and their friends, learning English was a major struggle. For years, I translated for them. There were no free schools, and no one could afford to pay for English classes. The students at The ILC, although from different countries and circumstances, are no different in their aspirations from my parents and their friends. They have the same motivation to succeed and the same deep appreciation for this country. For many, being in the United States is the first time in their lives that they experience security, freedom, and hope.

Every year, The ILC hosts a citizenship swearing-in ceremony. As these immigrants take the oath, holding a small American flag in one hand, the other hand over their hearts as they pledge allegiance to the flag and tears stream from their eyes, I am reminded of when I accompanied my parents at the age of eight as they were sworn in as American citizens. It was no different.

After 9/11, some of our students were afraid to come to school because strangers would yell terrible things at them—that they were unwelcome and should return to their native countries. Suddenly, people who weren't aware of the work I do began telling me that immigrants were the main problem with our country. On the radio and television, in newspapers and magazines, immigrants were portrayed as job stealers or welfare abusers who brought disease into the country, failed to learn English, and resisted integration into American society. I couldn't help but remember when my own parents were told that it was too bad Hitler had not killed all the Jews and that America had made a terrible mistake in permitting all these immigrants into the country. I saw how such slurs had affected my parents, but I also knew they and their friends had made meaningful contributions to this country and its economy.

In response to the post 9/11 anti-immigrant furor, The ILC expanded its mission by creating a Public Education Institute to educate the public about the positive impact immigrants have on this country, its economy, and its local communities. Of course, I was told that a small not-for-profit in Malden, Massachusetts, could not successfully take on such a national issue. But we were determined to try. We have commissioned and publicized ten university-based research studies that examine immigrants as entrepreneurs, workers, and consumers in various business sectors in Massachusetts and New England. Each study clearly shows that immigrants are a major positive force in the economy. These and other professional research studies show that immigrants and a liberal immigration policy are needed if the United States is to remain the world's foremost economic power in the twenty-first century.

The ILC Public Education Institute also hosts online teacher forums on teaching immigration across the curriculum to reach educators throughout the country. Recently, The ILC partnered with George Mason University to create an Institute for Immigration Research that will research the economic impact of immigrants nationally and publicize its research results. I am confident these national studies will show the same positive results that The ILC-commissioned studies have found in our region.

Every time I passionately responded to another outrage directed at a student or a distortion about immigrants in the media, my husband, Barry Portnoy, would mention a similar incident in history that some immigrant group experienced. There was the anti-Catholic and anti-Irish Know Nothing Party, the murder of striking European coal miners at Lattimer, Pennsylvania, the Chinese Exclusion Act, the South Omaha riot where so many Greek immigrants were killed, the refugee boats filled with displaced Arcadians in the colonial period or Jews released from Nazi concentration camps or modern-day Haitians and Cubans who were not permitted to land, and so on. It was during one of these conversations that we decided to write this book to add some historical context to the current dialogue about immigration.

In so many ways, nothing has changed. Immigrants continue to struggle, and immigrants continue to make major gifts to this country. From the very famous who serve in high political office or who found new enterprises employing thousands, to those small entrepreneurs who revitalize depressed neighborhoods with ethnic groceries or restaurants, this book shows that each wave of immigrants—regardless of their native country, religion, ethnicity, or skin color—have experienced what immigrants today are experiencing but have gone on to make major contributions to this country.

I hope this book helps to place current immigration issues in historical context and to persuade readers that today's immigrants are every bit as likely as yesterday's to make significant contributions to American life.

Thank you to my husband Barry, Charlie Riggs, and all the authors for making this book a reality.

September 10, 2012

Diane Portnoy
Founder, President and CEO
The Immigrant Learning Center, Inc.

For more information about The Immigrant Learning Center and its Public Education Institute, visit its website at www.ilctr.org or write to The Immigrant Learning Center, Inc. at 442 Main Street, Malden, MA 02148.

TABLE OF CONTENTS

Immigrants viewing the Statue of Liberty from Ellis Island

IMMIGRANT STRUGGLES

By Charlie Riggs

A LL AMERICAN HISTORY IS THE HISTORY OF IMMIGRANTS. At the remove of several generations from the immigration experience of their ancestors, many Americans seem to have forgotten this essential fact. But it holds true for all inhabitants of the United States, from those who arrived last year, to the grandchildren of turn of the century steerage passengers, to those who trace their descent to seventeenth-century English colonists, and arguably even to Native Americans, whose ancestors crossed the Bering Strait from Asia. All are bound together by a common—though by no means identical—migration experience.

This truth may seem banal, like saying that all human beings are bound together by the experience of childbirth, but it poses a special problem for those who seek to write the history of immigration and American life. The pervasiveness of immigration and ethnicity in America, as many students of both topics have discovered, makes them extremely difficult to address comprehensively. Oscar Handlin, one of the fathers of US immigration history, named the problem exactly in 1951: "Once I thought to write a history of the immigrants in America. Then I discovered that the immigrants *were* American history."[1]

One strategy (and the one used by Handlin, as well as by the contributors to this volume) is to avoid even trying to write such a comprehensive account; the chapters in this book do not form anything like a complete history of American immigration. At most, they are a set of revealing and suggestive snapshots of a much larger and more complicated drama. They suggest elements of a story that has been repeated time and again, with variations, for different immigrant groups and across different periods of American history. This story includes not just immigrants themselves, but also restrictionists and nativists: those who would have excluded the immigrants from entering and who resented their presence after they arrived. It is a story of striving against adversity, of achievement despite intolerance.

Each of the chapters in this book deals with the history of a particular immigrant group in the United States. The chapters—written by historians, sociologists, and anthropologists—all begin with a striking historical episode of nativism directed against a particular group of American immigrants. These incidents serve as departure points into the longer term histories of the targeted groups themselves, including their main reasons for migration, their obstacles to advancement and inclusion, their culture and occupational patterns in the United States, their assimilation and acculturation, and their accomplishments and contributions to American life.

Some of these histories will strike a contemporary resonance. Some deal with groups that still produce large numbers of American immigrants whose stories have yet to fully run their course. Other chapters concern older groups whose histories nevertheless contain suggestive parallels to the present. All of the essays collected here attempt to weigh the actual lived experiences of American newcomers against the nastiest things said about them in the times when they were considered least welcome.

By thus opposing the manifold accomplishments of American immigrants to the rantings of American nativists, this volume underlines a recurring pattern in the nation's immigration history: groups that were once stigmatized and thought to be inassimilable have contributed mightily to economic and social prosperity and over time won a secure place for themselves and their children in the American mainstream. Ironically, some immigrants have adjusted so well as to become themselves intolerant of foreigners or different racial groups. This pattern of triumph over prejudice, and its persistence among those it once targeted, is one of the more tragic and perennial themes of American immigration history.

The approach of this book is admittedly episodic. The groups covered in its pages do not necessarily represent the most important or even the most representative populations of American immigrants. No attempt has been made to set forth comprehensive theories of migration, pioneering scholarship, or watertight categories for the immigrant groups. A brief look at the table of contents will surely disappoint anyone seeking a consistent organizational framework for understanding the whole of American immigration history: some of the immigrants considered here are grouped by ethnicity (Italians, Greeks), others by geography (east Europeans), and still others by religion (Muslims, Jews). Some are racial *and* geographic (black West Indians), and some are defined by their political status (refugees). Rather than dwelling on the most appropriate taxonomies, the aim of this collection of essays is to pick out significant threads—especially those regarding nativism and immigrant achievement—across different groups and over a long period of time.

Although all of the chapters in this book deal with groups that relocated to the United States principally after the American Revolution, debates over immigration extend back to the colonial period. Intolerance, distrust, and maltreatment of newcomers were defining marks of life in the British colonies of North America from the beginning, whether in the rigid Puritanism of New England or the chattel slavery of the plantation South. The culture and social arrangements of the mostly Protestant, farming, Anglo American settlers of the seventeenth century had an incalculable influence upon later generations, forming the template to which all subsequent immigrant groups were made to assimilate and acculturate, for better or for worse.

On the other hand, the uneven development of the colonies and Britain's often flexible governance of its New World territories also led to a strain of religious and ethnic pluralism. The coastal regions north and south of New York City and along the Hudson River Valley, originally controlled by the Dutch, cultivated a tradition of ethnic diversity and religious liberty that persisted after the British assumed control of the region in the 1660s and 1670s. Pennsylvania became an even more radical model of ethnic and religious toleration upon its founding in 1682. Although William Penn originally designed the colony to accommodate his fellow Quakers, he also extended a more general ecumenical welcome and the region became a premier destination for disparate groups of Scotch Irish, Germans, French Huguenots, and others.

The revolutionary generation wrote extensively about immigration. In keeping with the prevailing mercantilism of eighteenth-century political elites, population growth was seen by many of the Founding Fathers as a key to political power and economic prosperity. Some colonists complained of the British government's willingness to settle Roman Catholics, convicts, and indentured servants in the New World. But the generally restrictive immigration policies of the British colonial government were a major grievance in the period leading up to the Revolution. The Declaration of Independence complained that King George III "endeavored to prevent the Population of these States; for that purpose, obstructing the Laws for Naturalization of foreigners, [and] refusing to pass others to encourage their migration hither."

The Founders also supported immigration on moral grounds. George Washington told a group of Irish immigrants in 1784 that "the bosom of America is open to receive not only the Opulent and respectable Stranger, but the oppressed and persecuted of all Nations And Religions."[2] At a time of political crisis and economic turmoil in much of Europe, the new nation of the United States was widely seen as a sanctuary for the oppressed and downtrodden of the world. It was a view bolstered by the civic republican principles cherished by the Founders and many late eighteenth-century Americans. Thomas Paine, himself an immigrant from England, reflected a common view in his widely read 1776 pamphlet *Common Sense*:

> Every spot of the Old World is overrun with oppression. Freedom hath been hunted round the globe. Asia and Africa have long expelled her. Europe regards her like a stranger and England hath given her warning to depart. O! receive the fugitive and prepare in time an asylum for mankind.[3]

After the outbreak of the Revolution, republicanism became the main marker of American citizenship rather than ethnic status (except for blacks and American Indians).

In practice, the "asylum for mankind" was slightly less than advertised. Article One of the United States Constitution empowered Congress to "establish a uniform Rule of Naturalization," which it did in 1790. The resulting Naturalization Act reflected the widespread prejudices of the times, only allowing "white persons" of "good moral character" to become citizens, and thus excluding slaves, free blacks, and indentured servants. In 1798, fears of war and French radicalism led John Adams's Federalist Party to pass the Alien and Sedition Acts, which empowered the president to deport politically hostile aliens. The laws, mostly targeted at Adams's domestic political opponents, led to very few deportations, caused a political backlash against the Federalists, and fell into disuse during Thomas Jefferson's administration.

In general, the early years of the American republic were hospitable towards immigrants. President John Tyler spoke for a broad pro-immigrant consensus when he delivered an annual message to Congress in 1841: "We hold out to the people of other countries an invitation to come and settle among us as members of our rapidly growing family."[4] In a sparsely populated and economically expanding country, immigrants were needed to settle the land, furnish capital and technical skills, and build basic infrastructure networks. Their numbers were still relatively small—in the first fifty years of the country's existence, only about one million people (predominantly English, Scotch Irish, German, and increasingly Catholic Irish) came to America.

The federal government left immigration largely unregulated. An 1808 statute banned the international slave trade, and an 1819 law required ship manifests to record immigration statistics. Otherwise, immigration policy was left to the coastal states. An immigrant ship would simply land at port, hand over its manifest to the customs agent, and allow its passengers to disembark. When states did bother with immigration, it was usually to boost their populations by offering bounties to entice immigrants. Only in 1849 did the Supreme Court rule (in the *Passenger Cases*) that the federal government was responsible for immigration policy. Even so, states continued to process the immigrants and to handle many other functions.

By then, a full sixty years after the founding of the nation, the pro-immigrant consensus had began to fracture. For example, the Massachusetts and New York statutes invalidated by the *Passenger Cases* had levied a head tax on all incoming immigrants to those states. Especially in the northeast, where Catholic Irish and German immigrants had been arriving in ever-greater numbers since the 1830s, state and local governments began to register the first stirrings of a popular anti-immigrant movement. Anti-Catholic riots broke out in Boston and Philadelphia. Several local anti-immigrant parties sprang up throughout northeastern cities, and in 1845 the Native American Party held its first national convention.

Although immigrants were often marked by natives for the less savory aspects of their lifestyles and their contribution to urban overcrowding, they very quickly assumed a vital economic function. Irish labor helped dig mines, build city infrastructures, and dredge the network of canals connecting the cities of the eastern seaboard to the Great Lakes region. German and Scandinavian immigrants settled throughout the Midwest, where they populated the growing cities of the region and imported farming techniques that helped revolutionize American agriculture (their experiences are treated in chapters by Anna Gressel-Bacharan and William G. Ross, respectively.)

Antebellum nativism reached its zenith during the 1850s and the extent of its success was something of a fluke. The "Know Nothing" movement—so called because its members were pledged to profess ignorance about the group's activities—emerged virtually overnight to capture several state legislatures and governorships in 1854 and 1855. Know Nothing candidates backed measures like lengthening the naturalization period, denying funds to Catholic schools, barring foreigners from elected office, and banning the sale of liquor (which was seen as an immigrant vice). The movement sprang not only from the anti-Catholic prejudices of many northeastern Protestants but also from the collapse of the Whig Party over the slavery issue and the growing sectional crisis. Slavery proved to be the Know Nothings' downfall as well, and the movement dissolved into electoral oblivion before its leaders had time to enact serious anti-immigrant measures in the states where they gained power.

When the Civil War erupted, immigration faded from the national political agenda as enmity between the sections eclipsed animosity between ethnic groups. In fact, the military service of hundreds of thousands of immigrants in both armies encouraged the acceptance of German and Irish immigrants as loyal Americans. The Northern Congress offered citizenship to immigrants who agreed to fight for the Union and also adopted a contract labor law in 1864 to meet wartime labor shortages.

The pro-immigrant mood continued through the boom years of the late 1860s and early 1870s. Railroads, steamship companies, and state governments all actively recruited foreigners to meet the voracious labor needs of an expanding industrial economy and its transcontinental railway network. States in the Midwest (intent on growing their populations), the South (eager to replace emancipated slaves), and the Southwest (determined to create a solid European base to balance the region's large Mexican presence) were particularly active in courting immigration. Michigan handed out free land, South Carolina offered immigrants a five-year tax exemption on real estate purchases, and Texas sent agents abroad to promote the state for European settlement.[5] A reasonably warm reception greeted the large numbers of German, British, Irish, Scandinavian, and French Canadian immigrants arriving during those years.

The same could not be said of the Chinese. Since the accession of California in the Mexican American War and the discovery of gold there in 1849, the West Coast had become the premier American destination for Chinese immigrants, largely comprising temporary laborers from Southern China. As their numbers grew in the following decades, the Chinese faced discrimination and violence from California's white and largely Irish American working-class population. The growing clamor in the West led Congress to enact the first major restrictive immigration law in American history, the Chinese Exclusion Act of 1882.

The designers of Chinese Exclusion—which barred entry to all Chinese, with exceptions for diplomats and merchants—argued that their actions would affect only one narrow group. In retrospect, that law was the first in a line of increasingly comprehensive measures over the next forty years. Just months after its passage, Congress enacted another, more general statute levying a head tax on all immigrants, barring the entry of those "likely to become a public charge" and creating a national immigration bureaucracy under the control of the Treasury Department. This small administrative agency, which was chronically thwarted by the deceptions and smuggling activities of undocumented Chinese immigrants, soon became a major institutional voice calling for new and tighter restrictions.

By then, American immigration was entering a new phase, its volume swelling and its composition changing dramatically. Starting in the 1880s, growing numbers of southern and eastern European immigrants, as well as those from East Asia, the Middle East, and the Caribbean, could be found alongside the continued waves of Irish, Germans, French Canadians, and Scandinavians. The falling cost of steamship travel, the attractive effect of remittances accompanied by colorful (and highly exaggerated) letters, and numerous European demographic crises initiated a wave of "America fever" in Italy, Greece, and parts of the Russian and Austro-Hungarian Empires. The early waves of the "new immigration" were heavily male and essentially formed the western frontier of a transatlantic industrial labor market.

Because the "new" immigrants often toiled at the margins of American life—as peddlers, domestics, factory workers, miners, and itinerant laborers—they sometimes escaped the notice of the general public. However, they quickly became the targets both of social reformers, who worried about their effects on overcrowded cities, and of working folk, who feared they would depress native wages. Mounting social unrest and incidents such as the Great Railroad Strike of 1877 and the Haymarket riots of 1886 focused a more widespread public anxiety on the "immigrant menace."

At first, the darkening mood on immigration led to no meaningful restriction. An 1891 law confirmed existing trends: centralizing the immigration administration and excluding further "undesirable" groups, such as convicted felons, paupers, lunatics, polygamists, etc. But the aim of federal policy was still to process and facilitate the entry of immigrants rather than to keep them out. The old immigrant depot at Castle Garden, administered by the State of New York, was replaced by a new federal facility at Ellis Island in New York Harbor in 1892. Over the next three decades, some twelve million immigrants would arrive in America through Ellis Island.

Before the late nineteenth century, American nativism had been a mostly popular phenomenon, finding its support among the likes of Know Nothing rowdies, railroad workers, and the urban petit-bourgeoisie, but in the 1890s it also became the province of elites. The growing disquiet in American labor markets sent ripples of concern through the ranks of businessmen and capitalists, who now worried about the radicalizing effects of foreign labor. Even more important, Anglo-Saxon racial ideas came into vogue among a highly influential class of patrician intellectuals. Drawing in equal parts from romantic myth and racial pseudoscience, racial thinkers like Prescott Hall and Madison Grant painted the dangers posed by an influx of "genetically inferior" eastern and southern Europeans to America's "great race" of Anglo-Saxons. In 1894, a group of Boston lawyers and intellectuals helped to found the Immigration Restriction League, which became the country's most effective exponent of racial thinking and its most powerful anti-immigrant lobbying group.

It was out of this noxious world of genteel bigotry that the first serious efforts emerged to staunch the flow of immigrants. The Immigration Restriction League championed numerical limits on immigration as well as increased head taxes, but its *cause célèbre* was a literacy requirement for prospective immigrants. Designed to exclude the poorest immigrants (particularly those from southern and eastern Europe), the literacy test passed Congress four times under the stewardship of Massachusetts Senator Henry Cabot Lodge, the public face of the League. Each time, it was vetoed—by President Cleveland in 1897, by President Taft in 1911, by President Wilson in 1915, and by Wilson again in 1917. The final time, Congress overrode Wilson's veto, and the literacy test became law.

In the intervening years, the anti-immigrant movement had gathered considerable momentum in the halls of power and in American society at large. Progressive reformers took a dim view of the immigrant presence in cities and urban political machines. President McKinley's assassination by a native born American with a foreign-sounding name (Leon Czolgosz) prompted Congress to outlaw the entry of anarchists in 1903. Anti-Japanese sentiment in California threatened to lead to another racist exclusion

IMMIGRANT STRUGGLES, IMMIGRANT GIFTS

After the Civil War, railroads, steamship companies, and many state governments actively recruited immigrants.

similar to the 1882 law directed against the Chinese. In the last case, however, Japan's status as a military power demanded more delicate measures. The so-called "Gentlemen's Agreement," concluded in 1907 between Japan and Theodore Roosevelt's administration, was designed to end Japanese immigration without humiliating the Japanese Empire itself. In return for America's restraint in not legislating "Japanese Exclusion," the Japanese government agreed to deny visas to those seeking to travel to the United States.

Throughout the period of high immigration around the turn of the century, whiteness conferred a significant advantage to those immigrants who could plausibly claim it, as compared to the Chinese, Japanese, Filipino, Caribbean, and other non-European immigrants who clearly dwelt on the other side of the color line. Nevertheless, the racially charged landscape of the early twentieth century—promoted in part by the problematic status of emancipated slaves—led to a heightened consciousness of alien "races" like Slavs, Italians, Celts, and Jews. Even as many of these groups enjoyed the legal advantages of whiteness, culturally and economically they occupied a murkier, "in between" status.[6] Erika Lee's chapter on Chinese immigrants and Nancy Foner's essay on black West Indians discuss the continuing role of race and the color line in American immigration and ethnicity.

Immigrants continued to arrive in the United States in huge numbers during the turn of the century period. Though many settled in the ethnic enclaves of large cities, they also dispersed to almost every part of the country. Some were sojourners who crossed back and forth many times before deciding to put down roots or return to their native countries. The immigrants performed work in every variety of occupation: on railroad gangs, in steel mills, on construction crews, in coal mines. Some immigrants became entrepreneurs, starting dry goods stores, diners, shoeshine stands, and innumerable other small businesses. Some founded larger concerns that persist to the present day.

With varying degrees of solidarity, immigrants built institutions and subcultures that nurtured their own inside the United States. These ranged from mutual benefit societies to churches to labor unions to urban political machines. The rich organizational life of turn of the century immigrants comes through especially well in the chapters on Italians (by Luciano J. Iorizzo), east Europeans (by Robert M. Zecker), Greeks (by Alexander Kitroeff), and Jews (by Deborah Dash Moore).

Immigration, then as now, produced strange political alliances. Progressive reformers and labor unions found themselves working with xenophobic nationalists for restriction while business leaders teamed with liberal humanitarians and immigrant rights groups to preserve the status quo. Nevertheless, a new consensus was slowly taking shape in Congress for a major restriction, particularly to halt the continuing influx of southern and eastern European immigrants and the smaller numbers of Asian newcomers.

In 1911, a special congressional commission chaired by Senator William Dillingham of Vermont produced a forty-two volume report that drew sharp distinctions between the permanent, industrious, easily assimilated, and in all other ways benign immigrants of the past and the supposedly transitory, degraded, and alien newcomers who had shown up since approximately 1880. The Dillingham Commission advised Congress to adopt a number of measures to limit the "new immigration," including the literacy test, an increased head tax, the exclusion of unaccompanied males, and in what would soon become the cornerstone of American immigration policy, annual quotas assigned to each European country.[7]

Congressional inaction and presidential vetoes blocked such measures from becoming law immediately, but the pressure for restriction mounted as the United States entered the First World War and much of the country embraced an aggressive, xenophobic nationalism. The "100 percent American" movement cast dark suspicions on the loyalty of German American immigrants, denounced all manner of other "hyphenated Americans," and enforced a vigilant and intense patriotism. The wartime Congress adopted several immigration measures, including the much debated literacy test (which after so much acrimony proved to be ineffectual, due to rising literacy rates in Europe) and a barred immigration zone directed mostly at newcomers from India (the so-called "Asia Pacific Triangle").

Whereas the Civil War had burnished the image of the foreign born and provided an opportunity for many immigrants to demonstrate their loyalty to the United States, World War I left a feeling of suspicion and intolerance in its wake. In the context of rising unemployment caused in part by the shutdown of war industries, a nationwide steel strike, and the unexpected success of the Bolshevik Revolution of 1917, wartime patriotic energies turned quickly against foreign-born radicals—real and imagined—in America's midst. Thousands were arrested and hundreds deported in the Palmer Raids of 1919–1920. In the face of this scrutiny, large numbers of immigrants rushed to prove their loyalty by becoming naturalized citizens.

Immigration had fallen off sharply during the war years, and when it resumed in the early 1920s, the American public was in no mood to receive it as before. Even among the former champions of immigration, the main policy question was now not whether to enact limits but rather how sharp they should be and what form they should take. Severe restrictionists, led by Albert Johnson in the House of Representatives, favored an immediate suspension of all immigration until new rules could be designed. In 1921, the more moderate Senate prevailed in passing a bill that set a hard, low numerical cap and quotas for European immigrant groups. The quotas were based on the percentages of foreign-born residents in the United States reported in the 1910 census.

The 1921 law, signed by the new Republican president Warren Harding, was the most restrictive American immigration law to date, but it was merely a stopgap measure. When Congress passed a more permanent law in 1924, it reduced the annual cap even further and based its quotas on the 1890 census so that fewer southern and eastern Europeans would find available spots. A panel of experts was put in place to determine—with pseudoscientific accuracy—the "national origins" of the American people, on which the allotment of future quotas was based. This panel, which issued its conclusions in 1928, confirmed the bias against southern and eastern Europeans. Immigrants from the Western Hemisphere, in particular the Mexican laborers then becoming vital to agriculture in the western states, were exempted from the quotas, as were some immigrants who would be admitted as family members. Despite the prior existence of Chinese Exclusion and the Japanese Gentleman's Agreement, the 1924 Act placed an outright ban on all "aliens ineligible to citizenship" in what became known as "Oriental exclusion."

The Reed Johnson Act of 1924 defined American immigration policy for the next forty years, but it did not fully meet the expectations of its framers. A considerable flow of immigration continued throughout the 1920s. Migrant workers from Canada, Mexico, and Puerto Rico filled labor shortages caused by the reduced flow from Europe. Smaller but not insubstantial numbers of southern and eastern Europeans (9,000 Poles and 22,000 Italians in 1930, for example) entered mostly as non-quota immigrants, many employing the new preferences for family members.[8] One immediate and unforeseen impact of the law was to sharply reduce return migration, effectively freezing what had been circular migration patterns.

The Great Depression was much more potent than any legal barrier in reducing immigration. The dire economic situation in the United States diminished the "pull" that had drawn immigrants across the oceans and borders for generations; on the contrary, substantial numbers of people left the country during these years, so that migration to and from the United States was essentially equal. Some 500,000 Mexican immigrants, including many naturalized American citizens, were deported or otherwise pressured to return to Mexico by "repatriation" campaigns undertaken at all levels of government. Meanwhile, the Roosevelt administration did very little to aid asylum-seeking Jewish exiles from Hitler's Germany.

Even as most of the population was buffeted by economic hardship during the Depression, the 1930s proved to be an important time of assimilation and acculturation for many of the groups that had arrived in the early twentieth century. The growing labor movement and the housing reforms of the New Deal allowed many white ethnics to cling to a modest prosperity during the lean Depression years and beyond. The internal migration of African Americans from the South to the Northeast and Midwest also meant that previously marginal groups of first- and second-generation immigrants were now brought unambiguously into the white fold.[9]

The Second World War had a mixed effect on American immigration policy. On the one hand, in one of the worst civil liberties violations in the nation's history, it led to the internment of over 100,000 Japanese Americans in the wake of Japan's attack on Pearl Harbor. On the other hand, the war marked an important turning point towards the liberalization of policy. A small refugee program was designed and executed under presidential authority, setting a precedent for postwar refugee admissions. Another program recruited about 225,000 agricultural workers, many of them Mexican "braceros," or manual workers, to meet labor shortages in the southwest. The exigencies of war also convinced Congress to lift the longstanding Chinese Exclusion law as a gesture to America's wartime alliance with China, although China still only received a token quota of 101 spots. Other laws ended the bans for Filipinos and Indians and allowed the foreign born wives of American servicemen to enter on a non-quota basis.

The "golden door" to America continued to crack open slightly in the immediate postwar years. The Displaced Persons Act of 1948 allowed for the entry of about 415,000 refugees from Eastern and Central Europe, a mix of ethnic Germans, Baltics, and Jewish Holocaust survivors. The McCarran-Walter Act of 1952, which established the Immigration and Naturalization Service and re-codified the general principle of "national origins" quotas, was widely seen as an anti-immigrant measure at the time of its passage. But the law also expanded some of the non-quota categories and jettisoned the more blatantly racist exclusions in the laws of the early 1920s. Meanwhile, large numbers of immigrants continued to enter the United States outside of the quota system, using special categories for Displaced Persons, spouses, and other relatives of American citizens.

The Displaced Persons Act had been a congressional statute that technically preserved the quota system, but most postwar refugee policy was conducted under presidential authority and in a more ad hoc fashion. Foreign policy and particularly the Cold War came to dominate the selection of refugees. When the Soviet Union sent in troops to crush the Hungarian Revolution of 1956, President Eisenhower used his executive parole power to accept and resettle 38,000 Hungarian exiles. Presidents Kennedy and Johnson adopted similar spur-of-the-moment programs for Cubans in the aftermath of Fidel Castro's 1959 takeover of Cuba, as did Presidents Ford and Carter for Indochinese refugees after the Vietnam War.

The Cold War was also a crucial impetus for the most significant immigration legislation of the modern era, the law that still largely governs legal immigration in America: the Immigration and Nationality Act of 1965. With the United States competing with the Soviet Union for world leadership, the old national origins system began to seem like an embarrassing outcrop from an earlier, racist era. The 1965 law, navigated through Congress by Senator Edward Kennedy and signed by President Johnson, ended the Asia-Pacific Triangle and replaced national origins quotas with caps on overall immigration in each global hemisphere, caps of 20,000 for individual countries in the Eastern Hemisphere, and a preference system that favored skilled immigrants and, especially, family reunification.

10

Writing in retrospect in 1981, journalist Theodore White called the 1965 Act "noble, revolutionary—and probably the most thoughtless of the many acts of the Great Society."[10] The assessment is hard to dispute. The Hart-Celler Act received nothing like the attention that accompanied the Civil Rights Act of the previous year. Its advocates claimed that they were simply redressing an historic wrong and revising the prejudicial assumptions that governed the old quota system. They felt that if the law stimulated any new immigration it would come from southern and eastern Europe, the region that had been most affected by the restrictive laws of an earlier time. What they did not realize was that Europe's economy had rebounded and economic "push factors" from places like Greece and Italy had slackened in the postwar era.

Policymakers also appear to have not fully understood the dynamics of chain migration. The provisions for family members, both within and outside the preference system, came to overwhelmingly dominate the immigrant stream. Rather than being used by southern and eastern Europeans as the legislators expected, the new family reunification slots were used instead by Asians, Latin Americans, and others from the so-called "Third World." Even for groups with relatively small populations in the United States before 1965, the new openness to family members facilitated a process whereby the presence of just one individual could eventually lead to the immigration of an entire extended family network.

The most variable category in the post-1965 period was refugees, whose need for spots naturally depended more on international events than on predictable economic asymmetries. The 1965 immigration statute set aside only six percent of the slots within the preference system for refugees, a number that proved completely inadequate in coping with crises abroad such as the end of the Vietnam War. To bring order to what had been a more or less haphazard process, Congress passed and President Carter signed the Refugee Act of 1980. Fifty thousand slots were given to "refugees," those screened overseas by the United Nations, while a separate system processed "asylees," those screened upon arrival. In addition, a bureaucracy was put in place to resettle refugees and the president was given the emergency prerogative to raise the number of admissions. David Haines's essay in this book tracks the mixed success of the Refugee Act and changing American attitudes about refugees generally.

Several factors contributed to a resurgence of anti-immigrant rhetoric and sentiment during the 1980s. The Mariel boatlift of 1980, in which Fidel Castro allowed the exit of thousands of economically destitute Cubans—including a small number of criminals and inmates of insane asylums—caused widespread public alarm and brought immediate chaos to the newly established refugee procedures. Several lobbying groups, such as the Federation for American Immigration Reform (FAIR), successfully focused anti-immigrant rhetoric on economic, environmental, and other concerns. And the political conversation increasingly turned to the issue of "illegal immigration", particularly from Mexico.

Even though the 1965 Hart-Celler Act was in most respects a liberalizing immigration measure, the law also set an unprecedented annual cap for the Western Hemisphere of 130,000 slots. Organized labor and old-guard restrictionists in Congress had demanded the Western Hemisphere cap as a price for the more liberal elements of the law.[11] The nearly simultaneous expiration of the WWII-era Bracero Program meant that there were far fewer avenues for legal Mexican migration in the post-1965 period than before. The border was not fortified, however, and the seasonal migration of Mexican workers went on as previously, with the implicit approval of western growers but without the sanction of law.

By the 1980s, the presence of large numbers of undocumented workers had begun to rankle some in the political system and the population at large. After over five years of contentious debate, the Democratic Congress and the Republican Reagan administration worked out a compromise known as the Immigration Reform and Control Act (IRCA) of 1986. Despite its title, on balance, IRCA actually increased immigration. The law built up the border patrol and imposed sanctions against employers who hired illegal immigrants. But the former measure proved ineffectual while the latter went largely unenforced. The law's main effect was to provide a path to citizenship for over three million undocumented immigrants and to establish a pro-diversity program for countries with low numbers of immigration slots under the existing preference system.

The legal regime that governed immigration continued to grow in scope and complexity during the late twentieth century. Another overhaul of immigration law in 1990 consolidated several elements of IRCA. The diversity program installed in 1986 was originally designed to find immigration slots for Ireland, as a legislative sweetener for congressmen with large Irish American constituencies. But in 1990 it was reformed into a proper vehicle for promoting geographical diversity. This statute also created several categories of specialized, temporary visas and raised many of the annual legal caps to better reflect the reality of immigration numbers in recent years.

Otherwise, however, immigration policy during the 1990s evinced a striking disconnect between the quality of legislation, which focused on "controlling the border" through tighter enforcement, and the reality of immigration, which continued largely impervious to policy. A number of laws proposed to "get tough" on illegal immigration by pouring more resources into the INS and Border Patrol. Other laws aimed at making life more difficult for those who had already managed to cross illegally. In California, voters passed the controversial ballot measure Proposition 187, which denied health care, public education, and state benefits to undocumented immigrants. Although later struck down by the courts, Prop 187 initiated a raft of similar measures in other states and in the national Congress. Wayne Cornelius addresses this recent turn against immigration in his chapter on Mexican immigrants.

Around the turn of the twenty-first century, the sour atmosphere surrounding immigration policy seemed to mellow slightly and prospects looked bright for some kind of legalization program for undocumented immigrants. Then came the September 11 attacks on the World Trade Center, conducted by a group of Islamic terrorists who had entered the country under legal temporary visas. The aftermath of 9/11 included incidents of anti-Muslim violence and thousands of specious arrests and deportations, documented in David Reimers's chapter on Muslim immigrants. In time, these events will likely take their place alongside other infamous bouts of nativist hysteria. The post-9/11 period also brought an administrative reshuffling that disbanded the INS and distributed its functions among several agencies within the newly created Department of Homeland Security.

Immigration, meanwhile, has for the most part continued apace, both within and outside the legal visa system. In every year since 2005, over a million people have gained legal permanent residency status in the United States, to say nothing of the hundreds of thousands of undocumented immigrants who have arrived every year. The newcomers have hailed from all parts of the world, with Mexico, China, the Philippines, and India producing the largest numbers in recent years. The immigrants are making their presence felt in every region of the country, but numerically their concentration has been heaviest in populous states like New York, California, Texas, Pennsylvania, New Jersey, and Illinois.

Just as in the past, the immigrants make tremendous social and economic contributions to American life. Their annual contribution to Gross Domestic Product is currently estimated to be about one-eighth of the American economy. Because most of today's immigrants tend to be either highly skilled professionals or low-skilled laborers, they have been able to fill niches at either end of the economic spectrum without displacing many native-born American workers. On the contrary, their presence has stimulated new hiring, labor market mobility, neighborhood revitalization, and a vibrant culture of entrepreneurship. The immigrants are doing their share. As in the past, however, their success in integrating into American society will depend in part upon the type of welcome they are accorded.

Thus stands, in broad outline, American immigration today: what it is and how it got that way. But the bare details of law, policy, and demography, as always, do scant justice to the flesh-and-blood human beings who traveled great distances, confronted prejudice up close, and through their sweat and striving made a better life for themselves and their children. It is to these richer stories, and their impact upon America, that the individual chapters of this book now turn.

Endnotes

[1] Oscar Handlin, *The Uprooted* (Boston: Little, Brown, 1951), 3.

[2] George Washington, "Address to the members of the Volunteer Association and other Inhabitants of the Kingdom of Ireland who have lately arrived in the City of New York," December 2, 1783, in *The Writings of George Washington from the Original Manuscript Sources, 1745–1799*, ed. John C. Fitzpatrick (Washington: Government Printing Office, 1931), XXVII: 254.

[3] Thomas Paine, *Common Sense* (Forgotten Books: 2008, orig. 1776), 40.

[4] Roger Daniels, *Guarding the Golden Door,* (New York: Hill and Wang, 2004), 7.

[5] John Higham, *Strangers in the Land: Patterns in American Nativism, 1860–1925* (New Brunswick, NJ: Rutgers University Press, 1955), 17–18.

[6] James R. Barrett and David Roediger, "Inbetween Peoples: Race, Nationality and the 'New Immigrant' Working Class," *Journal of American Ethnic History* 16 (Spring 1997): 3–44.

[7] United States, *Abstracts of Reports of the Immigration Commission: with conclusions and recommendations, and views of the minority* (Washington: Government Printing Office, 1911), 47–48.

[8] Reed Ueda, *Postwar Immigrant America: A Social History* (Boston: Bedford St. Martin's, 1994), 25.

[9] See David Roediger, *Working Toward Whiteness: How America's Immigrants Became White* (New York: Basic Books, 2005).

[10] Otis Graham, "The Unfinished Reform: Regulating Immigration in the National Interest," in Daniels and Graham, *Debating American Immigration,* 149.

[11] Aristide Zollberg, *A Nation by Design: Immigration Policy in the Fashioning of America* (Cambridge: Harvard University Press, 2006), 324–333.

The son of German immigrants, William Boeing (center), founded the giant aircraft manufacturing firm that bears his name.

CHAPTER 1

GERMAN AMERICANS

By William G. Ross

A DOZEN FIFTH GRADE students were reading aloud from a book of German language Bible stories during their daily German lesson at a Lutheran parochial school near Hampton, Nebraska on an afternoon in May 1920, when a stranger entered the one-room schoolhouse without knocking. The students were particularly apprehensive of outsiders because vandals had recently ransacked a neighboring school operated by their congregation, blasting out the windows with shotguns and ripping up German language books.

The stranger listened for a while and then had a brief whispered conversation with their teacher, Robert T. Meyer, after the teacher had spoken to the students in German. Meyer had never met the stranger, but he knew that he was Frank F. Edgerton, the Hamilton County Attorney, and that he had come to this classroom to determine whether Meyer was violating a Nebraska statute prohibiting instruction in foreign languages to students who had not yet passed the eighth grade. Like many other teachers in Lutheran schools, Meyer had defied the law as he felt his students needed to understand German in order to prepare for their confirmation and to participate in German language church services.[1] "I had my choice," Meyer later told his lawyer. "I knew that, if I changed into the English language, he would say nothing. If I went on in German, he would ... arrest me. I told myself that I must not flinch. And I did not flinch. I went on in German." Meyer explained that he had a duty to teach his students "the religion of their fathers in the language of their fathers."[2]

Meyer was fined twenty-five dollars for violating the statute, which the legislature had enacted in the wake of the First World War primarily to prevent the teaching of German in parochial schools. Many Nebraskans believed that such instruction impeded the assimilation of German Americans, even though most religiously affiliated schools, including the one at which Meyer was employed, taught German only as a second language and offered all other instruction in English. Although members of Meyer's congregation offered to pay the fine, Meyer declared, "I shall not pay the fine. It is not a matter of money. This is a question of principle. If I go to jail for doing what I know is right, I go to jail. I shall not compromise with what I know is not right."[3]

The Nebraska Supreme Court upheld Meyer's conviction, but the US Supreme Court overturned it in *Meyer v. Nebraska*, a landmark decision in 1923. The ruling invalidated the Nebraska law and similar statutes in twenty-one other states on the ground that the state had failed to demonstrate that teaching German posed any threat to the public welfare. Although the decision was based in part upon long-established principles of property rights, the court for the first time held that the Fourteenth Amendment's "due process" clause protected non-economic personal liberties from unwarranted intrusion by a state. The court explained that this included the right to marry, raise children, worship God in one's own way, and "to acquire useful knowledge."[4] This decision marked the beginning of the court's modern role as a guardian of civil liberties and has served as precedent in many cases sustaining rights that are not specifically listed in the US Constitution.[5]

The Court's decision in *Meyer v. Nebraska* closed the most tragic chapter in the history of German Americans. Although they had suffered from many of the same prejudices, suspicions, and discrimination to which other immigrant groups were subjected throughout American history, German Americans had only rarely encountered virulent or violent hostility until World War I. Since most were Protestant and lacked physical characteristics that distinguished them from the population at large, relatively few encountered racial or religious discrimination. Although cultural conflicts had periodically sprung up between the large German American minority and the Anglo American majority, the latter generally regarded German Americans as a model ethnic group, admiring their work ethic, orderliness, and high cultural standards. Although some German Americans preferred to maintain their language and customs, often in isolated ethnic enclaves, others assimilated rapidly and without much difficulty. After the United States declared war on Germany in April 1917, however, German Americans suddenly became the targets of ferocious campaigns to extirpate all vestiges of German American ethnicity.[6]

Since German Americans were the country's largest ethnic minority—numbering 8.3 million first and second generation immigrants in the 1910 census—federal, state, and local governments feared that they had the power to subvert the war effort. Discomfort with German Americans reflected the government's broader fear that Americans would not support an unparalleled level of mobilization for a foreign war, which had unclear goals and which could require unprecedented sacrifice in lives and treasure. The government particularly feared that dissident German Americans would join together with socialists, pacifists, and other anti-war elements of the population, including some Irish Americans who objected to American participation in a war allied with Great Britain.

In order to keep wartime patriotism stoked to a white heat, the Federal Committee on Public Information and countless newspapers churned out an immense quantity of propaganda depicting Germany and Germans as depraved enemies of civilization. In particular, the committee and the news media attempted to convince Americans that various acts of savagery by German military forces in Belgium and France were characteristic of German society generally. Although most of this propaganda was not consciously directed against German Americans, it inevitably bred hostility in many of the native-born toward their German American neighbors. Public and private organizations formed to promote the war effort became vehicles for attack on the German American community.

As war hysteria spread, acts of violence against German Americans and their property intensified and accelerated. In perhaps the most egregious incident, a mob in Collinsville, Illinois lynched a young German immigrant in April 1918, even though the victim protested his loyalty to the United States. A jury summarily acquitted members of the mob. Countless other German Americans, including clergymen who conducted church services in German, suffered beatings or damage to their homes and other possessions. On several occasions during the war, President Woodrow Wilson publicly exaggerated the extent of German American disloyalty. His subsequent denunciation of mob violence during the middle of 1918 was muted and arrived too late.

Much of the anti-German animus was directed against the German language, which was the most visible aspect of German ethnicity in the United States in the early twentieth century. German was used in a multitude of churches, in an extensive network of thousands of Lutheran and Roman Catholic parochial schools, and in many businesses and social clubs. German was the primary and often sole language of millions of German Americans, who dominated communities ranging from large sections of rural counties to entire neighborhoods of large cities throughout the Midwest and the Northeast. Efforts to repress the German language sometimes had an almost comical aspect, as when many Americans began calling sauerkraut "liberty cabbage," transforming hamburger into "salisbury steak," and raising "liberty pups" where once they had bred dachshunds. This movement, however, also exhibited a more sinister aspect. German street names in cities all over the country were renamed or anglicized. In many states and counties, public officials urged German Americans to use only English in public, including in church services. Despite the merely advisory nature of these warnings, they often carried at least veiled threats. Since many German Americans, particularly the elderly, spoke little or no English, restrictions on their right to speak their native tongue created some real hardships.

In May 1918, Iowa Governor William L. Harding went further, issuing a proclamation that prescribed English as the sole means of communication in all public places, including churches, and over telephones—this, at a time when operators could overhear conversations. Although Harding later issued dispensations to some pastors of heavily German congregations, he declared in June 1918, "there is no use in anyone wasting his time praying in other languages than English. God is listening only to the English tongue."[7] The South Dakota State Council of Defense prohibited the use of German in public and private schools, public meetings, and church services in the spring of 1918. The council later outlawed the use of German over the telephone and in assemblies of three or more persons in any public place, except in emergencies. Violation of the order carried a maximum penalty of one year in jail and a fine of $1,000, the equivalent of approximately $15,000 today.[8]

In many states, mobs took the initiative in suppressing the German language. In March 1918, a horde of rabble-rousers stormed the local high school in Lewistown, Montana, harassing the principal for continuing to permit German language instruction, and burning German textbooks while bellowing out patriotic songs. Two Mennonite churches in Oklahoma and a German Lutheran church in rural Kansas were burned to the ground, a Lutheran church in Indiana that refused to stop teaching German was destroyed by dynamite, and a Lutheran school in Missouri that continued to offer instruction in German, too, was put to the torch.[9]

The anti-German hysteria also created severe hardships for German language periodicals and educational organizations. Many German newspapers could not afford to provide the English language translations that the federal government demanded, while others suffered harassment ranging from raids on offices by public officials to the destruction of issues by mail carriers and pseudo-patriotic citizens. Nearly half of the 522 German language periodicals that existed at the beginning of the war had closed their doors by the end of 1919.[10] At the same time, scores of German parochial schools were shuttered to avoid public opposition to their use of the German language.

Alleging that German music was as dangerous as the German tongue, officials in many cities banned the performance of music by German composers. Some symphonies dropped these compositions from their programs voluntarily. Vague suspicions of disloyalty led to the firing, arrest, and detention of two prominent German-born conductors, Ernest Kunwald and Karl Muck. Muck's downfall came in 1917 when a group of patriotic organizations, suspicious of the composer's German roots, petitioned his Boston Symphony Orchestra to play "The Star Spangled Banner" at a visiting performance in Providence, Rhode Island. The orchestra's management ignored the request and Muck himself did not learn of it until after the performance. Newspapers interpreted his failure to play the national anthem as a slight to American patriotism, and Muck found himself denounced from all quarters. The *New York Times*, former president Theodore Roosevelt, and even Walter Damrosch, the German-born conductor of the New York Symphony Orchestra, all called Muck's loyalty into question.

German American Mennonites, whose pacifist beliefs precluded their enlistment in the military, suffered considerable persecution during the war. Although many served in noncombatant capacities, they were subject to various forms of abuse from officers and enlisted men in the camps where they were stationed. Approximately 130 Mennonites were incarcerated for long terms at Fort Leavenworth and Alcatraz prisons for refusing to obey orders to which they had expressed conscientious objections. At least two died from the brutal conditions to which they were exposed in prison. Countless other Mennonites suffered beatings, vandalism, and other indignities because their religious beliefs prevented them from saluting the flag or purchasing war bonds.[11]

The service of hundreds of thousands of German Americans in the American military forces and the patriotic activities of countless German American civilians helped ameliorate hostility against the community. Even conspicuous shows of loyalty, however, were not enough to satisfy some super-patriots, or "100 percent Americans," as they sometimes called themselves. A clergyman in Nebraska who delivered a short German language sermon at the funeral of a deceased soldier received the vehement rebuke of a local Council of Defense, while in other places German immigrants were tarred and feathered or forced to kiss American flags. Rumors circulated widely that a massive sabotage campaign was underway and that German American women were placing broken glass in bandages that they knitted for soldiers.

Although the armistice in November 1918 marked the end of most acts of violence against German Americans, many legislators, educators, social scientists, labor unions, and fraternal lodges concluded that the nation needed to continue the push for rapid assimilation of immigrant groups, particularly the Germans. Pointing out that

IMMIGRANT STRUGGLES, IMMIGRANT GIFTS

AN AMERICAN IN NO MANS LAND.

A GERMAN IN AMERICA

New York Herald **editorial cartoon, 1917. Karl Muck was fired from his position as conductor of the Boston Symphony Orchestra during the anti-German frenzy of the World War I years.**

many men who volunteered or were drafted for military service had little or no knowledge of the English language, assimilationists claimed that insular enclaves of immigrants were a threat to national security.

During a two-year period following the war, twenty-two legislatures enacted statutes imposing various prohibitions and restrictions on the teaching of foreign languages. Some applied to all modern languages other than English, while others were limited to German. Most, like Nebraska's, applied only to elementary schools. At the same time that courts were reviewing this legislation in cases that culminated in *Meyer v. Nebraska*, nativists were conducting a nationwide campaign to eliminate private and parochial education by requiring all children to attend public schools. Although some advocates of compulsory public education sincerely hoped that it would ameliorate class differences, many were attracted by the simple prospect of closing Roman Catholic schools, German and otherwise. The Ku Klux Klan, which reached the zenith of its power during the early 1920s, enthusiastically supported compulsory education, as did many powerful fraternal lodges. Some Protestant clergy also championed the movement. A Methodist bishop in Detroit proclaimed, "the parochial school is the most un-American institution in America, and must be closed."[12]

Compulsory education, like the movement to restrict instruction in foreign languages, met its end in the courts. The movement was dealt a setback in 1920 when Michigan voters rejected a compulsory education law, but it regained momentum in 1922 when Oregon voters approved a similar measure. A broad coalition including Roman Catholics, German American Lutherans, Jews, and Seventh Day Adventists were prominent in mounting constitutional challenges to the Oregon statute, which the US Supreme Court invalidated in *Pierce v. Society of Sisters* (1925). Relying heavily on its decision in *Meyer*, the court held that parents have a constitutional right to decide where their children should be educated.[13]

Outright hostility toward German Americans faded after the mid-1920s, although prejudice lingered. During the early 1930s, newspapers emphasized the German birth of Richard Bruno Hauptmann, the man convicted of kidnapping Charles and Anne Morrow Lindbergh's infant son. Newspapers rarely mentioned that Norman Schwarzkopf, Sr., the New Jersey chief of police who was instrumental in obtaining Hauptmann's conviction, was himself the son of German immigrants.

World War II saw no virulent revival of hostility against German Americans, despite the horrors of Nazism. During the pre-war years, some German immigrants had formed a German American Bund and other organizations promoting American support for fascism, but these groups never attracted more than a tiny fraction of German Americans to their ranks and quickly dissolved when the war began. In the Second World War as in the First, countless German Americans served in the US armed forces, and their loyalty was largely beyond reproach. The war against Germany and the monstrous barbarities of Nazi Germany undoubtedly caused some German Americans to mute their ethnic identity even more than before.

The widespread attacks on German American ethnicity during the era of the First World War and its aftermath were a trauma that fundamentally changed the German American community. The war sharply hastened the assimilation process and marked the end of a distinctive, assertive, and self-confident German American identity. In particular, the war's intolerance of German as the language of a multitude of schools, churches, periodicals, and social clubs deprived the German American community of the major factor in its cohesion.

Language was particularly important because German Americans were (and are) such a diverse group. German-speaking persons worshipped many different faiths and came to the United States not only from the areas that comprise present day Germany but also from the German speaking cantons of Switzerland, modern-day Austria, and large regions of Eastern Europe formerly under the rule of the Hapsburg and Russian empires. These regions, all home to large numbers of ethnic Germans, include parts of modern Hungary, the Czech Republic, Romania, and Poland.

During the decades following World War I, German American identity was further eroded through many of the same social factors that diminished ethnic identity among other groups. Many German Americans migrated from tight-knit ethnic communities in rural areas to cities. Then, many of the heavily Germanic neighborhoods in the big cities of the Midwest and Northeast lost their distinctive ethnic character when urban Americans of all ethnicities moved in large numbers to the suburbs and to the Sun Belt after World War II.

Although German Americans remained the country's largest single ethnic group at least as late as the year 2000, when seventeen percent of Americans—42.8 million people—identified themselves as German American and many millions more had at least some German ancestry, most today have little sense of ethnic identity. The descendents of German immigrants, who are found throughout the country but who are concentrated in an arc stretching from eastern Pennsylvania though the Dakotas, no longer vote in blocs or participate widely in Germanic organizations. Aside from the occasional Oktoberfest or Steuben Day Parade, there is little public evidence of German ethnicity. Most seem to prefer to blend into the Anglo American majority and to identify themselves as generic Americans or as old-stock Americans of "Nordic" descent. Although the United States Congress in 1987 declared October 6 as National German American Day, this commemoration receives little attention even among most persons who identify themselves as German American.

Germans have been part of the nation's history from the very beginning. A German may have been among the first settlers at Jamestown, Virginia, in 1607, as many artifacts found at Jamestown bear German inscriptions. In smaller numbers than their mostly British contemporaries, German settlers trickled into the colonies throughout the seventeenth century. The first Germans to enter the colonies as a group were Mennonites, an Anabaptist religious sect that fled Germany to escape persecution in 1683 and settled in what is now Germantown, Pennsylvania, near Philadelphia. Quaker leaders in Pennsylvania welcomed Mennonites, who resembled Quakers in their pacifism, strong work ethic, emphasis on simple living, and disdain for religious ritual. Even today, eastern Pennsylvania remains a stronghold of Mennonite sects in the United States, particularly the Old Order Amish. A large proportion of these groups, which are also found in Indiana, Ohio, and other parts of the upper Midwest, continue to speak German dialects and to adhere to old German customs.

The British government encouraged immigration of German Protestants to the American and Canadian colonies in order to counteract the strength of French Catholics in Quebec. Germans began moving into Virginia in substantial numbers in 1714, when a group of settlers from Nassau-Siegen established a colony at Germanna, near what is now Culpeper, Virginia. During the 1730s, thousands of "Salzburgers," Lutherans who had been expelled from the Tyrol region by the Roman Catholic archbishop of Salzburg, arrived in Georgia. Members of the German-speaking Moravian sect began arriving during the 1750s in North Carolina, where the Moravian presence can still be felt today. Pennsylvania continued to be the most popular destination for Germans coming to the American colonies. By the time of the American Revolution, German immigrants and their descendants constituted approximately one-third of the colony's population.

German-born American Revolutionary War hero Friedrich Wilhelm von Steuben later became the focus of German American ethnic pride.

However, German Americans also had a strong presence in colonial New York, New Jersey, Maryland, and South Carolina—nearly ten percent of all of the colonists were of German origin.

Most Germans, like emigrants from virtually every part of Europe through the nineteenth century, came to the New World to escape a society in which social and economic mobility was highly circumscribed. The fondest hope of many of these newcomers was to own and tend their own land. As was true of the large majority of their fellow colonists, German Americans were generally farmers, and many introduced innovative agricultural practices to the New World. Some were craftsmen renowned for their skill in carpentry and cabinet making, stone masonry, and glass blowing.

Most Germans in the colonies appear to have favored independence during the American Revolution. After the outbreak of hostilities in 1775, German regiments in Pennsylvania and Maryland were quickly raised to support the cause of independence from Great Britain. Although King George III retained many of the German connections of his grandfather, George I, the King of Hannover, colonial German Americans felt little affinity for the British motherland. Like his father and grandfather, George III remained the monarch of Hannover and privately worshiped as a Lutheran. Even though the Church of England in the colonies tended to regard Lutherans as honorary Anglicans, German colonists of all religions balked at the special privileges enjoyed by the English Church in New York and the southern colonies, where it was the established religion.

Generations of German Americans have cherished the (possibly apocryphal) tale of John Peter Gabriel Muhlenberg, a Lutheran pastor who astonished his Virginia congregation by stripping off his clerical vestments during a Sunday service to reveal the uniform of an officer of the Continental Army. There is, Muhlenberg is said to have declared, "a time to pray" and "a time to fight."[14] Many other German Americans also fought for independence during the Revolution. Even the British troops sent to suppress the rebellious colonists contributed to German immigration. Loyalist forces included approximately 30,000 Germans whom the British hired from the armies of various German states, particularly Hesse-Cassel. Several thousand of these so-called "Hessians" remained in the United States after the war, while others resettled in Canada.

Baron Friedrich Wilhelm von Steuben played a critical role in the American Revolution. Von Steuben, who learned military tactics in the Prussian Army, served for several years as a close aide to Washington and introduced Prussian methods of drilling, discipline, organization, and sanitation into the ragtag American forces. Von Steuben became a major general of the United States Army, was naturalized as an American citizen after the war, and lived out his life in New York. Many cities observe annual von Steuben Days on or near September 17, the anniversary of his birth, which provide an occasion for celebrating German American ethnicity. Some of these festivals include parades, the largest of which is on Manhattan's Fifth Avenue.

Several factors, including the Napoleonic Wars and the accompanying military blockades that encircled much of Europe, caused German emigration to the United States to taper off during the decades following the American Revolution. Immigration began to rise again around 1830 and it increased sharply between 1845 and 1855 as the result of economic, political, and religious turmoil in Germany. Unlike nineteenth-century immigrants from many other places, Germans frequently arrived with at least some capital, literacy, or artisanal skills—sometimes all of these. Even German peasants tended to have picked up more sophisticated farming techniques than their counterparts from other countries. Conditions on German immigrant ships were not quite as horrific as on those departing from most other countries, and Germans were less likely to die en route to America or to arrive in a diseased or debilitated condition. The combination of capital and agricultural skills enabled many German immigrants to avoid the overcrowded cities of the East and to move west, where they purchased farms shortly after their arrival. German immigrants were more agriculturally inclined than any immigrant group besides the Scandinavians, and farming enabled many to attain a high level of prosperity more quickly than immigrants from most other places.

Unlike some immigrant groups, particularly Italians and east Europeans, most Germans came to the United States in family groups with the intention of making America their permanent home. Relatively few returned to Germany during any period. The concentration of Germans in rural areas, however, tended to isolate them from mainstream American life, to make their presence less visible to other Americans, and to impede the movement of later generations into non-agricultural businesses and the professions.

Although German Americans settled heavily in the mid-Atlantic and midwestern states (especially Wisconsin and Minnesota), German immigrants spread to every part of the United States. While fewer Germans settled in the South than in other areas, most southern states contained pockets of significant German settlement. During the 1840s, a particularly large number emigrated to Texas, where they congregated in what is known as the Hill Country in the central part of the state.

Not all Germans settled in rural areas or in small towns, and when they were drawn to large cities they made major contributions to the development of urban life. Cincinnati, Milwaukee, St. Louis, Baltimore, Chicago, Buffalo, Cleveland, and New York City all had especially large German American contingents. Like other immigrant groups, they often dominated particular neighborhoods, many of which became known as *klein Deutschlands* (little Germanies). These urban immigrants and their children performed a variety of different kinds of work, from toiling in factories to opening small businesses as shopkeepers or master craftsmen.

Although immigrant farmers and other workers acknowledged that life in the United States included no quick road to riches and demanded labor at least as hard as they performed in Germany, most agreed that their new work was more profitable and satisfying. Christian Kirst, an immigrant who settled near Pittsburgh, wrote to a friend in Germany in 1882 saying, "here you work harder than over there," but he added that the United States was a "land of Canaan where milk and honey flow," where a thrifty and hardworking person "can save more money in a short time than he could in a lifetime in Germany."[15]

Similarly, Wilhelm Stille, an immigrant from Westphalia who settled in Ohio, explained in a letter to his parents and siblings in 1836 that immigrants at first faced "an uphill climb" because of the difficulty and costs of immigration and the trouble of learning a new language, "but when they've been here for a while and get a feel for freedom, and see the good crops growing here and all without manure, and that the land is so easy to work, then they think differently, and then they feel sorry for their friends who are still in Germany, and spending all day from early morning to late evening working to pay their taxes, and having to eat such bad food, not even meat every day, [which here we eat] even three times a day."[16]

Roman Catholic Germans first began arriving in large numbers in the 1840s due to economic conditions exacerbated by a potato famine in southwestern Germany and the Rhineland. After the unification of Germany in 1871, many Catholics left Germany when the new, predominately Protestant, German Empire began to suppress Catholicism through its *Kulturkampf* (cultural struggle). Lutherans also came to the United States during the 1840s and 1850s to escape the growing secularism of the German churches or to avoid the Prussian government's confederation of the Lutheran and Reformed churches. Many of these Germans settled in the St. Louis area, where they founded the Lutheran Church-Missouri Synod, today the second largest Lutheran denomination in the country. Mennonites and members of other dissident Protestant sects continued to emigrate to evade religious persecution. Also, throughout the nineteenth century, young German men emigrated to escape compulsory military service, first in the Prussian army and later in the forces of the united Germany.

After the failed revolutions of 1848, many Europeans fled to the United States to escape political retribution. Generally more secular and better educated than earlier immigrants, the German contingent of "Forty-Eighters" continued to work in the United States on behalf of the progressive ideals for which they had fought unsuccessfully in Germany. They formed Turner societies (*Turnverein*) that encouraged sporting activities and physical fitness, sponsored musical performances and lending libraries, spoke out on issues of concern to the German American community, and occasionally supported political or social reforms. Perhaps their biggest contribution to American society was the role they played in introducing physical education courses in public schools. The several dozen Turner societies that remain today in the United States are apolitical and promote sports, music, and other cultural activities.

The post-Civil War period in the United States offered a number of inducements to Germans of various social and economic stripes. These included higher manufacturing wages for skilled technicians, the falling cost of steamship travel for the impoverished, and free land for farmers provided under the Homestead Act of 1862. The last major wave of German immigration occurred between 1881 and 1892, a time of economic depression in Germany, when 1.7 million Germans arrived in the United States. Like other immigrants during this period, Germans arriving in New York were greeted by the Statue of Liberty (as of 1886), the iconic American statue sculpted by Frederic Auguste Bartholdi, a Lutheran of German descent. Bartholdi, a French citizen who strongly opposed Germany's annexation of his native Alsace after the Franco-Prussian War in 1871, modeled the face of the statue on the faces of his wife and mother, both of whom were of German origin.

Although Lady Liberty may have worn a German visage, Americans have not always greeted German immigrants with the sympathy of fellow countrymen. From the beginning, the customs and language of German immigrants subjected them to at least some prejudice from other groups, especially Americans of British origin. Like other ethnic groups, German Americans generally attracted the most hostility when they were arriving in large numbers. When German immigration to Pennsylvania was peaking during the middle of the eighteenth century, Benjamin Franklin famously assailed "the Palatine boors" and expressed anxiety that German settlers would become "so numerous as to Germanize us, instead of our Anglifying them." German immigrants in Franklin's Philadelphia during the eighteenth century were sometimes ostracized for being infected with Yellow Fever, leading some colonists to refer to the disease as "Palatine Fever."

Until World War I, the tendency of German Americans to insist upon their traditions and their strong sense of ethnic identity caused friction with other Americans. Some German immigrants regarded their native culture as superior to that of the United States and preferred to make Americans more German rather than to amend their own customs. British Americans, for their part, regarded the Germans in their midst as clannish, stubborn, and deficient in social graces. They also complained that German Americans were unduly traditional and resistant to modern ideas in agriculture and business, despite the German provenance of many new ideas in the New World.

German Americans typically regarded British American Protestants, whom they called "Yankees" regardless of geography, as prosaic philistines and puritans who lacked the intellectual and cultural attainments of Germans and German Americans. They frequently accused the Yankees of placing too much emphasis on the acquisition of money; conversely, the Yankees complained that their German American neighbors were unduly parsimonious. During the late nineteenth century, however, when pseudo-scientific theories of race became popular among educated Anglo Americans, Germans were usually grouped with the British, Dutch, and Scandinavians as supposedly superior in physical, moral, and intellectual qualities. This widespread Anglo American belief in the superiority of northern Europeans culminated in the enactment of the Immigration Act of 1924, which sharply curtailed immigration from southern and eastern Europe while favoring immigration from northern Europe. Germans received more than one-third of the annual quota of 155,000 immigrants.

"Nordic" solidarity, however, did not prevent serious cultural and social cleavages between Anglo and German Americans. In particular, German Americans overwhelmingly opposed the growing movement to prohibit the production and consumption of alcoholic beverages, and they rarely adhered to strict observance of Sunday as a solemn day of rest. Germans often scandalized their more puritanical neighbors by spending parts of their Sundays playing games, participating in athletic activities, enjoying secular music, dancing, or socializing in the beer gardens that dotted German American communities. At a time when saloons had unsavory reputations and were patronized almost entirely by adult men, Anglo Americans looked askance at the convivial atmosphere of the German beer gardens, where both men and women imbibed alcohol in the company of their children and where even clergymen participated in the festivities. German Americans ardently opposed "blue laws" that restricted the operation of businesses, including beer gardens, on Sundays.

Anglo Americans were less resistant toward the adoption of German holiday customs. German American Lutherans and Roman Catholics were influential in introducing more festive celebrations of Christmas and Easter into a nation in which many British American Protestants regarded those holidays as pagan or "Papist" until well into the nineteenth century. In particular, the tradition of the Christmas tree came to the United States largely through German Lutheran immigrants.

Some German Americans suffered from the rise of nativism during the late 1840s and 1850s, which coincided with sharp increases in both German and Irish immigration. Roman Catholics were especially vulnerable since nativists regarded their religion and church as antithetical to democracy. Rather than attempting to curtail immigration itself, nativists sought to impose various legal disabilities on immigrants, including the longer waiting periods for naturalization and limits on voting and office holding for the foreign born. Hostility toward immigrants in this period culminated in the short lived but briefly powerful Know Nothing movement, so called because its adherents were sworn to secrecy about their beliefs. After widespread electoral success in state and local elections in 1854, especially in the Northeast, the Know Nothings (officially the American Party) received twenty-three percent of the vote in the 1856 presidential election. Soon after, the movement fell asunder, partly because of internal conflicts over slavery, but also because the newly formed Republican Party occupied the vacuum created by the decline of the Whigs while a concurrent decline in immigration ameliorated alarm about the impact of immigrants.

In most parts of the country, the nativist hostility of the late antebellum period targeted the Irish more than it did the Germans, who were generally more prosperous and relatively less visible because of their geographic dispersal. Since the nativist movement was largely motivated by anti-Catholicism, Protestants of German extraction tended to be spared the worst slings of nativism. In fact, Know Nothing candidates received the votes of large numbers of Lutheran and Reformed German Americans. Nonetheless, some American Protestants regarded Lutheranism with suspicion because its liturgy and doctrine in many ways resembled Roman Catholicism more closely than Anglo American Protestantism.

The nativist agitation of the 1850s sometimes took a violent turn. One of the worst attacks on German Americans occurred in August 1855 in Louisville, Kentucky, where approximately forty percent of the population was German-born. Riots fanned by the Know Nothings generated fatalities that may have exceeded one hundred and damaged or destroyed dozens of homes and businesses. Most victims were German Catholics, but German Protestants and German Jews were also targeted, along with Irish Catholics. In the wake of the riots, large numbers of immigrants fled the city, which suffered from their loss particularly because many of them were highly educated Forty-Eighters.

Throughout the nineteenth century, some politically conservative Americans suspected the new German arrivals of socialist or revolutionary tendencies. Especially after the failed and controversial pan-European revolutions of 1848, such Americans feared that Europe was exporting its worst troublemakers across

German immigrants sometimes scandalized their Anglo neighbors by spending their Sundays drinking, carousing, or otherwise enjoying themselves—as in this 1897 photo of a Wisconsin picnic.

the Atlantic. The fear grew more acute in the 1870s and 1880s, a time of industrial unrest and growing conflict between management and labor in the United States. In this context, Germany—the land of Karl Marx and the German Social Democratic Party—was frequently regarded as a hotbed of socialist and anarchist politics. This sentiment peaked in 1886, when the bombings at Haymarket Square in Chicago led to the arrest of seven German born anarchists and a national outpouring of anti-radical xenophobia. "The enemy forces," a Chicago newspaper wrote after the bombings, "are not American [but] Hussite desperadoes with such names as Wazinski, Hitt and other Cossack and Teutonic appellations ... rag-tag and bob-tail cutthroats of Beelzebub from the Rhine, the Danube, the Vistula and the Elbe."[17]

Jewish German immigrants experienced different and often more severe prejudices than other Germans, being denied certain rights or privileges reserved only for Christians. For example, Jews had difficulty persuading Congress to provide Jewish chaplains for the Union Army during the Civil War. Until well into the twentieth century, Jews—including German American Jews—suffered from quotas in university admissions, exclusion from elite social clubs, and discriminatory hiring practices at universities, large law firms, and other powerful institutions. Jews of German origin, however, tended to suffer less than those who arrived from Poland and Russia during the late nineteenth and early twentieth centuries, in part because the former group arrived earlier and in smaller numbers and because German Jewish immigrants tended to be more secularized and prosperous, thus making them virtually indistinguishable from other German immigrants.

Another category of German immigrants that faced special forms of prejudice in the United States was the approximately 100,000 ethnic Germans who arrived from Russia (often in large extended families) during the late nineteenth century. These immigrants, known as the Volga Germans, were descended from Germans whom the Russian czars had invited to settle in western Russia during the eighteenth and nineteenth centuries to facilitate Russian economic development. After Russia revoked their exemption from military service and began to interfere with their cultural autonomy, many sought refuge in the United States, where they formed vibrant and distinctive communities throughout the Dakotas, Kansas, and Nebraska. In the early twentieth century, especially during World War I and the anti-communist "Red Scare" of 1919–20, the Volga Germans were targeted for both their German and their Russian backgrounds. Their relative poverty (most had been unable to remove their wealth from Russia) also made them vulnerable to discrimination. Their strong resistance to assimilation, the result of a history of embattled German identity under difficult conditions in Russia, also made them special targets of nativism.

For German Americans, as for so many other ethnic groups, churches were the principal vessel for the maintenance of ethnic identity. German immigrants established hundreds of predominately German parishes of the Roman Catholic Church, which permitted the development of ethnically homogeneous congregations. These parishes, concentrated in the Midwest and Northeast, acted as a focal point for German culture. Few German parishes exist today, as most have been merged with other parishes or have lost their German identities. Several German American synods exist within the 4.6 million-member Evangelical Lutheran Church in America. Most German American Reformed churches have merged with various Anglo American bodies. The largest merger occurred in 1957, when the Evangelical and Reformed Church, a predominately German American denomination, merged with the Congregational Church to form the United Church of Christ. This union of a German church with the denomination founded by the Pilgrims was in a way symbolic of the manner in which German Americans have been transformed into "old stock" Americans.

Another sign of weakening ethnic identity was the drifting of many German American Protestants from their original congregations. Affluent second- and third-generation German Americans often left the Lutheran and German Reformed churches to become Episcopalians or Presbyterians, while the less prosperous became Methodists or Baptists. Reasons for departure included theological disputes, intermarriage with non-Germans, a desire to assimilate more rapidly, and the slow adoption in many Lutheran and Reformed congregations of the English language for religious services and instruction.

One legacy of German American churches was the development of universal elementary education in the United States. Most German Lutheran congregations during the eighteenth and nineteenth centuries operated their own elementary school, often building the schoolhouse before the church. Until at least the end of the nineteenth century, German Lutherans had the country's largest network of parochial schools, and throughout most of the twentieth century the Lutheran Church-Missouri Synod maintained a parochial school network second in size only to that of the Roman Catholic Church. The success of German schools appears to have helped to encourage the rapid growth of public schools in the northern states during the antebellum period.

Although churches were the main sources of social cohesion for Germans in the United States, an array of fraternal lodges, social clubs, and other organizations helped to perpetuate German customs and foster a sense of German American identity. The largest of these was the National German American Alliance, which claimed 2.5 million members before the First World War. Formed in 1901, the organization was particularly active in opposing the prohibition of alcohol and the growing movement to restrict immigration in the first two decades of the twentieth century. Although it strongly supported the war against Germany, it disbanded in 1918 in the wake of hostility against German Americans and after a US Senate investigation determined that it had received much of its financial support from the brewing industry. Several present day organizations, including the German American National Congress and the Steuben Society of America, foster German American ethnicity.

German Americans also established various organizations to assist their communities, many of which still flourish. For example, the Legal Aid Society of New York, the country's oldest and largest provider of legal services for the indigent, was founded in 1876 by German Americans and was modeled after legal aid societies in Germany. Thrivent Financial for Lutherans, a Fortune 500 financial services company and the nation's largest fraternal benefit society, is a successor to the Aid Association for Lutherans, which was founded in Wisconsin in 1902 to provide reliable life insurance for German Americans at a time when the unregulated insurance industry often preyed on immigrants.

The vulnerability of German and other immigrants to the unregulated industrial economy of the late nineteenth and early twentieth centuries had tragic consequences for the large German American community in Manhattan. On June 15, 1904, more than 1,000 persons, mostly German American women and children from St. Mark's Lutheran church on the Lower East Side, drowned or were burned to death when an excursion boat, *The General Slocum*, caught fire on the East River during a church picnic outing. Although the boat was not chartered exclusively to immigrant or ethnic groups, its failure to maintain proper safety equipment furnished a grisly example of the hazards to which many working class persons, a large number of whom were immigrants, were subjected.

During the period from 1850 to 1917, when German ethnicity was at its zenith, German Americans disagreed about the extent to which they wanted to assimilate. So-called "soul Germans," who adhered to an almost mystical belief in the superiority of German culture, wished to retain their use of the German language and many of the basic traditions of the old country and to extend German influences throughout Anglo American society. Meanwhile, "stomach Germans" were content to become

Americanized while continuing to enjoy German food, music, and other customs that did not unduly impede their assimilation.

During this period, many German Americans shared the views of Carl Schurz, who often urged his fellow German Americans to combine the best of both German and American traditions. Schurz's career exemplified his own advice. Perhaps the most notable German American of the second half of the nineteenth century, Schurz served in many high federal offices and was prominent in a large variety of social and political reform movements over the course of six decades.

Schurz, a newspaper editor and military officer, had supported the democratic German revolutions of 1848–49. After the uprisings failed, he fled Germany and eventually settled in Wisconsin. There, he became an outspoken advocate of the abolition of slavery. In the 1860 presidential election, Schurz stumped for Abraham Lincoln among the German American community. During the Civil War, he served as a major general in the Union army and as ambassador to Spain, where he successfully dissuaded the Spanish government from recognizing the Confederacy.

In the postbellum period, Schurz became something of a political celebrity, bouncing between various political offices and newspaper editorships. In 1868, he visited his homeland (from which he had been exiled for almost twenty years) and was granted an audience with Otto von Bismarck. In a late-night chat with the Prussian chancellor, the highly egalitarian Schurz sang the praises of his adopted country to an impressed Bismarck, noting pointedly that "in a democracy with little government things might go badly in detail but well on the whole, while in a monarchy with much and omnipresent government, things might go very pleasingly in detail but poorly on the whole."[18]

The following year, Schurz became the first American senator of German descent, representing the state of Missouri. From his platform in the Senate, Schurz continued his long crusade against corruption in government. As secretary of the interior from 1877 to 1881, he promoted land conservation and established a civil service system that provided a model for the federal Civil Service Act of 1883. In the years before his death, he was an outspoken critic of American foreign policy.

Like Schurz, many German Americans were outspoken abolitionists before and during the Civil War. The large German population in the St. Louis area may have been responsible for keeping Missouri in the Union despite strong secessionist elements in the state, in which slavery remained legal. German immigrants also voted for Lincoln and fought in the Union Army in disproportionate numbers. In the postbellum period, German American party allegiances became more fluid, with entire voting blocs sometimes swinging their support to the party that most successfully courted their interests.

German American Catholics (like other Roman Catholics) have tended to be Democrats. German American Protestants for generations tilted toward the Republican Party because it had opposed rebellion and slavery during the Civil War and because they identified it with honest government and "sound" money (the gold standard). However, Republican drives to prohibit alcohol, restrict Sabbath activities, and impose other moralistic measures antagonized some German American voters, as did periodic bouts of nativism among Republican Protestants. In 1890 elections in Wisconsin and in 1892 elections in Illinois, for example, German Americans helped to defeat Republicans who had supported statutes requiring the use of English in parochial schools. As a cohesive group, German Americans were a major force in national elections for the last time in 1920, when they retaliated against the Democratic Party for its attacks on German ethnicity in conjunction with its support of the First World War, and again in 1924, when the Progressive Party's candidate Robert M. LaFollette attracted widespread support among German Americans in his home state of Wisconsin and throughout the Midwest and West.

During the late nineteenth and early twentieth centuries, LaFollette and other progressives, mostly Republicans, appealed to German American voters with a variety of social welfare measures, some of which were pioneered in Bismarck's Germany. German American voters tended to favor systematic public action to improve educational opportunities, promote public and individual health and safety, conserve natural resources, protect consumers, and provide assistance to the elderly. Espousing an organic vision of society that sometimes conflicted with the individualism of their Anglo American neighbors, German Americans voters helped to ensure the election of local, state, and federal officials who constructed the modern administrative state.

Many working class German immigrants had been affiliated with Germany's thriving trade union movement. They and their descendants helped to encourage the development of organized labor in the United States. Walter, Victor, and Roy Reuther, whose father emigrated from Germany, were driving forces in the American labor movement during the mid-twentieth century. Walter Reuther, who organized workers in Detroit automobile factories during the 1930s, later served as president of the United Autoworkers Union and as president of the Congress of Industrial Unions (CIO) He helped to merge the CIO with the American Federation of Labor (AFL) in 1955 to form the AFL-CIO, the country's largest labor union.

The socialist movement that thrived in the United States during the early twentieth century also owed much of its prominence to German Americans, who voted in disproportionate numbers for Socialist Party candidates. Emil Seidel, the son of German immigrants, became the first Socialist mayor of a large American city (Milwaukee) in 1910, and a German immigrant, Victor Berger, became the first Socialist elected to Congress that same year.

Far from rejecting capitalism, however, many German Americans have been prominent entrepreneurs and business leaders who have contributed materially to making the United States an industrial and technological giant. John Jacob Astor, a native of the Palatinate, immigrated to the United States as a young man during the American Revolution and developed a fur trading business that eventually stretched from coast to coast. He later became a prominent real estate investor and philanthropist in New York City and probably was the richest person in the country when he died in 1848. Although Astor retained close ties with the German community, his descendants were quickly and thoroughly absorbed into the Anglo elite. Frederick Louis Maytag, the son of German immigrants, was the first major manufacturer of washing machines. Isaac Merritt Singer, the son of a German immigrant father, perfected and marketed the modern sewing machine. Charles Pfizer, an immigrant from Wurttemberg, founded the pharmaceutical giant that bears his name. William Boeing, the founder of one of the world's largest aircraft manufacturers, too, was the son of German immigrants.

Many major beer brewing companies were founded during the nineteenth century by German immigrants—Eberhard Anheuser, Adolphus Busch, Adolph Coors,

Frederick Miller, Frederick Pabst, and Joseph Schlitz are all household names. German Americans have also made major contributions to the food industry. The H.J. Heinz food conglomerate was founded in Pennsylvania in 1899 by Henry J. Heinz, the son of German immigrants. William Entenmann, a German immigrant who learned the baking trade from his father in Stuttgart, opened his pastry business in Brooklyn in 1898. An immigrant from Wurttemberg, Oscar Mayer founded his iconic sausage company in the late nineteenth century. German Americans are credited with introducing hot dogs, pretzels, and hamburger steak into the American diet, and they helped to popularize beer and sausage. Although restaurants that specialize in German cuisine are much less common than they once were, many continue to thrive, particularly in cities and neighborhoods that have high concentrations of German Americans.

German Americans also distinguished themselves as engineers. John Augustus Roebling, (an immigrant from Thuringia) and his son, Washington Augustus, planned and supervised the construction of many major bridges, including the famous Brooklyn Bridge. German Americans were also prominent in the development of the American automobile industry. The Duesenberg brothers, August and Frederick, were instrumental in engineering the modern automobile; they successfully manufactured high-quality automobiles for several decades during the early twentieth century. The Studebaker Company of South Bend, Indiana, traced its origins to a German American family of wagon makers. The company remained one of the nation's largest car manufacturers from 1902 to the 1960s.

Publishing and journalism have been other areas of special German American prominence. Martin Luther's German translation of the Bible was the first of its kind printed in the American colonies in a western language. John Peter Zenger, a German immigrant who published the New York *Weekly Gazette,* won a major victory for freedom of the press in 1735 when a jury acquitted him of seditious libel against the governor. The case established the enduring principle that truth is an absolute defense against defamation. Joseph Pulitzer, an acolyte of Carl Schurz and one of the nation's leading newspaper publishers, was a German-speaking immigrant from Hungary who was active in German American affairs in St. Louis. Henry Villard, a Bavarian immigrant, became the owner of *The Nation* and the *New York Evening Post* during the 1880s. He used these publications (and his considerable fortune) to promote various progressive causes, including suffrage for women.

Thomas Nast, whose parents emigrated from the Palatinate in 1846 to escape the political upheaval of the period, grew up to become one of the most influential editorial cartoonists in American history. Working for *Harper's Weekly* from 1862 to 1886, Nast popularized the modern image of Santa Claus as a rotund, bearded, jolly fellow, and the donkey and elephant as symbols of the Democratic and Republican Parties. Throughout his long and prolific career, Nast relentlessly satirized urban political corruption while championing civil service reform, the gold standard, and the rights of marginalized groups such as American Indians, freed blacks, and Chinese Americans. However, he also roundly attacked the Roman Catholic Church and was guilty of characterizing Irish Americans as apish, uncivilized sub-humans.

H.L. Mencken, a longtime reporter and columnist for the *Baltimore Sun* and founder of the *American Mercury,* was one of the country's most celebrated journalists during the first half of the twentieth century. An acerbic critic of what he regarded as the hypocrisy,

pretentiousness, and insularity of the American middle class (what he called the "booboisie"), Mencken took particular relish in satirizing the foibles of prominent politicians. He was also a

Margarethe Meyer-Schurz, photographed here in her Watertown, Wisconsin classroom, is credited with introducing the concept of kindergarten to the United States.

noted philologist who authored *The American Language*. A true iconoclast, Mencken was a lapsed Lutheran who was deeply proud of his German heritage; he once boasted that he had faith only in Bach, Beethoven, and German beer.

Given the high premium placed on education by the German American community, it is no surprise that there have been a number of eminent educational reformers among its ranks. The modern American kindergarten is modeled in large part on a school founded in Wisconsin in 1854 by Margarethe Meyer-Schurz, the wife of Carl Schurz. Born into a highly educated and wealthy Hamburg family, Margarethe studied under tutors who were influenced by the progressive educational concepts of the German child advocate Friedrich Froebel, who pioneered the idea of kindergarten ("children's garden"). As an adult, she became acquainted with Froebel, under whose auspices she opened kindergartens in various German states. When her sister fled to England after the failed revolutions of 1848 and opened a kindergarten of her own, Margarethe became a teacher there. It was in London that she met and married Carl Schurz. They lived briefly in New York before heading west to Watertown, Wisconsin. She started a kindergarten that attracted the attention of childhood development experts, who in turn opened private kindergartens throughout the United States. By the early twentieth century, kindergarten had become a ubiquitous element of the public school curriculum. Meyer-Schurz died in 1876 at the age of forty-three of complications arising from the birth of her son, but the kindergarten she founded in Watertown survived until the First World War, when it became the victim of anti-German hysteria.[19]

American higher education, too, would not be what it is today without the influence of German Americans. German immigrants were present on American college faculties from at least the early nineteenth century. One of the most famous was Francis Lieber, a Prussian immigrant who attained distinction as a scholar of law and political science. Lieber produced the country's first encyclopedia, the *Encyclopedia Americana*, published between 1829 and 1832, and wrote the first modern treatise on the laws of war, the *Lieber Code*. During the late nineteenth century, German universities pioneered sophisticated methods of scholarship and became the model for the modern research university. Large numbers of aspiring American academics earned degrees in Germany and many American colleges hired prominent German scholars. During the 1930s, American universities were enriched by an influx of intellectuals who fled Nazi Germany. This galaxy included Albert Einstein, political theorist Hannah Arendt, and noted psychologist Bruno Bettleheim. Drawing upon the rich intellectual traditions of German Protestantism, German American theologians from Reinhold Niebuhr to Paul Tillich have had a profound influence upon various politicians and other twentieth-century secular figures.

German Americans also have enriched the nation's musical life. The glorious tradition of German music tended to make Anglo Americans more appreciative of their Germanic neighbors during periods of cultural tension in the nineteenth and early twentieth centuries. German Americans often helped to organize, conduct, and perform in American symphony orchestras. The translation of many German hymns into English by Catherine Winkworth and John Mason Neale during the mid-nineteenth century also helped burnish German American cultural credentials. These hymns became standard works in many British American denominations, particularly the Episcopal, Methodist, and Presbyterian Churches. Widely admired for their choral societies, German Americans regularly presented both religious and secular music to large audiences in hundreds of American towns and cities. They also have distinguished themselves as manufacturers of musical instruments—the renowned Steinway Piano Company, for example, was founded in New York in 1853 by Heinrich Steinweg, a German immigrant.

Although German Americans are known for their high voter turnout in elections, surprisingly few persons with close ties to German American communities have achieved prominence in national politics. Frederick Augustus Muhlenberg, a Pennsylvania congressman, was the first speaker of the US House of Representatives, serving from 1789–91 and again from 1793–95. John Peter Altgeld, a German immigrant who served as governor of Illinois from 1893–97, presided over the enactment of an array of progressive measures, including factory safety legislation and increased support for public education. Several presidents, such as Herbert Hoover and Dwight D. Eisenhower, can claim German ancestry, but none have identified with their German ethnicity.

Indeed, the central paradox of German American influence on the United States is that it is both inestimably large yet virtually invisible today. In addition to the German immigrants and second-generation German Americans discussed in this chapter, countless persons with at least some German ancestry have made distinctive imprints on almost every aspect of American life. German Americans have so successfully overcome prejudices and so fully integrated into American society that most are not regarded as German Americans, but simply as Americans. German American assimilation may in fact have been too thorough, for the demise of a distinctive German American identity has dimmed one of the most vibrant tiles of the American ethnic mosaic.

Endnotes

[1] William G. Ross, *Forging New Freedoms: Nativism, Education, and the Constitution*, 1917–1927 (Lincoln: University of Nebraska Press, 1994), 3.

[2] Arthur F. Mullen, *Western Democrat* (New York: W. Funk, 1940), 218.

[3] Ibid.

[4] *Meyer v. Nebraska*, 262 US at 399 (1923).

[5] Ross, Forging New Freedoms, 185–200.

[6] Frederick Luebke, *Bonds of Loyalty: German-Americans and World War I* (DeKalb: Northern Illinois Press, 1974), 226–59.

[7] Ross, *Forging New Freedoms*, 45.

[8] Ibid., 44–45.

[9] Ibid., 45–46, 47.

[10] Luebke, *Bonds of Loyalty*, 271.

[11] Ibid., 258–59

[12] Ross, *Forging New Freedoms*, 68.

[13] *Pierce v. Society of Sisters*, 268 US 510 (1925).

[14] Paul A.W. Wallace, *The Muhlenbergs of Pennsylvania* (Philadelphia: University of Pennsylvania Press, 1950), 117–119.

[15] Walter D. Kamphoefner, Wolfgang Helbich, and Ulrike Sommer, eds., Susan Carter Vogel, trans., *News from the Land of Freedom: German Immigrants Write Home* (Ithaca: Cornell University Press, 1991), 477–478.

[16] Ibid., 69.

[17] Harry Barnard, *Eagle Forgotten: The Life of John Peter Altgeld* (New York: Duell, Sloan and Pierce, 1938), 132–133.

[18] Carl Schurz, *The Reminiscences of Carl Schurz*, vol. 3, 1863–1869 (London: J. Murray, 1909), 277–278.

[19] Hannah Werwath Swart, *Margarethe Meyer-Schurz: A Biography* (Watertown: Watertown Historical Society, 1967).

Left: the first Irish American president of the United States, Andrew Jackson (1829–1937).

Below: the first Catholic Irish American president of the United States, John F. Kennedy (1961–1963).

CHAPTER 2

IRISH AMERICANS

By Anna Gressel-Bacharan

I N 1854, A SEMI-SECRET POLITICAL PARTY dubbed the "Know Nothings" won an astonishing string of victories in American state and local elections. Largely unknown up to that point, the party campaigned on an anti-immigrant and anti-Catholic platform that proved wildly popular with voters in many northeastern and midwestern cities, where a surge of mostly Catholic Irish immigrants had roused deep nativist anxieties in the preceding years. The Know Nothings' victory was most dramatic in Massachusetts, where Henry Joseph Gardner was elected governor in a landslide while his fellow Know Nothings won control of the state legislature. The state of Delaware also fell into Know Nothing hands, as did the mayoralties of Philadelphia, Chicago, and San Francisco. In New York, the Know Nothing James Barker came very close to claiming the mayor's office, coming in second in a four-way race and garnering nearly a third of the vote.[1]

The Know Nothings appeared to emerge from nowhere, erupting onto the national scene out of an obscure collection of secret fraternal societies that had developed during the late 1840s. The Whig and Democratic parties, already fracturing under the strain of the debate over slavery, were thrown into disarray. "Nearly everybody appears to have gone altogether deranged on Nativism," wrote one Pennsylvania Democrat in the run-up to the 1854 election. Other politicians referred to the Know Nothing surge of 1854 as a "tornado," a "hurricane," and a "freak of political insanity."[2] Most Know Nothing voters were relatively young; some of them had never before participated in politics. When asked about their organization or its membership, affiliates uniformly replied that they "knew nothing," a response that proved more durable than the organization's official name, the American Party.

Although most Know Nothings did not propose to restrict immigration per se, their platform promised to delay naturalization periods and to limit certain jobs and services to those born in the United States. In their rhetoric, the Know Nothings singled out recent Irish Catholic immigrants in the most overwrought and conspiratorial terms. In August 1854, Patrick Lynch, an Irish Catholic newspaper editor and letter writer to the *New York Times,* summed up the Know Nothing diatribes then being heard across the country:

> You have at present opposed to you a bitterly inimical and powerful secret society called the "Know-Nothings"—opposed to you—to us Irishmen, particularly—on the grounds that we are impudent and voracious cormorants of petty places under Government; that we are ignorant, turbulent and brutal; that we are led by the nose and entirely controlled by our clergy; that we are willing subjects of a "foreign prince," the Pope; that we are only lip Republicans; that we are not worthy of the franchise; that by the largeness of our vote and the clannishness of our habits and dispositions we rule or aspire to rule in America; that we are drunkards and criminals; that we fill the workhouses and prisons; that we heap up taxes on industrious and sober and thrifty citizens; and that for these and other reasons we should be deposed from our citizenship, and in fact, rotted out of this American nation, as a body, by every fair and foul means.[3]

If Lynch's characterization was slightly over-the-top, then so were the Know Nothing attacks.

Because of the organization's semi-secret status, it was sometimes difficult to divine the true positions of Know Nothing candidates. Know Nothings frequently averred that Catholicism, rather than immigration, was their true *bête noire*. Levi Boone, the new mayor of Chicago, raised the specter of Catholic despotism in America in his inaugural address:

> When, however, I come to count the true friends of our country, and those to whom our institutions may be safely committed, I am frank to confess, gentlemen, ... I cannot be blind to the existence in our midst of a powerful politico-religious organization ... boldly avowing the purpose of universal dominion over this land, and asserting the monstrous doctrine, that this is an end to be gained, if not by other means, by coercion and at the cost of blood itself.

Yet even when they seemed to disavow prejudice against immigrants as such, Know Nothings could usually not resist working nativism into their proposals. Levi Boone went on:

> I ask ... to whom can the affairs of this country, the administration of its laws, it liberties and its constitution, be so properly committed, in whose hands can it be hoped they will be so safe as in those of the men who were born under their shadows, whose first vital breath was drawn in their atmosphere, whose youth as well as manhood has drank into their spirit, whose fathers planted, and whose fathers blood nourished them into life?[4]

Upon assuming office, Know Nothing officials initiated a variety of measures to limit the influence of immigrants in public life. In Chicago, Boone barred all immigrants from city jobs. In Massachusetts, the legislature disbanded the state's Irish militia company.

Anti-Irish and anti-Catholic sentiment in the 1850s was not limited to campaign rhetoric or legal restrictions. In 1854 alone, Know Nothing riots targeted the Irish in Massachusetts, Missouri, Maine, New York, New Jersey, Louisiana, and Kentucky. Mobs of Know Nothing rowdies served as election-day enforcers in many southern and midwestern cities. In early August 1854, a mob in St. Louis threw stones and brickbats into homes and stores and at anyone who seemed suspiciously foreign. An even larger riot took place the following year in Louisville, Kentucky. On August 6, 1855, rioters looted, destroyed, and set fire to over a hundred buildings. At least twenty-two people were killed in the melee.

The elections of 1854 were the apogee of the Know Nothings' political power. Although the American Party won significant victories in a few southern and mid-Atlantic states in 1856 and 1858, the movement in the South turned increasingly away from its anti-immigrant origins to become a refuge for former Southern Whigs. In 1856, the Know Nothings recruited former president Millard Fillmore to run atop their presidential ticket, but Fillmore only carried one state, Maryland. In light of the slackening immigration tide and the escalating national debate over slavery, the Know Nothing vocation of "chasing Paddy" came to be seen as a distraction from the weightier issues of the time. The American Party died a quiet death in 1860.

Yet Know Nothingism was only the most dramatic and the most public expression of the era's profound anti-Irish and anti-Catholic animus. And while it could not sustain a mass political movement in the midst of a nationwide crisis over slavery, it tapped a reservoir of deeply rooted prejudice. Anti-Catholicism was a way of life for many nativists of English, Scottish, or even Irish Protestant descent. Since the very advent of Protestantism in the sixteenth century, an Old World tradition of "anti-Popery" cast Catholics as players in an international papal conspiracy to subdue free peoples around the world, running from the Spanish Armada through John Foxe's *Book of Martyrs* to the latest alleged perfidies of Pope Pius IX. Transplanted to the New World, these antagonisms sometimes grew even sharper in a context where occasionally extreme Protestant sects were liberated from a moderating Anglicanism.

When Catholic immigrants from both Ireland and Germany began to arrive in large numbers in the 1830s, the reaction was swift and allergic. Serious riots targeted the Catholic Irish of Boston in 1835 and of Philadelphia in 1844. The growing power of the Roman Catholic Church in the United States provoked the ire and anxiety of both conservative Protestants, who hated Catholicism for traditional reasons, and some liberal democrats, who saw the Church as an enemy to progress. Public funding for parochial schools and the governance of Catholic orders and parishes became particular flashpoints. In 1836, the purported memoirs of a reformed Canadian nun were published as *The Awful Disclosures of Maria Monk*. The pamphlet, later revealed to be a hoax, detailed the sexual perversions of her Montreal convent and convinced a wide American readership of the evils of Catholic institutions in the New World.

The ancient bigotries of Protestant anti-Popery mingled with newer resentments against the Irish immigrants. Immigrant Catholics, and particularly Irish Catholics, tended to take a more relaxed view of alcohol than the native-born Protestant population, and immigrants quickly gained a reputation as disorderly, drunken brawlers. The temperance movement, which had persuaded many middle and working class Protestants to abandon drink during the early nineteenth century, met a stubbornly recalcitrant element in Irish and German Catholic immigrants, for whom alcohol was a mainstay of social and family life. Horace Greely's *New York Tribune* encapsulated the aggressive tone of the dry crusade: "It is liquor which fills so many Catholic (as well as other) homes with discord and violence … fills our prisons with Irish culprits, and makes the gallows hideous with Catholic murderers."[5]

Disease became another Irish immigrant stigma. Overcrowded, disease-ridden immigrant ships delivered many Irish men and women to America in a diseased or otherwise debilitated condition. Fear of cholera, sometimes known as the "Irish disease,"[6] was widespread and may explain the death of fifty-seven miners at Duffy's Cut, Pennsylvania, in 1832. The miners, recent arrivals from Ireland who were helping to build the Philadelphia and Columbia Railroad, were long thought to have been cholera victims denied care by local residents and other railroad employees. Recent forensic evidence excavated from the Irish mass grave, however, suggests that the area's residents may in fact have massacred the sick miners from fear of an epidemic. A similar fear of diseases borne by immigrants led a mob to burn down the hospital at the Staten Island quarantine station in 1858.[7]

Anti-Irish and anti-Catholic feeling long outlived the 1850s and the mania of Know Nothingism. The 1870s saw several coal field riots in which different immigrant factions targeted Irish laborers.[8] In the 1880s, the American Protective Association was founded to counter the influence of the Catholic Church and singled out Irish Americans for abuse and ridicule. In the twentieth century, acts of violence against Irish immigrants decreased even as some of the underlying sentiments remained. The 1928 presidential campaign exposed the extent of these latent views when Al Smith, the Irish American governor of New York, became the Democratic candidate for president. Smith's 1928 campaign elicited a vitriolic mix of nativism and anti-Catholicism. Protestant ministers and the recently revived Ku Klux Klan spread rumors that Smith would take direct orders from the Pope.[9]

One of the most surprising and salient features of anti-Irish feeling in America is that its source was itself often Irish. Irish Protestants filled out the ranks of the Know Nothing movement, the American Protective Association, and numerous anti-immigrant mobs, including the one that rampaged through the streets of Louisville in 1855 and the one that burned down the Staten Island quarantine station in 1858. An embattled minority within Ireland, Irish Protestants sometimes took an even dimmer view of Irish Catholics in the United States than did the descendants of British immigrants. In fact, as more and more Catholic Irish immigrants arrived in America during the middle decades of the nineteenth century, Irish Protestants gradually abandoned the label "Irish" altogether. Since most Irish Protestants in America were descended from seventeenth-century Scottish families who had been relocated to Ulster (northern Ireland), they came to prefer the terms "Scotch Irish" or "Scot Irish."

Although there were Catholic immigrants in America from the time of the earliest European settlements, it is largely with these Irish Protestants that the story of Irish America begins. The Scotch Irish, as they later would be known, began coming to North America in large numbers during the eighteenth century, less than a century after their ancestors first established a significant presence within Ireland. In 1602, the English government began an aggressive "plantation" policy whereby the former lands of conquered Gaelic noblemen were ceded to English overseers, who tenanted their new lands

The publication and wide dissemination of *The Awful Disclosures of Maria Monk* in the 1830s fed American anti-Catholicism with false reports of sexual exploitation at a Montreal convent.

AWFUL DISCLOSURES
OF
MARIA MONK
OR THE SECRETS OF THE BLACK NUNNERY REVEALED.

MARIA MONK

with mostly Presbyterian settlers from lowland Scotland. Over the course of the seventeenth century, a large, self-conscious, and intensely Protestant settler population formed in Ulster. Even though they were originally settled by British policy, the Presbyterians, as religious dissenters, were still denied many religious and landholding privileges reserved for members of the established Church of Ireland.

It was most often economic distress and lack of opportunity that caused Irish Presbyterians to leave Ulster for the American colonies. From the time of the first plantations, Presbyterians had been an economically marginal group in Ireland, toiling on rocky northern farmland or in the region's unstable linen industry. When crop failures struck, as they did repeatedly throughout the eighteenth century, or when linen exports collapsed, as they did in the 1770s, emigration to America became the only means of avoiding complete destitution. The Presbyterian migrants would make their way from the countryside to emigrant ports like Belfast, Londonderry, and Newry, and thence on ships across the Atlantic. Many could not pay for the cost of their passage and arrived as indentured servants. The main American port of entry for these early Irish immigrants was Philadelphia.

Irish American life was largely rural in the eighteenth century. Some settled in New England, where the names of towns like Bangor, Maine, and Londonderry, New Hampshire testify to the Scotch Irish influence. More frequently, however, they spread out in frontier communities in the Pennsylvania backcountry and beyond. The "Old Philadelphia Road" proved to be the most heavily trafficked immigration corridor of the period, conveying the Scotch Irish west and south into the trans-Allegheny region, the Shenandoah Valley, the backcountry of the Carolinas, and as far south as Georgia. Colonial governments in those areas sometimes encouraged the Irish to settle as a "frontier shield" because they had a reputation for ruggedness and hostility toward Native Americans. But these frontier communities also had a tendency to chafe at the authority exercised by tidewater elites.

At the same time, much smaller numbers of Irish Catholics also had made their way to the colonies. Although there were some wealthy Catholics who fled the confiscation of their lands in Ireland, in general Irish Catholics were much likelier than their northern Presbyterian counterparts to be poor, to arrive as indentured servants, and to settle in the port cities. But they could be found in the hinterland and throughout the southern colonies as well. Charleston, South Carolina had a particularly notable Catholic Irish presence. Due to small numbers, the dearth of Catholic churches and clergy, and the intense hostility to their religion in the New World, many Catholics converted to Protestantism or otherwise muted their faith. Cut off from sizable ethnic enclaves, many were simply absorbed into the larger communities that surrounded them.

By 1775, fully one-sixth of those living in the nascent United States were either born in Ireland or could claim Irish descent. That year marked the beginning of the Revolutionary War, a conflict in which the Irish American role was mixed but generally supportive of the American cause. Occasionally, the antagonisms between backcountry settlements and the more prosperous coastal regions moved the Irish to oppose the Revolution and even to take up arms as loyalists. An "Irish Volunteer" unit, made up of both Catholics and Protestants, served in the army of the British general Charles Cornwallis. On the other hand, over a third of George Washington's Continental Army was Irish born or had close Irish roots. Eight Irish Americans, three of whom were immigrants, signed the Declaration of Independence and one served as secretary to the Continental Congress. The prevalence of Irishmen among the American revolutionaries even led some in Britain to wonder whether the loss of the colonies could have been prevented if Ireland and the king's Irish subjects had been treated better. "America was lost by Irish emigrants," as one Anglo-Irish Member of Parliament put it in 1784.[10]

After the Revolution, as a more well-to-do Irish Presbyterian element formed in cities like Philadelphia, Baltimore, and Pittsburgh, Irish Americans made their presence increasingly felt in the politics of the young republic. Especially after 1798, when a failed uprising in Ireland sent a new class of revolutionaries into American exile, the Irish population was known for its devotion to radical causes. One unsympathetic observer touring western Pennsylvania reported of the region's Irish, "with very few exceptions they are United Irishmen, Free Masons, and the most God-provoking democrats this side of Hell."[11] It was partly to keep out such rabble-rousers that John Adams's Federalist Party passed the Alien and Sedition Acts in 1798. The move provoked a tremendous backlash, however, and Irish voters were instrumental to Thomas Jefferson's election to the presidency in 1800.

The most prominent Irish American politician of the early United States was Andrew Jackson, a figure who embodied many of the democratic and Anglophobic political tendencies of the Irish Protestant population in America generally. Raised on the North Carolina and Tennessee frontier as the son of Ulster immigrants, Jackson was a decorated general in the War of 1812 who made his reputation by defeating the British at the Battle of New Orleans in 1815. Despite the place John F. Kennedy holds in the popular imagination, Jackson in fact became the country's first Irish American president when he was elected to office in 1828. In addition to founding the modern Democratic Party, successfully opposing the Second National Bank of the United States, and opening the patronage system to a wider swath of the population, Jackson also cultivated a political identity strongly tied to his rough-and-tumble Irish Protestant ethnicity.

Irish immigration, Protestant and Catholic, eased during the early years of the nineteenth century due in part to British restrictions on passenger ships meant to discourage emigration. British policy also shaped the pattern and dispersal of the immigrant traffic that did come to America. Various restrictions meant that the cost of passage to the United States was often more expensive than heading to British Canada. Hundreds of thousands of Irish immigrants, among them rising numbers of Catholics, sailed for eastern Canada to participate in the region's booming lumber trade with Britain. From there, a significant portion of new Irish arrivals headed south, sometimes on foot, filtering throughout the New England countryside and into large cities, such as Boston.[12]

In Ireland, meanwhile, social and demographic pressures bore down upon an overwhelmingly impoverished population. Quite simply, the problem was that there was not enough land to go around. During the Napoleonic Wars, when Irish markets were protected from European competition, Ireland had experienced a period of relative economic prosperity and rapid population growth. But the final defeat of Napoleon in 1815 and the resumption of trade with Europe led to a precipitous drop in agricultural prices and new pressure on landlords to create grazing space by clearing tenants from their properties. The ranks of the poor swelled with subtenants and newly landless laborers As these pressures increased, immigration to the United States became an increasingly attractive proposition.

Many of the new Irish arrivals to America joined other immigrant groups at work on the giant transportation and infrastructure projects then underway in the United States. The Irish contribution to the country's growing network of canals in this period was tremendous. Between 1800 and 1865, Irish immigrants worked on some 4,000 miles of canals.[13] The Erie Canal, which connected the Eastern seaboard to the Great Lakes, was a project especially indebted to Irish labor, and Irishmen settled throughout upstate New York along the path of the canal after its completion in 1825. Another huge project was the New Canal in New Orleans, whose debt to Irish diggers was commemorated by a popular song:

Ten Thousand Micks, they swung their picks
To dig the New Canal.
But the choleray was stronger 'n they,
An' twice it killed them all.[14]

The estimate of twenty thousand deaths seems implausibly high, but canal building was dangerous work indeed.

The first immigrants to leave Irish families were often the young, ambitious men, who could be relied upon to find work and send home remittances. Irish Catholic immigration was thus heavily male throughout most of the early nineteenth century. Irish women began to show up in large numbers during the 1840s, often joining husbands or finding work on their own as domestics or mill workers. New England mill towns like

Lowell and Lawrence in Massachusetts became hubs for Irish immigrant women while bourgeois households throughout the United States soon included an Irish maid, or "Bridget" as she was stereotypically known.

Although the long-term Irish pattern of mass emigration to America was already in place by the 1830s, the Great Famine of 1845–1852 (called the Great Hunger in Ireland) nevertheless marked a watershed for both Irish and Irish American history. Throughout the period of population growth and shrinking land holdings in the early nineteenth century, the potato had become a mainstay in the diet of most Irish peasants. Families sold what crops they could, at ever diminishing prices, and were only able to stay alive by eating potatoes from their garden plot. So when a particularly devastating potato blight struck Ireland starting in 1845, it initiated a crisis of unprecedented magnitude, made worse by rampant disease and widespread evictions. Many tenant farmers were reduced to eating the potato crops slated for the following season, which perpetuated the crisis into subsequent years. The calamity went all but unaddressed by two successive governments in London.

The Great Famine changed Ireland—as well as the heritage of those who left the "auld sod." The island lost half its population, of which roughly one half died in the Famine and the other half emigrated. Those who were able to flee Ireland did so in droves, making their way not only to America but also to England, Scotland, Canada, and Australia. While exact numbers are not available, it is estimated that between 1.7 and 2.5 million men, women, and children came to the United States as a direct result of the famine.[15] The flow of immigrants accelerated as conditions deteriorated in Ireland. Between 1840 and 1850, some 800,000 Irish men and women made their way to the United States. In 1851 alone, at the height of the famine, at least 220,000 arrived. Traveling aboard what would come to be known as "coffin ships," thousands did not survive the voyage.[16]

This great, sudden wave of immigrants was most visible in the large cities of the Northeast. In Boston, many new immigrants crowded in tiny cellars, sometimes up to forty in one space. In the decade before the famine began, an average of five to six thousand Irish arrived in the city every year. In 1847, that number suddenly swelled to over 33,000. The Irish population in Boston grew so quickly that it went from representing a fiftieth of the city's inhabitants in 1854 to a fifth in 1885.[17] New York City was an even bigger recipient of Irish newcomers. By 1850, over a quarter of those living in New York were Irish born. Including the second and third generations, a full third of the city was Irish. A decade later New York had become the largest Irish city in the world, with some 200,000 Irish men and women calling it home.[18] Other major Irish American cities included Baltimore, Pittsburgh, Chicago, St. Louis, and Detroit.

The reaction to this influx ranged from guarded suspicion to outright hostility. The profile of famine immigrants—poorer, less educated, less skilled, and more Catholic than earlier Irish arrivals—did not aid their prospects for an easy acceptance in America. Particularly in large cities like Boston, New York, and Chicago, recent immigrants did sometimes contribute to crime and overcrowded living conditions. Religious animosity also affected the tone of nativist rhetoric and action. It was during the 1840s and 1850s that the Know Nothing movement rose to brief prominence, that a wide-ranging movement of legislators strove to close down Catholic parochial schools, and that Irish Protestants began self-identifying as Scotch Irish to distinguish themselves from the Irish Catholic rabble.

Anti-Irish sentiment might have taken even deeper root in American national politics had it not been for the American Civil War. In addition to fracturing the Know Nothings, the war proved an unexpected boon to the acceptance and assimilation of Irish immigrants in the United States. Irishmen marched in the ranks of both armies, but there were more in the Union Army due to their higher concentration in the Northern states. The Irish gained a reputation as fierce fighters, in particular at the battles of Fredericksburg, Antietam, and Gettysburg. Several states raised Irish regiments, the most famous of which was the "Fighting 69th," a regiment in the vaunted "Irish brigade" from New York. Able-bodied male Irish immigrants arriving in New York City were sometimes given citizenship and military enlistment papers at the moment they stepped off the boat. At the same time, some Irish soldiers resented their military service on behalf of an increasingly anti-slavery cause and played a leading role in the infamous New York Draft Riots of 1863.

Some Irish who enlisted did so fully aware that fighting on behalf of their new country would allow them to claim full rights as American citizens and perhaps influence American politics on behalf of Ireland. On a more practical level, some even saw the war as an opportunity to gain military experience they might later use against Britain. Many immigrants continued to see affairs in Ireland through the lens of their exile, or that of their forebears, sometimes misunderstanding the reality the Irish "back home" were facing. As a result, Irish nationalism was frequently more intense and militant in America than in Ireland. In 1858, Irish American immigrants were crucial in the formation of the Fenian Brotherhood, an Irish republican organization that later played a major role in the politics of Ireland. During the late 1860s, the Fenians staged a series of raids on Canada from south of the American border, in a somewhat far-fetched bid to ransom Canada back to the British in exchange for Irish independence. The invasion failed, halted by the American government, but the Irish American diaspora would continue to insert itself in the affairs of the homeland in years to come.

For the vast majority of first generation immigrants, however, making a living overrode most other considerations. The typical Irish immigrant had spent most of his life on a farm, but unlike his German or Scandinavian counterpart lacked any capital to buy land. His main economic asset was his willingness to work hard. In the cities, Irish navvies labored on sewers, streets, water works, and other construction projects. But they also went wherever unskilled jobs could be found, often propelling them into the western states and territories. As railroads gradually superseded canals as the country's principal construction projects, they also became the major agents of Irish American dispersal. Concentrations of Irishmen would appear wherever there was railroad building to be done. Data from the 1870 census, for instance, can be mapped onto the path of the Union Pacific-Central Pacific railway line that connected Omaha to San Francisco: large groups of first- and second-generation Irish lived all along the route.

The backbreaking nature of railway work was such that mid-nineteenth century deaths of Irish Americans also followed the railroads. Some of the working conditions were so dire that Boston and New York newspapers ran advertisements warning new immigrants away from accepting employment with certain railway lines. For the most part, however, the Irish went anyway. Rail operators touted their high wages and free-flowing liquor, neglecting to mention that diggers would see most, and sometimes all, of their pay go to reimbursing their trip to the building site, their lodging, and the inflated costs of food and daily necessities that could only be acquired from railroad company stores.[19]

Irish immigrants not only helped build the railroads, they also dug up the coal that powered the trains. Estimates vary, but as many as half the coal miners in nineteenth-century Pennsylvania and West Virginia, for instance, may have been Irish. Like canal and railroad projects, the mining industry called for vast numbers of inexpensive unskilled laborers and found many Irishman willing to fill that need. In the same way that railroads and canals had dispersed earlier Irish immigrants, mining sent Irishmen in large numbers throughout the American West. Butte, Montana, for example, today hosts one of the largest Saint Patrick's Day parades in the country, mostly as a result of the large community of Irishmen drawn there by copper mining in the mid-to-late nineteenth century.

In a very different fashion, other forms of mining also drew newly minted Irish Americans west. The lure of finding a lode of silver, gold, or oil proved as irresistible to the Irish as it did to many other Americans. As news spread of the vast riches in California and Nevada, so did the movement of immigrants towards those regions, along the very railways they or their compatriots had helped to build. Most prospectors failed to strike it rich, but a few did so quite spectacularly. In the 1860s, James Fair, James Flood, John Mackay, and William O'Brien became known as the Silver Kings (or sometimes the Bonanza Kings) thanks to the Comstock Lode in Virginia City, Nevada. The four men, who all shared similarly impoverished backgrounds, partnered and eventually managed to break the "Bank Ring" monopoly that then dominated Nevada mining.

Of the four, John Mackay stands out for his drive and accomplishments. Born in Dublin and raised as a street urchin on the streets of New York City, Mackay moved to Sierra County, California, at the height of the gold rush only to find that there were few viable claims left. Mackay worked tirelessly as a laborer to send money back to his mother in New York. In 1859, when he heard news of what would become the Comstock Lode in Nevada, he joined his close friend William O'Brien in setting out for Virginia City. Share by share, mine by mine, they built up a holding that transformed their lives and the history of the region. After making his name and fortune in silver, Mackay went on to found the Commercial Cable Company and the Commercial Pacific Cable Company, which would pioneer communications across the Atlantic and Pacific Oceans, respectively.[20]

Although the success of John Mackay and his fellow Bonanza Kings was outsized even for their time, in some ways they represented a rising Irish American business class in the post-Civil War American West. Away from the crowded cities where most Irish continued to live, opportunities abounded for energetic and ambitious men. It was exactly this sort of Irish immigrant who frequently chose to head west, where some profited handsomely even as others struggled or died working on large infrastructure projects. The canals and railroads allowed a small number of Irishmen to rise through the ranks to become supervisors, surveyors, engineers, and even financiers. The Irish provided not only the labor that extracted American copper, but also some of the industry's financial leadership. Marcus Daly, a famine immigrant from County Cavan, became one of Butte's famous "Copper Kings" in the 1880s and 1890s, fighting for control of the copper industry and its tremendous wealth. Daly helped to found the Amalgamated

Copper Mining Company, which later became Anaconda Copper Mining Company, with Daly as its president.

Cities like San Francisco and Los Angeles came to be major gathering points for Irish immigrants. Throughout the West, the presence of Chinese and Japanese laborers in the workforce tended to "promote" the status of the Irish above the lower socioeconomic rung they occupied in many eastern cities. In addition to a middling population of miners and laborers and an active labor movement, San Francisco's Irish community produced some notable business successes. Like many other Irishmen, Peter Donahue made his way to California during the gold rush days. From the blacksmith's shop he opened with his brothers, Donahue created the Union Iron Works, a foundry that would come to symbolize industrial San Francisco. The business kept expanding and Donahue became the owner of the San Francisco Gas Company, through which he would light the streets of San Francisco in the mid-1850s.

Donahue's eastern counterpart was Martin Maloney, one of many almost unbelievable examples of Irish American entrepreneurial achievement. Maloney was eight years old when he left Ireland and arrived in the United States in 1854. Before he died in 1929, he had worked in a coal mine until the age of fifteen, opened a grocery store in Scranton, founded a plumbing company, and illuminated the streets of Philadelphia, Pittsburgh, Jersey City, and Camden. Among his many inventions was a highly improved gasoline burner that could be used for street lamps. In 1882, he partnered with other businessmen to found the United Gas Improvement Company of Philadelphia, the precursor to the Philadelphia Electric Company. Maloney's interests and influence extended far beyond Philadelphia. He played a key role in organizing the Electric Company of America, one of the first multi-state power and electric corporations.[21]

As some Irishmen gained an economic foothold or even made fortunes in the United States, they helped to build and shape the major institutions of Irish American life. Chief among these was the Roman Catholic Church, a major beneficiary of both philanthropic giving and rising membership from the influx of Irish and other Catholic immigrants. Although French priests were the main players in the early Church hierarchy, the somewhat austere and occasionally aggressive Irish take on Catholicism came to dominate the American Catholic Church as it grew. Occasionally, tensions boiled over between the overwhelmingly Irish clergy and the varied German, Italian, and east European immigrant parishioners in the late nineteenth century, some of whom hoped to break into the hierarchy or to establish ethnic parishes. But the sheer numbers of Irish immigrants, and their presence during the first major growth of Catholicism in the United States, mostly ensured their dominance within the church hierarchy.

The Catholic Church was not the only carryover from the Old Country. The Irish also brought with them a particular aptitude acquired from decades of subterranean organizing—where a man's word mattered more than any formal structure—and resistance against British rule. Coupled with the natural English language skills other immigrant groups lacked, this experience drew more than a few Irish immigrants into local politics, where they and their children came to exercise an outsize influence. From the 1830s, most Irish Catholics owed their political allegiance to the Democratic Party, which unlike the Whigs or the Republicans, favored immigration and opposed temperance. It was to the distinct advantage of the Irish that the Democratic Party was in virtual shambles after the Civil War, leaving room for a new political group to organize from below. Almost more important than the stance of the Democratic Party was the opportunity to join, benefit from, and expand the political patronage model. The Irish quickly worked their way up through the major urban political machines as block captains, ward heelers, and "bosses." Much of local politics in this vein was corrupt, and it attracted withering criticism and intermittent attempts at reform. But the political machines also provided real services in return for votes, handing out city jobs or helping constituents to navigate the often biased or corrupt legal system.[22]

Labor unions were another manifestation of the Irish American genius for organizing. As early as the 1860s, Irish laborers began to combine for better working conditions, higher pay, shorter hours, and protection against arbitrary firings. First- and second-generation Irish assumed a place at the top of unions all across the country, from John Mitchell of the United Mine Workers to Terrence Powderly at the head of the Knights of Labor to Michael J. Quill among New York City's transport employees. By the time of the Great Railroad Strike of 1877, fully one third of the striking workers against eastern railways were Irish.[23] Although the popular imagination tended to associate Irish union activity with the extreme violence of quasi-terrorist groups like the Molly Maguires in the coal fields of eastern Pennsylvania, much more common were moderate unionists belonging to the American Federation of Labor (AFL). Later, during the twentieth century, Irish labor leaders like Philip Murray and George Meany presided over the merger of the AFL and the Congress of Industrial Organizations (CIO) to form the AFL-CIO, currently the country's largest labor union.

One outstanding union leader, unusual but not unique in being a woman, was Mary Harris Jones, known popularly as Mother Jones. Born the daughter of a tenant farmer in Cork, Harris (later Jones) immigrated with her family to Canada during the famine years. She worked as a teacher at a convent in Michigan and as a dressmaker in Memphis before her husband and children suddenly died in an epidemic of yellow fever. Jones moved to Chicago to start her business anew, but her dressmaking shop burned down along with much of the rest of the city in the Great Chicago Fire of 1871. Jones turned to union organizing work, at first for the Knights of Labor and then for the United Mine Workers. In time, Jones became a famous and fiery orator who visited various hotspots of labor and management conflict, from a drive to abolish child labor in 1903 to the famous and bloody Colorado coal strike of 1913. Jones cultivated an adamant, matronly persona and frequently defined her vocation as "raising Hell."

Most traditional histories treat Irish American immigration as a strictly mid-nineteenth century phenomenon quite separate from the influx of Italians, Jews, east Europeans, and others who began arriving in the years surrounding the turn of the century. But even though Irish immigrants made up a smaller share of the overall immigrant stream than before, the absolute number of Irish immigrants continued to be high, with over 2.6 million arriving in the decades after 1860.[24] Irish settlement remained quite urban, although there was a shift away from some of the traditional destinations like Boston and Philadelphia. Still, most Irish settled in enclaves where other Irish lived, thus masking the effect of their arrival. Whereas famine migration had largely been a family affair, in the years after 1860 the immigrant flow was dominated by young single men and women.

Young women were a particular feature of post-famine Irish immigration, and female immigrants slightly outnumbered men in those years. The mass death and departure of so many Irish men during the famine combined with the decline of the domestic cottage industries meant that there were very few opportunities for young women in Ireland, either for marriage or for independent employment. As in earlier times, Irish women immigrants joined upper or middle class households as maids or found jobs in the mills and factories of the Northeast. Nuns were accorded great respect in Irish culture, and convent life became an appealing option for many immigrant women. Others, usually the better educated, became schoolteachers and thus contributed to the upward mobility of the second generation.

Irish miners in Butte, Montana, 1908. The mining industries drew Irish laborers to communities throughout the American West.

As the sons and daughters of famine immigrants came of age in the early twentieth century, they gradually surpassed the modest stations of their parents. Irish American activism in politics and organized labor, which persisted even after the Irish lost their numerical superiority in inner city voting districts, paid off handsomely in this regard. Rather than toiling as unskilled workmen, second-generation Irish frequently attained city employment, union jobs in the skilled trades, and white-collar work. As during the nineteenth century, Irish Americans tended to be more prosperous in the West than in large eastern cities, but upward mobility reached urban areas as well. Through family, friendship, and political connections, Irish immigrants and their sons dominated various kinds of city jobs. The "Irish cop" (and his "paddy wagon") became something of a cliché, and to this day Irish Americans are well-represented in police forces and fire departments throughout the country.

Irish acceptance within the American mainstream was buttressed by several high-profile successes. Thomas Murray was one of twelve children born to an Irish immigrant family in upstate New York. Murray's father died when he was nine years old and to support his family he quit school and lit gas lamps for the city of Albany. By the time he died in 1929, he was a multimillionaire, the patriarch of a large upper class Irish family, the owner of all the major electric companies in the New York City area, and the holder of more patents than any individual in the United States apart from his fellow inventor and business partner Thomas Edison. Edison may have invented the light bulb, but Murray invented sockets, fuse boxes, switches, circuits, dynamos, and numerous other components that delivered power to the incandescent bulb. Murray also played a role in the transformation of New York City's social life. While his family initially had to create its own outpost of New York society, the Murray clan became so established that they later looked askance at what would become the United States' iconic Irish American family, the Kennedys, viewing them as parvenus.[25]

More generally, the Irish were moving up in society. In addition to Murray, other high profile Irish successes included James Farrell, the head of the United States Steel Corporation from 1911 to 1932; James Butler, the owner of a giant grocery chain and numerous horse racing tracks; and Michael Cudahy, the head of a prominent Nebraska meatpacking family. Even when the Irish were not quite so ostentatiously successful, they made their presence felt in small businesses, in the trades, and in the professions. In 1900, men of Irish origin constituted about ten percent of the business elite.[26] Large numbers moved out of inner city shantytowns into the developing suburbs, where they became known, pejoratively to those left behind, as "lace curtain Irish." Gradually, the departure and social dispersal of urban Irish men and women meant the disappearance of many of the old Irish ethnic enclaves, particularly in medium-sized cities.

One of the reasons Irish neighborhoods shrank was that they were no longer being as steadily replenished by new arrivals. Although Ireland was largely unaffected by the restrictive quotas of 1921 and 1924, which made generous provisions for "old stock" immigrants like the Irish, there was an unmistakable slowing of Irish American immigration starting in the 1920s. Although much of the population in Ireland remained impoverished, the would-be American flow was increasingly diverted to Britain, another country where the Irish had a strong migratory tradition and where greater opportunities for workers and domestic servants proliferated in the decade after the First World War. Throughout the twentieth century, the twists and turns of the Irish economy would send periodic bursts of migration to the United States, especially during the 1950s, but the flow from Ireland never again came close to the heights of the Famine era. The Irish presence among the foreign-born especially fell off after the passage of the 1965 Hart-Celler Act, which relaxed immigration restrictions generally but limited the visa opportunities for unskilled workers.

For most of the twentieth century the saga of Irish America was mostly the story of the follow-on generations. As Irish Americans continued their social and economic climb, they gradually broke out of recognizable employment patterns to occupy places in high-level politics, entertainment, and literature. The extent of Irish American— emphasis on the American—success in these fields is sometimes made most plain by the understated nature of their Irishness.

In politics, the nomination of New York governor Al Smith as the Democratic Party's candidate for president in 1928 to some extent signified the mainstreaming of America's Catholic Irish, even as the subsequent general election showed the persistence of anti-Catholic bigotry in many quarters. Before he ran for president, Smith was also an

ambitious reformer and fierce opponent of Prohibition. Several talented Irish American politicians wielded power throughout the latter half of the twentieth century: John Fitzgerald Kennedy, who won the presidency in 1960, was the most famous of these, but others included his brother Attorney General Robert Kennedy, Senator Eugene McCarthy, Speaker of the House Thomas Philip ("Tip") O'Neill, and Senator Daniel Patrick Moynihan.

The contributions of the Irish to the American film industry are manifold. Some of the iconic figures were first generation immigrants, including Maureen Sullivan, who played Jane to Johnny Weissmuller's Tarzan, and Maureen O'Hara, whose many credits include *Miracle on 34ᵗʰ Street*. Two famous Kellys, Gene and Grace, both had Irish forbears. The all-American dancer Gene Kelly starred in such classics as *Singin' in the Rain* and *An American in Paris* while the unrelated Grace made her movie career with *Mogambo* and would later join both Hollywood and European royalty. Spencer Tracy, who was nominated for nine Oscars and won two for Best Actor in 1937 and 1938, had Irish grandparents. Among those whose ancestors had come in the earliest waves of Irish Protestant immigration are Judy Garland and Bing Crosby.

The Irish have also exercised their influence in Hollywood from behind the camera. Director John Ford's influence on American cinema cannot be overstated. Best known for his westerns, such as *Stagecoach* and *the Man Who Shot Liberty Valance*, the second-generation Ford was a prolific director whose work would earn him a record four Academy Awards for Best Director. Leo McCarey developed a very different, but similarly iconic, body of work. His comedies *The Awful Truth* and *Going My Way* garnered multiple awards, including three Oscars for McCarey (two for directing and one for Best Picture).

Interestingly, many of the most eminent Irish American writers had a somewhat strained relationship with their ethnic roots. Nobel laureate Eugene O'Neill's father was an Irish-born actor who achieved a modest level of fame on the American stage. Several of the son's plays, such as *Beyond the Horizon* and *Long Day's Journey Into Night* (both Pulitzer Prize winners) document his tortured relationship with his family and the tangled relations between Irish Catholics and Protestants in America. F. Scott Fitzgerald, literary innovator and mainstay of American literature classrooms, belonged to a well-to-do Irish Catholic family from Minnesota, but attended Princeton and fell in with the Protestant establishment. His novels—notably *This Side of Paradise* and *The Great Gatsby*—betray an arriviste anxiousness about this transition.

Irish American history is of course still in progress, and Irish American ethnicity remains strong. In fact, Saint Patrick's Day today is a far more elaborate, boisterous affair in the United States than it has ever been in Ireland. Thousands of Americans every year discover, rediscover, or sometimes even invent their Irish heritage. But the ongoing ties and debt to those who made the difficult voyage from Ireland to the United States are real. According to census data, over forty million Americans claim Irish ancestry. Of those, some thirteen percent identify as Scotch Irish. The remainder either proudly proclaim their Irish Catholic roots or embrace their Irishness without concern for ethnic or religious divisions. In the end, it is difficult to argue with the impact of those Irish immigrants that forty million people are proud to claim as ancestors.

Endnotes

[1] Cormac Ó'Gráda, *Black '47 and Beyond: The Great Irish Famine in History, Economy, and Memory* (Princeton, NJ: Princeton University Press, 1999), 121.

[2] Quoted in James MacPherson, *Battle Cry of Freedom: The Civil War Era* (New York: Oxford University Press, 1988), 130.

[3] Patrick Lynch, "The Coming Elections," *New York Times*, August 30, 1854.

[4] Levi Boone, "Inaugural address of Mayor Levi Boone," *Daily Democratic Press* (Chicago), March 14, 1855.

[5] MacPherson, *Battle Cry of Freedom*, 134–35.

[6] Charles Rosenberg, *The Cholera Years: The United States in 1842, 1849, and 1866* (Chicago: University of Chicago Press, 1987), 59; James Gallman, *Receiving Erin's Children: Philadelphia, Liverpool, and the Irish Famine Migration, 1845–1855* (Chapel Hill: University of North Carolina Press: 2000), 109–10.

[7] "The Quarantine Incendiaries," *New York Times*, September 3, 1858; "The Quarantine Conflagration," *New York Times*, September 4, 1858.

[8] Seamus P. Metress and Eileen K. Metress, *Irish in Michigan* (East Lansing: Michigan State University Press, 2006), 56–62.

[9] Kevin Kenny, *The American Irish: A History* (Edinburgh: Pearson, 2000), 219.

[10] Owen B. Hunt, *The Irish in the American Revolution: Three Essays* (Philadelphia: O. Hunt, 1976), 45–102; Thomas Addis Emmet, *Irish Emigration During the Seventeenth and Eighteenth Centuries* (New York, 1899), 12.

[11] Maldwyn A. Jones, "Scotch-Irish," in *The Harvard Encyclopedia of American Ethnic Groups*, eds. Stephen Thernstrom, Ann Orlov, and Oscar Handlin (Cambridge: Belknap Press of Harvard University Press, 1980), 904.

[12] Donald Akenson, *Being Had: Historians, Evidence and the Irish in North America* (Ontario: P.D. Meany, 1985), 13–36.

[13] Dennis Clark, "The Irish in the American Economy," in *The Irish in America: Emigration, Assimilation and Impact*, ed. P.J. Drudy (Cambridge: Cambridge University Press, 1985), 234.

[14] Roger Daniels, *Coming to America: A History of Immigration and Ethnicity in American Life* (New York: Harper Collins, 1990), 137.

[15] According to R. F. Foster, between one and 1.5 million people emigrated from Ireland between 1815 and 1845. During the Famine years and their immediate aftermath, at least three million left the country. R.F. Foster, *Modern Ireland, 1600–1972* (London: Penguin, 1989), 345.

[16] Tim Pat Coogan, *Wherever Green is Worn: The Story of the Irish Diaspora* (London: Hutchinson, 2000), 253–63, 280–85.

[17] Stephan Thernstrom, *The Other Bostonians: Poverty and Progress in the American Metropolis, 1880–1970* (Cambridge: Harvard University Press, 1973), 112, 136–47.

[18] Ó'Gráda, *Black '47 and Beyond*, 114 15; George E. Reedy, *From the Ward to the White House: The Irish in American Politics* (New York: Charles Scribner's Sons, 1991), 63.

[19] James H. Ducker, *Men of the Steel Rails: Workers on the Atchison, Topeka and Santa Fe, 1869–1900* (Lincoln: University of Nebraska Press, 1983), 11–12, 65–68.

[20] Michael J. Makley, *John Mackay: Silver King in the Gilded Age* (Reno: University of Nevada Press, 2009). See in particular chapters 5, 6, and 15.

[21] "Martin Maloney Dies in 83rd Year" *New York Times*, May 9, 1929.

[22] Reedy, *From the Ward to the White House*, 12, 26–31, 50; Stephen P. Erie, *Rainbow's End: Irish-Americans and the Dilemmas of Urban Machine Politics, 1840–1985* (Berkeley: University of California Press, 1988), 25–66, 140–61.

[23] Patrick Blessing, "Irish" in *Harvard Encyclopedia of American Ethnic Groups*, 538.

[24] Daniels, *Coming To America*, 140.

[25] Stephen Birmingham, *Real Lace. America's Irish Rich* (London: Hamish Hamilton, 1976), 38–39.

[26] Dennis Clark, "The Irish in the American Economy," 241.

Mulberry Street, Little Italy, New York City, c. early 1920s.

ITALIAN AMERICANS

By Luciano J. Iorizzo

SSASSINS SHOTGUNNED CHIEF OF POLICE David C. Hennessy in the dead of night on a New Orleans street on October 15, 1890, but their intended victim did not die outright. There were no known eyewitnesses, and though the fatally wounded policeman conversed with friends that evening at the hospital, he named no assailant. On the following day, Hennessy took a turn for the worse and suddenly expired, supposedly murmuring on his deathbed to Captain William O'Connor, "Dagoes did it." Thus began to unfold one of several episodes that would unfairly mark Italian immigrants as members of an innately criminal race, unworthy of the status of American citizens.

Hennessy was no stranger to violence. He had made his reputation in the New Orleans police by beating two thieves with his bare hands and dragging them to the station house. He had also been acquitted of the murder of a police department rival, Captain Thomas Devereaux, by reason of self-defense. When he became chief, Hennessy sided with the Provenzano crime family in its battle with the Matranga clan for control of illicit commerce at the port of New Orleans. The Matranga gangsters were the prime suspects in Hennessy's murder.

Immediately after the shooting, hundreds of Italians in New Orleans were rounded up; nineteen were eventually indicted for the crime. Several of those indicted were members of the Matranga faction, but most had no known criminal connections. Of the nine who went to trial on February 16 to March 13, 1891, six were acquitted and three avoided convictions through mistrials. Jurors later claimed they had acted on the evidence (or more precisely, the lack of evidence) presented by the prosecutors at trial. But local newspapers and politicians cried foul, claiming that the jury had been compromised, bribed, or coerced by a mysterious entity known as "the Mafia" to hand down its verdicts.

The acquittals were a scandal. Encouraged by community leaders and a special Committee of Fifty appointed by the mayor, an inflamed mob of well over a hundred met on March 14, 1891, broke into the jail, and lynched eleven Italians, crying "Kill the

Dagoes!" Some of those lynched had been incarcerated on lesser charges, simply found in the wrong place at the wrong time. Five more Italian prisoners died later of injuries suffered in this vigilante attack.[1] No one was ever charged for these murders.

The newspaper reactions around the country were mixed. Some papers, particularly in the East and the Midwest, condemned the "lawless and uncivilized" behavior of the mob, but many expressed the view that justice had been served. The victims were described as sneaky and cowardly Sicilians, sworn to kill and maraud as members of criminal societies. The day after the attacks, the sensational headline in the *New York Times* read, "Chief Hennessy Avenged; Eleven of His Italian Assassins Lynched by a Mob. An Uprising of Indignant Citizens in New-Orleans—The Prison Doors Forced and the Italian Murderers Shot Down."[2]

Other newspapers used the incident to discuss unfavorable trends in American immigration. New York City's *Irish American* applauded the actions of the lynch mob and lamented that the United States had become a "garbage dump" for European countries seeking to discharge their least desirable inhabitants. In general, coverage of the Italian criminal element in New Orleans overwhelmed any attention to the actions of the mob. Next to the Italian suspects, the *New York Times* claimed, the members of the lynch mob were noblemen.

The public acclaim for vigilante justice was not universal. Italian American communities around the country, who felt they and their kind had been unjustly maligned and grossly mistreated, showed their outrage in a number of public demonstrations. The government of Italy, meanwhile, complained bitterly about the treatment of Italian citizens in the United States. Three of the lynched victims were Italian nationals, whose families were later awarded $25,000 by the United States government under intense pressure from Italy—the families of Italian American victims received nothing.

Far from countering anti-Italian sentiment, what pushback there was seems to have provoked new anger and ironically added credence to the claim that Italian crime was an international and far-reaching conspiracy. The *New York Times* warned darkly that the anti-lynching demonstrations could lead Americans to believe even law abiding Italian immigrants supported the Mafia atrocities in New Orleans. Italy's very public anger over the lynchings was seen as an even greater provocation. The nationalist American press pilloried Italy's response in the most bellicose terms, foreshadowing the jingoistic rhetoric that would lead the United States into war with Spain a decade later.

Hostility with Italy didn't lead to war, but the taint of criminality would linger for years to come. The events of 1890 and 1891 appear to be the occasion when the word "Mafia" first came into common usage among Americans, as shorthand for a powerful network of Sicilian criminals. As late as the mid-twentieth century, bigots would taunt Italian Americans with the phrase, "Who kill-a the Chief?" in reference to the Hennessy shooting. The enormous amount of nationwide publicity given to the incident did much to lay the foundation for the practice of identifying Italian Americans as Mafia associates.

In the 120 years since the Hennessy affair, Italian Americans have carried the burden of criminality in general and of the Mafia in particular. Why has this been the case? That some Italian Americans were involved in organized crime during this period is undeniable. From "Black Hand" extortionists in the late nineteenth century to the rise of bootlegging during Prohibition to the consolidation of New York City's criminal gangs during the 1930s, it is true that there have been real pockets of Italian American organized crime in the United States. From Al Capone to Lucky Luciano, some of the major figures in the criminal underworld have been Italian Americans. There certainly was and is a Sicilian Mafia, whose practices some immigrants may have brought with them to the United States, but the evidence is that its organizational reach barely touched mainland Italy, much less Brooklyn, New Jersey, Chicago, or Las Vegas. In fact, many of the most successful criminals in the United States (such as Capone and Luciano) were fully Americanized second-generation Italian Americans rather than immigrants. The popular notion of a massive, interrelated, Sicilian-based crime conspiracy with connections deeply embedded in the fabric of American society is pure fantasy.

Artist's rendition of the 1891 New Orleans lynching. The murder of Chief of Police David Hennessey led to the bigoted popular taunt against Italian Americans, "Who kill-a the chief?"

Crime has been a small piece of nearly every American ethnic group's process of assimilation and upward mobility over the past two centuries. During the supposed heyday of Italian American criminality of the 1920s and 1930s, numerous other ethnic groups—such as Jews, Irish, Puerto Ricans, and African Americans—can be found in the ranks and leadership of criminal organizations, including Al Capone's notorious Chicago gang. In fact, the emergence of other, newer groups in criminal activity lends credence to the theory that ethnic succession in organized crime is a "queer ladder" of upward social mobility.

Nevertheless, while other groups have managed to shake the stigma of organized crime affiliation, it has followed Italian Americans with dogged persistence. Even as the details of the Hennessy incident have passed into obscurity, the shiftless, scheming *Mafioso* who featured so prominently in the news reports of 1891 has become a recognized caricature. In part, this image is a cultural one, shaped by the books, movies, and television programs that routinely depict the Italian American community as being steeped in a culture of organized crime. Mario Puzo's trilogy of *Godfather* books presented an unflattering and largely fictional representation of Italian Americans; still, the story was widely read and later transformed into one of the most successful movie franchises of the 1970s. Al Capone, a figure of widespread popular fascination in his own day, continues to be the model for numerous movies and television shows. Re-runs of *The Untouchables* and *The Sopranos* present the negative side of Italian Americans to new generations.[3]

Magnifying the importance of crime has also become a habit among some Italian Americans themselves. Especially after *The Godfather*, which managed to romanticize Italian Americans even as it overstated their involvement in organized crime, the Mafia has acquired an admired, even glamorous, image in some quarters. Like all other Americans, Italian Americans are more likely to have experienced crime as victims than perpetrators. Yet the culture has become so saturated with the Mafia myth that for many it functions as a source of ethnic pride, as a marker of community and family solidarity. It seems that almost everyone in the Italian American community claims to know someone (or to know someone who knows someone) who is a bookmaker, a numbers runner, a loan shark, a drug dealer, or the acquaintance of a gang member who can right a wrong for you (or make someone "an offer they can't refuse").

The persistence of the Mafia mystique has also been the deliberate work of politicians and the police. American law enforcement has shown a remarkable tendency to assume the link between Italian immigrants and crime, beginning with the Hennessy killing, in which the Gang of Fifty used the homicide as an excuse to indiscriminately round up hundreds of people in New Orleans whose only "crime" was having an Italian surname. Decades later, in 1970, the arrest of New York City mobster Hugh Mulligan illustrated this dynamic once again. Mulligan was a known Irish American bookmaker in Hell's Kitchen whose career spanned thirty years. When asked to explain why it took the police department so long to uncover his activities, a spokesman for the New York District Attorney's office responded; "We never really heard about him before two years ago. When we went after organized crime we only went after Italians."[4]

Politicians have been little better. The Dillingham Commission Report of 1911, tasked with researching the social and economic effects of immigration for the United States Congress, purposely presented its statistics to paint a picture of rampant Italian American criminality when the data in fact showed the opposite.[5] Interest in the Mafia resurfaced during the 1950s and 1960s with politically driven spectacles from the Kefauver Committee to the sensational testimony of mobster turned informant Joe Valachi. Politicians like Estes Kefauver and John McClellan more or less ignored the multi-ethnic and multi-racial composition of organized crime and fixated on the Mafia conspiracy theory—the implication being that Italians ruled the criminal underworld.

The impact of what is essentially wholesale character assassination has been devastating for the Italian American community. Thousands of ordinary men and women have had their careers blocked or stymied by rumors of Mafia ties. Prominent Italian Americans who have thrived in politics, from Geraldine Ferraro to Mario Cuomo, have been haunted by similar scuttlebutt. The Mafia myth, though past its peak, is still deeply embedded in American lore.

To many Italian Americans, its persistence and prevalence is puzzling. The everyday lives of Italian immigrants and their descendants belies the ubiquitous, tawdry tales of organized crime that persist in following them. Instead, the history of the Italians in America reveals them to be a tremendous asset to the United States. Their values, their striving to overcome adversity, their manifold talents in music and the arts, their brilliance in physics and medicine, their heroism in military service, their vibrant culture and family life all attest to a vast reservoir of talent and strong values that they have brought with them to this country.

The history of the Italians in America begins as early as that of any European group. The European "discoverer" of the Americas, Christopher Columbus, was an Italian, as were many of the other early European explorers, including Giovanni Caboto (who landed on Newfoundland in 1497 and is widely known today by the Anglicized cognomen of John Cabot), Giovanni da Verrazano (who explored the Atlantic coast including New York Harbor during the 1520s), and Amerigo Vespucci (who lent his name to the continents of the New World). Several hundred Italians also served in the armies of explorers and conquistadors like Hernando de Soto and Robert de La Salle. Particularly noticeable among the early Italians were the missionaries, who could be found scattered throughout the Southwest and the vast trans-Mississippi region that would later form the Louisiana Purchase. But because Italy did not become a politically unified nation until the nineteenth century *Risorgimento* (literally, Resurgence),[6] there were no Italian colonies in the fashion of the French, English, Spanish, and Dutch settlements in the New World.

Italians were among the many European groups that poured into the American backcountry during the colonial period. Compared to groups like the English and the Scotch Irish, their numbers were relatively small: before the 1880s, fewer than 100,000 Italians came to America. The vast majority of these immigrants were professional, middle-class, educated, skilled, and Catholic (both clerical and anti-clerical). A minority included peasants, illiterates, unskilled workers, Protestants, and Jews. Most of the early immigrants came from the more economically developed regions of Northern Italy. Since many had previously experienced new cultures by migrating to northern Europe or to Spain before their American journeys, they were able to adapt to America with relative ease. A number of other northern Italians in this same period also migrated to South America, especially Argentina and Brazil.

When the American War of Independence broke out in 1775, several Italians lent crucial support to the American cause. Filippo Mazzei came to America in 1773 with a cohort of other Italians, including gardeners, weavers, cabinet-makers, musicians, and vine growers (who introduced the grape and olive to Virginia). A noted physician and pamphleteer, Mazzei shared his views on political and religious freedom with his fellow Virginians James Madison and Thomas Jefferson. Some have even claimed that Jefferson borrowed the famous phrase "all men are created equal" from Mazzei's writings. While some of his Italian countrymen took up arms in the revolution, Mazzei became an agent for the state of Virginia and set out for Florence to obtain money for the revolutionary cause.[7]

Francesco Vigo, from the Piedmont region of Italy, was another important personality of revolutionary America. Vigo made his way via the Spanish army to New Orleans, where he became interested in the fur trade. He won friends and garnered influence among the French and Indians along the Mississippi and established a successful fur trading business in St. Louis in 1772. Vigo placed his entire fortune at the disposal of American militia commander George Rogers Clark, who won the stunning victories over the British at Kaskaskia and Vincennes that ended British influence in the "Old Northwest" to establish American claims to that land. At war's end, Vigo moved to Vincennes and became a naturalized citizen. He is memorialized today in having a township and county in Indiana named after him.

After the War of Independence, many Italian clergymen achieved prominence in the new nation's Catholic churches and other religious institutions. Father Giovanni Grassi served as president of Georgetown University from 1812 to 1817, admitting non-Catholics for the first time and transforming it from a small parochial school into a respected, degree-granting institution of higher education. Starting in the 1830s, Italian clergy helped to meet a severe shortage of priests caused by the influx of mostly Catholic Irish, German, and French Canadian immigrants. Samuel Charles Mazzuchelli, a Dominican missionary from Milan, was one of the most successful of those to attend to the newcomers. He spent most of his career in the Midwest helping establish new parishes, ministering to American Indians, and founding religious and other schools. A man of many talents, Mazzuchelli also served as chaplain for the first territorial legislature of Wisconsin, drew up plans for the county courthouse in Galena, and designed the first Iowa statehouse in Iowa City.

Hundreds of other less renowned Italian priests also made their way across the country, long before the arrival of their countrymen on a mass scale. Father Lewis Griffa is an example of the proverbial unsung parish priest. As pastor of St. Mary's church in Oswego, New York from 1867 to 1885, he ministered to large groups of English-speaking parishioners and facilitated the entry of the French-speaking Father J. F. X. Pelletier from Quebec to take care of the equally numerous French Canadians. Eventually, Griffa encouraged the Francophones to leave St. Mary's and start their own church. Thus was born the Roman Catholic Church of St. Louis. [8]

Most visible in the general population were Italian artists, who helped close the significant cultural gap between the New World and the Old. The nineteenth century produced an impressive number of Italian American musicians, teachers, concert artists, painters, and sculptors. The United States Marine Corps band made famous by John Philip Sousa was built around a group of Italian musicians brought to America by Thomas Jefferson; four Italian maestros headed the band during the nineteenth century. Another productive and renowned artist was Constantino Brumidi, who introduced the art of fresco to the new country. His Michelangelo-like "Apotheosis of Washington," is a magnificent work that graces the dome of the rotunda of the capitol building in Washington, DC.

Prior to the Civil War, a small but influential group of Italian businessmen, merchants, and industrialists could be found scattered from coast to coast. Eugene Grasselli hailed from a long line of chemists in Torno, Italy who produced such disparate concoctions as gunpowder and perfume. Grasselli immigrated in 1836 and soon thereafter began building a chemical empire in Cincinnati. After the Civil War, his company made its headquarters in Cleveland and became one of the nation's leading manufacturers of zinc alloys. Another businessman, Giuseppe Tagliabue arrived in New York around 1831. A noted scientist and inventor, he manufactured thermometers and other glass instruments and performed important work for the United States Coast and Geodetic Service.

The dispersal of Italians around the country before the Civil War was fairly even. With the exception of the Great Plains states, Italians settled in almost every part of the country. Several ill-fated attempts at launching agricultural colonies attracted Italian immigrants to Georgia and Florida. The Gold Rush of 1849 was a magnet to California for Italians, and when the mines gave out, the immigrants turned largely to agriculture and fishing for their livelihood. For many years, Louisiana had the highest incidence of Italian immigrants of any state in the nation. The newcomers were drawn to this entrepôt by opportunities in fishing, retail, importing, dock-work, and agriculture (especially on sugar plantations).[9] In the antebellum years, Italians (like many Americans) pulled up stakes and moved west; many settled in Texas, where the major attractions were railroad work, farming, and small business. In 1878, a group of Sicilians laying a rail line in Bryan, Texas decided to stay on and develop a cotton colony there when the road was completed.

Although Italians trickled into New York State, both before and after the American Revolution, it was not until around 1880 that New York became the premier urban destination for Italian American immigrants. Most of the early Italians in New York worked on upstate farms; some were bricklayers and stonemasons, others worked as fishermen, waiters, cooks, and confectioners. A small but highly visible number made a living as peddlers and organ grinders. New York City was also the home of a significant exile community of Italian nationalists, socialists, and freethinkers. Eleutario Felice Foresti, a university professor and later US consul to Italy, taught Italian language and literature at Columbia University and New York University from 1839 to 1856. Giuseppe Garibaldi, one of the great heroes of the *Risorgimento*, briefly took residence in New York and worked at a candle factory on Staten Island during the early 1850s.

The vast majority of these exiles were sympathetic to the unionist, antislavery cause of the North during the Civil War. The Italian American community in New York contributed a company of soldiers to the multiethnic Thirty-ninth New York Volunteer Infantry Regiment, known as the "Garibaldi Guard." Three Italian Americans won the Congressional Medal of Honor during that war, and Italian American military service in general did much to temper whatever small degree of anti-Italian sentiment had built up during the antebellum years.[10]

Starting around 1880, Italian immigration to America entered a distinct new phase. In the four decades around the turn of the twentieth century, over four million Italian immigrants came to the United States—more than fifty times the number that had come between 1820 and 1880.[11] After 1880, the geographical source of Italian immigration also shifted southward. Whereas most of the early and mid-nineteenth century immigrants had come from the cities of northern Italy, after 1880 they increasingly came from either Sicily or the Mezzogiorno, the region south of Rome.

The new influx was due, in part, to changing conditions in the old country. Life had long been difficult for unskilled laborers and peasant farmers in southern Italy, but the traditions of rural life kept most *contadini* (peasants) tied to their families and farms.

After the *Risorgimento*, conditions in the south worsened. The new northern-dominated Italian government pursued an economic policy that ultimately benefitted the entire country, but in the short term favored the industrialization of the north; the south was often treated as though it was a colonial possession. Overpopulation, high taxes, and the inequities of the land ownership system held out little hope for the individual farmer to improve his lot.

Under these circumstances, the siren song of the United States beckoned Italian immigrants. Skilled and unskilled laborers in America could earn three times their pay in Italy (a paltry thirty cents to $1.40 per day). And in America, their dollar went further and their workweek was shorter. The growth of American cities also proved a powerful attraction. Amenities like running water, indoor bathing, toilet facilities, and central heating were still wanting in many parts of southern Italy. In America they could be found in abundance. Throughout the Italian countryside, labor recruiters and the agents of steamship companies spread the word of the wealth that awaited immigrants to America.

Many, if not most, of the initial immigrants in the post-1880 wave never intended to stay permanently in the United States. They were known as *ritornati*, or "birds of passage." With the goal of earning enough money to improve their lives in Italy, they would stay as briefly as a season or as long as several years. Some made multiple journeys back and forth before either returning permanently to Italy or putting down roots in the United States. In the early years, they worked largely in the manual labor jobs—railroad-building and construction—that had recently been the province of Irish American immigrants.

In the 1880s and 1890s, much Italian immigration to the United States was mediated by a system of *padroni*, or labor bosses. Generally English-speaking Italian immigrants themselves, the padroni functioned as interpreters and agents, connecting large companies with the cheap immigrant labor they sought. Sometimes these men would ruthlessly prey on the new arrivals, meeting immigrants at the docks and promising them irresistible opportunities and then charging exorbitant commissions, colluding with exploitative employers, and forcing women into prostitution. But the padroni were also important intermediaries who provided real assistance to otherwise isolated individuals. In addition to supplying jobs, they offered a multitude of personal services such as banking, loans, legal advice, translating, money transfers, and letter writing that enabled the immigrants to make their way in the new society.

By the time of the heaviest Italian immigration in the decade before the First World War, the padrone system had already ceased to be the major force it once was in Italian American life. Muckraking journalists exposed the abuses of the system and legislatures passed laws limiting the activities of these intermediaries. Also, as Italian American communities became more established, the immigrants were able to provide for themselves and the padroni lost much of their influence. Increasingly, immigrants were met by family connections, who could advise them on how to navigate the legal system or find a job. In some cases, large contingents or entire Italian villages immigrated to particular small towns or neighborhoods in America, facilitated by those already in place. This process of chain migration was instrumental in encouraging the birds of passage to change their life goals and settle permanently in the United States.

Remittances were another crucial impetus to accelerating Italian immigration during these years; from the 1870s to 1914, immigrants sent close to three-quarters of a billion dollars to Italy.[12] The impact of such remittances was electric; fresh capital bolstered the Italian economy and fueled a continuous flow of new immigrants to America. Previously, many southern Italians had been extremely reluctant to leave home. For much of the nineteenth century, going abroad was considered an admission of failure at home. As a result of this stigma, many of the early immigrants from Sicily or the Mezzogiorno led their kin to believe they were working in northern Italian cities rather than in the United States. But the large sums of money they sent home betrayed them, and the much-needed flow of funds from across the Atlantic gradually changed Italian attitudes about emigration. Soon, the most attractive young women were willingly marrying Italian Americans and the preferred destination for those leaving their hometowns was the United States.

Coming to America was one thing, picking a place to settle was another. During the period of major Italian immigration, ninety-seven percent of all Italian immigrants entered the United States at New York City. Many stayed, and the Italian population of New York ultimately eclipsed that of Florence, Venice, and Genoa combined. [13] Italian quarters, replete with ethnic businesses and crowded tenements, sprung up in lower Manhattan, Brooklyn, Queens, and the Bronx. But the immigrants also dispersed throughout the country: in large cities like Boston and Chicago, in areas already previously settled by generations of Italians such as Louisiana and Texas, and all along the railroad lines in frontier outposts like Yuma, Arizona. At the end of a railroad job, work gangs found themselves deep in the interior of the country with their pay and their compatriots; some formed the hub of future Italian American communities.

Most Italian men worked in the unskilled trades, but over time they also moved into other fields such as the garment industry, where they were very active in the labor movement through unions like the Amalgamated Clothing Workers Union and the Ladies Garment Workers Union. Italians also started small businesses. Because most Italian immigrants had little capital, they worked from small shops or pushcarts selling fruits, vegetables, meats, fish, and staples to the immigrant community. Some set up as barbers or shoemakers. Bootblacks set up chairs on street corners or other busy locations where they could service commuters. Those skilled as carpenters and masons worked from their homes as independent contractors and handymen.

At the turn of the twentieth century, immigration restrictionists complained that Italian immigrants failed to take up farming, like German or Scandinavian immigrants before them. To a certain extent, this was true and quite understandable: by the 1880s and 1890s, land acquisition and ownership had become much more difficult for those without significant capital. Even if they could acquire land for themselves, former *contadini* were in many cases reluctant to travel thousands of miles only to return to the farm. It was a time of enormous industrial expansion when cities were desperate for workers, and urban jobs held out the promise of decent pay and significant upward mobility. In this respect the Italians were part of an exodus from country to city by natives as well as immigrants; in this time, the lure of the city was turning America into an urbanized industrial powerhouse.

Of course, some Italians did take up agriculture. Louisiana had several fairly large Italian rural communities, especially in sugar cane territory. The cotton colony in Bryan, Texas, led to other farming ventures and by 1908, Texas had more Italian American rural communities than any other state. Most Italians in New Jersey were small farmers who would work at nearby factories or mills and spend their spare time clearing land. It was the mass migration of Italians to America that sparked the rise of the domestic Italian cheese industry; a group of Italian dairy farmers (mostly Genoese) in Wisconsin and Michigan started this industry.[14]

The largest Italian farming communities were located in California. By 1900, over half of the state's 60,000 Italians worked in agriculture. Starting as tenant farmers of greens and tomatoes, they peddled their harvest in farmers' markets in and around San Francisco. Eventually, as they acquired land of their own, they developed thriving businesses that catered to wholesalers, large hotels, and restaurants throughout the state. The vineyards and wineries of Sonoma and Mendocino counties, north of San Francisco, were manned—and in many cases owned—by Italian immigrants. Andrea Sbarboro and Pietro C. Rossi, pioneers in California viniculture, established a cooperative Italian-Swiss colony that gained international fame for wines that could compete with the best from France and Italy.

Over the course of the late nineteenth century, several large concerns came to dominate California agriculture, and Italian Americans often led the action. Marco J. Fontana introduced large-scale canning operations essential to the phenomenal growth of agriculture in that state. His Del Monte brand, established in 1889, became the largest fruit and canning operation in the world. Joseph and Rosario Di Giorgio were friends of Fontana. They ran the hugely profitable Atlantic Fruit Company in Baltimore before moving to California in 1911. Their Di Giorgio Fruit Company became the largest shipper of fresh fruit in the world, and their S&W label of fancy canned goods was highly sought after by consumers throughout the twentieth century.

Many of these agricultural ventures, especially in California, were assisted or underwritten by Italian American bankers and financiers. The most successful of these lenders was A.P. Giannini, who is widely credited with democratizing American banking practices. Born to Italian immigrants in San Jose, California, Giannini got his start as a produce broker and dealer. Noting that the large immigrant population around San Francisco was underserved by the city's banks, Giannini founded the Bank of Italy in 1904. Despite its moniker, the Bank of Italy served the general community, granting loans that were often backed by nothing but the good character of the borrower. After the disastrous earthquake that devastated San Francisco in 1906, Giannini was one of the first bankers to restore lines of credit. He encouraged small business growth, furnishing loans as well as business advice on how to turn a profit. He also encouraged branch banking, an innovative practice enabling him to shift funds around in a timely fashion to serve farmers in need of capital. In 1929, Giannini merged the Bank of Italy with the Bank of America and became the head of what would later be one of the world's largest commercial banks.

California's active and energetic Italian American community furnished other success stories in business and industry. Domingo Ghirardelli hailed from a line of confectioners in Italy. After failing to strike it rich in the California gold fields, he turned his attention to chocolate. Partnering with his son-in-law, F. Barbagelata, and Carlo Peters, Ghirardelli formed a company that specialized in importing, jobbing, and manufacturing sweets. The firm failed in 1870, and tradition has it that he was bailed out by Italian American fishermen, a major source of merchant capital for California's Italians in the nineteenth century. In 1877, Ghirardelli's firm came out of receivership and thereafter became a story of sweet success. Today, the company's chocolates are found in countless retail shops across America.

Italian entrepreneurs were not limited to the West Coast. Amedeo Obici came to America in 1888 at age eleven to join an uncle in Scranton, Pennsylvania. As he spoke no English, Obici's destination was written on a label attached to a buttonhole on his coat during his journey. But he was accidentally diverted on the train ride from New York to Scranton and found himself in Wilkes-Barre, Pennsylvania, where he grew close to the only Italian family in town. With little education, Obici took a variety of odd jobs, one of which was at a peanut stand. He discovered a process of roasting peanuts that led him to join with M. Peruzzi to establish the Planters Peanut Company. Before long, they were selling peanuts throughout America and Canada. Planters became an internationally known brand and Obici was crowned the "Peanut King."

The first generation of Italian immigrants in the period after the Civil War spoke little or no English. Since few had much leisure time, their socialization was limited to what family they had and possibly to fellow Italians from their hometowns. Although native born Americans tended to lump all Italians together, the immigrants often drew sharp distinctions among themselves. Many considered themselves to be *paesani*, that is, citizens of a particular region, rather than Italians. A unified Italy was scarcely thirty years old when the masses started migrating to America and some immigrants felt little attachment to the national government or to their nominal compatriots. Neapolitans settled near Neapolitans, Sicilians were drawn to fellow Sicilians, and so on. If, for example, a Neapolitan wanted to marry a Sicilian, both families might object on the grounds that it was a "mixed marriage." Regionalism of this sort still lingers among Americans of Italian descent.

Regional identification among Italian immigrants also led to tight-knit social groups. Early on, the main opportunities for family socialization were birthdays, weddings, wakes, funerals, and christenings. Family visited one another from house to house and entertained themselves with music, card playing, eating, and drinking. Traditional Italian cuisine became very important at these events, even though most immigrants had never enjoyed such rich dishes when they were peasants in Italy. Musicians and vocalists provided much of the spontaneous entertainment at these gatherings. The internationally acclaimed duo of guitarist Giuseppe Massaro (also known as Eddie Lang) and violinist Joe Venuti got their start playing at these neighborhood affairs in early twentieth-century Philadelphia.

Italian immigrants, like many other ethnic groups, also established fraternal clubs and mutual benefit societies. These groups held dances, celebrated holidays, played bingo, sponsored sports teams, and in general opened their doors for weekly dinners and casual card playing or conversation. Mutual benefit societies functioned like insurance companies (though less efficiently), collecting dues and then distributing funds to pay for medical care or burials for their members. In the early years, membership was determined on the basis of town or regional origin, and as a result the groups were frequently too small to function effectively. In time, the more successful groups like the Sons of Italy relaxed their membership rules to admit any Italian, regardless of regional origin. But they could not require their members to associate with other members, and regional cliques developed in which *paesani* would seek out their own kind within the organization.

The intense regionalism of Italian Americans faded somewhat among members of the second generation, who socialized outside the tight-knit circles of their parents. The sons and daughters of immigrants went to American schools, learned English, attended religious services with a mixed membership, and made friends in and out of the immigrant community. These children were sometimes more adept at navigating the American environment than their parents, a dynamic that often caused friction within households. Boys had significant opportunities to join a wider circle of friends, as they participated in various athletic events such as baseball, basketball, and bowling, usually sponsored by churches or local service clubs. But girls also moved beyond the compass of the family, sometimes by earning wages as garment workers.

In the early years of mass Italian immigration, the Roman Catholic Church was less important to Italians than to other Catholic ethnics in the United States, such as the Irish or Poles. Italy had a strong tradition of anti-clericalism, buttressed by the church's opposition to Italian nationalism and the *Risorgimento*. Moreover, the Catholic Church in the United States was overwhelmingly dominated by Irish clergy and many immigrants found its practices to be austere or rigid. Italian-speaking priests struggled to find a place in the American Catholic hierarchy, even in parishes near Italian neighborhoods, making certain rituals, such as frequent confession, out of the question for many parishioners.

Gradually, the church became more accessible to Italians with the establishment of ethnic Italian parishes. More likely to be staffed by Italian-speaking priests, these parishes offered many of the same support activities as those of the benefit societies. And like the benefit societies, they were frequently riven by infighting. Selecting a site for a church could become a major problem, with each regional group insisting on building near its own neighborhood. When Italians gained their own churches they were able to celebrate feast days peculiar to Italian Catholics. Churchgoers and non-churchgoers alike welcomed the opportunity to gather with family and friends during a religious holiday, whether it was a widely celebrated one—such as Easter or Christmas—or a regional favorite like San Rocco for Romans, San Gennaro for Neapolitans, or San Bartolomeo for Sicilians.

One exemplary Italian American religious figure in this period was Francesca Cabrini, better known as Mother Cabrini, the first American citizen to be canonized by the Roman Catholic Church. In 1880, this Italian nun was the driving force in the establishment of the

Italian-born Amedeo Obici, the "Peanut King," founded the Planters Nut and Chocolate Company in 1908.

Missionary Sisters of the Sacred Heart of Jesus, and she continued to function as the institute's superior general until her death. Pope Leo XIII sent her to New York City in 1889 to assist Italian immigrants. In America she founded an orphanage, known today as Saint Cabrini Home in Ulster County, New York, as well as over sixty other institutions located throughout North America, South America, and Europe. She built hospitals, cared for orphans, operated nurseries and schools, and generally looked out for the welfare of immigrants, earning her the epithet of "patron saint of immigrants." Though she mainly worked in New York and Chicago, a number of shrines, schools, hospitals, and housing projects across the United States and Canada stand as monuments to her selfless service.[15]

Italian American politicians were not numerous throughout most of the nineteenth century. Low naturalization rates among the early immigrants prevented the formation of meaningful voting blocs. Some Italian Americans found posts in municipalities or state legislatures, but before the First World War only two became members of Congress: New York City's Francis B. Spinola and California's Anthony Caminetti, who later became Woodrow Wilson's commissioner of immigration. As Italians began to naturalize and vote throughout the twentieth century, immigrant leaders emerged to win political power. Native-born political leaders were also quick to recognize the value of the ethnic Italian voters and solicited their support by doling out political favors. Patronage jobs abounded in law enforcement agencies and fire departments. Party leaders encouraged immigrants to form their own political clubs and to use them as stepping-stones to political careers as ward leaders or local officials. Some went on to high office as members of legislatures and judgeships. Carmine De Sapio became the top boss of New York City's Tammany Hall, a post from which he frequently lent his assistance to fellow Italian Americans.[16]

Almost as soon as they began arriving in large numbers, Italians attracted prejudice and resistance from the native-born population. One of the earliest points of friction was in the labor markets. During the 1870s, several thousand immigrants from Italy and Eastern Europe arrived under contracts to work in the Pennsylvania coalfields, principally as strikebreakers. Although many would later join the union movement, the immigrants quickly developed a reputation among the native-born miners as hapless, degraded pawns in the struggle between capital and labor. They were further set apart by their appearance and demeanor: they were poor, illiterate, strangely dressed, and ignorant of the English language.

As the mass migration of Italians expanded and accelerated, the immigrants were also castigated for their lawlessness and their affinity for carrying (and wielding) knives. They were criticized for living in unsanitary ghettoes and for eating "strange" foods such as broccoli, escarole, lentils, eggplant, anchovies, and tripe—all heavily seasoned with exotic herbs. American writers frequently cited the scent of garlic as a cause for alarm among Americans. A visitor entering an Italian tenement might be overcome by the unfamiliar aromas permeating the atmosphere. To the uninitiated, the smells were a stench associated with filth.

These stereotypes fueled racial resentments. Most Italians were lighter skinned than African Americans, but darker than Anglos. In the early twentieth century, census takers identified some very dark Italians as "Black Italians." The appellation persisted as late as the 1970s in parts of the Midwest. The racial situation was particularly tangled in the South. Italian merchants in southern states offered their goods and services to black customers as well as white ones, thus threatening the unwritten code of racial segregation. In Louisiana, where many worked on sugar plantations, Italians were seen as surrogates for African slaves, being characterized as a swarthy "in between" race. Italians were frequently the target of lynchings or other forms of mob violence, most sensationally in New Orleans in 1891, but also in Pennsylvania, Mississippi, Colorado, North Carolina, Florida, and Illinois.[17]

In the early years of the twentieth century, stereotypes about Italians melded with a more generalized anti-immigrant animus. Italians took their place alongside Jews, Slavs, Greeks, Arabs, and numerous other groups thought to be "degrading" and "diluting" the Anglo American population. These arguments were expressed in intellectual and scientific circles as well as popular culture. The prominent sociologist, eugenicist, and criminologist E. A. Ross wrote bluntly that southern and eastern Europeans were ugly with crooked faces, coarse mouths, heavy jaws, low foreheads, and dark and oily skin—all evidence of their "low mentality." If these negative physical attributes were not enough reason to keep the immigrants out of America, restrictionists argued that the ethnic interlopers were responsible for urban slums, lower living standards, increased crime, and outbreaks of venereal disease.[18]

Until the First World War, the growth of political nativism failed to translate into changes in immigration law. Efforts by the Immigration Restriction League to pass a literacy test that was largely intended to exclude Italian and east European immigrants consistently foundered on presidential vetoes. When the war broke out, Italian immigration fell off sharply. It resumed in the years following the war, by which time the restrictionists were ascendant. The literacy test finally passed in 1917 but proved largely ineffectual in keeping the immigrants out. The enactment of restrictive quotas in 1921 and 1924 finally succeeded in drastically curtailing the influx of immigrants. Italian immigration continued to wane through the 1920s, and the quotas marked the beginning of the end of the mass Italian immigration to the United States.

Decreasing immigration notwithstanding, the Italian American community made significant social and cultural contributions to their new homeland. Politics was one area in which this progress was highly visible. By the 1930s it was not uncommon for Italians to campaign for and win high political office. Running as a Republican, Fiorello H. LaGuardia was elected to the US House of Representatives in 1916. He was a staunch advocate of Italian American causes and instrumental in the passage of the 1932 Norris-LaGuardia Act that banned judicial injunctions in non-violent labor disputes, as well as "yellow dog" contracts forcing employees not to join labor unions. In 1933, LaGuardia became mayor of New York City and served for three terms. Responsible for modernizing the city's infrastructure and public transit, reforming of the civil service, and effectively fighting the influence of organized crime, LaGuardia is widely credited as one of the most effective mayors of the twentieth century.

The most enduring progress made by Italian Americans was not at the level of high politics; rather, it was in the lives of thousands of ordinary men and women, who spent generations ascending the socio-economic ladder in twentieth-century America. Known only to each other and to friends, their quiet success is nevertheless central to the improving image of the Italian American community in our own time. The history of one such family illustrates the tribulations and triumphs of Italian Americans more generally.[19]

The Neapolitans Giovanni Caruso and his wife Graciela were the first in the family to leave Italy in the late 1870s for New York City.[20] A stonemason by trade, Giovanni eventually sent for their son, Luigi (also a stonemason), and their three daughters, Paolina, Alphonsina, and Giovanna. None of the family had much formal education, speaking broken English for the most part, and all the children married other Italian Americans. Luigi married Maria Castellano, a widow and daughter of immigrants, who brought four children from her previous marriage to the union. Maria's first husband had left her some money, which she invested in real estate—buying, selling, renting, and speculating on property in Brooklyn. She was among the first in the community to move out of the Italian section of South Brooklyn and into the more affluent neighborhood of Park Slope.

Luigi and Maria added three more children to the family, two boys and a girl. In 1922, the forty-two-year-old Luigi succumbed to the flu pandemic then sweeping Europe and America. Even during the Depression years, Maria did well enough in her business ventures to send her two youngest daughters to college. One went to pharmacy school and the other, Giannina, to medical school in Italy (a rarity among Italian American women). When they married, Maria's children chose Italian spouses. Giannina wed a first generation Italian doctor and they opened a family practice together. The others married first- or second-generation Italian Americans. Maria's sons did not attend college. One became a successful businessman manufacturing ladies' handkerchiefs. Another took factory work and put together a band that played at local social events. The third chose a military career; a survivor of the Battle of the Bulge, he also served in the Korean War.

In the fourth generation, many of Maria's grandchildren intermarried with individuals of Irish, German, English, Puerto Rican, Greek, and Swedish extraction. The fourth generation resembles a cross-section of the upwardly mobile American middle class. The men and women are mostly college educated and have careers in medicine, teaching, investing, media, small business, and sports (one son became a key administrator for the New York Yankees). A few remained in blue-collar positions requiring no higher education. The fifth and sixth generations continue the lifestyles of their parents. The family now has added an infusion of French Canadian, Polish, and Czechoslovakian blood. All of the adult descendents of Luigi and Maria, some of whom spent years crowded in tenements, came to own their own spacious houses.

The record of this Caruso clan is noteworthy in that the women have achieved remarkable success. The family worked gradually from manual labor to white-collar jobs and the professions. The individual members have served their country in peacetime and in war. They worked hard to get out of the immigrant neighborhoods in which their forbears settled. While Giovanni, Graciela, Maria, Luigi, and many of their children are buried in cemeteries in New York City, none of the family lives there today. They can be found in Connecticut, New Jersey, Pennsylvania, and various counties of upstate New York, geographical markers of their social and economic mobility.

This pattern of advancement, typical of Italian Americans at large, occurred against a backdrop of tumultuous world politics. The Italian American community was deeply divided by the advent of fascism in Italy during the 1920s and 1930s. Especially in the 1920s, many Italian Americans were attracted by Italy's newly elevated stature in world affairs and by Mussolini's successful attempts to forge a concordat between the Italian state and the Roman Catholic Church. As the darker side of Italian fascism became apparent, with numerous exiles seeking refuge in the United States, opinions of Mussolini became more divided. Support for fascist Italy within the Italian American community collapsed outright after the United States entered the Second World War on the side of the Allied powers.

During World War II, Italian Americans were notable for their military service. Some of the hundreds of thousands who fought against the country of their forbears did so with a heavy heart, but they did so all the same. Among the many celebrated Italian American war heroes were Captain Don Gentile and Sergeant John Basilone. An ace fighter pilot, Gentile was credited with destroying thirty enemy planes, thus breaking Eddie Rickenbacker's World War I record. After receiving the Congressional Medal of Honor for his actions at the Battle of Guadalcanal in 1942, Basilone voluntarily left his cushy stateside military post to rejoin his comrades fighting in the Pacific theatre. He was killed on the first day of the Battle of Iwo Jima. His sacrifice is honored on several monuments, and he has a US Navy destroyer and a Sons of Italy lodge named after him.[21]

Before, during, and after the Second World War, a small stream of highly skilled Italian exiles immigrated to the United States. Several were luminaries in the humanities as well as the sciences, including the orchestral conductor Arturo Toscanini, the

Harvard historian Gaetano Salvemini, the journalist Max Ascoli, and the Yale medievalist Robert Lopez. A number were prominent scientists, the most famous of whom was the physicist Enrico Fermi. Known by his close asso-

Italian-born Amadeo Giannini founded what is now the Bank of America in 1904 to provide services to San Francisco's immigrant community.

ciates as "the Pope" for his apparent infallibility, Fermi had the rare ability to combine theory, experimentation, and engineering. His discoveries in the atomic field were crucial to the success of the Manhattan Project that yielded the first atomic bomb. Other émigré Italian scientists in America include Franco Rasetti, Ugo Fano, Emilio Segre, Salvador Luria, and Renato Dulbecco, the last three of whom, along with Fermi, were awarded Nobel Prizes.

These notables were allowed to come to the United States due to their special status as uniquely talented or skilled individuals. It was not until the 1960s that the gates would be reopened to other Italians not so advantaged. In 1965, Congress passed and President Lyndon Johnson signed the Hart-Cellar Immigration and Nationality Act, which abolished the quota system of the 1920s and put all countries on a more equal immigration footing. Although its main effect would be to spur immigration from Asia, Latin America, and the Caribbean, the law was intended to benefit immigrants from southern and eastern Europe. The fact that lawmakers now curried favor among Italian Americans, rather than demonizing them, spoke volumes about the progress made by the generations that came during the mass migration and after.

In the decade after the 1965 law was passed, some 226,000 Italians entered the country.[22] Although many of these new immigrants were kin to Italians already in the United States, and therefore taking advantage of the family preference system of the new law, there was also a significant contingent of professionals and highly trained technicians working in medicine, nursing, the natural sciences, engineering, accounting, drafting, and all levels of education. In addition, there were also those skilled in business, banking, investments, and politics. Many were part of the broader European "brain drain" that had been gathering momentum since the 1930s. These newcomers defied the old stereotypes.

In the post-WWII era, Italian Americans benefitted from the country's general economic prosperity. Returning veterans availed themselves of the educational and borrowing provisions of the GI Bill, going on to careers in business, professional, or white-collar work. Italians like the archetypical Carusos continued their move from urban enclaves into the suburbs. Older Italian American institutions like the mutual benefit societies faded in importance, and as Italian American priests, archbishops, and even cardinals found an ever more secure place in the Catholic Church hierarchy, the Church came to be the main means of maintaining Italian American ethnic identity. Since the 1970s, there has seen a major revival in ethnicity and many Italians are publicly proclaiming their pride in their ethnic heritage.

Italian Americans are increasingly well represented in business. The auto tycoon Lee Iacocca is a sterling example. Coming from a family hit hard by the Great Depression, Iacocca earned degrees in industrial engineering from Lehigh University and mechanical engineering from Princeton. He worked his way up the ladder at Ford, where he engineered the remarkably popular Mustang. After serving as Ford's president (and subsequently being fired from that post), he moved on to become the president and CEO of the troubled Chrysler Corporation. He resurrected the company by rallying labor, union leaders, suppliers, bankers, and governmental agencies—the latter of which guaranteed $1.5 billion worth of loans. Customers responded favorably to his personalized TV ad campaign that championed quality and fuel economy in American-made small automobiles.[23]

The postwar era has also seen changes in Italian American political involvement, which has become both extensive and diffuse. Members of the second and third generations have been particularly successful. Mario Cuomo and Geraldine Ferraro both dabbled in presidential politics during the 1980s, with Ferraro becoming the first major-party female candidate for the vice presidency. Italian Americans have continued to win big city mayoral races, from Boston (Thomas Menino) to New York (Rudy Guliani) to Baltimore (Thomas D'Alesandro, Jr). D'Alesandro's daughter, Nancy Pelosi, became a congresswoman from California and speaker of the house from 2006 to 2010. Cuomo's son, New York Governor Andrew Cuomo, is already being touted as a top Democratic candidate for the presidency in 2016. Antonin Scalia and Samuel Alito (both of whom are the second-generation Italian Americans) sit as justices on the US Supreme Court.

Indeed, in the modern era, Italian American success has advanced so far that in many fields it becomes impossible to name even the most eminent. They are a potpourri of the obvious and the unexpected, men and women with Italian blood lines not clearly apparent from their names: Bernard De Voto, John Ciardi, Lawrence Ferlinghetti, Richard Russo, and Don DeLillo in history, linguistics, and literature; Joe DiMaggio, Rocky Marciano, Yogi Berra, and Vince Lombardi in sports; Alan Alda, Al Pacino, Bernadette Peters, Robert De Niro, and Sylvester Stallone in drama; Frank Capra, Francis Ford Coppola, and Martin Scorsese in film directing; Frank Sinatra, Tony Bennett, Dean Martin, Bruce Springsteen, and Madonna in popular music.[24]

The ease with which many Italian Americans blend into life in the United States today is cause for both celebration and concern. It is remarkable that those whose ancestors were widely thought to be "greasers," "wops," "dagoes," "ginzos," and "guineas" are now accepted into the mainstream of American society. Still, a good deal of this progress has only occurred because Italians have muted their ethnic identity—assimilation is a constant balancing act.

Endnotes

[1] A succinct and insightful account of the New Orleans incident is contained in Dwight C. Smith, Jr., *The Mafia Mystique* (Lanham, Md.: University Press of America, 1990), 23–45.

[2] "Chief Hennessy Avenged," *New York Times*, March 15, 1891.

[3] See Luciano J. Iorizzo, *Al Capone* (Westport, CT: Greenwood Press, 2003).

[4] "Police-Crime Link is Under Inquiry," *New York Times*, July 24, 1970.

[5] Oscar Handlin, *Race and Nationality in American Life* (Boston: Little, Brown, 1957), 93–138.

[6] Scholars generally agree that this transitional period of Italian unification began in 1815 with the Congress of Vienna and concluded with the capture of Rome in 1870.

[7] Many of the Italians in colonial America are profiled in Giovanni Schiavo, *The Italians in America Before the Civil War* (New York: Vigo, 1934). Sr. Margherita Marchione, ed., *Philip Mazzei: Jefferson's "Zealous Whig"* (New York: American Institute of Italian Studies, 1975) will appeal to those seeking a more in-depth treatment of Mazzei.

[8] This paragraph and the one following are drawn from the copiously documented account of the first Italian Americans. Luciano Iorizzo, *Italian Immigration and the Impact of the Padrone System* (New York: Arno Press, 1980), 7–30.

[9] See Vincenza Scarpaci, *Italian Immigrants in Louisiana's Sugar Parishes* (New York: Arno Press, 1980).

[10] Aldo E. Salerno, "Medal of Honor Winners," in *The Italian American Experience: An Encyclopedia*, ed. Salvatore LaGumina (New York: Garland, 2000), 365–66.

[11] Humbert Nelli, "Italians," in *The Harvard Encyclopedia of American Ethnic Groups*, eds. Stephen Thernstrom, Ann Orlov, and Oscar Handlin (Cambridge: Belknap Press of Harvard University Press, 1980), 547.

[12] Iorizzo, *Italian Immigration*, 134–60.

[13] Nelli, "Italians," *Harvard Encyclopedia of American Ethnic Groups*, 548.

[14] Today, Italian cheese production is firmly rooted as a major subdivision of the American dairy industry. See Vinzenza Scarpaci, "Agriculture," in *Italian American Experience* and Luciano Iorizzo and Salvatore Mondello, *The Italian Americans*, 3rd ed. (Youngstown, NY: Cambria, 2006), chap. 9.

[15] See Mary Louise Sullivan, *Mother Cabrini: Italian Immigrant of the Century* (New York: Center for Migration Studies, 1992).

[16] Salvatore J. LaGumina, "Politics" in *Italian American Experience*, 480-86.

[17] John Higham, *Strangers in the Land* (New Brunswick, NJ: Rutgers University Press, 1955), 90–91, 169, 180, 264. Also see Iorizzo, *Italian Immigration*, 212–14.

[18] E. Digby Baltzell, *The Protestant Establishment: Aristocracy and Caste in America* (New York: Random House, 1964), 96–98. See also Edward A. Ross, "Racial Consequences of Immigration," *Century Magazine* 87 (February 1914), 616, 621.

[19] This account is drawn from the author's research and interviews with members of the family. Their names have been changed to protect their privacy.

[20] The names of the family members have been changed in order to protect their privacy.

[21] Valentine Belfiglio and Salvatore J. LaGumina, "Wartime Military and Home Front Activities," in *Italian American Experience*, 672–73.

[22] Nelli, "Italians," *Harvard Encyclopedia of American Ethnic Groups*, 558.

[23] Luciano J. Iorizzo, "Business and Entrepreneurship," in *Italian American Experience*, 73–82; Adele Maiello, "Ligurian Entrepreneurs in the United States," in ibid., 83–84.

[24] See Nick J. Mileti, *Closet Italians A Dazzling Collection of Illustrious Italians with Non-Italian Names* (Xlibris Corporation, 2004).

Although often identified as the "Ellis Island of the West," the Angel Island Immigration Station in San Francisco Bay often served as a detention center to enforce the Chinese Exclusion Act and other restrictive laws.

CHAPTER 4

CHINESE AMERICANS

By Erika Lee

O N FEBRUARY 28, 1882, Senator John F. Miller of California opened debate in the United States Congress on a bill to bar the entry of Chinese immigrant laborers from the country. Over the next two hours, the California Republican spelled out the imminent danger posed by Chinese immigration to the United States and exhorted his colleagues to support the bill that would become known as the Chinese Exclusion Act. According to Miller, Chinese immigrants were members of a "degraded and inferior race." Other senators compared the Chinese to "rats," "beasts," and "swine." "Oriental civilization," they claimed, was incompatible with America and threatened to corrupt the nation.

Miller felt Chinese immigrant laborers also posed an economic threat. They competed with white workers with their "machine-like" ways and their "muscles of iron." The American workingman—whether on the farm, at the shoemaker's bench, or in the factory—simply could not compete with his low-paid Chinese counterpart. A vote for Chinese exclusion was thus a vote for both American labor and for the "public good" of the country, Miller proclaimed.

The debate over the law did engender a modicum of opposition. Former Radical Republicans, like Senator George Frisbie Hoar of Massachusetts, called Chinese exclusion "old race prejudice," a crime committed against the Declaration of Independence. Overall, however, politicians in both the Senate and the House quickly agreed on its rationale. Discrimination was acceptable if conducted in defense of the nation, they believed. "Why not discriminate?" Miller asked. "Why aid in the increase and distribution over … our domain of a degraded and inferior race?" If the stream of Chinese immigration was not stopped, "these stubborn invaders" would threaten "American Anglo-Saxon civilization itself."[1]

The Chinese Exclusion Act became law on May 6, 1882. The new measure barred the entry of Chinese laborers for a period of ten years, allowed only certain "exempt" classes of Chinese (students, teachers, travelers, merchants, and diplomats), and prohibited all Chinese from obtaining naturalized citizenship. It was the country's first significant restrictive immigration law as well as the first to restrict a group of immigrants based on their race, nationality, and class.[2]

The Chinese Exclusion Act was a crucial turning point in the long history of Chinese immigration to America. A trickle of Chinese began coming to the Americas as early as the sixteenth century, and today there are 3.8 million people of Chinese descent in the United States.[3] Their experiences in the United States reflect the histories of global mass migration, and racism and xenophobia, as well as the spirit, perseverance, and striving common to so many immigrant groups.

Chinese began coming to the United States in large numbers during the mid-nineteenth century in search of *gum saan,* or Gold Mountain. Among the thousands of gold seekers who rushed to the West Coast during the California Gold Rush were 325 Chinese "forty-niners." In 1850, 450 more came. Within a year, the rush of Chinese gold seekers had begun in earnest: 2,716 Chinese came to California in 1851 and 20,026 in 1852. Only a few struck it rich in the gold fields, but there were enough economic opportunities in America as well as problems back home in China to make the prospect of new lives in America worth pursuing. By 1870, there were 63,000 Chinese in the United States, a large majority of them (seventy-seven percent) in California.[4]

Most of the Chinese who came to the United States during the late nineteenth and early twentieth centuries came from the Pearl River Delta in Guangdong Province. A population explosion, natural disasters, and political upheaval (like the Opium Wars with Great Britain from 1839–1842, and the Taiping Rebellion of 1850–64) created an environment of crisis in the region. Unequal treaties between China and western imperial powers often meant higher taxes on local peasants. More frequent contact with the West also brought the establishment of regular steamship routes between Hong Kong and San Francisco, Seattle, Vancouver, and a host of ports along the west coast of North America. Farmers who could no longer make a living on their small plots of land began to migrate, first from the countryside to the coastal cities. There they encountered American traders, missionaries, and labor recruiters. Thoughts of America and journeys across the Pacific soon followed.

In the early-twentieth century, political, economic, and social crises in China deepened as attempts to restore order under the Qing Empire faltered and Japan defeated China in the Sino-Japanese War (1894–1895). European imperialist powers tightened their grip on China's economy by forcibly occupying new territory, including key port cities. When the 1911 Chinese Revolution led by Sun Yat-sen failed to bring stability, powerful warlords emerged as the dominant power brokers in many parts of China. Internal rivalry between the Guomindang (Nationalist Party) and the Communists beginning in the late 1920s and a full-scale war with Japan in the 1930s continued to breed chaos in all spheres of life and provided additional incentives for many of the more ambitious Chinese to seek work and permanent resettlement abroad.[5]

Meanwhile, industrialization and the expansion of American capitalism whetted an almost insatiable appetite for labor in the United States. A massive labor force was needed particularly in the developing western states to exploit natural resources and to build a transportation infrastructure. Chinese immigrant laborers, who worked cheaply, quickly became indispensable as miners and as railroad and farm hands. They were hired again and again for jobs that were believed to be too dirty, dangerous, or degrading for white men and were paid on a separate and lower wage scale from whites.

From 1865 to 1869, Chinese laborers were instrumental in building the country's first transcontinental railroad. Hired by railroad barons Charles Crocker, Leland Stanford, Collis P. Huntington, and Mark Hopkins, 12,000 Chinese laborers made up ninety percent of the work force of the Central Pacific Railroad, which stretched eastward from Sacramento, California to Promontory Point, Utah. They cleared trees, laid track, and handled explosives for boring tunnels through the mountainous regions.

At the close of the nineteenth century, Chinese laborers had been pushed out of the mines and railroads and began to migrate back to the central valleys and cities of the Far West. An increasing number entered agriculture, fishing, trade, and manufacturing. By 1873, Chinese laborers were producing over fifty percent of California's boots and shoes, and in 1882, the Chinese made up from half to three-quarters of the harvest labor in some California counties. Chinese laborers constructed an intricate irrigation system that turned vast marshes in California's central valley into some of the most productive and fertile farmland in the country.[6]

Chinese American communities were predominately made up of men during the late nineteenth and early twentieth centuries. Like many European immigrant groups, Chinese immigrants often came to America as sojourners, immigrants who intended to return home after a stint of work lasting anywhere from months to years. Chinese women did immigrate to the United States, but their numbers were small. During the nineteenth century, the traditional Chinese patriarchal family system discouraged and even forbade "decent" Chinese women from traveling abroad. Those married to migrants were expected to remain in China and to take care of their spouse's parents, thus performing the filial duties of their absent husbands. Marriage and children tied the sojourner to his family and village, insuring that he would dutifully send remittances, and possibly return home some day. Other deterrents to female immigration included the harsh living conditions in California, high levels of anti-Chinese violence, expensive trans-Pacific transportation, and the lack of available jobs for women. As a result, women made up less than ten percent of the Chinese immigrants to the United States between 1910 and 1940.[7]

Immigration laws also presented formidable barriers to female Chinese immigration to the United States. The 1875 Page Act barred Asian women suspected of prostitution as well as Asian laborers transported to the country under duress. The Exclusion Act of 1882 discouraged the entry of Chinese women, though they were not explicitly barred. The exempt categories listed in the exclusion law—merchants, students, teachers, diplomats, and travelers—were almost exclusively peopled by men in nineteenth-century China.[8]

Most Chinese immigrant families during the late nineteenth and early twentieth centuries were therefore split across the Pacific Ocean, with fathers and husbands working and living in the United States while their wives and children remained in China.[9] Until the early-twentieth century, when more Chinese women began to pursue higher education and became students, there were no provisions in the law that allowed them to immigrate on their own. Over time, the easing of cultural restrictions on Chinese female emigration and the desire for economic security in the United States also prompted more Chinese women to move abroad as the wives and daughters of Chinese merchants and American citizens.[10]

The Chinese who entered the United States in the late nineteenth century were only a small fraction of the total immigrant population of the United States. From 1870 to

1880, a total of 138,941 Chinese immigrants entered the country. They made up just 4.3 percent of the total number of immigrants (3,199,394) who came during the same decade.[11] Nevertheless, their presence in the United States sparked some of the most violent and destructive racist campaigns in American history. Belief in white superiority and the doctrine of Manifest Destiny were among the factors driving America's expansion westward. Indian wars, struggles over slavery, and the conquest of the West were all tied to race-based ideas of who belonged in America and where they fit into America's racial hierarchy. Chinese were the largest group of voluntary nonwhite immigrants to the United States, and questions about their status in American life were raised as early as the initial phase of the gold rush in California.

Industrialists praised Chinese immigrants as a means to an end. They provided an ample source of cheap, available labor to build the transcontinental railroad and help develop the lumber, fishing, mining, and agricultural industries of the American West. At the same time, others believed Chinese immigrants represented unfair economic competition, since they were willing to accept low wages and poor working conditions. The opponents of Chinese immigration also fretted over the alleged vices (drug use, prostitution, gang activity) that the mostly male population of Chinese immigrants brought with them to America, in addition to the obvious racial threat they were believed to pose to white civilization in America.[12]

Demagogues, such as California Workingmen's Party leader Denis Kearney, capitalized on the deep sense of economic insecurity among the white working classes in San Francisco during the economic depression of the 1870s. Blaming Chinese workers for unfavorable wages and the scarcity of jobs, labor leaders such as Kearney charged that Chinese workers were imported "coolies" engaged in a new system of slavery that degraded American labor. Chinese immigrants' purported diet of "rice and rats" was cited as a clear sign that they had a lower standard of living, one that white working families could not, and should not, degrade themselves by accepting. Chinese men were also depicted as a sexual threat, preying upon white women. Further, they were characterized as an affront to acceptable gender roles in American society, as they often engaged in "women's work" of cooking, cleaning, and related domestic roles.[13]

Anti-Chinese sentiment manifested itself in legislative and extralegal efforts to bar Chinese from mainstream American institutions as well as from certain occupations and even entire geographical regions. State laws in California often explicitly discriminated against the Chinese. As early as 1850, Chinese miners were required to pay a special tax on foreign miners in California. Though the law was aimed at all foreigners, it was primarily enforced against the Chinese.[14] In 1854, the California Supreme Court ruled that Chinese immigrants, along with African Americans and Native Americans, should be prohibited from giving testimony in cases involving a white person. In support of its decision, the Court argued that Chinese immigrants were a "distinct people ... whom nature has marked as inferior."[15] In 1855, California Governor John Bigler approved a bill that taxed any master or owner of a ship found to have brought Asian immigrants to the state.[16] The following year, the state assembly issued a report that again described the Chinese as a "distinct and inferior race," a "nation of liars," and a danger to white labor.[17]

Not surprisingly, anti-Chinese sentiment often turned violent. Beginning in the 1850s and continuing through the nineteenth century, Chinese were systematically harassed, rounded up and driven out of cities and towns across the West.[18] In the spring of 1852, white miners attacked a group of Chinese miners along the American River in the Sierra district. Over the next few months, Anglo miners in El Dorado County set up barricades to prevent Chinese from passing through. Ruthless evictions continued throughout California's gold country. During the winter of 1858–59, a veritable race war broke out in the gold fields as armed mobs forced Chinese out of various campsites and towns. By the end of the 1850s, only 160 Chinese miners remained in California's Shasta County, down from 3,000 in 1853.

On October, 24, 1871, seventeen Chinese were lynched in Los Angeles after a policeman was shot by a Chinese assailant. A mob of nearly 500—almost a tenth of the population of the city—gathered to force its way into the Chinese quarter. The attackers dragged Chinese men out of their homes, while others hastily erected gallows downtown to hang the victims. Police stood by and did nothing as a broad cross-section of the citizenry, including women and children, assisted the mob in their grisly work. The Chinese massacre in Los Angeles was the largest mass lynching in American history.[19]

The violence and expulsions were not confined to California. On September 2, 1885, gangs of white miners attacked Chinese miners who refused to join their strike at Rock Springs, Wyoming. Twenty-eight were killed, another fifteen were wounded, and hundreds were driven out into the desert. On November 3, 1885, a mob of 500 armed men descended upon Tacoma, Washington's two Chinese neighborhoods and forced nearly 1,000 Chinese residents out of the city. Some of the victims of this "racial cleansing" were dragged from their homes and forced to watch their businesses being pillaged and their belongings thrown into the streets. By the afternoon, Chinese residents were being marched out of town in a heavy rain to the Lake View Junction railroad stop to be shipped away. Ironically, the line was part of the Northern Pacific Railroad that Chinese laborers—quite possibly some of the very people who were being forcibly evicted from Tacoma—had originally built during the 1870s. Others struck out afoot, walking as far as 100 miles to Oregon, to British Columbia—to anywhere but Tacoma. Three days later, the City of Seattle demanded that all of its Chinese residents leave town.[20]

The passage of the Chinese Exclusion Act of 1882 reflected a national consensus on the issue of restricting Chinese immigration. The edict was extended in 1892, made permanent in 1904, and remained on the statute books until 1943. Three hundred-thousand Chinese managed to enter the United States during the exclusion era from 1882 to 1943 as returning residents and citizens, exempt-class merchants, and family members. Thousands of Chinese immigrants circumvented the exclusion laws altogether and found ways to come to the United States with fraudulent documents, fabricated relationships, and false identities as "paper sons" and "paper daughters." The first to be restricted, Chinese were the first "illegal immigrants."[21]

One hundred-thousand Chinese entered the United States through the Angel Island Immigration Station in San Francisco. While popularly called the "Ellis Island of the West," the station on Angel Island was in fact very different from its counterpart in New York. Ellis Island enforced American immigration laws that restricted, but did not exclude, European immigrants. Angel Island, on the other hand, was the chief port of entry for Chinese and other immigrants from Asia. As such, officials at Angel Island enforced immigration policies that singled out Asians for long detention and exclusion. Chinese immigrants faced harsh interrogations, humiliating medical examinations, and long detentions. The Chinese made up the overwhelming majority (seventy percent) of the detainee population at Angel Island, and their average stay was two to three weeks, the longest of all the immigrant groups. Law Shee Low, who was detained there in 1922, recalled the anxiety and despair in the women's barracks over the interrogation: "One woman was questioned all day and then deported. She told me they asked her about life in China: the chickens and the neighbors, and the direction the house faced. How would I know all that? I was scared."[22]

Many Chinese poems like the one below were carved into the barrack walls by angry, frustrated, and homesick immigrants. They are powerful reminders of the costs and hardships of immigration under such a discriminatory regime; they are also evidence of resistance and perseverance. And it is this indomitable immigrant spirit that draws hundreds of thousands of visitors to the Angel Island Immigration Station—now a National Historic Landmark—every year:

I clasped my hands in parting with my brothers and classmates.
Because of the mouth [hunger], I hastened to cross the American ocean.
How was I to know that the western barbarians had lost their hearts and reason?
With a hundred kinds of oppressive laws, they mistreat us Chinese[23]

If Chinese made it off Angel Island and into the United States, they were forced to retreat into the segregated confines of Chinatowns or they found themselves isolated in larger communities. The only work available was menial: in restaurants, laundries, and garment factories. Second generation Chinese Americans repeatedly sought bridges to mainstream white society, but were often met with rejection and unequal treatment.

Despite exclusionary laws and the violent anti-Chinese sentiment in the United States during the late nineteenth and early twentieth centuries, Chinese immigrants continued to come in limited numbers, settle in the United States, form vibrant communities, and raise families. Lue Gim Gong, Wong Kim Ark, and Mamie Tape are three stellar examples of Chinese immigrants who made America their home and left a deep imprint on their adopted country.

Lue Gim Gong was an agricultural pioneer. Originally from a village near Canton, China, Lue was living in San Francisco when he answered the call for Chinese labor by Calvin T. Sampson, a shoe manufacturer in North Adams, Massachusetts. Lue traveled east in 1870 at a time when there were fewer than a hundred Chinese in the eastern states. In North Adams, Lue attended Sunday school and became very close to his teacher, a woman named Fanny Burlingame. Lue converted to Christianity and became a Baptist. He cut off his queue, and adopted Western clothing and manners. Fanny adopted Lue as her son, and he followed her south when she moved to DeLand, Florida, in the late 1880s. Lue managed the Burlingame family's orange groves and began to conduct experiments to develop an orange that could withstand sudden cold snaps. He ultimately succeeded in growing a substantial, juicy orange that could be shipped around the country in large quantities. In 1911, the Lue Gim Gong orange won the American Polomological Society's distinguished Wilder Silver Medal.

Lue went on to develop a new grapefruit strain and several other unusual plant combinations as well, but he never made a profit from his agricultural innovations. Indeed, after his citrus improvements failed to yield financial dividends, he became highly mistrustful of relinquishing any control over his orchards or of participating in the burgeoning mass market of Florida citrus growers in the early twentieth century. But he garnered deep respect among Florida growers and citizens of DeLand, and many came to his aid when he suffered financial setbacks that threatened to rob him of his land and his home. When he died in 1925, Lue Gim Gong, the so-called "citrus wizard," was memorialized for the significant role he played in the Florida citrus industry.[24]

Wong Kim Ark was a native born American citizen of Chinese decent whose 1898 Supreme Court challenge affirmed the constitutional status of birthright citizenship for all persons born in the United States, despite the immigration status of their parents. A restaurant cook and native of San Francisco, Wong was twenty-four years old in 1894 when he returned to California after a visit to China. To his sur-

Lue Gim Gong, the "citrus wizard," was a pioneer in the development of the Florida citrus industry.

prise, he was denied entry into the United States. John H. Wise, collector of customs, claimed that Wong, though born in the United States, was not a citizen because his parents were Chinese nationals who were ineligible for citizenship under the Chinese exclusion laws. According to Wise, Wong's claim to citizenship was invalid and he should be excluded as a laborer "of the Mongolian race." A self-described "zealous opponent of Chinese immigration," Wise attempted to apply the exclusion laws as broadly as possible, including second-generation Chinese Americans. Wise ordered that Wong be returned to China.

Wong and his lawyers challenged the decision with a writ of habeas corpus. He claimed that he had a right to be re-admitted into the United States based on his status as a United States citizen under the Fourteenth Amendment. The question for the court was: how does the United States determine citizenship—by *jus soli* (by soil) or by *jus sanguinis* (by blood)? The District Court for the Northern District of California ruled for Wong, but the US

Attorney appealed the decision and the case was argued before the United States Supreme Court in March 1897. With a majority opinion by Justice Horace Gray, the court ruled in Wong's favor. *Wong Kim Ark v. United States* affirmed that all persons born in the United States were, regardless of race, native-born citizens of the United States and entitled to all the rights of citizenship. The Court has not reexamined this issue since this ruling.[25]

In 1884, Mary and Joseph Tape went to enroll their daughter Mamie in San Francisco's Spring Valley School. School officials and the San Francisco School Board refused their application, citing state education codes that allowed schools to exclude children who had "filthy or vicious habits, or children with contagious or infectious diseases." Characterizing all Chinese children as dangerous or diseased, the school board trustees used these codes to keep Chinese students out and maintain a strict policy of racial segregation in the public schools. Because there was no other public education option available to the Tapes, the family launched a legal fight for equal access to education. They sued the San Francisco Board of Education and argued that as a native-born citizen of the United States, Mamie was entitled to the free education that was every American's birthright. San Francisco Superior Court Judge Maguire agreed. In 1885, he ruled, "to deny a child, born of Chinese parents in this State, entrance to the public schools would be a violation of the law of the State and the Constitution of the United States."

While the school board appealed the decision to the state supreme court, Spring Valley school officials continued to bar Mamie from the school. Mary Tape wrote a letter of protest to the Board of Education: "I see that you are going to make all sorts of excuses to keep my child out of the Public Schools. ... Is it a disgrace to be born a Chinese? Didn't God make us all!!! What right! Have you to bar my children out of the school because she is of chinese Descend." The San Francisco School Board responded by establishing a separate Chinese primary school in the Chinatown district. Mamie and her younger brother Frank were the first two students to show up for class when the school opened in April, 1885.[26]

Chinese Americans like Lue Gim Gong, Wong Kim Ark, and the Tapes all struggled with discrimination in the United States throughout the early twentieth century. In addition to the exclusion laws that restricted Chinese immigration and barred them from naturalizing, there were state "alien land laws" that prevented Chinese and other Asian immigrants from owning, and sometimes even leasing, land. Immigration officers seeking to deport Chinese immigrants staged terrifying raids in Chinese communities in Cleveland, Chicago, Boston, Philadelphia, New York, San Francisco, and other cities during the first two decades of the twentieth century. In 1923, the San Francisco Chinese community charged that they lived under a "veritable Reign of Terror." "No matter how long their residence or how firm their right to remain, Chinese are being arrested, hunted, and terrorized," the Chinese Six Companies organization reported to President Woodrow Wilson in 1918.[27]

The decade of the 1930s brought even more hardship for Chinese in America, with the Great Depression in the United States, the invasion of China by Japan, and the beginning of the Sino-Japanese War. Like their fellow Americans, Chinese Americans suffered from economic insecurity, but they were also distressed about the safety and wellbeing of family and friends in war-ravaged China. Then came the Japanese attack on Pearl Harbor, and American views of China and Chinese Americans changed dramatically, almost overnight. For decades, the Chinese in America had been publicly vilified as "Chinks," "heathen Chinese," and "inassimilable aliens." After Pearl Harbor, public opinion quickly shifted in favor of the Chinese, whose homeland had been under attack by Japan since the early 1930s. After the United States entered the war and became allies with China, Chinese Americans were now officially labeled "friends." The Chinese in America energetically threw themselves into the war effort. Communities organized "Rice Bowl" parties in over seven hundred cities across the nation to raise money and spread propaganda for war relief in China. In 1938, more than 200,000 people packed San Francisco's Chinatown as part of its first Rice Bowl party.[28]

Twenty thousand Chinese men and women served in all branches of the US military during the Second World War, the majority in the army. Maggie Gee was one of two Chinese American women to transport military aircraft around the country with the Women's Airforce Service Pilots Program (WASP). Inspired by Amelia Earhart, Gee endured the same lengthy and rigorous flight training as her male counterparts. "We flew the open cockpit Stearman … the 650-horsepower AT-6," she explained, "which had radio and retractable landing gear—the kind of plane used in combat in China." WASPs completed three fourths of all domestic aircraft deliveries by 1944 and were known for flying longer hours and having fewer accidents than male pilots. Opposition from the Army Air Force, however, caused the female flight program to be disbanded a few months before the war ended and the WASPs were not granted veteran status until 1977. Maggie Gee returned to Berkeley and trained to become a physicist. She also worked as a political activist.[29]

Before World War II, Chinese Americans had long been excluded from occupations outside of Chinatown, but the war economy opened up new, well paying jobs in shipyards and factories, where they could earn stable wages and mix with other ethnic groups. The biggest wartime change for Chinese Americans, however, was political. On December 17, 1943, President Franklin D. Roosevelt signed the Magnuson Act repealing the Chinese Exclusion Act. Chinese immigration was placed within the same quota system regulating European immigration under the 1924 Immigration Act.[30] The repeal was an important symbolic gesture of friendship to China, now a wartime ally against Japan, and in his signing statement the president cited the need to "correct a historic mistake."[31]

The repeal had mixed results. Because the quota system had been designed to favor "old stock" western European immigrants, only 105 Chinese were allowed to enter the country per year and America's gates remained largely shut to Chinese immigration.[32] The Magnuson Act did, however, allow Chinese immigrants to become eligible for naturalization. Several war-related measures also expedited naturalization for Chinese American members of the armed forces, and the War Brides Acts of 1945 and 1947 permitted citizen members of the military to bring their foreign born spouses and minor children into the United States outside of the small Chinese quota.[33]

Demographically speaking, these new naturalization and immigration opportunities for Chinese Americans had a much bigger impact than the formal end of Chinese exclusion. In the immediate postwar period, more Chinese women entered the United States than ever before. From 1948 to 1952, an estimated ninety percent of new Chinese immigrants were women joining their husbands after years of separation.[34] Chinese

Mary Tape (far right) fought for the right of her daughter Maimie (center) to attend elementary school in San Francisco in the 1880s.

sojourners and transnational families gave way to family reunification and permanent settlement in the United States.

During the 1950s, Cold War politics and the rise of Communist China placed Chinese Americans in a vulnerable position once again. In 1949, Chinese communist leader Mao Zedong emerged victorious over his nationalist rival, Chiang Kai-shek, in China's long civil war. The positive feelings toward China and the Chinese that had prevailed during World War II quickly evaporated. Chinese Americans came under particular scrutiny in 1950, when China intervened in the Korean War. An anti-Communist campaign led by politicians and government officials sought to expose alleged Chinese Communist spies in the United States.

American authorities also began investigating Chinese American communities to root out those who had entered the country during the exclusion era with fraudulent documentation. The so-called "Confession Program" was created to encourage Chinese Americans to confess their misuse of immigration documents and expose any relative or friend who had also committed an immigration-related crime; coming clean would result in amnesty. The confessions set off a domino effect that wrought havoc in the Chinese American community. Immigrants in a position to legalize their status could adversely affect their paper relatives or even their real relatives who were reluctant to confess. Many Chinese Americans described the Confession Program as a "no-win situation." Altogether, some 30,530 Chinese immigrants confessed. In return, they were granted legal status to remain in the United States as long as they were not involved in any Communist or "subversive" activities.[35]

But even as the Cold War created an environment of suspicion, it also facilitated the entry of a new generation of Chinese immigrants. Professional and elite Chinese began to arrive in the United States from Taiwan and Hong Kong in the 1950s as part of government-sponsored programs to recruit scientific workers and engineers in the field of military technology. They joined a small group of Chinese students who chose to remain in America after the Communist takeover in 1949.[36]

One of these new immigrants was Chang-Lin Tien. He arrived from Taiwan in 1956 and ultimately became the first Chinese American chancellor at the University of California, Berkeley—the first Asian American to head a major research university in the United States. His parents had been prosperous and politically active in China, but lost all of their wealth when the Japanese invaded in the 1930s. When the Communists came to power in the following decade, the family escaped to Taiwan. Life was hard: squeezed into one tiny room, the parents and their ten children slept in shifts. Chang-Lin took on odd jobs to help support the family while he attended school. He graduated from National Taiwan University and then applied to 240 schools in the United States in hopes of winning a scholarship. He attended the University of Louisville, where he experienced racial discrimination firsthand. It was this unsavory experience that led to his later advocacy of affirmative action in higher education. Tien completed his master's degree in one year, while two more years of study yielded a doctorate from Princeton. After having served as a professor of mechanical engineering at the University of California, Berkeley he moved into academic administration, serving as the school's chancellor from 1990 to 1997 [37]

The passage of the Hart-Celler Immigration and Nationality Act of 1965 was a major turning point for Chinese Americans. The statute abolished the national origins quota system, institutionalized a family reunification program and ushered in a new surge in immigration from Asia and Latin America, a trend that continues to this day. These momentous changes were felt almost immediately in Chinese American communities across the country. In 1960, the Chinese population in the United States was only 237,000. This number grew to 812,000 by 1980 and exploded to well over three million by 2010.

The normalization of relations between China and the United States in 1979 was predictably followed by a surge of immigration. This latest group of immigrants, or *san yi man,* is an extremely diverse set. It includes both men and women, members of the working and professional classes, and Cantonese and Mandarin speakers.

Many Chinese who first arrived in the 1960s pursuing educational opportunities helped to initiate an extensive "chain migration" under the family preference categories of the 1965 immigration act. This part of the law allowed them to sponsor their spouses and children, parents, brothers, and sisters. Once naturalized, these new Americans could in turn arrange for the entry of their spouses and children as well, and as a result the Chinese immigrant community in America has grown at an exponential pace.[38]

Chinese immigrants come to the United States for a variety of reasons. Some seek political asylum; Chinese emigration shot up dramatically from Taiwan and Hong Kong after the Tiananmen Square massacre of 1989. The imminent handoff of British control of Hong Kong to mainland (Communist) China in 1997 resulted in a similar exodus. In the 1980s, surveys of Hong Kong residents found that sixty percent of its lawyers, seventy percent of its government doctors, and forty percent of its civil engineers made plans to leave the colony before 1997. Many paid tens of thousands of dollars to establish themselves in Canada, Australia, and the United States.[39]

Other new Chinese immigrants have very diverse backgrounds. There are "uptown, high-tech Chinese" who are English speaking scientists, real estate moguls, capitalist entrepreneurs, and professional elites. Then there are the "downtown, low-tech" Chinese who are low-skilled, blue-collar workers, waiters, domestics, cooks, and laundrymen.[40] Elite and professional Chinese immigrants arrive in the United States with education, savings, and skills that are sometimes much higher than the average American. Statistics published for 2004 reveal that fully half of adult Chinese Americans and two-thirds of immigrants from Taiwan (twenty years old or more) had attained four or more years of college education. In comparison, thirty percent of non-Hispanic whites achieved this academic benchmark. Chinese Americans were also shown to be more likely to work in professional occupations than non-Hispanic workers (fifty-two percent versus thirty-eight percent), and the annual median household income for Chinese Americans was higher. Many of these professional immigrants formed new ethnic enclaves in the suburbs, complete with Chinese-owned banks, restaurants, malls, and Chinese language newspapers. Monterey Park in Southern California, where Chinese made up more than one third of the city's population, was nicknamed "the first suburban Chinatown."[41]

Another feature of elite and professional Chinese immigrants is their strong ties to their homeland. Like earlier generations, contemporary Chinese immigrant families are sometimes stretched across the Pacific Ocean. Some Hong Kong and Taiwanese families choose to split up the family unit in order to make the most of business opportunities in Asia and educational opportunities for children in the United States. Thus "astronaut" or "spacemen" Chinese fathers shuttle across the Pacific for business while their wives and children live and attend school in the United States. Some Taiwanese "parachute" kids are left alone in the United States or with caretakers and relatives to go to school and improve their chances of gaining admission to a prestigious American university while their parents stay behind to work in Taiwan.[42]

The "downtown, low tech" immigrants often labor in difficult working conditions in crowded garment factories in American cities, and struggle with high poverty rates.[43] Others include those who have entered the country without proper documentation, sometimes with the help of smugglers, or "snakeheads." With neither professional skills nor relatives already in the United States who could sponsor their legal immigration, an estimated 150,000 Chinese entered without documentation during the 1990s.[44] Many come from the coastal province of Fujian hoping to strike it rich. They pay huge sums and take great risks to fulfill deep-rooted American dreams. "Before I came here, I imagined America would be a wonderful place to live," said one thirty-eight-year-old woman. "I thought that if I ever had the opportunity to come to the United States, my life would not be wasted. [Everyone says,] 'The United States is better than China.'"[45]

Under the control of smugglers, immigrants are often forced to take long, circuitous, and dangerous journeys in order to get to the United States. Some head to Africa or Europe first. Others are deposited in Canada and Mexico and then cross the land border without documents. An unknown number have died en route. In 1995, eighteen Chinese suffocated to death inside a sealed trailer on its way to Hungary. Five years later, fifty-eight dead Chinese were found inside a refrigerated container full of rotting tomatoes in Dover, England. In 1993, a ship called the *Golden Venture* ran aground on Rockaway

Peninsula near New York City with 260 Chinese immigrants aboard. Urged by the crew to swim ashore, the Chinese jumped overboard. Ten drowned in the attempt.

Even if they survive the journey to the United States, undocumented Chinese immigrants often face years of exploitation at the hands of the "snakeheads" who brought them to the United States. Hidden in urban centers, they spend years working menial jobs in an effort to pay back the exorbitant smuggler's fees (often as much as $60,000 to $70,000) and to send money back home to waiting relatives. Some are imprisoned, beaten, and forced to work for extremely low wages. Some repay these dubious debts and buy their freedom—a few have even become financially successful. Many find only hardship and sometimes death in the United States.[46]

Two other groups of recent Chinese immigrants include ethnic Chinese from Vietnam and adopted Chinese children. The victory of the North Vietnamese forces in Vietnam in 1975 instigated the migration of 1.5 million Vietnamese, Laotian, and Cambodian refugees of which around 450,000 came to the United States. After the beginning of the Sino-Vietnamese War in 1979, Chinese businesses, schools, and newspapers in Vietnam were shut down and discrimination against ethnic Chinese became government policy. Beginning in 1977, ethnic Chinese were systematically expelled from Viet Nam. By 1979, 65,000 were being forced out each month. Many escaped by any means possible, often under the cover of darkness in barely seaworthy vessels. Traveling with only their most precious possessions, these so-called "boat people" fell victim to pirates who terrorized and often killed their refugee victims. Some estimates claim that thirty to fifty percent of these refugees lost their lives during their escape.[47]

Le Tan Si and his family fled Vietnam in 1979 in a boat with fifty-eight people on board. "The trip was full of hardship," he reported years later. The engine broke down and the boat was repeatedly approached by groups of Thai pirates who robbed the refugees of their possessions, raped the girls and women, and killed all who resisted. Eventually, the survivors made their way to Malaysia with the help of a group of Thai fishermen. Le Tan Si and his family lived in two refugee camps for fourteen months with the support of the United Nations. In 1980, just as the United States was formalizing its refugee admission procedures, he arrived in Seattle. "I then really had freedom and a new life in this country," he wrote.[48]

Adopted children from China began to arrive in the United States during the 1990s. Strict enforcement of the Communist government's one child policy established in 1979 to curb population growth led many families to put children up for adoption or to abandon them outright. Because of patriarchal values that led families to value sons over daughters, a large majority of these children have been girls. Orphanages became overcrowded and abuse was commonplace. In 1992, the People's Republic of China (PRC) began to encourage large-scale international adoption. The United States became a major receiving nation for children adopted from China. Many childless couples frustrated with the American bureaucracy eagerly turned to China for adoption. The Chinese adoption program provided healthy young infants free of ties to birth families. They soon acquired a reputation as "model adoptees." Adoption was viewed as a humanitarian act, in that American couples felt they were rescuing "unwanted" children; it also served as a potent symbol of progress for multicultural America. By 2000, China became the leading provider of children put up for international adoption, with over 5,000 Chinese adoptees arriving in the United States that year.[49]

As the Chinese American community has become more diverse in the late twentieth and early twenty-first centuries, Chinese Americans have been received in conflicting ways. Beginning in the 1960s, the image of Chinese Americans began to change. Caricatures of Chinese as inassimilable coolie laborers faded into the background as Chinese and Japanese Americans came to acquire the status of a "model minority." Economically and academically successful, such model minorities were said to have achieved success the old fashioned way—through hard work and perseverance.[50]

By the 1980s, these outwardly positive portrayals of Chinese and other Asian Americans took a darker turn as some complained that Asian Americans were taking the place of deserving whites at the nation's best institutions of higher education. Some made tongue in cheek references to schools allegedly overrun with Asians. MIT was said to mean "Made in Taiwan," while UCLA was supposedly the "University of Caucasians Lost Among Asians."[51] These sentiments were often overlaid with anxieties about American economic decline and international rivalries. With the demise of the Soviet Union in 1989, China slowly began to emerge as a military and economic power that might some day rival America. At the same time, the United States de-industrialized and sank into a recession in the 1980s and again in the early twenty-first century.

The People's Republic of China is now seen in America as both an important business partner and a dangerous rival. By 2003, the United States had a trade deficit of $489.4 billion, $129 billion of which came from a shortfall in trading with China.[52] Sensationalist bestsellers like *Hegemon: China's Plan to Dominate Asia and the World*; *When China Rules the World: The End of the Western World and the Birth of a New Global Order*; *Death by China: Confronting the Dragon—A Global Call to Action*; and *China Shakes the World: A Titan's Rise and Troubled Future—and the Challenge for America* have fueled Americans' growing unease with China. They claim that China's rise to power will topple European and American hegemony and reshape global trade and politics. Some even go so far as to describe China's ascent as an all-out assault on America. As evidence, some outspoken commentators contend that China gobbles up the world's natural resources while exporting "poisoned food, spiked drugs, toxic toys" that injure or kill Americans ever year.[53]

Many in the federal government, the national media, and academia have also expressed concern. According to the *Washington Post*, an anti-PRC group of politicians, congressional staff members, analysts, political operatives, journalists, lobbyists, and academics known as the "Blue Team" have been vocal in expressing the belief that "a rising China poses great risks to America's vital interests." In 1999, Representative Christopher Cox (R-California) released a 700-page report that charged China with stealing classified data on American nuclear weapons. That same year, Senator Richard Shelby (R-Alabama), who was then chairman of the Select Committee on Intelligence, told reporters that the "Chinese are everywhere, as far as our weapon's systems [are concerned]. ... They're real. They're here. And probably in some ways, very crafty people."[55]

This general atmosphere of suspicion, rivalry, and insecurity with China has also spilled over into perceptions of Chinese Americans and their role in American life. As in the past, Chinese in the United States have been continuously conflated with China. When Chinese fighter jets intercepted a US Air Force surveillance plane flying over the South China Sea, Chinese Americans took the brunt of American angst. A Springfield,

Chang-Lin Tien, professor of mechanical engineering, applied from Taiwan to 240 universities in an effort to win a scholarship for graduate work in the United States. He later became chancellor of the University of California, Berkeley (1990–1997), the first Asian American to lead a major American research university.

Illinois radio talk show host angrily advised his listeners to boycott all Chinese restaurants, declaring that all Chinese in the United States should be sent home to "their country." California Representative Christopher Cox made unsubstantiated charges that Chinese government-owned firms in the United States might be acting as fronts for the Chinese People's Liberation Army and then conflated Chinese American scientists, students, and businesspeople with Chinese government personnel.[56]

Chinese American scientists have often been accused of spying for China. The most egregious case involved Wen Ho Lee, a Taiwanese-born Chinese American physicist and research scientist at Los Alamos National Laboratory in New Mexico. Lee came under investigation in 1999 when the *New York Times* alleged that an insider at the Los Alamos lab had been passing nuclear warhead technology to China; intelligence officers were convinced that a Chinese spy was responsible. Because of his ethnic background and access to the secret data, Wen Ho Lee was identified as the prime suspect. News of the investigation was leaked to the press and Lee was arrested, shackled, and placed in solitary confinement for nearly seven months. After five years of intensive investigation, the US government unearthed no evidence of espionage activity by Lee. Eventually, it was conceded by various experts that the case had been severely mishandled. Robert Vrooman, former head of the counterintelligence unit at Los Alamos, went so far as to say that the entire investigation had been "built on thin air," and that the reason that the federal government had targeted Lee in the first place was because he was Chinese. The US District Court judge in New Mexico in charge of Lee's case issued a formal apology: "I believe you were terribly wronged by being held in custody pretrial ... under demeaning, unnecessarily punitive conditions. ... [Top government officials] have embarrassed our entire nation."[57]

Beginning in the 1980s, Asian Americans were increasingly targeted by a rash of hate crimes, including intimidation and murder. The first high-profile case occurred in Detroit, where the American auto industry was in serious economic decline while Japanese and Korean auto manufacturers flourished. It was not uncommon for autoworkers and the media to blame Japanese imports for Detroit's economic woes. In 1982, Vincent Chin, a Chinese American engineer, was beaten to death with a baseball bat by two white autoworkers who equated him with Japan's increasing power in the auto industry. The two men reportedly called Chin a "Jap" and yelled, "It's because of you, motherf***ers that we're out of work!" The men were convicted of manslaughter and sentenced to three years probation and $3,780 in fines and court costs. The murder and the incredibly light sentence prompted protests from the Asian American community and civil rights organizations across the country.[58]

Even as the Chinese American community is facing increased scrutiny and sometimes harassment and violence at the beginning of the twenty-first century, it is also sending forth some of its most committed visionaries in a variety of fields to lead the United States into the future. Gary Locke traces his roots to an ancestor who settled in Olympia, Washington, in 1874, worked as a domestic servant, and became a leader of the Chinese American community in Seattle. Locke's father served in World War II and Gary spent his early years living in public housing for veterans' families in Seattle. After graduating from Yale University and Boston University Law School, Locke returned to Washington and began a career in state politics. In 1996, he was elected governor of Washington, the first Chinese American governor in the nation's history. In 2003, he delivered the Democratic Party's response to President George W. Bush's State of the Union Address. His comments emphasized his own story, which exemplifies Chinese immigrants' role in achieving the American Dream: "My grandfather came to this country from China nearly a century ago and worked as a servant. Now I serve as governor just one mile from where my grandfather worked. It took our family one hundred years to travel that mile. It was a voyage we could only make in America."[59]

After a two-year stint as President Obama's Commerce Secretary, Locke was named as the US ambassador to China. In his new role, Locke has sought to dispel notions of Sino-American rivalry. In his first speech in China in September of 2011, he announced, "President Obama and I reject the notion that China and the United States are engaged in a zero-sum competition, where one side must fall for the other to rise. We can and must achieve security and prosperity together."[60] He insists that this process requires China to open important sectors of its economy to foreign investment and relax online censorship.[61] Ambassador Locke has proven to be extremely popular among everyday Chinese. A photograph of him buying his own coffee and carrying his luggage at the Seattle airport on his way to his new posting was widely circulated throughout China. The image of a high-ranking government official performing such mundane tasks for himself shocked many Chinese, who are not used to seeing the same behavior displayed by their own officials. "This is something unbelievable in China," said ZhaoHuiTang, a Chinese American who snapped the photo. "Even for low-ranking officials, we don't do things for ourselves. Someone goes to buy the coffee for them. Someone carries their bags for them."[62]

Activist and author Grace Lee Boggs is another leader charting a new future for Chinese Americans. Born in 1915 to Chinese immigrant parents, Boggs grew up in Providence, Rhode Island. She attended Barnard College and then went on to Bryn Mawr where she received her PhD in 1940. Unable to find a post in academia, she relocated to Chicago where she became involved in African American civil rights activism through her work with West Indian Marxist C.L.R. James. She was inspired by African Americans' struggle for civil rights, especially labor leader A. Philip Randolph's successful campaign to establish fair hiring practices in American defense plants during the 1940s. "When I saw what a movement could do I said, 'Boy that's what I wanna do with my life,'" Boggs recalled.[63] She married African American activist James Boggs and moved to Detroit in 1953. The pair worked together for decades playing a key role in the many social and "humanizing" movements of the late twentieth century, including civil rights, Black Power, labor issues, women's rights, antiwar campaigns, environmental concerns, and Asian American rights.[64]

At the age of ninety-five, Grace Lee Boggs still expresses her steadfast belief in the power of ideas. She published her autobiography, *Living for Change*, in 1998 and a collection of essays, *The Next American Revolution: Sustainable Activism for the Twenty-First Century*, in 2011. Her words continue to inspire all Americans: "These are times that try our souls," she writes of the global economic crisis, divisive politics, war, and disinvestment in cities and public education. "How are we going to build a twenty-first-century America in which people of all races and ethnicities live together in harmony ... ?"[65] The answer, she claims, is openness and activism: "We must open our hearts to new beacons of Hope. We must expand our minds to new modes of thought. We must equip our hands with new methods of organizing."[66]

Contemporary Chinese Americans are also great innovators in business and technology. Jerry Yang was born in Taiwan in 1968. His father died when he was two years old and his mother, fearing that her sons would be drafted into the Taiwanese army, moved the family to San Jose, California when Jerry was ten. He spoke very little English, but rose to the challenge. "We got made fun of a lot at first," he recalled. "I didn't even know who the faces were on the paper money. But when we had a math quiz in school I'd always blow everyone else away. And by our third year, my brother and I had gone from remedial English to advanced-placement English." While studying electrical engineering at Stanford University during the early 1990s, Yang and his friend David Fillo started an Internet company they initially named "Jerry and Dave's Guide to the World Wide Web." Later, it came to be known as Yahoo!, one of the world's foremost search engines. Yang served as the company's CEO from 2007 to 2009.[67]

Chinese Americans have a long history in the United States; trans-Pacific journeys brought gold prospectors, prostitutes, merchants, students, and families from China to the United States. They struggled to forge new lives in a strange land while suffering the indignity of racism and discrimination. Today's diverse community of Chinese Americans comes from many different political, economic, and social backgrounds, a reflection of the changing face of America. As one of the fastest growing immigrant groups, Chinese Americans will continue to shape America's future—just as they did America's past.

Endnotes

[1] Congressional testimony, cited in Andrew Gyory, *Closing the Gate: Race, Politics and the Chinese Exclusion Act* (Chapel Hill, University of North Carolina Press, 1998), 223–38.

[2] Erika Lee, *At America's Gates: Chinese Immigration During the Exclusion Era, 1882–1943* (Chapel Hill: University of North Carolina Press, 2003), 40–43.

[3] "UCLA AASC: 2011 Statistical Portrait of Asian Americans, Native Hawaiians, and Other Pacific Islanders," UCLA Asian American Studies Center, accessed October 6, 2011, http://www.aasc.ucla.edu/archives/stats2011.asp.

[4] Ronald Takaki, *Strangers from a Different Shore: A History of Asian Americans* (Boston: Little, Brown, 1989), 79.

[5] Erika Lee and Judy Yung, *Angel Island: Immigrant Gateway to America* (New York: Oxford University Press, 2010), 70–71.

[6] Sucheng Chan, *This Bittersweet Soil: The Chinese in California Agriculture* (Berkeley: University of California Press, 1986), 51–78; Takaki, *Strangers*, 84–94.

[7] Women made up less than ten percent of the Chinese immigrants to the United States between 1910 and 1940. Sucheng Chan, "Exclusion of Chinese Women," in Sucheng Chan, ed., *Entry Denied: Exclusion and the Chinese Community in America, 1882–1943* (Philadelphia: Temple University Press, 1991), 95–99; Judy Yung, *Unbound Feet: A Social History of Chinese Women in San Francisco* (Berkeley: University of California Press, 1995), 55–63.

[8] The Page Law is formally passed as Act of March 3, 1875 (18 Stat. 477). On its effects on Chinese female immigration, see George Anthony Peffer, *If They Don't Bring Their Women Here: Chinese Female Immigration Before Exclusion* (Urbana: University of Illinios Press, 1999). On the Exclusion Act's impact, see Chan, "Exclusion of Chinese Women."

[9] Madeline Hsu, *Dreaming of Gold, Dreaming of Home: Transnationalism and Migration Between the United States and South China, 1882–1943* (Stanford: Stanford University Press, 2000), 90–123.

[10] Chan, "The Exclusion of Chinese Women;" Yung, *Unbound Feet*, 55–63.

[11] US Department of Commerce and Labor, *Annual Report of the Commissioner-General of Immigration* (Washington: Government Printing Office, 1906), 43; Fu-ju Liu, "A Comparative Demographic Study of Native-born and Foreign-born Chinese Populations in the United States" (PhD diss., University of Michigan, 1953), 223; Helen Chen, "Chinese Immigration into the United States: An Analysis of Changes in Immigration Policies," (PhD diss., Brandeis University, 1980), 201.

[12] Elmer Clarence Sandmeyer, *The Anti-Chinese Movement in California* (Urbana, IL: University of Illinois Press, 1973, 1991), 14–15, 20–21, 30. See also Robert Lee, *Orientals: Asian Americans in Popular Culture* (Philadelphia: Temple University Press, 1999), 15–50, 57–82.

[13] R. Lee, *Orientals*, 83–105; Karen J. Leong, "'A Distant and Antagonistic Race:' Constructions of Chinese Manhood in the Exclusionist Debates, 1869–1878," in *Across the Great Divide: Cultures of Manhood in the American West*, eds. Laura McCall, Matthew Basso, and Dee Garceau (New York: Routledge, 2000), 131–48.

[14] The Act (Act of April 13, 1850, ch. 97, Cal. Stat. 221, 221–22) was popularly known as the Foreign Miner's Tax. Though it survived a challenge to its constitutionality in court in 1850, it proved impossible to enforce and was repealed in 1851. It was reinstated in 1852. See Charles McClain, Jr., *In Search of Equality: The Chinese Struggle Against Discrimination in Nineteenth-Century America* (Berkeley: University of California Press, 1994), 10n9, 289.

[15] *People v. Hall*, 4 Cal. 399, 405 (1854), as cited in Lucy Salyer, *Laws Harsh as Tigers: Chinese Immigrants and the Shaping of Modern Immigration Law* (Chapel Hill: University of North Carolina Press, 1995), 8.

[16] Foreshadowing the use of Chinese and other Asians' inability to become naturalized citizens as a means of excluding them from the country, the 1855 law was entitled "An Act to Discourage the Immigration to this

State of Persons Who Cannot Become Citizens Thereof." In 1857, in *People v. Downer,* the California Supreme Court ruled that the law was an impermissible interference with the national government's exclusive power to regulate foreign commerce. See Charles McClain, *In Search of Equality,* 17–18.

[17] Assembly Committee on Mines and Mining Interests, *Report,* Cal. Assembly, 7th Sess., Appendix to the Journal of the Assembly (1856) 3, 9, 13, as cited in McClain, *In Search of Equality,* 20.

[18] Jean Pfaelzer, *Driven Out: The Forgotten War Against Chinese Americans* (New York: Random House, 2007), 10–16.

[19] John Johnson, "How Los Angeles Covered Up the Massacre of 17 Chinese," *LA Weekly,* March 10, 2011, accessed September 13, 2011, http://www.laweekly.com/2011-03-10/news/how-los-angeles-covered-up-the-massacre-of-18-chinese/.

[20] Pfaelzer, *Driven Out,* xv–xvi, 262.

[21] E. Lee, *At America's Gates,* 147–50.

[22] Lee and Yung, *Angel Island,* 88–89.

[23] Ibid., 69.

[24] Ruthanne Lum McCunn, *Chinese American Portraits: Personal Histories, 1828-1988* (Seattle: University of Washington Press, 1988), 32–39.

[25] *United States v. Wong Kim Ark,* 169 U.S. 649 (1898); Erika Lee, "*Wong Kim Ark v. United States*: Immigration, Race, and Citizenship," in *Race Law Stories,* Devin Carbado and Rachel Moran, eds., (New York: Foundation Press, 2008), 89–109.

[26] McCunn, *Chinese American Portraits,* 41–45; Mae Ngai, *The Lucky Ones: One Family and the Extraordinary Invention of Chinese America* (New York: Houghton Mifflin, 2010), 43–57.

[27] Lee, *At America's Gates,* 228–31.

[28] R. Lee, *Orientals,* 147–48; Yung, *Unbound Feet,* 239.

[29] Yung, *Unbound Feet,* 252, 257.

[30] "An Act to Repeal the Chinese Exclusion Acts, To Establish Quotas, and For Other Purposes," Act of Dec. 17, 1943, (57 Stat. 600; 8 U.S.C. 212(a).

[31] "President Urges Congress Repeal Chinese Exclusion Act as War Aid," *New York Times,* October 12, 1943.

[32] Despite the small quota allocated to Chinese immigrants, Chinese could continue to enter as non-quota immigrants if they were returning citizens or returning residents from visits abroad. Members of certain professional classes were also allowed in outside of the quota. Ministers, professors, and their wives and minor children were non-quota immigrants. So were students and the wives and minor children of US citizens. David Reimers, *Still the Golden Door: The Third World Comes to America* (New York: Columbia University Press, 1985), 11–22.

[33] Lee and Yung, *Angel Island,* 105–109.

[34] On the dramatic changes occurring in the Chinese American community following the Second World War, see Zhao, *Remaking Chinese America: Immigration, Family and Community* (New Brunswick, NJ: Rutgers University Press, 2002), chaps. 3–4; Reimers, *Still the Golden Door,* 28.

[35] E. Lee, *At America's Gates,* 240–42.

[36] Peter Kwong and Dušanka Dušana Miščević, *Chinese America: The Untold Story of America's Oldest New Community* (New York: New Press, 2005), 231–33.

[37] Kate Coleman, "Reluctant Hero," *San Francisco Focus,* December 1996, cited in Iris Chang, *The Chinese in America: A Narrative History* (New York: Penguin, 2003), 300–303.

[38] Takaki, *Strangers,* 422–23.

[39] Chang, *Chinese in America,* 337; Kwong and Miščević, *Chinese America,* 343–8.

[40] Takaki, *Strangers,* 425; Peter Kwong and Edith Wen-Chu Chen, "Chinese Americans," Edith Wen-Chu Chen and Grace J. Yoo, eds., in *Encyclopedia of Asian American Issues Today,* vol. 1, (Santa Barbara, California: Greenwood Press, 2010), 19–20; Kwong and Miščević, *Chinese America,* 233–36; Chang, *Chinese in America,* 349–88.

[41] Min Zhou, *Contemporary Chinese America: Immigration, Ethnicity, and Community Transformation* (Philadelphia: Temple University Press, 2009), 47, 83; Timothy Fong, *The First Suburban Chinatown: The Remaking of Monterey Park, California* (Philadelphia: Temple University Press, 1994).

[42] Chang, *Chinese in America,* 338–46; Zhou, *Contemporary Chinese America,* 202–20.

[43] Zhou, *Contemporary Chinese America,* 47. On Chinese immigrant garment workers, see "Immigrant Women Speak Out on Garment Industry Abuse," in Judy Yung, Gordon Chang, and Him Mark Lai, *Chinese American Voices from the Gold Rush to the Present* (Berkeley: University of California Press, 2006).

[44] The United States grants the People's Republic of China an annual quota of 20,000 immigrants per year, but these mostly go to the highly educated and others with official connections or relatives already in the country. Chang, *The Chinese in America*, 376.

[45] Ko-lin Chin, *Smuggled Chinese: Clandestine Immigration to the United States* (Philadelphia: Temple University Press, 1999), 22.

[46] Chang, *Chinese in America*, 375–88.

[47] Carl L. Bankston III and Danielle Antoinette Hidalgo, "The Waves of War: Immigrants, Refugees, and New Americans from Southeast Asia," in Zhou and Gatewood, *Contemporary Asian America*, 2nd ed. (New York: New York University Press, 2007), 143–48.

[48] "Le Tan Si Writes a College Essay About His Terrifying Escape by Boat from Vietnam," in Lon Kurashige and Alice Yang Murray, *Major Problems in Asian American History*, 394–97; Takaki, *Strangers*, 451–54.

[49] Sara Dorow, *Transnational Adoption: A Cultural Economy of Race, Gender, and Kinship* (New York: New York University Press, 2006); "International Adoption Facts," Evan B. Donaldson Adoption Institute, accessed October 17, 2011, http://www.adoptioninstitute.org/FactOverview/international.html.

[50] R. Lee, *Orientals*, 10, 145–53.

[51] Chang, *Chinese in America*, 329; Takaki, *Strangers*, 479.

[52] Kwong and Miščević, *Chinese America*, 428.

[53] Steven W. Mosher, *Hegemon: China's Plan to Dominate Asia and the World* (San Francisco: Encounter Books, 2001); Martin Jacques, *When China Rules the World: The End of the Western World and the Birth of a New Global Order* (New York: Penguin, 2009); James Kynge, *China Shakes the World: A Titan's Rise and Troubled Future—and the Challenge for America* (Boston: Houghton Mifflin, 2007). Peter W. Navarro and Greg Autry argue that China is strategically attacking the United States from within and without in *Death by China: Confronting the Dragon—A Global Call to Action* (Upper Saddle River, NJ: Pearson Prentice Hall, 2011).

[54] The term is borrowed from American military training simulations, in which the "good guys" are always the blue team, while the so-called "Aggressor" force is the red team. It is no coincidence that the color red is also associated with communism.

[55] Chang, *Chinese in America*, 355–56, 365.

[56] Kwong and Miščević, *Chinese America*, 430, 438.

[57] Ibid., 423–26; Chang, *Chinese in America*, 359–69; Wen Ho Lee and Helen Zia, *My Country versus Me: The First-hand Account by the Los Alamos Scientist Who Was Falsely Accused of Being a Spy* (New York: Hyperion 2001).

[58] Helen Zia, *Asian American Dreams: The Emergence of an American People* (New York: Farrar, Straus and Giroux, 2001), 55–81; Judy Yung, Gordon Chang, and Him Mark Lai, "Anti-Asian Violence and the Vincent Chin Case," *Chinese American Voices*, 345.

[59] "About the Governor," Digital Archives, State of Washington, accessed October 15, 2011, http://www.digitalarchives.wa.gov/governorlocke/bios/bio.htm; "Governor Gary Lock's Inaugural Address," January 15, 1997," Digital Archives, State of Washington, accessed October 15, 2011, http://www.digitalarchives.wa.gov/governorlocke/speeches/speech-view.asp?SpeechSeq=107; "Democrats Respond to Bush's State of the Union," *Washington Post*, January 28, 2003, http://www.washingtonpost.com/wp-srv/onpolitics/transcripts/demstext_012803.html.

[60] "China's Reception of New US Ambassador Gary Locke," Public Radio International's "The World," September 9, 2011, accessed October 15, 2011, http://www.theworld.org/2011/09/chinas-reception-of-new-us-ambassador-gary-locke/.

[61] "New U.S. Envoy Urges China to Relax Business Restrictions," *New York Times*, Sept. 20, 2011, accessed October 15, 2011, http://www.nytimes.com/2011/09/21/world/asia/ambassador-gary-locke-urges-china-to-open-wider-to-investment.html.

[62] "Gary Locke, US Ambassador To China, Photographed Ordering Coffee In Airport," Huffington Post, August 16, 2011, accessed October 15, 2011, http://www.huffingtonpost.com/2011/08/16/gary-locke-us-ambassador-_n_928534.html.

[63] "Grace Lee Boggs," Bill Moyers Journal, June 15, 2007, accessed October 18, 2011, http://www.pbs.org/moyers/journal/06152007/profile2.html.

[64] Grace Lee Boggs with Scott Kurashige, *The Next American Revolution: Sustainable Activism for the Twenty-first Century* (Berkeley: University of California Press, 2011), 4, 29.

[65] Ibid., 33, 30.

[66] Ibid., 50.

[67] "How a Virtuoso Plays the Web: Eclectic, inquisitive, and academic, Yahoo's Jerry Yang reinvents the role of the entrepreneur," *Forbes Magazine,* March 6, 2000.

East European immigrants often quickly embraced American forms of patriotism. Pictured below is a second-generation Slovak American girl dressed as the Statue of Liberty for the Labor Day flag-raising ceremony at South Philadelphia's Slovak Hall.

CHAPTER 5

EASTERN EUROPEAN AMERICANS

By Robert M. Zecker

OR THE EAST EUROPEAN COAL MINERS of Lattimer, Pennsylvania, the change at the mule barns was the final straw. At the end of the summer of 1897, the Lehigh and Wilkes-Barre Coal Company announced that henceforth, its mule skinners would have to make their way to a remote barn in the village of Audenried to fetch the animals that hauled the coal cars and return them to the barn at the end of the work day. Previously, mules had been readily available at several nearby sites, but newly implemented cost-cutting measures meant the muleteers had to walk an hour to fetch their teams and repeat the process after nine or ten hours of back-breaking work underground. Just so there would be no misunderstanding, the company stressed that, as they produced no coal, these journeys would be considered unpaid "dead work."

Two or more hours of unpaid work for laborers who cleared eight dollars in a good week was bad enough, but the change to the mule barns was only the last in a long line of such outrages. Immigrant miners' helpers, breaker-boys, and loaders toiling in the mines controlled by the Pardee family and other absentee owners had suffered one indignity after another. Wage cuts were arbitrarily imposed, often with little advance notice or explanation beyond vague references to something called "the market." At the end of the summer of 1897, pay rates in eastern Pennsylvania's anthracite coal region were again slashed by ten percent. Whether at low rate or high, Pardee's outfit and other companies paid their employees sporadically, sometimes only once a month, leaving cash-strapped workers with little alternative but to turn to mine managers and the "company store" for credit against future wages to buy food and other necessities.

Companies already siphoned off a bewildering series of deductions from meager paychecks—for tools, blasting powder, and company housing—and the erratic pay only exacerbated the situation. The company store—or "pluck me," as the miners called it— was another ingenious device that allowed management to hold back a large portion of the pay packets they so guardedly doled out. At the company store, food, clothing, furniture, and other household items were sold to miners at monopoly prices, often three times those charged by independent retailers in nearby towns. In the bituminous coal fields of western Pennsylvania, an enterprising immigrant who rode the trolley into Johnstown to buy groceries would later find the price of his purchases deducted from his paycheck, as if he had done his shopping at the company store. In economic downturns, many of these company stores were more profitable than the actual mining of coal. Detectives on the company's payroll stood watch on the only road leading out of town and noted who was returning with non-company goods or conversing with suspect outsiders bringing news of the United Mine Workers union. Indeed, the hated Coal and Iron Police and other private detectives were a further grievance to miners. Such a mercenary army—the "Cossacks," Slavic immigrants persistently called them—stood ready to crack the heads (or worse) of those miners who agitated for a union contract.[1]

The piecework system for "inside workers"—company employees who actually worked underground at the coal face—was prone to arbitrary abuses, too. Coal operators paid miners and their helpers not by the hour but according to tonnage. Miners were allocated cars that, when filled with coal, were weighed by a company functionary, the "checkweighman." But not all that was loaded in the car was credited as coal. What counted for a "miner's ton" might soar to as much as 2,800 pounds when it came time for the checkweighmen to tabulate a miner's tonnage. The excess, uncompensated weight was discounted as worthless pigeon coal, slag, or rock. Miners' demands for an honest, independent checkweighman were regularly ignored.

In addition, dead work—such as blasting through rock, traveling to or from the coal face, or propping up the mine shaft's pillars—was all necessary work that went uncompensated by the company. All that mattered was the tonnage calculated by the checkweighman, in very subjective, company-friendly weighings. Not surprisingly, work that was already dangerous often became lethal as miners scrimped on uncompensated timber work or otherwise cut corners. States such as Pennsylvania did not provide workmen's compensation until 1916. Slovaks, Poles, and other immigrants injured on the job turned instead to minimal accident or death benefits available from their own fraternal associations.

Subjective payments in tonnage remained the norm for decades. Class consciousness developed quickly under such circumstances, especially among the Slavic American second generation. One son of east European immigrants who later took a lead in the United Mine Workers' organizing drive in Windber recalled his early days underground helping his father clear rock from a new coal face. After ten or more hours, he began speculating to his father about how much money they had earned that day. His father replied with a bitter, resigned laugh: "Son, we made nothing today. You didn't load no coal. You only get paid when you load coal." Like so many other east European miners, the son rejected his father's fatalism, proclaiming "From now on I'm a strong union man. If a guy says we're on strike, … I'm on strike, Dad, I don't care what you do. … I do not intend to work for nothing."[2]

The refusal of coal operators to deal with "outside agitators" was possibly the most important grievance in the summer of 1897, for in the absence of a signed contract all the miners' other complaints persisted. At that time, a rejuvenated organizing drive by the UMW was sweeping through eastern Pennsylvania. Organizer John Fahy repented of his earlier flirtation with nativism (an original and recurring sin of America's labor movement) and now deployed organizers and local union officers fluent in Polish,

Lithuanian, Slovak, Magyar, and other eastern European languages to explain the benefits of collective bargaining to immigrant workers. The UMW even elected Polish and other immigrant officers, though the top positions remained the preserve of Welsh, Irish, and other "old stock" miners. When such organizers approached the miners they were met with the full force of company-hired detectives, who also issued blunt threats to the "Hunky" workers who showed any interest in the union.

In spite of such hurdles, by the end of August thousands of east Europeans joined the "American" miners in the UMW, thus bridging a barrier many old-stock Americans had recently thought insurmountable. Slavs, Magyars, Lithuanians, and other new immigrants had widely been thought docile and unorganizable, "broad of back but weak of mind." In 1897, however, they joined the picket lines with demands for a union contract, restored wage rates, a fair checkweighman, and compensation for dead weight.

In response to the wage cuts and the change to the mule barns, several dozen muleteers walked off the job on August 14, 1897. After a hated mine supervisor threatened strikers with physical force, the walkouts spread, and within days thousands of Slavic, Magyar, and Italian mine laborers were out on strike. When one of the affected operators in the village of Coleraine sought to break the strike by importing a new batch of Slavic immigrants as strikebreakers, the ploy backfired; the would-be strikebreakers joined the picket line and signed up with the union. One of the nativist stereotypes about the Poles, Slovaks, and Ukrainians—as docile Hunkies who, as journalist Henry Rood claimed, "could be handled like so many domestic cattle"—was exposed for the libel it was.[3]

On Labor Day 1897, thousands of east European immigrants marched peacefully through villages such as Pittston, McAdoo, and Mahanoy City, shutting down mines along the way as other immigrants downed their tools and joined the procession. Fahy and other union officials such as Harwood local president Joe Mahalko urged demonstrators to avoid any hint of violence that might provide the Coal and Iron Police with the pretext they needed to retaliate. Although Polish and other Slavic women taunted the few miners who broke the picket by tossing pennies and stale bread, the flying pickets were mostly peaceful. For good measure, the unarmed marchers made sure to walk behind two large American flags, broadcasting their intention to seek justice.

In this period, the flag was a malleable symbol that immigrant laborers and bosses variously deployed to claim the mantle of American values. In seeking to end the 1913 Paterson silk strike in New Jersey, city business leaders hung a large flag above a downtown thoroughfare. An accompanying banner proclaimed "We Live Under the Flag, We Work Under the Flag, We Will Defend this Flag." To which the Polish, Ukrainian, and other immigrant silk workers responded by parading with a flag and banner of their own: "We Wove the Flag, We Dyed the Flag. We Live Under the Flag, But We Won't Scab Under the Flag." Such patriotic gestures offered the immigrants little protection, however, and for decades to come the nativist press ran cartoons of savage-looking Hunkies menacingly brandishing fists and clubs while waving the Stars and Stripes. To many immigration restrictionists, an uncivilized Pole or Ukrainian embracing the flag made a mockery of the "white man's republic."[4]

Up to 10,000 miners were on strike in eastern Pennsylvania by the first week of September 1897, and the Coal and Iron Police was unequal to the task of suppressing the uprising. On September 8, the owners demanded that Schuylkill County Sheriff

East European mine workers marched to their slaughter outside Lattimer, Pennsylvania, on September 10, 1897.

Alexander Scott arrest the thousand or so miners who had forced the closing of a pit near Pottsville. Scott had already declared that the disturbances in his county did not constitute a riot and that unarmed men and women had a right to march, even if they were Poles and Slovaks. Now he added insult to injury by denying the coal barons' demands and refusing to arrest anyone. In Gilded Age Pennsylvania, coal company executives were unaccustomed to being refused, even by sheriffs.

The owners had better luck with Luzerne County Sheriff James Martin, who deputized around one hundred men to serve as peacekeepers in the strike. Many of these men worked in managerial capacities for the coal company or had vested financial interests in the suppression of the strike. Others had worked for the companies' hated Coal and Iron Police. The deputies—virtually all of them Protestant native-born citizens of middle-class background—were the kind of people who for years had been reading inflammatory propaganda about the "horde of Hungarians, Slavs, Polanders, Bohemians, Arabs, Italians, Sicilians, Russians, and Tyrolese," "the scum of the Continent," that were bringing ruin to eastern Pennsylvania. Now they were given guns and authorized to keep the peace among such an invading horde.[5]

On September 10, Martin learned that striking east Europeans at the village of Harwood, west of Hazleton, were marching to Lattimer. The Italian and Slavic workers at this mine patch had requested the assistance of the UMW to bring their own pit's work force out on strike. Martin and the deputies hastened to head the marchers off, boarding the interurban trolley cars. At times the strikers walking beside the trolley tracks could see the armed deputies inside the cars. As the marchers reached the outskirts of West Hazleton, a squad of deputies jumped off the trolley and blocked their progress. Martin ordered the marchers to disperse and several deputies drove the point home with rifle butts to skulls. Deputy Ario Pardee Platt, a relative of the coal company owners and the operator of a local company store, grabbed the American flag from a

IMMIGRANT STRUGGLES, IMMIGRANT GIFTS

Slovak marcher and tore it to shreds. The only desecration of the flag to occur on the day of the Lattimer Massacre came not from the east European rabble, but from the native-born defenders of the status quo.[6]

As workers picked up rocks and faced off against the deputies, help arrived from an unlikely quarter. City Police Chief Edward Jones confronted Martin, announcing that he and his deputies had no jurisdiction within West Hazleton city limits. Furthermore, he declared, the sheriff had no business interfering with the Slavs' march along a public highway. Either out of jurisdictional jealousy or perhaps disgust with the coal barons' high-handedness, Jones finally managed to disperse the deputies, who cursed as they boarded their trolleys, vowing to catch up with the Hunky marchers again.

Jones next turned to the strikers and explained that while they were free to march along the highway, they could not take their protest through the congested streets of Hazleton. Although the most direct line of march passed straight through the city, the police chief offered to show the miners a slightly more circuitous route that skirted his city but that would nevertheless bring them to Lattimer. Following Jones' suggestion and picking up the one American flag that Deputy Platt had not destroyed, the Slovaks and Poles continued on their way.

In their second confrontation with Martin and his deputies, the miners were not so lucky. The sheriff and his forces again accosted the crowd of roughly 400 marching workers as they approached the village of Lattimer. Unlike at West Hazleton, however, the bulk of the deputies this time set up a defensible position in the ditches to the side of the road, aiming their rifles at the marchers as one might seek to cut off the advance of an invading army. Martin and several deputies bounded into the middle of the road, but the marchers continued on. Grabbing the sleeve of the nearest man, the sheriff waved his pistol in the marcher's face, hollering for the miners to disperse in a language that most of the immigrants could not understand.

What happened next is disputed. Men in the rear of the march may have continued pushing forward, or perhaps the man the sheriff had grabbed pushed back. In either case a brief scuffle ensued. While Martin would later testify he gave no order to shoot, the deputies opened fire on the miners. Nineteen Slavic miners were killed, most shot in the back as they fled the melee. As many as forty-nine others were seriously wounded. Men who witnessed the carnage later testified that the deputies continued firing even as the Slavs scrambled for cover in the hills; the undertaker who prepared eleven of the bodies for burial said that nine of the men had been shot in the back. Still other witnesses related that the deputies had boasted of going Hunky hunting earlier in the day.[7]

Initially, English-language papers such as the *Hazleton Daily Standard* deplored the violence. Shooting men in the back, even if they were Slavs, apparently crossed a line. But by the time Martin and seventy-three of his deputized gunmen were brought to trial the following February, the dominant narrative depicting lawless, brutal Hunkies reasserted itself, with stories recounting the threatened, heroic sheriff saved from a mob by his deputies' quick, if regrettable, action. By March, the verdict was handed down: not guilty. No one was ever punished for the shootings.

The Lattimer Massacre was the bloodiest and most vivid instance of anti-Slav sentiment in late-nineteenth century America, but it was far from the only one. Long-established tropes of Slavic barbarism depicted the newcomers as imperiling and impoverishing the country. Mine managers dismissed Slavs as subhuman, listing employees under separate categories as "Slavs" or "white men."[8] Other writers questioned the mental capacities of Slavs; one sociologist cited a school superintendent's absurd claims that the children of Poles and Slovaks had retardation rates well above fifty percent. This sort of racial pseudoscience may have been the genesis of the enduring jokes about unintelligent Poles.[9]

Other slurs stressed the Slav's degraded or bestial nature. Writers variously portrayed the Slovaks, Poles, Ukrainians, and Rusyns in the United States as dull-witted drones threatening "white men's" wages or as brutes innately predisposed to violence. To the Protestant minister Peter Roberts, writing only a few years after the Lattimer Massacre, Slavs represented "possibly the lowest grade of European workmen that can be imported." Roberts went on to say, "when the brute is aroused in the Sclav by a mixture of whisky and lager, he becomes more fierce than the red-toothed beast of prey." Earlier killings of striking immigrants were similarly justified as the only way to deal with unruly Slavs or "Huns." After ten striking miners were killed and fifty wounded during the 1891 strike at Henry Frick's coke works in Morewood, Pennsylvania, officers justified the slaughter as the only way to deal with "races" who "fill up with liquor and cannot be reasoned with."[10]

Slavs and other immigrants were suspected of importing dangerous ideas, too, and cartoons of bomb-wielding Slavs frequently graced the pages of popular magazines and newspapers. When the anarchist Leon Czolgosz assassinated President William McKinley in 1901, nativists were quick to denounce not only Czolgosz's political views, but also his dangerous gene pool. A correspondent to the left wing *Socialist Spirit* declared, "Czolgosz is the type of Hun and Vandal, which Macaulay, the English historian, declared long ago in a letter to Thomas Jefferson would ravage our republic in the twentieth century." Czolgosz's American birth was discounted. Another writer, a self-proclaimed expert on *The Diseases of Society*, pointed out that Czolgosz "was a Pole by birth, and had a long line of revolutionary ancestry behind him. The Polish race of all others is the most likely to advocate revolution and assassination as 'reform' measures." This "inborn" Polish principle of violent revolution, the writer added, was exacerbated by Polish immigrant culture: "What heredity had begun education completed, for he was trained in Polish parochial schools." The Catholic school, in the fervid mind of this writer, was thus transformed from one of the immigrant community's strongest bulwarks of social conservatism into a hotbed of anarchist politics. Two years after McKinley's assassination, Congress enacted a ban on suspected anarchists' immigration to the United States, the first time political beliefs were to be scrutinized at ports of entry.[11]

This association between Slavs and radicalism gradually came to dominate nativist rhetoric in the early twentieth century. It reached its apex in the aftermath of the First World War, when steel workers engaged in a nationwide strike and the Russian Revolution bred widespread fear of the communist contagion. In the midst of this crisis, the *American Legion Weekly* pointed to "the autocracy of imported ignorance and alien viciousness ... the unbalanced temperament of virulent Slav radicalism."[12]

In part, this anti-radical strain was a reaction to the increasing role immigrants were playing in organized labor and socialist politics. Where Slavs had once been seen as mindless drones, fodder for the capitalist machine, they now appeared in the nativist imagination as dangerous revolutionaries, capitalism's most potent threat. Some writers

Immigrant Struggles, Immigrant Gifts

squared this contradiction by claiming it was the docility of the Slav that explained the ease with which he was held in line by unions, which "[took] advantage of the habits of subordination." Earlier, when Slavs were dismissed as a scab race, this imagined docility had been thought to work on behalf of the operators. Evidently the newcomers could not win.[13]

In the face of such defamation, many Slavic groups could point to a heritage that included colonial and early republic settlers as well as heroes of the American Revolution, even if such luminaries were atypical of the later mass emigration to America. Highlighting the military achievements of east Europeans was one of the ways Slavic and Magyar groups countered xenophobic rhetoric and established their American bona fides. Quite early in their American odyssey, Poles foregrounded generals Casimir Pulaski and Thaddeus Kosciusko, Polish heroes of the American Revolution. Pulaski in particular was a binational patriotic symbol to which Poles pointed with pride. Upon his arrival in America, Pulaski had written to George Washington, "I came here, where freedom is being defended, to serve it, and to live or die for it." Kosciusko, meanwhile, was the military engineer instrumental in the Continental Army's defense of Philadelphia; later, he led the 1794 Polish uprising against the Russian Empire.

Other Slavic groups had less prominent early heroes, although some Czechs discovered that Maryland's William Paca, a signer of the Declaration of Independence, had Bohemian (Czech) roots. Paca's ancestry is sometimes claimed by Italians as well. In any case, by 1776 he was a thoroughly Anglicized statesman. Czechs also pointed out that the Moravian Brethren, Protestant dissenters, had in the eighteenth century established the founding settlement in Bethlehem, Pennsylvania, a pedigree that resonated with America's love for her Puritan New England heritage of yearning for religious freedom. Other early Bohemians included Bedrich Filip, who in 1647 arrived in New Amsterdam. The merchant prince of New York later Anglicized his name as Philips, and his family became one of the wealthiest landowners in the Hudson Valley. By the 1860s, a small Czech and Slovak contingent had settled in Chicago, where some formed Bohemian regiments that were decorated by Lincoln for meritorious service to the Union.[14]

The earliest Polish settlement in the United States was established in 1854 at Panna Maria, Texas. Czechs likewise put down roots in central Texas before the Civil War, settling in Cat Spring, Fayetteville, New Ulm, and Nelsonville by 1855. Less prominent were early economic migrants to America, such as the Slovak *drotári*, itinerant tinkers who repaired pots and pans, and manufactured and peddled all manner of wire goods. By the seventeenth century these tinkers had traveled as far afield as Vienna, Siberia, the Balkans, and Armenia, so it was perhaps not surprising that as early as the 1840s, some enterprising *drotári* appeared on the streets of New York and Philadelphia, as well as in the South.[15] Such early arrivals were few and far between, however. Less than 2,000 Poles were estimated to have arrived in the United States before the Civil War, and this early Slavic heritage remained half-submerged, distant from many later immigrants' consciousness.

Only during the late nineteenth and early twentieth centuries did mass migration of Slavs and Magyars take place. One scholar has estimated that at the beginning of the twentieth century, one-third of adults in Hungary (including Slovakia, Subcarpathian Rus' and Transylvania), Poland, west Ukraine, Croatia-Slavonia, northern Serbia and Slovenia had lived or worked outside their birthplaces. From 1860 to 1914, approximately six million people in Hungary migrated from hometowns, either as seasonal laborers or transoceanic migrants.[16] Between 1908 and 1923, approximately 2.3 million east Europeans made it to the United States, including 788,000 Poles, 225,000 Slovaks, and 226,000 Magyars, although many returned to Europe, too. East European migrants gravitated chiefly to the coal, steel, railroad, and textile centers of Pennsylvania, New York, New Jersey, Illinois, Michigan, Ohio, Connecticut, and Wisconsin.[17] By century's end, the tidal forces of economic dislocation had torn east Europeans loose from local communities for decades.

The main groups who arrived in America were Poles, Ukrainians, Serbs, Croatians, Czechs, Slovaks, Magyars, and Rusyns, although other peoples from the Balkans, the Baltic areas, and other regions of Austria-Hungary, Germany, and tsarist Russia arrived as well. Most groups had been ruled for centuries by outsiders, and clung to faith and local customs for a sense of peoplehood and communal solidarity. Rusyns, for example, more closely identified with their faith (Byzantine Rite Catholicism) than an ethnic identity, while Poles recalled their pre-partition kings but also their Roman Catholicism under rule by Orthodox Russia or Lutheran Germany. Magyars are ethnic Hungarians and not a Slavic group; rather, they are descendants of central Asian peoples who arrived in present-day Hungary as early as the ninth century CE. Although subjects of the Habsburg Empire, after 1867 the Magyars were granted some autonomy in the Hungarian part of Austria-Hungary. While Magyars frequently chafed at rule by Vienna, they themselves extended no such local self-government to Slovaks and other Slavs under their rule. Many Slavic groups had virtually no history of self-governance prior to 1918, and for many rural peasants, only a slight ethnic consciousness prior to immigration to the United States.

For simplicity's sake, current immigration historians speak of Slovaks, Rusyns, and Poles as unified and distinct groups. But ethnic identity in the period around the turn of the twentieth century was very fluid and in many cases only dimly conceived. While national awakenings had begun among Poles, Magyars, Slovaks, and others, these movements were the handiwork of urban elites (priests, poets, and newspaper editors), and many immigrants to America still identified with a village of origin or at best a region, rather than an imagined ethnic nation. In Philadelphia, for example, battles broke out among "Slovaks" when immigrants from western Trenčín refused to sit with parishioners from eastern Zemplín province, whom they dismissed as "these foreigners here."

Later ethnic ascription was often a matter of circumstance. In 1891, when lay immigrants in Yonkers petitioned New York's archbishop to found what later became the Slovak parish, they did so as "Austrians." It was only fifteen or more years later that parishioners began to embrace a Slovak identity. As one Brooklyn immigrant quipped around 1900, "Us Slovaks didn't know we were Slovaks until we came to America and they told us!" As late as 1941, some members of New York's Slovak parish of Saint Elizabeth's registered ethnically based protests. Rudolph Petz wrote to Cardinal Spellman demanding that the word "Slovak" be avoided in the prelate's homily celebrating the parish's golden jubilee. "Our parents and friends who organized this parish did it for the benefit and sole purpose: that the *Slavish people* could pray, sing and hear the sermon in their native Slavish language, the language they were taught by their parents in the northern part of Hungary," claimed Petz. "I hope it is plain to you that this parish is *not* Slovak, but *Slavish.*" No wonder Irish Catholic bishops often found their east European parishioners difficult charges.[18]

Whatever they called themselves, by 1920 several million east Europeans were the prime movers that made America's mines, mills, and factories hum; Slavic immigration was instrumental in America's rise to economic and political preeminence in the early twentieth century. The height of eastern and southern European emigration from roughly 1880 to 1914 coincided with the building of America's industrial might and fortunes, and the vast majority of Slavic, Magyar, and Mediterranean migrants filled the laboring positions in mines, mills, and factories. Slavs, though, had particularly high rates of return migration, with around forty percent of Poles and Slovaks returning home. Many migrants made several trips, and immigrant newspapers circulated across America and back to eastern Europe to alert migrants to the job situation in various cities.[19]

Because many east Europeans initially conceived of themselves as sojourners in the United States, they exhibited high rates of savings, often living in boarding houses as frugally as possible in order to save money with which to buy a bigger farm in one's home village *na staru kraju* (in the Old Country). Many of those who mined coal or milled steel had already worked those same jobs in Germany or in other locales closer to home before immigrating to the United States, but comparatively higher wage rates increasingly beckoned them to cross the Atlantic. This transience among the immigrants raised suspicion among the native born that east Europeans were draining the country of wages, and some writers addressed the Slavic "bird of passage" with venom. In 1891, Henry Rood complained that eastern Pennsylvania had become "diseased by thousands and tens of thousands of foreigners who have no desire to become Americans, who emigrate to the United States for a few years to make money."[20]

Other Anglo-American writers were more ambivalent, allowing that these "Sclavic" "hewers of wood and the carriers of water" were necessary to "perform menial toil which is shirked by wage-earners on a higher social plane." The minister Peter Roberts, who wrote frequently on the Slavic immigrant "problem" cautioned that "the fact that the brawn and muscle necessary for the production of coal has been furnished by them should never be lost sight of." Even if the authorities had to keep a watchful eye on such uncivilized people, Roberts argued, the country still needed them.[21]

An appreciation for their economic necessity did little to dull resentment against these "superfecund Slavs," as another writer called them, who "could live in dirt that would kill a white man."[22] Wrote Roberts:

> The thousands of immigrants added to our population have lowered our standard of living, have bred discontent, and have brought elements that are utterly un-American in ideas and aspirations into our communities. These, by their adherence to their language and customs, remain unassimilated after years of residence in the United States. This works disintegration in our industrial and social life, and unless counteracting forces are set in motion, will result in a lower type of manhood and womanhood in these communities."[23]

Like many other writers on the immigrant problem circa 1900, Roberts's remedy was Social Darwinism. "Under the laws of nature the brood of the unfit would soon be eliminated," he wrote, "but under our social relations they are fed, clothed and educated free of charge to the parents … [S]ome means should be used to eliminate this parasitic class from the social body." Even decades before workmen's compensation, minimum wage laws, and unemployment insurance or old-age pensions, nativists claimed that the largesse of the state coddled "unfit" ethnic groups.

East European immigrants themselves had other ideas on how to survive in America. In the immediate aftermath of the Lattimer Massacre, thousands of Slavic immigrants flocked to the UMW banner. Ignoring the more conciliatory line of the old-stock national and district leadership, by October 1897 east European miners signed up in the union by the thousands and walked off the job. Districts One and Nine consistently elected Poles and other Slavs to leadership positions in the union. In subsequent job actions in 1900 and 1902, it was the ostensibly sheeplike Slavs, Magyars, and Italians who brought about de facto recognition of the union by enforcing discipline in the walkouts.[24] Even those Slavs who initially intended to return to home villages in Austria-Hungary or Russia with their savings in order to live like a *pán* (mister, lord, big shot) had a vested interest in improving pay at American job sites, and thus joined union locals.

Perhaps most importantly, hundreds of thousands of east European immigrants brought families to join them and altered their life goals to remain in American cities rather than returning to Europe. In Slavic parts of Chicago and other cities, east Europeans began to exhibit extraordinarily high rates of home ownership, exceeding that of native-born whites. Modest bungalows were often built or purchased with the assistance of parish-based or ethnic fraternal society building and loan associations.

This trend of home ownership was noted quite early by Anglo-American observers. One noted that "hardly a Ruthenian [Rusyn] but has from fifty to two hundred dollars at least saved and put away," and that "out of their savings [they] buy lots and build houses in America."[25] But even immigrants' thrift and high savings rate were interpreted as menacing signs. In 1891, the future senator Henry Cabot Lodge warned the native-born, middle-class readers of the *North American Review* that in the coal mining regions,

> their whole purpose [is] to accumulate by parsimonious, rigid, and unhealthy economy a sum of money and then return to their native land. They live in miserable sheds like beasts; the food they eat is so meagre, scant, unwholesome, and revolting that it would nauseate and disgust an American workman, and he would find it difficult to sustain life upon it. Their habits are vicious, their customs are disgusting, and the effect of their presence here upon our social condition is to be deplored.

Lodge concluded his screed, which also drew invidious comparisons between Slavic and Chinese labor, by demanding the United States impose a literacy test to "shut out a large part of the undesirable portion of the present immigration." After he gained election to the Senate, Lodge spent twenty-four years lobbying for such a literacy test, and eventually succeeded in 1917.[26]

As part of the broader set of immigration restrictions imposed in the wake of the First World War, Congress passed a quota act in 1921 that set low annual immigration levels for eastern Europe. Only three percent of each ethnic group enumerated in the 1910 US Census was permitted to immigrate each year. Three years later, the quotas—which nativists asserted were still too generous to suspect Magyars, Slavs, and southern Europeans—were revised downward so that only two percent of each ethnic group enumerated in the 1890 census was allowed to enter the country each year. The revised

figures gave generous, and annually unfilled, quotas for England, Germany, and other "Nordic" countries, while Slavic immigration slowed to a trickle.

One of the unintended consequences of this policy was that it hastened the assimilation of Slavs and other immigrants from southern and eastern Europe. Migrants who prior to World War I may have made multiple trips back and forth between Poland and Chicago, for example, now decided to remain permanently in the United States rather than risk getting caught on the other side of a closing immigration door. In the earlier era, the annual arrival of tens of thousands of newcomer Poles, Ukrainians, Slovaks, and Croatians had meant that immigrant neighborhoods steadily received new "customers" for ethnic parishes, foreign language newspapers, and ethnic businesses. With the immigrant stream now slowed to a dribble, and the first-generation immigrants aging and passing from the scene, second-generation Slavic Americans were no longer surrounded by large numbers of newcomers demanding services and institutions in the language of the homeland.

In the 1920s, 1930s, and especially following World War II, the children of immigrants began the move from reading *New Yorský denník* to perusing the *Daily News*. Performances in the parish *divadlo* (ethnic theater) were replaced with viewings of Milton Berle in the comfort of one's suburban home. While particular neighborhoods of northern and midwestern cities such as Chicago's Ukrainian Village or Brooklyn's Greenpoint retained definite Slavic influences (as they do today), the enjoyment of mass

> **Sports helped acculturate immigrants to America. Slavic, Magyar, and German immigrants from Hungary starred on the Garfield, New Jersey Belmont Hilltops who, as the banner notes, were "1919 Baseball Champs."**

culture and mass consumer goods facilitated the second generation's gradual move from an ethnic niche market into the American mainstream.

While popular culture and the consumer marketplace hastened immigrants' assimilation, it would take another forty years after Lattimer before Slavs and others in the UMW and other unions won for blue-collar Americans a measure of economic security and advancement into the middle class. Other pitched union battles were fought between management and Slav labor at such places as McKees Rocks, Lawrence, Paterson, Ludlow, and Passaic. But the gains from such efforts were slow and halting. Home ownership, disposable income, and other markers of middle-class status arrived on a broad scale only during the Second World War and the postwar period.

During the Roosevelt years and beyond, east Europeans continued to play an instrumental role in the national economy in two ways. To begin with, as even some nativist commentators pointed out, the Slavic, Magyar, and other east European immigrants contributed the muscle, brains, and talents in mine and mill that created the industrial infrastructure of the United States: its docks, railways, factories, meatpacking plants, textile mills, and mines. It is difficult to imagine such twentieth-century industrial behemoths as United States Steel, General Electric, General Motors, or the Pennsylvania Railroad without the labor of east European immigrants. But the transplants' efforts also yielded another, even more lasting and important laurel—job security and living wages, won in tandem with key social legislation of the New Deal. These achievements contributed materially to the growth of a broad-based American middle class.

On a smaller scale, east European immigrants were the clientele for local success stories—grocers, restaurateurs, realtors, funeral directors, and other merchants, whose businesses were patronized by a blue-collar customer base. It was the steel workers, miners, and textile workers whose purchases enabled a handful of east European immigrant entrepreneurs to thrive. Representative of this class was Michael Bosak of Scranton, whose First National Bank was popular with fellow Slovaks before he was wiped out in the Great Depression. P.V. Rovnianek, an immigrant realtor and president of the National Slovak Society, likewise rode the roller coaster of ethnic entrepreneurship, amassing a small fortune selling land and homes to his countrymen but finally going bust during the Depression and dying penniless. The Slovenian immigrant Vertin family experienced more long-term success; their department store in the copper mining region of Calumet, Michigan, billed itself as the largest such establishment in the upper Midwest.

East European immigrants were also instrumental in establishing parishes, social halls, and hundreds of local chapters of fraternal self-insurance societies that created vibrant, enduring ethnic neighborhoods in cities like Chicago, Philadelphia, and New York. Slovak, Rusyn, Polish, Croatian, Ukrainian, and other immigrant communities built parishes of their own with financial contributions and "sweat equity." In smaller cities, too, Slavs established enduring, awe-inspiring centers of worship and community. A present day traveler to the former textile town of Garfield, New Jersey, will drive past nondescript, modest frame houses, only to crest Outwater Lane and encounter the jaw-dropping grandeur of gold-domed Three Saints Russian Orthodox Church. Similar icons of faith abound wherever east Europeans settled.

Each parish was not just a site of worship, but a social and civic center in which lessons in American citizenship were rehearsed via primers published by national ethnic fraternal associations such as the National Slovak Society.[27] Americanism also blended with ethnic identity in churches, where immigrant theater troupes, choral societies, and musical bands flourished. Slavs often believed they were bringing culture to dour, puritanical America with their immigrant bands and singing societies. Whether such a message of "immigrant gifts" reached many native-born Americans is debatable, but in immigrant papers such as *Slovák v Amerike*, east Europeans made the case that their life-affirming culture was an antidote to the Anglo-Saxon land of the time clocks. Parish theater and music societies also raised money for parishes and took the edge off life in the steel mill or coal mines.

While faith certainly was central to immigrants' lives, the parish and fraternal society were also means of attaining individual advancement through collective action, a pooling of resources and talents. As east Europeans took on an increasingly active role in the labor movement, the community organizations became centers of political and union activity. In Philadelphia, meetings for locals of the Amalgamated Clothing Workers were held in Slovak Hall, and ushers at Slovak Roman Catholic parishes participated in collections to aid striking anthracite workers. Other fraternal organizations, like the National Slovak Society, enabled individuals to purchase homes or to weather sickness and industrial accidents.[28]

For all the venom directed toward east Europeans by nativists, Slavs, Magyars and other European immigrants possessed certain advantages over blacks and Asians. Slavs never faced the legal bars placed before black advancement or the federal statutes prohibiting Asian migration or naturalization from the 1880s into the mid-twentieth century. In the very years that east Europeans were beginning to own homes and make their presence felt in industrial unions, Asians were excluded from eligibility for citizenship and African Americans were experiencing a regime of segregation, discrimination, and racial violence. While east European migrants toiled in wretched working conditions, their "whiteness," compared to other groups, gave them an advantage in the tough competition for housing, jobs, and the vote that characterized the racially charged American landscape during the era of mass migration. Establishing plausible claims to whiteness gave these newcomers very real, tangible benefits in the economic war of all against all.[29]

It was not only passively that Slavs benefited from the degradation of non-Europeans. Examining Slavic newspapers' coverage of race-related topics suggests the painful truth that many east European immigrants actively collaborated in the formation of an "anti-foreigner" ideology of their own, at least when it came to African Americans and Asian Americans. Slavic newspapers of the early twentieth century often expressed a growing concern with Asian immigrants as rivals depressing the "white" wage rate. *Jednota*, newspaper of the First Catholic Slovak Union, editorialized on the "Yellow Peril," a supposed flood of docile Asian laborers who worked for distressingly low wages. "Asiatics once inundated Europe," the editors warned. "The Huns of Attila were actually wild savages who slaughtered women and children like bloodthirsty animals. ... Why it is impossible to educate the world, that Japan similarly wants to destroy us, is difficult to say." Other foreign-language papers that spoke out against the immigration quotas for European immigrants following World War I nevertheless accepted or even encouraged the comprehensive ban on all immigration from the Far East.[30]

Blacks were likewise demeaned as a scab race—the same calumny that had dogged east Europeans themselves in the 1890s. The tensions grew especially intense in the 1910s and 1920s as southern blacks began migrating to the cities of the Northeast and upper Midwest. Even as early as 1899, however, Slovak newspapers applauded their countrymen's murder of black strikebreakers in Pana, Illinois, while at other times they approvingly reported efforts to drive blacks from job sites. After one strike, the Polish journal *Dziennik Chicagoski* editorialized, "We Poles should for our own good, and for the preservation of our honor as a people, leave the role of scabs, those drudges of capitalism, to the Negro and the Chinese."[31]

Of course, not all Slavs participated in, or excused, anti-black violence. During the 1919 Chicago race riot, some Polish businessmen were joined by Father Louis Grudzinski in publishing calls for calm in Polish-language newspapers. They urged their countrymen to refrain from attacking blacks, even as other Polish immigrants later boasted of having participated in the riots. Polish Chicagoans initially resisted stigmatization of blacks, battling them only when they served as strikebreakers; otherwise, they merely viewed them as one group among many in the competition for jobs. After 1919, however, Chicago's Polish papers carried articles urging their readers to join neighborhood improvement associations to enforce restrictive covenants against blacks buying homes in their neighborhoods. Similar efforts found support among Poles in Saint Louis and Detroit.[32] Even white ethnics who did not actively embrace anti-black animus benefited from institutions and mechanisms that distributed economic opportunity on an uneven racial playing field.

White privilege aside, formidable hurdles were placed before east Europeans upon their entry to America, and considering the circumstances their successes are striking. While most immigrants achieved relatively modest advances—a higher wage, a claim to respectability, opportunity for one's children—some rose to a laudable degree of fame and fortune. Especially in the second and third generations, many children of east European immigrants achieved remarkable success in artistic, scientific, business, military, and political occupations. Here, though, a distinction should be drawn between shared achievement—the gains made by the collective eastern European community—and individual attainment, a realm in which only a few east European Americans could shine. Many successful individuals were atypical even from the moment of emigration in that they often had attained education, training, or socioeconomic class advantages in Hungary, Russia, or Poland before setting out for America. Consider military affairs, an area of particular prominence for Americans of eastern European descent. Even before the mass migrations began in earnest, Slavic Americans were highly regarded for their martial qualities. As noted, during the Civil War Abraham Lincoln singled out the Bohemian regiment of Chicago, the "Lincoln Rifles," for commendation. During later conflicts, Slavic papers featured letters from immigrant soldiers serving with the US armed forces in the Spanish American War and in the Philippines. During World War I, Slovak readers of *Jednota* and *Národné noviny* were urged to subscribe to Liberty Loan drives, and photos of Slovak American soldiers serving "over there" were a regular feature of these ethnic tabloids.

Yet most of the Slavic American community's eminent military or defense figures have been skilled émigrés rather than typical steerage passengers. Pulaski and Kosciusko, the two Polish heroes of the American Revolution, were the first prominent east Europeans to serve in their adopted country's armed forces and security establishment. Others in this tradition include General (and later Chairman of the Joint Chiefs of Staff) John Shalikashvili, who was born in Poland of noble Georgian ancestry; National Security Council Adviser Zbigniew Brzezinski, whose father was a Polish diplomat; and

Secretary of State Madeleine Albright, who was born in Prague and came to the United States with her diplomat father in 1947 as the communist regime tightened its hold on Czechoslovakia.

East European Americans have served in political offices at almost all levels. While most were descendants of immigrants, some of the first generation also made significant marks in electoral politics. Adolph Sabath came to America from southern Bohemia in 1881, settling in Chicago. During his forty-four years in Congress, Sabath championed the first federal workmen's compensation legislation as well as old age pensions. He was instrumental in the passage of the Social Security Act in 1935 and pushed unsuccessfully for civil rights legislation as well as the liberalization of immigration laws. Sabath's fellow Czech Chicagoan, Anton Cermak, was the son of a coal miner who rose to the height of power in his adopted city. Although derided by some nativists as "Pushcart Tony," Cermak arguably was the founder of Chicago's modern Democratic machine. Elected Chicago's first (and so far only) foreign-born mayor in 1931, Cermak's tenure was cut short by an assassin's bullet intended for president-elect Franklin D. Roosevelt in 1933.

Other notable American political figures of eastern European background were Edmund Muskie, the senator from Maine, 1968 vice-presidential nominee, and secretary of state in the Carter administration; Watergate prosecutor and former president of the American Bar Association Leon Jaworski; and Senators Barbara Mikulski of Maryland and Roman Hruska of Nebraska. In the House of Representative, Michigan's John Dingell, Jr has served since 1955; he wielded the gavel of the influential House Energy and Commerce Committee when the Democrats were in the majority in Congress. Dingell was elected to succeed his father, who had Anglicized the family name from the Polish, Dzieglewicz. The only father-daughter team to serve as US senators, Alaska's Frank and Lisa Murkowski, have Polish roots, as does Ed Derwinski, congressman and first secretary of the federal Department of Veterans Affairs. Tom Ridge, former Pennsylvania governor and founding secretary of the Department of Homeland Security, can claim Slovak ancestry.

While most of America's leading Catholic clerics have been of Irish descent, the Polish American Edmund Szoka led the Diocese of Detroit from 1981 to 1990 before being called to Rome as the president of the Pontifical Commission for Vatican City State. Another Polish American, John Cardinal Krol, led the Philadelphia Archdiocese for twenty-seven years beginning in 1961. And Catholics venerate America's first male saint, Bishop John (Ján Nepomuk) Neumann, who presided in Philadelphia prior to the Civil War. A native of the southern Bohemian town of Prachatice, Neumann immigrated to New York in 1836 and became the Philadelphia Diocese's fourth bishop in 1852. The often contentious relationship between the primarily Irish hierarchy of the Catholic Church in America and Slavic parishioners, however, occasionally defied reconciliation. Some Polish Catholics who resented their treatment in America in 1898 followed Father Francis Hodur into an autonomous Polish National Catholic Church that remains active today.

In science, Nikola Tesla, born in the ethnically Serbian village of Smiljan in the Croatian province of Austria-Hungary, provided valuable contributions to the field of electromagnetism and conducted research that served as the basis of modern alternating current electric power. Tesla moved to America at age twenty-eight, with little more than a letter of introduction to Thomas Edison, who would later become his main rival.

Another immigrant scientist and success story was Michael Pupin, a Serbian who emigrated to the United States at age sixteen after the death of his father. Pupin later said, "I bless the stars that the immigration laws were different then than they are now." The United States might have blessed the stars, too, for after working menial jobs at New York biscuit factories and Delaware farms, Pupin graduated with honors from Columbia University, became a professor of physics at Columbia (the physics building there is named after him), and developed patents in loading coils that enabled American Telephone and Telegraph to dramatically improve the country's communications system in the first half of the twentieth century. Other Pupin patents led to modern X-ray technology. In addition, Pupin's autobiography, *From Immigrant to Inventor*, won the 1924 Pulitzer Prize.

East European immigrants have contributed their talents as journalists and writers as well. Vladimir Nabokov wrote many of his novels during his decades in America, where he also contributed scientific articles as a world-renowned entomologist. While Nabokov did not immigrate to the United States until he was past forty, much of his best writing (including *Lolita*) was done in America. Other writers, such as Louis Adamic, had more traditional immigrant journeys. Adamic was born in Slovenia and it was only in the 1930s, well after immigrating, that he made his mark as an investigative journalist, editor of *Common Ground*, and memoirist. His books include *Dynamite* (a study of militant workers), *Laughing in the Jungle: The Autobiography of an Immigrant in America*, and the bestselling *The Native's Return*.

In theater and film, many Slavic and Magyar Americans have made significant contributions. Volodymyr Palahniuk, a son of Ukrainian immigrants, toiled in his youth in the Lattimer mines several decades after the massacre of 1897. Volodymyr's father was also a miner, but the young man grew tired of the grim routine, deciding life as a professional boxer was preferable. Eventually he tired of boxing as well, concluding, "You must be nuts to get your head beat in for $200." Palahniuk drifted into acting, where he first made his mark on Broadway portraying another difficult Slav, Stanley Kowalski, in *A Streetcar Named Desire*. A career in Hollywood followed, where he became famous under his stage name, Jack Palance. Another film legend, Paul Newman, had a Hungarian-Polish Jewish father and Slovak Catholic mother, although he later somewhat flippantly said he identified with his Jewish roots, as "it's more of a challenge." Newman's contributions to film are legendary, including such credits as *The Hustler, Cool Hand Luke,* and *Butch Cassidy and the Sundance Kid*. He is also recognized for his philanthropic projects.

Fine art luminaries include the Rusyn Slovak American Andy Warhol, whose family hailed from Medzilaborce, Slovakia, and went by the name, Warhola. Several conductors with eastern European origins—including Eugene Ormandy, Leopold Stokowski, and Georg Solti—have wielded the baton in major American symphony orchestras. Antonin Dvořák, who was already famous as a composer in his native Bohemia before leading a conservatory in New York City and residing in Iowa, could also be included in this category. It was in New York that he composed his famous "New World Symphony."

Sports are an important way in which immigrant groups assimilate, and this has been true of Slavs as well as others. As early as the 1890s, newspapers such as the Rusyn

Amerikansky russky viestnik advertised immigrant baseball leagues, and by the early 1940s the magazine *The American Slav* ran features on the big leaguers who could form All-Slav football and baseball teams. Many such icons have enriched American popular sports culture: baseball Hall of Famers include pitcher Stan Coveleski, a Pole who hurled in the 1920s for Cleveland and Washington; the Red Sox immortal Carl Yastrzemski; Cardinals outfielder Stan Musial; and Pirates second baseman Bill Mazeroski. Yankees slugger Roger Maris, who held the single season home run record until the mythical sixty one was surpassed by Mark McGuire in 1998, was the son of Croatian immigrants. Football fans still lionize Chuck Bednarek, the Philadelphia Eagles center and linebacker who is the last man to play both offense and defense in the same game.

Michael Pupin, professor of physics at Columbia University, immigrated to the United States from Serbia at age sixteen. His inventions had practical implications in a range of areas including telecommunications and X-ray technology.

Bednarek may have learned his toughness in the steel mill city of Bethlehem, where he was a standout athlete with the Slovak Catholic *Sokol* lodge. The title card of great Slavic American boxers includes 1980s light heavyweight champ Bobby Czyz and two time middleweight champ Tony Zale (born Anthony Florian Zaleski in Gary, Indiana). One of the most celebrated early heavyweight title bouts featured Stanley Ketchel (Kiecal), who was persuaded to box above his weight class as a "great white hope" taking on the first African American champ, Jack Johnson. Although Ketchel went twelve rounds, he could not stop Johnson.

One final coda from very recent history illustrates both the persistence of nativism and the remarkable progress of east Europeans over the past hundred years. Today, the descendants of Slavic, Magyar, and Italian immigrants in Hazleton, Pennsylvania, the town where the immigrant miners began their ill-fated march in 1897, are fully integrated into the mainstream of the town. Far from being immigrant outcasts, some have taken up nativism themselves, joining other residents in the town to pressure the city council to bar the rental of apartments to undocumented Hispanics. It is in some ways encouraging that American Slavs have been so successful as to leave their own ancestors' travails in that very region a dim or forgotten irrelevance. But the persistence of nativism makes the task of reminding and remembering all the more urgent.

Endnotes

[1] Mildred Allen Beik, *The Miners of Windber: The Struggles of New Immigrants for Unionization 1890s-1930s* (University Park: The Pennsylvania State University Press, 1996), 197. For similar enforcement of the company store in eastern Pennsylvania's anthracite coal region, see Michael Novak, *The Guns of Lattimer* (New York: Basic Books, 1978), 47.

[2] Beik, *Miners*, 59, 68-69.

[3] Edward Alsworth Ross, *The Old World in the New: The Significance of Past and Present Immigration to the American People* (New York: The Century Co., 1914); Edward Alsworth Ross "The Slavs in America," *Century* 66 (1914), 590-98; Henry Rood, "The Mine Laborers in Pennsylvania," *Forum* 14 (1892): 110-22.

[4] William Adler, *Mollie's Job: A Story of Life and Work on the Global Assembly Line* (New York: Simon & Schuster, 2000), 48-49; Beik, *Miners*, 220.

[5] Harold W. Aurand, *From the Molly Maguires to the United Mine Workers: The Social Ecology of an Industrial Union, 1869-1897* (Philadelphia: Temple University Press, 1971), 139; George A. Turner, "The Lattimer Massacre and its Sources," Slovakia 27, no. 50 (Winter 1977): 9-43; Rood, "The Mine Laborers in Pennsylvania," as cited in Novak, *Guns*, 5.

[6] Novak, *Guns*, 121.

[7] Ibid., 130-32, 137.

[8] Michael A. Barendse, *Social Expectations and Perception: The Case of the Slavic Anthracite Workers* (University Park: The Pennsylvania State University Press, 1981), 62.

[9] Ross, *Old World*, 139.

[10] Peter Roberts, *Anthracite Coal Communities* (New York: Macmillan, 1904), 283; Katherine Mayo, *Justice for All: The Story of the Pennsylvania State Police* (New York: G.P. Putnam's Sons, 1916).

[11] "Pulpit Anarchy," *Socialist Spirit* 1, no. 2 (October 1901): 12-13; G. Frank Lydston, "Anarchy in its Relation to Crime," in *The Diseases of Society* (Philadelphia: Lippincott, 1906), 253-55.

[12] Quoted in Christopher Nehls, "'An Infallible Antidote': The American Legion's Americanism and Immigrants After World War I," paper presented at the American Historical Association Annual Meeting, January 8, 2005.

[13] Frank Julian Warne, *The Slav Invasion and the Mine Workers: A Study in Immigration* (Philadelphia: Lippincott, 1904), 93.

[14] Konštantín Čulen, *History of Slovaks in America*, trans. Daniel C. Nečas (St. Paul, MN: Czechoslovak Geneological Society, 2007), 2021.

[15] Karol Guleja, Reinhard Klimek, and Tomi Suchy, *Svet Drotárov: Umeleckohistorická etnograficko-technická sociálna monografia* ("The World of the Wire Workers") (Bratislava: Matica Slovenská, 1992), 15, 240-42; Katharina Kekelyova, *Drotárstvo* ("Wireworks") (Žilina: Povazske Museum, 1992), 7; Balch, *Our Slavic Fellow Citizens* (New York: Charities Publication Committee, 1910), 49, 97-99; Mano Somogyi, *A Hazai Vándoripar és Vandorkereskedés* ("Wandering Dealers and Workers") (Budapest, 1905).

[16] Ewa Morawska, *For Bread with Butter: The Life Worlds of East Central Europeans in Johnstown, Pennsylvania, 1890-1940* (New York: Cambridge University Press, 1985), 28.

[17] Mark Wyman, *Round Trip to America: The Immigrants Return to Europe, 1880-1939* (Ithaca: Cornell University Press, 1993), 9-12.

[18] Thomas J. Shelley, *Slovaks on the Hudson: Most Holy Trinity Church, Yonkers, and the Slovak Catholics of the Archdiocese of New York, 1894-2000* (Washington, D.C.: Catholic University of America, 2002), 49-50, 58-59, 61, 63, 84-85, 88; Robert M. Zecker, *Streetcar Parishes: Slovak Immigrants Build Their Non-Local Communities, 1890-1945* (Selinsgrove, Pennsylvania: Susquehanna University Press, 2010), 126-30, 136-41; Zecker, "'The Same People as Over Here': The Ethnic Fluidity of Slovak and Rusyn Immigrants in Philadelphia, 1890-1945," in *Committing Community: Carpatho-Rusyn Studies as an Emerging Scholarly Discipline*, ed. Elaine Rusinko (New York: Columbia University Press, 2009); "Golden Jubilee Souvenir of the Saint Joseph's Church of Calumet, Michigan, 1890-1940," housed at University of Minnesota, Immigration History Research Center; Roger Daniels, *Coming to America* (New York: HarperCollins, 1990), 218.

[19] John Bodnar, *The Transplanted, A History of Immigrants in Urban America* (Bloomington: Indiana University Press, 1987), xv; Morawska, *Bread*, 22-39; Wyman, *Round Trip*, 9-12; Marian Mark Stolarik, *Immigration and Urbanization: The Slovak Experience, 1870-1918* (New York: AMS Press, 1989), 25, 36; Caroline Golab, *Immigrant Destinations* (Philadelphia: Temple University Press, 1977), 34; Balch, *Our Slavic Fellow Citizens*;

Margaret Byington, *Homestead, The Households of a Mill Town* (New York: Charities Publication Committee, 1910); Beik, *Miners*, 41–42.

[20] Rood, "The Mine Laborers in Pennsylvania."

[21] Roberts, *Anthracite*, 13, 23.

[22] Ibid., 83; Warne, *The Slav Invasion*; Ross, *Old World.*

[23] Roberts, *Anthracite*, 345.

[24] Barendse, *Social Expectations and Perception*, 29, 53, 58; Greene, *The Slavic Community on Strike*, 128, 141–42, 183.

[25] Ivan Ardan, "The Ruthenians in America," *Charities and the Commons* 13 (December 4, 1904): 246–52.

[26] Henry Cabot Lodge, "The Restriction of Immigration," *The North American Review* 152, no. 410 (January 1891): 27–36.

[27] See *Cesta k Americkemu Občianstvo* ("The Road to American Citizenship"), play script, the Jankola Library, Mother House of the Nuns of Ss. Cyril & Methodius, Danville, Pennsylvania; *Krátke Životopisy Americkych Presidentov od Washingtona po Wilsona od roku 1789 do roku 1921* ("Short Lives of the Presidents from Washington to Wilson, From 1789 to 1921") (Pittsburgh: Ameriskeho Slovaka, 1922).

[28] Robert M. Zecker, *Streetcar Parishes*, 172–80.

[29] Thomas Guglielmo, *White on Arrival: Italians, Race, Color and Power in Chicago, 1890–1945* (New York: Oxford University Press, 2003).

[30] *Jednota*, September 14, 1904, 4; *Národné noviny*, June 16, 1920, 4.

[31] *Dziennik Chicagoski*, July 27, 1893, cited in Thaddeus Radzialowski, "The Competition for Jobs and Racial Stereotypes: Poles and Blacks in Chicago," *Polish American Studies* 33, no. 2 (Autumn 1976): 5–18.

[32] Frederic M. Thrasher, *The Gang: A Study of 1,313 Gangs in Chicago* (Chicago: University of Chicago Press, 1963; orig. published in 1927), 50–51, 327–28; Dominic Pacyga, "To Live Among Others: Poles and Their Neighbors in Industrial Chicago, 1865–1930," *Journal of American Ethnic History* 16, no. 1 (Fall 1996): 55–73. Robert M. Zecker, *Race and America's Immigrant Press: How the Slovaks Were Taught to Think Like White People* (New York: Continuum Press, 2011).

Russian-born Jewish American composer
Irving Berlin performing patriotic songs
aboard the USS *Arkansas*, 1944.

6

JEWISH AMERICANS

By Deborah Dash Moore

OW DO YOU FIGHT A LIBEL? Especially when its author is one of the most powerful and popular business heroes in the United States, the inventor of the famed Model T? This was the conundrum American Jews faced at the close of the First World War: "To answer feeds the vehemence of the attacks," mused Rabbi Henry Pereira Mendes, spiritual leader of New York City's Congregation Shearith Israel, the oldest Jewish synagogue in North America. "Not to answer seems unmanly, and gives the enemies a chance to say our silence acknowledges our guilt."[1] American Jews confronted a serious problem. What could possibly be said or done to counteract the extravagant and vehement lies of an American icon?

In 1919, the millionaire industrialist Henry Ford purchased a bankrupt local Michigan paper, *The Dearborn Independent*, and a year later, on May 22, 1920, published the first of ninety-one consecutive issues attacking Jews. Once a week over the course of almost two years, the series known as "The International Jew" appeared in the pages of *The Independent*. The first article in the series took "The Jew in Character and Business" as its theme. Among the many unsavory attributes evinced by Ford's portrait of international Jews was a "capacity for exploitation, both individual and social; shrewdness and astuteness in speculation and money matters generally; and Oriental love of display and a full appreciation of the power and pleasure of social position." Later topics in the series included "Jewish Testimony in Favor of Bolshevism," "Jewish Supremacy in the Motion Picture," and "How Jewish International Finance Functions."[2]

According to *The Independent*, "the Jews" controlled the media, corrupted American youth, dominated international finance, and pulled the strings in a vast yet murky conspiracy for global control. Ford's paper reproduced elements of *The Protocols of the Elders of Zion*, a forgery written by the Russian Tsar's secret police in 1905 that purported to describe a nefarious Jewish plot for world domination.[3] In 1921, even after *The Times* of London had debunked the authenticity of the *Protocols*, Ford publicly defended the book's premises, claiming darkly, "they fit in with what is going on."[4] For Ford and his editors at *The Independent*, this meant everything from the foreclosures of Midwestern farms to the spread of jazz music to the unsatisfactory conclusion of the Paris Peace Conference after World War I, not to mention the war itself.

Ford's most damaging publication appeared in book form in November of 1920: *The International Jew: The World's Foremost Problem*. The first of four volumes that reprinted articles from *The Dearborn Independent*, it contained no copyright protection, inviting reprinting and distribution around the globe as well as translations into dozens of languages. The publication's anti-Semitic tirades struck a popular chord and significantly boosted readership of *The Independent*. Ford's attacks appealed to Midwestern farmers and city folk alike, all of them bewildered by the fast pace of a rapidly urbanizing United States. He offered simple explanations of why the world was changing and who was to blame.[5]

The ironies in this attack were many. Despite his professed cultural conservatism, Ford was himself the agent of tremendous social and cultural change. Few individuals in early twentieth-century America were more directly responsible for the uprooting of tradition, the transformation of industry, and the growth of consumer culture—for better or for worse—than Henry Ford. Whereas most American Jews were relatively poor and many banks and employers discriminated against hiring them, Ford himself sat atop an international business empire of the kind he imagined was the exclusive province of his Jewish enemies. Ford was a modernizer who hated modernity, a capitalist who hated capital. He resolved his internal contradictions by projecting the anxieties inherent in his own ambitious project onto a secret cabal of Jewish financiers.

Ford, of course, was not the first, the only, or even the worst anti-Semite in America. A long tradition of Christian religious prejudice, carried over from Europe, depicted Jews as pariahs and "Christ-killers." Upper-class Protestants frequently condescended to Jews, especially wealthy ones, as materialist or pushy social upstarts. Jews figured in the imaginations of many late-nineteenth-century Populists as sinister, conspiratorial figures, agents of international capital and internal corruption. It was this last, paranoid strand of anti-Semitism that may have deeply affected Henry Ford, who grew up during the heyday of the Populist movement as a farm boy in Michigan and courted Populist sensibilities and politics.[6]

But Ford launched his attacks into a cultural environment unusually receptive to xenophobia in general and to anti-Semitism in particular. The end of the First World War meant the resumption of transatlantic migration along with the accompanying fears that immigrants, the "dregs of Europe," would swamp the United States. The Russian Bolshevik Revolution of 1917 and the massive and bitter American steel strikes of 1919 sent waves of panic rippling throughout American government and industry. Even unionized workers who went out on strike in 1919 feared competition from immigrant laborers willing to work for lower wages. Nativists, who had been lobbying for restrictive legislation since the 1890s, found a newly receptive audience and succeeded in passing restrictive quotas to limit immigration in 1921 and 1924. The era of open immigration from Europe to the United States had ended.[7]

The restrictionists, in many cases, were also driven by dislike of Jews. The Russian Revolution in particular was widely interpreted as a Jewish plot. Yet even as Jews were depicted as radical communists, they were also tagged as rapacious capitalists. Fear of anarchists, of communists, of capitalists, of bankers, of immigrants, of the "other," in all its teeming multiplicity, converged in the image of the Jew, already tarnished in Christian teaching as responsible for the death of Jesus. A newly revived Ku Klux Klan that targeted Jews together with African Americans and Catholics achieved significant political power in many cities in the Midwest and South. Varied constituencies Southern farmers, Midwestern Populists, New England businessmen, Western agrarians—all cultivated anti Semitism, with each group nursing its own particular grievances that could be blamed on "the Jews."[8] That many Americans had never even met or seen a Jew only contributed to anti-Semitism's flexibility and its capacity to focus ill-defined resentments.

Among the American Jewish community itself, Ford's attacks provoked a mix of righteous anger and caution. On the one hand, many Jews were justly furious that

Henry Ford's newspaper, *The Dearborn Independent*, regularly printed anti-Semitic tirades throughout the early 1920s.

Russian smears like the *Protocols of the Elders of Zion* had followed them to America. Some Jewish leaders, like Louis Marshall and Herman Bernstein, spoke out publicly, denouncing Ford's bigotry and offering evidence that the *Protocols* were a forgery.[9] Other Jews counseled a more conciliatory line. A respected Detroit rabbi met with Ford and tried unsuccessfully to convince him to stop. Some American Jews hoped that the lies would simply run their course and believed that nothing could be done in any case to stop them. The Constitution guaranteed freedom of the press, which included the freedom to publish hateful anti-Semitism. Furthermore, in each article there lurked a tiny kernel of truth. Jews did produce movies, write songs, and publish books. They figured prominently in the entertainment industry, though they did not control "the media." Many Jews expressed pride in Jewish contributions to American society, culture, and economic life. Ford twisted these achievements into menacing threats to America, perceiving every Jewish activity as part of a relentless drive to achieve dominance.[10]

Fortunately, Jews were not the only ones outraged at Ford's allegations. Many local car dealerships refused to distribute the paper or cancelled their contracts with the Ford Motor Company altogether. E. G. Pipp, the previous editor of *The Independent*, broke all ties to his former boss, declaring, "I regard Henry Ford's attacks upon the Jews as absolutely without reason, unfair, cruel, bigoted, and contrary to the American spirit."[11] In 1921, a Methodist minister named John Webster Spargo drafted a statement, "The Perils of Racial Prejudice," and solicited the signatures of eminent American Christians, including President Woodrow Wilson, President-elect Warren Harding, and former president William Howard Taft. "It should not be left to men and women of the Jewish faith to fight this … un-American and unchristian agitation," the statement averred.[12] Newspapers throughout the country carried headlines proclaiming that President Wilson had denounced anti-Semitism. Under the pressure of this intense public outcry, together with the criticism from Jewish leaders like Marshall and Bernstein, Ford halted the series in December 1921.[13]

Thereafter, the anti-Semitic attacks in *The Independent* were more sporadic but did not disappear altogether. One group of articles beginning in April 1924 assailed agricultural marketing cooperatives as pernicious schemes by Jewish bankers to rob farmers of their hard-earned profits. "Jewish Exploitation of Farmers' Organization—Monopoly Traps Operate Under Guise of 'Marketing Associations,'" blasted the headline.[14] These articles, which ran for an entire year, claimed that Aaron Sapiro, a Jewish lawyer, developed the cooperative concept to ruin American farmers. A sidebar even advanced the outrageous lie that Jewish powers also planned to take over boys and girls' farm clubs and to school them in "communistic ideas."

Ford's "International Jew" series named many Jews, but Aaron Sapiro took particular offense at the attacks. Born in Oakland California in 1884, the son of Jewish immigrants, Sapiro was orphaned at a young age and had struggled to emerge from childhood poverty. After entertaining ambitions of a life in the rabbinate, he left Hebrew Union College in Cincinnati to study law. Although legal practice became his ticket into the middle class, Sapiro retained his religious idealism, which he directed toward farming cooperatives. By the time he was forty, Sapiro had devoted much of his life to organizing California's farmers, encouraging them to create cooperatives to market their harvests and to eliminate middlemen and wholesalers. From California, Sapiro spread his gospel of cooperation to the nation at large and even to Canada. By 1925, 750,000 farmers had joined "Sapiro's Plan." According to *The Independent*, however, this plan was a mere ploy to siphon millions of dollars from farmers into the pockets of greedy Jewish bankers. Sapiro wrote a formal letter to Ford demanding a retraction of the entire series. He received no reply and the series continued.[15]

In February 1925, when *The Dearborn Independent* launched an attack on the Federal Reserve Bank as part of an alleged Jewish conspiracy to swindle Texas farmers, Sapiro had had enough. He sued Ford for libel. Twice Ford's lawyers sought and received six-month postponements. Finally, in March 1927, the trial date arrived. Under oath, Ford's lieutenants claimed that the auto executive himself knew very little about what was going on at the newspaper. This despite the later claims of others who worked at *The Independent*, who suggested that Ford was intimately involved in all its major editorial decisions, particularly relating to the "International Jew" series. Despite their efforts to shield him, the trial's relentless publicity damaged Ford's once-colossal reputation. A month later, a mistrial was declared and new trial date set for September.[16]

At this point, Ford abruptly changed his mind and decided to apologize rather than go to court. He announced his intention to shutter *The Independent* to his subordinates and began to explore an out-of-court settlement with Sapiro's lawyers. For advice on how to set things right, Ford turned to Louis Marshall, the head of the American Jewish Committee. A brilliant lawyer, Marshall had done his best to dissuade Ford when the initial series of articles appeared. Now Ford asked Marshall what needed to be done and the latter agreed to write an apology on Ford's behalf. On June 30, 1927, Ford signed the apology, without even bothering to read it. Newspapers around the country published the statement, but not *The Dearborn Independent*. Ford also settled the libel suit with Sapiro, agreeing to set up a scholarship fund to educate a needy orphan—a gesture toward Sapiro's own difficult childhood and his desire to help others—and to pay court costs and attorney's fees.

No apology, of course, could overturn the impact of seven years of scurrilous lies. Ford's publications continued to appear in new editions and in many languages around the world. They are still in print to this day. Many Jews suspected, with some justification, that Ford's sudden about face was purely cynical and that he would have continued the attacks had it not been for the threat to his public reputation (and by extension, his personal fortune). As the comedian Will Rogers quipped, "He used to have it in for the Jewish people until he saw them in Chevrolets, and then he said, 'Boys, I am all wrong.'"[17] In his later years, Ford continued to express anti-Semitic views in private but no longer gave vent to them in a newspaper with a readership thousands strong.

Anti-Semitism did not surprise Jewish immigrants, who had known it in Europe. Hatred of Jews prevented them from entering many occupations, from living in many cities, from traveling freely, and even from marrying. Until the French Revolution emancipated Jews in 1791, giving them citizenship rights as individuals, all European Jews were treated as corporate groups by their host countries. Emancipation spread slowly in the decades after the French Revolution, and did not arrive until 1917 for millions of Jews living in a restricted section of the Russian Empire called the Pale of Settlement. Because many European nations had officially recognized Christian denominations, Jews endured legal segregation and discrimination as a tolerated minority group. Jews had been expelled from Spain in 1492, and from Portugal five years later. While they settled in the Ottoman Empire as well as in Italian city-states and the Netherlands, the Spanish expulsion reverberated across the centuries, revealing the fundamental insecurity of Jewish life in Europe. Many Jews hoped things would be better in the New World. Still, their American history across several centuries included painful episodes of anti-Semitism as well as ongoing prejudice and discrimination.

The earliest Jews to arrive in the United States were Sephardim, the descendants of those who had fled the Spanish and Portuguese expulsions on the Iberian Peninsula. In 1654, a group of twenty-three Jewish refugees decided to relocate to North America from Recife, Brazil. How, exactly, did Jews end up in Brazil? For several decades, the Dutch government in Recife had allowed a small Jewish community to form there, until 1652 when control of the city was ceded back to the Portuguese. For the Jews of Recife, it was time to leave. Most dispersed to England or to the

Netherlands, but a small group came to New Amsterdam, one of the earliest Dutch settlements in North America.[18]

When these twenty-three Jewish refugees landed in New Amsterdam, they quickly discovered that the governor of the seaport, Peter Stuyvesant, did not like Jews. He called them "a deceitful race" and requested permission from the Dutch West Indies Company to expel the Jews from New Amsterdam, only to be told that they should be allowed to settle, trade, and participate in the life of the colony, as long as they kept their religious observances private and took care of their own poor. The Jewish newcomers, meanwhile, petitioned their fellow Jews back in Amsterdam, pleading for support to remain. Dutch Jews lobbied effectively on their behalf.

A relatively small Jewish community in New Amsterdam enjoyed these arrangements when the British conquered the city ten years later, renaming it New York. Gradually, the British extended additional privileges to Jews, allowing them to form congregations and to build a synagogue for public worship. By 1740 Jews in New York had received unprecedented rights to vote, to hold office, and to become naturalized citizens. Several other North American colonies also allowed Jews such standing. Britain's mercantile focus in the colonies prompted a tolerant attitude in matters of religious and ethnic diversity. By the time of the revolution, many Jews treasured not only their fellow citizens but also American Enlightenment ideals that enshrined freedom and equality. They were ready to risk their lives to support life, liberty, and the pursuit of happiness.[19]

Perhaps two thousand Jews lived in the colonies in the years leading up to the American Revolution; most had settled in five seaport cities: New York, Charleston, Newport, Philadelphia, and Savannah. The several hundred Jews in each town formed a minuscule percentage of the population but maintained a lively cultural and religious tradition. Jews earned their living through trade and crafts. Some prospered with extensive commercial ties to Jews in other ports around the Atlantic. Others did not distinguish themselves but contributed to each town's local economy; a few struggled in poverty. When their largely Protestant Christian neighbors noticed them, it was usually for their religion. Jews did not accept the divinity of Jesus and they considered themselves God's chosen people. Their Sabbath fell on Saturday, not Sunday, and they observed a different calendar of holidays and fast days. Jews prayed in Hebrew, with men sitting separately from women during worship. Yet in external appearance their synagogues resembled modest church buildings. The simple Touro synagogue in Newport, Rhode Island and the classical lines of the Congregation Beth Elohim (House of God) synagogue in Charleston blended well with the general architecture of these towns. In the public sphere, Jews seemed just like other colonists.[20]

But were they? On July 4, 1788, Philadelphia held a grand parade to celebrate Pennsylvania's ratification of the new Constitution. The Jews of the city lined up to march alongside their fellow countrymen. Gershom Mendes Seixas, who served as leader of Philadelphia's Mikveh Israel congregation, marched at the head of the parade linking arms with clergy of the different Christian denominations. At the parade's end, the weary but exuberant marchers were met with tables of food, including a kosher table. Historians debate how to interpret this event. Does the kosher table point to recognition of Jews' differences and a willingness to accept them? Did Jews march as Americans and dine as Jews? Or does the kosher table symbolize the impossibility of assimilating

IMMIGRANT STRUGGLES, IMMIGRANT GIFTS

Jews? Did their separation indicate their desire to remain apart? Such questions about Jewish differences and similarities from other Americans reverberated throughout the nineteenth century. Often they were posed in a spirit of goodwill, but sometimes with an edge of discomfort or dislike.[21]

In the new nation, Jews participated as political equals in some states, which assured freedom of religion, but not in others. The First Amendment of the new federal Constitution declared that Congress "shall make no law respecting an establishment of religion or prohibiting its free exercise thereof" and guaranteed freedom of speech, press, assembly, and petition. After George Washington was elected president, Jewish congregations sent him congratulatory letters, including one from Moses Seixas, warden of a synagogue in Newport, Rhode Island. Seixas praised the president and the new government of the United States for "generously affording to all liberty of conscience and immunities of citizenship." Washington was impressed by Seixas's phrases and replied, declaring religious liberty a natural right and describing the United States government as one "that gives to bigotry no sanction, to persecution no assistance."[22]

On the other hand, if a Jew ran for the state legislature in Maryland and won, he could not assume his seat without perjuring himself by reciting a Christian oath of office. It took almost a decade of debate for Christian legislators to change the requirements for office holding in Maryland, but the change came in 1826. Jews also faced legal disabilities in New Hampshire and North Carolina. Understandably, Jews gravitated to those states where their rights were recognized and to new territories under the jurisdiction and protection of the federal government. There they began to flourish.

Jewish immigrants started to enter the United States in larger numbers in the 1820s. Unlike the earliest Sephardic arrivals, the newer group comprised mostly Ashkenazi Jews, whose ancestors had settled along the Rhine in the Middle Ages. By the 1840s, a mass migration of Jews was underway from Europe. The largest numbers came at first from the German states, where anti-Semitic exclusions chafed and where peasant agriculture was in crisis. The United States seemed to offer Jews opportunities to improve their economic stations without having to compromise their religious beliefs. Many entered through the port of New York. From there they fanned out throughout the country, heading south and west to peddle goods in rural areas, small towns, and growing cities. Jewish peddlers, either carrying a pack on their backs or driving a wagon, became commonplace in the lives of many Protestant Christian American farmers. Most welcomed the peddlers as a source of useful goods and a connection to the market economy; some found Jews odd, having never seen one before; a few disliked and distrusted them, dubious of their honesty. Still, Jews fared no worse than Yankee peddlers, and usually managed to disarm whatever prejudice they encountered.[23]

In the cities, however, life was often more taxing and chaotic. Increasing numbers of Jewish immigrants chose to settle in New York and other booming cities. Substantial Jewish communities formed in Philadelphia, Richmond, Boston, Chicago, Omaha, Cleveland, Cincinnati, St. Louis, New Orleans, Charleston, Baltimore, Los Angeles, and San Francisco. Jews living in these towns earned a livelihood through trade and crafts, and often clustered in the poorer neighborhoods. Alongside German and Irish immigrants, Jews contended with crowded living conditions produced by rapid urbanization. Concentration, however, also heightened Jewish visibility and occasioned conflict with other ethnic groups, as did some of the types of work Jews performed.

Jewish immigrant Levi Strauss moved to San Francisco in 1853 to establish a branch of his brother's dry goods store. Twenty years later, in partnership with a Jewish tailor from Nevada, he patented the famous design for blue jeans that continues to bear his name.

Like other immigrants, Jews gravitated to ethnic occupational niches, particularly the garment industry. In the 1830s, a string of Jewish second-hand clothes dealers in New York City opened shops on Chatham Square, a particularly unsavory section of town. Nasty stereotypes of aggressive Jews circulated in the press as a result of their presence there, yet the dealers filled a useful economic task: they took cast-off tailor-made garments, mended and cleaned them, and sold them at cheap prices to sailors and servants. In time, some of the dealers started to manufacture inexpensive garments for slaves. By the time of the Civil War, the second-hand clothes shops had sparked a budding garment industry, which received a big boost with the tremendous demand for soldiers' uniforms.[24]

Jewish workers and entrepreneurs, in the garment industry and elsewhere, often relied on family connections. One celebrated example was the Jewish immigrant Levi Strauss, who originated from Bavaria and whose family ran a dry goods store in New York City. In 1853, Strauss settled in San Francisco, where his New York-based brothers hoped he would establish a new branch of the family business. Little did they anticipate that twenty years later Strauss's production and marketing of rivet-reinforced jeans would transform him into a household name. Strauss teamed with a Nevada tailor named Jacob Davis (also Jewish) to sew denim into a design for men's pants. The two men patented their wildly successful invention in 1873.

As during the Revolution, Jews identified strongly with their fellow Americans during the Civil War. Since more Jews lived in the North than in the South, a majority of American Jews fought for the Union. Even as soldiers, Jews did not forget their religion and tried to observe important Jewish holy days if possible. In 1862 in West Virginia, Jews in the Twenty-third Ohio Regiment improvised a makeshift Passover seder to celebrate the exodus of Israelites from Egyptian slavery. The soldiers managed to obtain two barrels of matzah from Cincinnati as well as a couple of haggadahs, the prayer book read during the seder meal. Along with two kegs of cider, some eggs, and a whole lamb, they proceeded with the celebratory meal.[25] In the South, Jews donned gray uniforms and fought for the Confederacy. Judah P. Benjamin, a Jew from Louisiana, served as Jefferson Davis's secretary of state and in this capacity helped to secure the finances of the Confederacy. The Civil War divided Jewish families just as it did those of other Americans. It did not matter that most Jews were relatively recent immigrants; like fellow German newcomers, they rallied to the cause.

Yet if the Civil War revealed the deep attachment of Jewish immigrants to their new country, north and south, it also produced one the nation's worst examples of anti-Semitism: an order of expulsion. General Ulysses S. Grant's General Order #11 expelled all Jews "as a class" from his army's jurisdiction, which covered parts of Tennessee, Kentucky, and Mississippi. Grant had been angered by profiteers and traders who exploited both ordinary citizens and soldiers. He then made the mistake of assuming that all traders were Jews and that all Jews involved in trade were war profiteers. Loyal Jews wrote to President Lincoln asking that the order be repealed. Other Jews living in Washington, DC also petitioned the White House for action. Lincoln immediately revoked Grant's order. Later, when Grant ran for the presidency, he apologized for the order and disavowed any prejudice toward Jews. Many Jews forgave Grant and voted in large numbers for his Republican ticket.[26]

The years after the Civil War saw the production and concentration of tremendous wealth in the United States. Those industrialists and financiers who benefited from the excesses of the Gilded Age famously earned the epithet "robber barons" while widespread poverty afflicted immigrants and the native born alike. Cycles of boom and bust added to the woes of poorer Americans. These economic extremes fed racism and anti-Semitism, nativism and populism. Americans looked to blame their sense of dislocation on scapegoats, and found them in newly freed African Americans, Chinese laborers, eastern and southern European immigrants, and Jews, both immigrants and the native born. By the 1880s, American Jews numbered around a quarter of a million, about one percent of the total American population. Despite the travels of Jewish peddlers, many Americans had never seen a Jew. It was easy to believe stereotypes about them: Jews were greedy, stingy and clannish; they corrupted the banking system; they lacked manners and were rude and selfish; they were arrogant and manipulative.

Prejudice and discrimination against American Jews took on new, more virulent, and increasingly complex forms even as the last of the states, North Carolina, abolished its remaining legal strictures on Jews holding office. The newer types of discrimination reached all strata of American Jewry—rich, poor, and middle class, immigrants and their native-born children. Indeed, the growth of anti-Semitism corresponded to a rapidly increasing population of Jewish immigrants, drawn to the economic opportunities of the United States and fleeing discrimination and dislocation in the Russian Empire.

In the 1880s and 1890s, economic and social conditions for Jews in the Russian Pale of Settlement deteriorated badly, propelling them to crowded, industrializing cities in search of work. State-sponsored violence against Jews—pogroms—made grisly headlines but seem to have motivated fewer Jews to emigrate than difficulties finding work. Gradually, adventurous young Jews set out from Russian cities for America, initiating a mass chain migration that would in time draw two million Jewish immigrants across the Atlantic.

Life had become so difficult that one out of three Russian Jews left the empire. Entire families uprooted themselves, leaving behind towns where Jews had lived for centuries.

Men, women, and children all cast their lot with America, willing to start over to build new lives and communities. Of course, not everyone came. Among those who stayed were the prosperous, the deeply impoverished, who could not raise funds to travel, and the religiously observant, who feared the "unkosher" environment of the New World. But larger and larger segments of Russian Jewish society were pulled into the flow, and those who did migrate rarely returned to Russia.[27]

By the 1870s, Jewish immigrants who had arrived prior to the Civil War had secured a foothold in the economy and were prospering; a few even had acquired significant wealth. One example among many was the banker and businessman Joseph Seligman. Seligman emigrated from Bavaria to New York in 1837 and began his American career, as many Jewish immigrants did, as a peddler. He soon opened a series of stores with his brothers and then entered the fledgling garment industry as a manufacturer of cheap clothing. Orders for uniforms during the Civil War, paid by government bills of deposit, prompted him to enter banking. Seligman joined other wealthy New Yorkers to found the Union Club and sold millions of dollars of bonds for the Union cause during the war. In the post-war period, he became active in numerous financing ventures and was even offered the post of secretary of the treasury by President Grant.

Seligman's influence and affluence did not shield him from prejudice or discrimination. In June 1877, when Seligman arrived to register at his favorite hotel in Saratoga Springs, he confronted a rude surprise. Judge Henry Hilton, the hotel manager, turned Seligman and his family away. Newspapers buzzed with news of the snub and lively debate over whether it was right to exclude Jews from hotels.[28] Those who defended Hilton claimed that as private businesses, hotels could choose their own patrons. Jews, they said, drove away valuable non-Jewish clientele who did not want to vacation alongside Jews with their poor manners and ostentatious displays of wealth. Seligman's backers argued that discrimination destroyed Jews' equal rights under the law.

American Jews and their defenders lost the day. Soon many hotels adopted policies of discrimination, advertising "Christians Only" or "Hebrews will knock vainly for admission." Gradually exclusion spread to private schools, to country clubs, and by the end of the nineteenth century to the very Union Club that counted Jews among its founders. These forms of discrimination particularly affected middle- and upper-class Jews who had assumed that their economic achievements and efforts at assimilation would win them acceptance among fellow Americans.[29]

Other types of bias found expression on the stage and in the press, where especially crude stereotypes flourished of Jews as buffoons, arsonists, swindlers, and lecherous immigrants. Vaudeville skits based on stereotypes reached working- and middle-class men and women, who laughed at the rude routines and absorbed their prejudices. Residential and economic discrimination took root as well. Jews soon discovered that they could not rent apartments in many sections of cities, nor could they find employment in whole areas of the economy. Legally, however, Jews possessed equal political and religious rights denied to African Americans and Asian minorities.

Jews responded in diverse ways to these expressions of anti-Semitism. Unable to convince Christians to rent them hotel rooms, Jews built their own hotels that let rooms to one and all, though in practice Jews mostly patronized these establishments. Similarly, they started their own clubs and fraternal associations. The earliest Jewish fraternal society, B'nai B'rith (Sons of the Covenant) began in New York in 1843 and combined elements from the Masonic order with Jewish ritual practices. By the 1880s, B'nai B'rith lodges had spread to Europe and Palestine, one of the first American Jewish exports.[30]

Jews also worked assiduously to elaborate their own ethnic occupational niches. The garment industry was expanding rapidly in the late nineteenth century to manufacture not only men's but also women's and children's clothing. Jews owned most of the factories, employing largely Jewish and Italian immigrants as laborers, especially in the cities that formed industry centers like New York and Chicago. By the turn of the century, roughly half of all Jewish immigrants in New York City worked in small sweatshops sewing clothing for Jewish owners. Unlike many immigrant groups, Jews could be found at all levels of the social and occupational ladder. As one observer remarked in 1905, "Almost every newly arrived Russian Jewish laborer comes into contact with a Russian Jewish employer, almost every Russian tenement dweller must pay his exorbitant rent to a Jewish landlord."[31]

Jews' participation in retail trade also grew as department stores emerged in cities and mass consumption began to

Joseph Seligman, a Jewish immigrant from Bavaria, became a prominent New York businessman and banker and helped finance the Union cause during the Civil War. In 1877, he was turned away from a Saratoga Springs hotel, igniting public debate over the exclusion of Jews from hotels, restaurants, and other privately owned businesses.

fuel the American economy. The most famous of these enterprises was Macy's, purchased and greatly expanded by a family of Jewish immigrants in New York City in the 1880s. But on a more local level as well, in cities and towns throughout the United States, Jews set up shops on Main Street, selling dry goods, jewelry, furniture, and shoes. They also established drug stores, newsstands, and bookstores. In the early twentieth century, Jews entered new unrestricted fields, like motion pictures, music recordings, and radio. Finally, Jews developed alternative, parallel ethnic sections of the economy. Jewish carpenters, glaziers, plumbers, and electricians found work with Jewish builders. They constructed apartments open to Jewish tenants, allowing Jewish immigrants to move out of crowded slum neighborhoods.[32]

Yet many considered these responses inadequate. Jewish immigrants and their children strove not only after economic advancement but also for widely available social and political freedoms. In 1916, Horace Kallen, a young professor of philosophy at the

University of Wisconsin, wrote an article on "Democracy and the Melting Pot." The son of an orthodox rabbi and an immigrant himself from Silesia, Kallen argued against the ideal of the melting pot—whereby differences among ethnic groups were overwhelmed by the common culture—in favor of cultural pluralism. He compared immigrant groups to different instruments of the orchestra, each with its own timbre. When all of the instruments played together in a symphony, they made beautiful music. Kallen's vision of cultural pluralism slowly became part of the American lexicon.[33]

Jewish political diversity complicated this picture. Some Jews, particularly those involved in the burgeoning labor movement, espoused varieties of socialism and awaited the end of racial prejudice once capitalism had been overthrown. Other Jews were Zionists, who held out little hope of acceptance in America and placed their hopes instead in a Middle Eastern Jewish homeland. Some well established Jews, particularly the sons and daughters of those who arrived from Germany in the mid-nineteenth century, blamed their more recently transplanted coreligionists for stirring up prejudice by speaking Yiddish and concentrating in city slums. The tensions among these contending factions played themselves out in the often fractious Jewish associational life of the turn of the century. Ultimately, however, most American Jews coalesced around a view that favored some forms of assimilation and shunned discrimination on the grounds of race, religion, or national origin—whatever the group involved. Allegiances often overlapped, and Jewishness was an extremely flexible concept in America.[34]

Jews developed additional responses to American anti-Semitism. When New York City's police commissioner declared in 1908 that Jews made up less than a quarter of the city's population but half its criminals, New York Jews decided to organize. The statistics were false (the police commissioner apologized) but community leaders recognized that it was nevertheless important to confront the problem of Jewish crime, which did exist in New York City. Jews therefore established the New York Kehillah, or Jewish Community, with bureaus for education, religious life, social welfare, and, of course, crime. An ambitious experiment to unite Jews across class and ethnic lines, the Kehillah failed to bring religious Jews and Jewish socialists together. It did manage briefly to overcome differences between recent east European immigrants and American Jews of German background, but it did not survive long.[35]

During its short lifetime, the Kehillah served as the local New York arm of a new type of American Jewish organization, the American Jewish Committee. Established in 1906, the AJC, as it came to be known, assumed the mantle of leadership of American Jews by virtue of the authority of the men who created it. Prominent American Jews, such as the banker and philanthropist Jacob Schiff, the former US commerce and labor secretary Oscar Straus, and the lawyer Louis Marshall agreed to pool their accumulated prestige, wealth, and experience to defend the precarious situation of Jews worldwide. In the past decade, hundreds of pogroms had raged through Russia; anti-Semitic political parties had won elections in Austria; the Jewish Captain Alfred Dreyfus had been falsely accused, tried, and convicted of treason in France; and Great Britain had restricted immigration of Jews from eastern Europe. The AJC and other organizations took up the challenge of fighting these global abuses.

Marshall, who would later lead the fight against Henry Ford, became identified with the AJC because he remained at its helm from its founding in 1906 until his death in 1929. Born and raised in Syracuse as the son of immigrant Jews, Marshall trained at Columbia

Law School and participated in a wide variety of different causes from Jewish advocacy to environmental conservation. Deep legal training and political acumen accompanied a profound commitment to oppose all forms of prejudice and discrimination. In 1913, under Marshall's guidance, New York State passed one of the first laws outlawing discrimination in public accommodations. It did not matter, the law said, that hotels or restaurants were privately owned; they were required to treat all customers equally.[36]

That same year, the case of Leo Frank presented Marshall with his first major national challenge as a Jewish community leader. Frank was a Texas-born Jew raised in Brooklyn who, while serving as the manager of an Atlanta pencil factory, was accused of murdering one of his employees, a thirteen-year-old white Christian girl named Mary Phagan. The evidence against Frank was suspect, and he pleaded innocent, but he was nevertheless convicted by a white Christian jury that had been inflamed by politically motivated newspaper accounts. Marshall worked largely behind the scenes on Frank's behalf, worrying that involvement by a New York Jewish lawyer would only make matters worse for Frank by playing into the anti-Semitic portrait of a Brooklyn Jew who came south to exploit innocent working girls. In the waning hours of his term in office, Georgia governor John Slaton commuted Frank's sentence to life imprisonment.

But the Frank saga was not finished. A lynch mob soon overturned the governor's decision, taking Frank from his bed in a state prison and driving him back to Mary Phagan's hometown of Marietta, Georgia where they strung him up on a tree. Photographs snapped that day of Frank's dead body circulated throughout the state. Marshall's approach had helped to save Frank's life only to see it snatched away by a lynch mob. Frank's murder traumatized the Jews of Atlanta and the country at large. It took many years before Atlanta's Jews were willing to confront the outrage and to seek a full pardon for Frank from the state.[37] Even as efforts to protect one of their own failed on the national stage, however, the effect of such injustices occasionally galvanized American Jews, creating a sense of solidarity.

In this, American Jews had a special advantage over many other ethnic groups because most Jews, by the second decade of the twentieth century, lived in relatively tight proximity. In the early twentieth century, New York's Lower East Side became the country's premier Jewish enclave. So crowded was the area that it rivaled Bombay in density. Jewish immigrants from various parts of Europe—Rumania, Poland, Russia, Austria—as well as the Middle East managed to live alongside one another in ethnic subsections of the Lower East Side. By 1914, over a million Jews lived in New York, roughly half of the entire population of American Jews.[38] The next largest city, Chicago, contained a quarter of a million. In all of the cities where Jews settled, they gravitated to the poor immigrant parts of town but rarely did they form a majority of an area's population except in New York.

On the eve of the First World War, the United States was home to approximately two million Jews, or 2.2 percent of the country's total population. Jews were distinct among other growing ethnic groups in having large percentages of women (forty-four percent) and children under fourteen (fourteen percent) as well as low rates of return to their home countries (seven percent). As a rule, Jewish immigrants came as families and intended to stay in the United States. Most of these families traveled separately, with husbands often arriving to find work before sending for their wives and children. Wives did their best to contribute to the household income. They worked behind pushcarts and in small shops selling items, took in boarders to help pay the rent, or did piecework, sewing garments at home where they could mind their children. But husbands knew that they had to earn enough for an entire household, or else the children had to go to work. Many did, finding jobs in an expanding garment industry.[39]

This family migration stimulated Jews to establish a wide array of organizations that reflected their commitment to settle in the United States. From Hebrew schools to hospitals, synagogues to burial societies, settlement houses to philanthropies, Jews elaborated a culture of organizations so diverse that few could keep track of all of them. They also created political organizations, including socialist clubs, the Workmen's Circle, and various Zionist groups. Jews were very active in labor unions, especially in the garment industry. Women developed their own organizations separate from men although both shared many of the same ideologies and religious beliefs.[40]

During World War I, an infantry company comprising mostly Jews was recruited from New York City. The men trained on Long Island, often under the leadership of Jewish officers. Military service inspired one Russian Jewish immigrant recruit, Irving Berlin, to write a song for an army revue, "God Bless America." Although he did not popularize the song until the 1930s, when it became a renowned patriotic anthem, many Jewish immigrants shared its sentiments.[41] For them, America was indeed the land that they loved, although most of them had never seen its prairies and had only glimpsed its mountains and oceans. They were eager to have other Jews join them in the United States and they assumed that immigration would resume when the war ended in 1918.

Members of the growing movement for immigration restriction had other ideas. Led by the New England-based Immigration Restriction League, nativists had repeatedly pressed for a literacy requirement throughout the early twentieth century, even though the political radicals feared by the restrictionists usually knew how to read and write. In 1920, however, the League finally convinced Congress to restrict all immigration by setting up a quota system based on country of origin. Jews, who did not have their own country but came from various European countries not favored by the new quota system, realized that the doors were slamming shut. A number of Jews testified before Congress against the new quota laws.

These efforts were unavailing, as were Jewish efforts to fight the rise of a new Ku Klux Klan. The Klan, resurrected on Stone Mountain outside of Atlanta and inspired in part by hatred roused by the Leo Frank case, recruited hundreds of thousands of members throughout the United States. Nativist sentiment swept the nation, though the general mood of bigotry targeted Blacks, Jews, and Catholics as much as immigrants per se. Fear of radicals, especially communists, fueled cruel nighttime raids in 1919 that led to the arrest and deportation of thousands of immigrants, including the outspoken Jewish anarchist Emma Goldman. An immigrant from Russia, Goldman championed women's rights and birth control in addition to opposing wealthy men who exploited their foreign workers. But these roundups did not seem to satisfy the nativists. Prohibition, often construed as an attack on immigrant socializing patterns, entered the Constitution. Republicans swept the White House with the handsome Warren Harding winning the votes of newly enfranchised women.

Louis Marshall died in 1929, just as the United States headed into the Great Depression and before the rise of Adolf Hitler to power in Germany. In the absence of

Marshall, American Jews looked to varied leaders as they confronted a decade of rising anti-Semitism amid economic hardship worldwide. Some supported the fiery orator Rabbi Stephen S. Wise, who championed a boycott of Nazi Germany; others trusted the AJC to continue to work behind the scenes; still others turned to radical political parties, both socialist and communist. Union leaders also established a new organization, the Jewish Labor Committee, to help rescue German socialists and to coordinate labor's response to fascism. By 1936, however, the vast majority of American Jews rallied behind the New Deal programs of President Franklin Delano Roosevelt. Roosevelt was fighting the Depression with imaginative programs that put men and women back to work; he advocated social welfare legislation, including Social Security; he supported the rights of workingmen and women to organize unions to secure decent wages and conditions; and he opposed the threatening fascism of Adolf Hitler.[42]

While Hitler honored Henry Ford with a Grand Cross of the German Empire in 1937, Roosevelt brought talented Jews into his administration at all levels, from cabinet positions (Henry Morgenthau was secretary of the treasury) down to civil service jobs. He also followed Woodrow Wilson, who had appointed the distinguished jurist Louis Brandeis to the Supreme Court, by appointing another Jew, Felix Frankfurter, to the bench. When Wilson had originally nominated Brandeis, who grew up in Kentucky and made a reputation as a militant champion of working men and women as well as free speech, members of Congress spoke openly against putting a Jew on the Supreme Court. But by the time Roosevelt nominated the immigrant Frankfurter, the Senate did not object at all. Both justices became voices for a generous vision of social justice during their time on the court.[43]

As Jews faced an escalating crisis in Europe, German Jews initially urged their American counterparts not to stir up trouble. But silence seemed to mean acquiescence in the outrageous Nazi laws that stripped German Jews of their livelihoods, rights, property, citizenship—and ultimately, their lives. Quotas for German immigrants to the United States were relatively large, but Jewish refugees faced numerous bureaucratic hurdles in attempting to immigrate. Because of the Great Depression, prospective immigrants needed to prove that they would not become a public charge. Individual American Jews, therefore, had to vouch that they would sponsor and support each refugee.

The movie producer Carl Laemmle signed hundreds of affidavits for Jewish residents of his hometown, Laupheim, Germany. Laemmle had emigrated early in the twentieth century and started to exhibit films, initially in nickelodeons. Soon he realized he had a talent for producing and distributing the films and he merged with several firms to create the Universal Film Manufacturing Company, predecessor of Universal Studios. In 1912, Laemmle left New York City for Los Angeles to put a continent between himself and the Motion Picture Patents Company, a trust of non-Jews that wanted to control the new film industry through monopoly. Laemmle saw movies as a democratic institution, allowing rich and poor to mingle. Reflecting such sentiments, he wrote a regular weekly column in Universal's trade journal called "The Melting Pot."

A host of talented Jewish moviemakers fled Europe, including the directors Billy Wilder and Otto Preminger. But most Jews did not have the resources or gumption of Carl Laemmle. The paperwork required in his effort on behalf of German Jews was mind-boggling. Both Nazi Germany and the United States erected paper walls: Germany to fleece emigrants of their remaining funds and possessions, and the United States to delay as many immigrants from entering the United States as possible. So effective was

Carl Laemmle, one of several eminent Jewish immigrant filmmakers, helped a number of Jewish residents from his hometown of Laupheim to escape from Hitler's Germany.

this combination that only in 1938 did the United States fully use its German quota. And after the outbreak of the Second World War in 1939, suspicions about espionage subjected potential immigrants to even greater scrutiny.[44]

Nazi persecution during the 1930s drove many accomplished European Jews to escape to the United States. The most famous of this group was Albert Einstein, the Nobel Prize-winning theoretical physicist whose theories of relativity transformed our understanding of space and time. Einstein accepted a position at Princeton University's Institute for Advanced Studies during the early 1930s. In addition to the scientific émigrés, artists and musicians, such as Marc Chagall, Rudolf Serkin, and Artur Rubenstein also found refuge in America. Many of these figures had already established impressive international reputations before leaving Europe, but others, such as the political philosopher Hannah Arendt, had only just begun their careers. Numerous academic fields—such as psychoanalysis, sociology, and theology—were also infused with the intellectual and artistic talents of Jewish émigrés.[45]

By the time the United States entered the war in 1941, the German conquest of most of Europe, and the onset of Hitler's extermination of European Jewry, had already changed the equation of how to rescue Europe's Jews. Jewish refugees from all parts of Europe struggled to flee the Nazi onslaught, first from Central Europe including Austria and Czechoslovakia, then from Poland and finally from the USSR as well. Persecuted Jews also fled, in smaller numbers, from Western Europe, including France, Holland, Belgium, and Italy. Only Denmark managed to save the majority of its Jews in a daring rescue operation that brought them to neutral Sweden.

American Jews raised money for rescue, held massive rallies and protests, and tried to mobilize political support in Congress for a bill to allow children to enter the United States outside the quota limits. But nothing availed. American Jews did not even manage to convince President Roosevelt to allow 900 Jewish refugee passengers aboard the ocean liner *St. Louis* to land in 1938, even though they held immigration visas for later years.[46] So American Jews did one of the few things open to them: they enlisted in the armed forces of the United States in record numbers. Approximately one half of all Jews eligible for the draft served in the military during World War II—half a million American Jewish men. Jews served in all branches of the service and in all theaters of war. Many fought not only to defend their country but also to defeat the murderous Nazi regime then exterminating Europe's Jews.

As servicemen, Jews finally saw the prairies, mountains, and oceans Irving Berlin had praised in his hymn to America. As members of religiously integrated units, they met all sorts of other Americans from small midwestern towns and the rural South. Given the small percentage of Jews in the American population, most Americans had never met a Jew. And since Jews living in large cities like New York grew up in predominately Jewish neighborhoods, frequently attending public school with other Jews, they, too, had not met many white Christian Americans.

The shared experience of military service changed both Jew and gentile alike. Jews learned to explain to their GI bunkmates that no, they did not have horns, while also debunking more serious anti-Semitic calumnies like claims that they shirked military service or served only behind the lines. These personal encounters were occasionally difficult for Jews, who sometimes got into fights with anti-Semites to defend their honor. But the contacts also produced profound changes. The military, for its part, did its best to promote acceptance of Judaism, along with Protestantism and Catholicism, as one of the three fighting faiths of democracy. Jewish chaplains and Jewish religious holidays received equal recognition with Christian chaplains and Christian holidays. The idea of a "Judeo-Christian tradition" upholding American democratic ideals as opposed to fascism became commonplace in the armed forces. When Dwight D. Eisenhower became president in 1953, he brought these values to Washington, DC and national politics.[47]

Jews, in turn, learned a great deal from their military service, including the importance of fighting for their country, their people, and their rights. When they returned to their families after the war ended in 1945, these veterans were no longer willing to tolerate the widespread anti-Semitic discrimination that had become common during the interwar years. Jews had risked their lives to defend the United States and now justly felt themselves entitled to a life without restrictive covenants that prevented them from buying a house in a nice area, or quotas that limited the number of Jews allowed to attend university or medical school, or employment discrimination that forced Jews to self-employ or to seek work only from other Jews. These Jewish veterans connected

American prejudice with European genocide, and they determined to change both attitudes and practices. They turned to the courts, to legislatures, to education, and to public opinion. Jews cooperated in this mammoth task, with each organization adopting a different approach to achieve similar goals.[48]

Zionism, which already had significant support among American Jews before the Second World War, flourished in its aftermath. American Jews came back from the war convinced that the survivors of the Holocaust could not return to Europe and that Jews needed a state of their own. Many lobbied in the United Nations and in the United States Congress for a Jewish state, even as they also successfully pressured Congress and the president to admit Jewish refugees to the United States by passing the Displaced Persons Act of 1948. That same year saw the establishment of the State of Israel. But even before the Israeli Declaration of Independence, American Jews rallied to the state's support, raising money, purchasing arms, and outfitting ships to carry Holocaust survivors to Palestine. Some even volunteered to defend the beleaguered state.

During the 1950s Jews enjoyed prosperity and social advancement, as did other white Americans. Jewish veterans took advantage of the GI Bill to attend college or to obtain professional training, which led to secure middle class jobs. They also used low cost mortgage benefits to buy homes, usually in the suburbs. Yet tens of thousands of American Jews returned from the war and decided that the other America they had seen, particularly those palm tree paradises of Los Angeles and Miami, were too lovely to resist. So they packed up their bags and moved, initiating a major redistribution of the Jewish population away from the Northeast and Midwest.[49]

Jewish political activism paid off. Quotas in universities were gradually dismantled. The Supreme Court declared restrictive covenants illegal. As Jews moved out of cities, they found homes next door to white Christians. Jews slowly battered down barriers in employment. After the war they still couldn't work at many firms on Wall Street, in elite law firms, in large insurance and utility companies, and in heavy industries. But corporations slowly began to accept a token Jew. "Company Jew coming through," one such Jew announced every day as he came to work in a large insurance firm.[50] Hollywood dramatized a plea for change in the 1947 movie, *Gentleman's Agreement*, in which an intrepid Christian reporter decides to pass as a Jew for six weeks in order to expose "polite" anti-Semitism. Changes came gradually. By the 1960s, a generation of Jewish baby boomers was growing up with very little personal experience of anti-Semitism.[51]

Yet even as their personal experience of prejudice diminished, many Jews remained committed to a more universal notion of an integrated society that included African Americans and Asians as equals to white Americans. Numerous Jews threw themselves into the Civil Rights movement and supported the integration of schools and other public spaces. They joined marches in the South to end segregation and participated in rallies in northern cities against employment discrimination and de facto segregation in housing. Other Jews stood on the sidelines, fearful to oppose their white Christian neighbors. Still others supported desegregation in principle but not in practice, nervous about the prospect of living alongside African Americans and Hispanics. Yet the Civil Rights movement inspired many Jews, who subscribed to its vision of a more just and equitable American society.[52]

For Jews, that vision included women as equal to men. Betty Friedan, born Bettye Goldstein, had grown up in the Midwest, attended an elite women's college, and then pursued a career in journalism before marrying, having children, and moving to the suburbs. In all outward respects her life appeared to fulfill the American dream but she discovered a profound unhappiness among middle-class American women as she conducted a study of her college classmates. She called it "the problem that has no name."[53] Friedan named the problem, women's subordination, and proposed the solution, women's equality. In doing so she drew upon an activist radical background in labor union politics. Friedan founded the National Organization of Women (NOW) in 1964 and helped to inaugurate a second wave of American feminism. NOW demanded that women should be free to work at any occupation, should receive the same pay as men, and should have the right to open bank accounts and receive credit for themselves rather than on behalf of their husbands. Just as Jews had previously struggled to fight employment discrimination against themselves and other ethnic groups, Jewish women like Friedan now rallied to end discrimination against all women. [54]

A few Jewish women lived lives guided by feminism and Judaism even before the 1960s. Rosalyn Yalow, only the second American woman to win a Nobel Prize in medicine, discovered *radioimmunoassy*, an application of nuclear physics to clinical medicine that uses radioactive tracers to measure even minute amounts of biological material. Yalow combined motherhood with research in the 1950s when it was very difficult to obtain a job as a married woman.[55] Yet she was only one of many eminent Jewish doctors and scientists who transformed the lives of Americans. Albert Sabin and Jonas Salk both invented vaccines to inoculate people against the polio virus. Other Jewish scientists, like Robert Oppenheimer and Richard Feynman, shaped new directions in physics.

The Immigration and Nationality Act of 1965, proposed by Emanuel Celler, a Jewish congressman from Brooklyn, ended the quotas of the 1920s. But most Jewish immigrants who settled in the United States in the second half of the twentieth century came as refugees, outside the normal visa system. In the 1970s Jewish immigrants from the Soviet Union arrived as a result of extensive efforts by American Jews to pressure the American government to fight for freedom of religion for all peoples in the Soviet Union. The Jackson-Vanik amendment of 1974 tied free trade to free religious practices and prompted the Soviet Union to allow some Jews to emigrate. Many went to Israel but thousands came to the United States.[56] Then in 1979 a revolution overthrew the Shah of Iran and thousands of Iranian Jews came to America. Other Jews fled political repression in South Africa and a number of states in South America, including Cuba. By the 1990s, immigrants constituted approximately ten percent of the American Jewish population. These estimates included a contingent of Israeli Jews who came to the United States for economic reasons. Unlike the vast majority of other Jewish immigrants, Israelis had a homeland to which they could—and often did—return.[57]

American Jews today resemble other Americans in many ways. They live in suburbs and cities, they work at diverse occupations, and they attend university. And yet Jews still differ from other Americans, not only in their religious practices and beliefs, but also in numerous sociological particulars. Jews, for example, tend to be liberal in politics even as the definition of "liberal" continues to evolve. Over ninety percent of American Jews attend college, a much higher proportion than the rest of the American population, and a significant percentage possess professional degrees. Jews still concentrate in certain sections of the country and in certain cities and suburbs, although they are far more dispersed than in the past. Jewish women are more likely to work in the same fields as

Jewish men, such as law, medicine, academia, and business.[58] Finally, Jews share a consciousness of being different that is often difficult to articulate. Sometimes it is lodged in history or heritage or memory. Sometimes it relates to the traumas of the twentieth century—particularly the Holocaust. Sometimes it stems from a special, intimate tie with Israel as a Jewish state.

Despite many difficulties, Jewish immigrants embraced America even as they did their best to help it live up to its democratic ideals of freedom and justice for all. They have succeeded in numerous realms from science to literature to politics to academia. Then again, the most frequent barrier to Jewish acceptance in America has never been too little success, but rather the suspicion of "too much." As American anti-Semitism slowly falls into eclipse, perhaps the Jews of the United States may begin to enjoy a more straightforward pride in their many accomplishments.

Endnotes

[1] Quoted in Neil Baldwin, *Henry Ford and the Jews: The Mass Production of Hate* (New York: Public Affairs Press, 2001), 108. Baldwin's book is the best historical account of Ford's anti-Semitic attacks on Jews and Jewish efforts to counter them.

[2] Steven Watts, *The People's Tycoon: Henry Ford and the American Century* (New York: Knopf, 2005), 379.

[3] Baldwin, *Henry Ford*, 108–33.

[4] Watts, *People's Tycoon*, 381.

[5] *The International Jew: The World's Foremost Problem* (Dearborn, MI: Dearborn Publishing Co., 1920–1922).

[6] Richard Hofstadter, *The Age of Reform: From Bryan to FDR* (New York: Vintage Books, 1955), 70–81.

[7] John Higham, *Strangers in the Land: Patterns of American Nativism 1860–1925* (New York: Atheneum, 1970), 300–30.

[8] Ibid., 264–99.

[9] Herman Bernstein, *The History of a Lie: "The Protocols of the Wise Men of Zion," A Study* (New York: Ogilvie Publishing, 1921).

[10] Baldwin, *Henry Ford*, 109–33, 162–71.

[11] Watts, *People's Tycoon*, 381.

[12] Baldwin, 150.

[13] Ibid., 134–51.

[14] Ibid., 209.

[15] Ibid., 204–17. See also Grace H. Larsen and Henry E. Erdman, "Aaron Sapiro: Genius of Farm Co-operative Promotion," *Mississippi Valley Historical Review* 49, no. 2 (September 1962): 242–68.

[16] Victoria Saker Woeste, "Suing Henry Ford: America's First Hate Speech Case," accessed April 15, 2012, http://www.americanbarfoundation.org/research/project/19.

[17] Watts, *People's Tycoon*, 396.

[18] Eli Faber, "America's Earliest Jewish Settlers, 1654–1820," in *The Columbia History of Jews and Judaism in America*, ed. Marc Lee Raphael (New York: Columbia University Press, 2010), 21–26.

[19] See Howard Rock, *Haven of Liberty: New York Jews in the New World, 1654–1865* (New York: New York University Press, 2012).

[20] Beth S. Wenger, "They Came to Stay, 1654–1880," in *The Jewish Americans: Three Centuries of Jewish Voices in America* (Garden City, NY: Doubleday, 2007), 1–6.

[21] For accounts of this parade and different interpretations, see Jonathan D. Sarna, *American Judaism: A History* (New Haven: Yale University Press, 2004), 38; Hasia R. Diner, *The Jews of the United States, 1654 to 2000* (Berkeley: University of California Press, 2004), 57.

[22] Quoted in Sarna, *American Judaism*, 38–39.

[23] For a good overview of this migration see Hasia R. Diner, *A Time for Gathering: The Second Migration 1840–1880* (Baltimore: Johns Hopkins University Press, 1992).

[24] Annie Polland and Daniel Soyer, *Emerging Metropolis: New York Jews in the Age of Immigration, 1840–1920* (New York: New York University Press, 2012).

[25] J.A. Joel, "A Union Soldier's Passover Seder," in *The Jewish Americans*, 87–113.

[26] For the most complete treatment of this incident and its implications see Jonathan D. Sarna, *When General Grant Expelled the Jews* (New York: Schocken, 2012).

[27] Beth S. Wenger, "A World of Their Own, 1880–1924," in *The Jewish Americans*, 87–113.

[28] For a comprehensive discussion of American anti-Semitism in general and the Seligman affair in particular, see Leonard Dinnerstein, *Antisemitism in America* (New York: Oxford University Press, 1994), 35–57.

[29] John Higham, "Social Discrimination against Jews, 1830–1930," in *Send These to Me: Jews and Other Immigrants in Urban America* (New York: Atheneum, 1975), 138–73.

[30] Deborah Dash Moore, *B'nai B'rith and the Challenge of Ethnic Leadership* (Albany, NY: SUNY Press, 1981), 1–51.

[31] Arthur A. Goren, "Jews," in *The Harvard Encyclopedia of American Ethnic Groups*, eds. Stephen Thernstrom, Ann Orlov, and Oscar Handlin (Cambridge: Belknap Press of Harvard University Press, 1980), 582.

[32] Wenger, "A World of Their Own," 87–113.

[33] Daniel Greene, *The Jewish Origins of Cultural Pluralism: The Menorah Association and American Diversity* (Bloomington, IN: Indiana University Press, 2011), 63–71.

[34] Eric Goldstein, *The Price of Whiteness: Jews, Race, and American Identity* (Princeton, NJ: Princeton University Press, 2007), 86–137.

[35] On the New York Kehillah see Arthur A. Goren, *New York Jews and the Quest for Community: The Kehillah Experiment, 1908–1922* (New York: Columbia University Press, 1970).

[36] On the American Jewish Committee see Naomi W. Cohen, *Not Free to Desist: The American Jewish Committee 1906–1966* (Philadelphia: The Jewish Publication Society of America, 1972).

[37] There is extensive scholarship on the Leo Frank case. Among the best treatments are: Leonard Dinnerstein, *The Leo Frank Case* (New York: Columbia University Press, 1968); Albert Lindemann, *The Jew Accused, Three Anti-Semitic Affairs (Dreyfus, Beilis, Frank), 1894–1915* (Cambridge: Cambridge University Press, 1991); Steve Oney, *And the Dead Shall Rise: The Murder of Mary Phagan and the Lynching of Leo Frank* (New York: Pantheon, 2003).

[38] Moses Rischin, *The Promised City: New York's Jews 1870–1914* (1962, rept.; Cambridge, MA: Harvard University Press, 1977), 76–94.

[39] Goren, "Jews," 582.

[40] Ibid., 583–88.

[41] Christopher M. Sterba, *Good Americans: Italian and Jewish Immigrants During the First World War* (New York: Oxford University Press, 2003), 105–10.

[42] Henry L. Feingold, *A Time for Searching: Entering the Mainstream, 1924–1945* (Baltimore: Johns Hopkins University Press, 1992), 189–224.

[43] See Robert A. Burt, *Two Jewish Justices: Outcasts in the Promised Land* (Berkeley: University of California Press, 1988).

[44] Of the extensive corpus of scholarship on this period, see especially David S. Wyman, *Paper Walls: America and the Refugee Crisis, 1938–1941* (Amherst: University of Massachusetts Press, 1968); Henry L. Feingold, *The Politics of Rescue: The Roosevelt Administration and the Holocaust* (New Brunswick, NJ: Rutgers University Press, 1970); and Richard Breitman and Alan M. Kraut, *American Refugee Policy and European Jewry 1933–1945* (Bloomington, IN: Indiana University Press, 1987).

[45] Laura Fermi, *Illustrious Immigrants: The Intellectual Migration from Europe, 1930–1941* (Chicago: University of Chicago Press, 1968); see also, Anthony Heilbut, *Exiled in Paradise: German Refugee Artists and Intellectuals in America from the 1930s to the Present* (New York: Viking Press, 1983).

[46] David S. Wyman, *The Abandonment of the Jews: America and the Holocaust 1941–1945* (New York: Pantheon, 1984); Feingold, *A Time for Searching*, 225–65.

[47] Deborah Dash Moore, *GI Jews: How World War II Changed a Generation* (Cambridge, MA: Harvard University Press, 2004).

[48] Ibid., 248–64; Stuart Svonkin, *Jews Against Prejudice: American Jews and the Fight for Civil Liberties* (New York: Columbia University Press, 1997).

[49] Deborah Dash Moore, *To the Golden Cities: Pursuing the American Jewish Dream in Miami and L.A.* (New York: Free Press, 1994), 1–20.

[50] Rich Cohen, *Tough Jews: Fathers, Sons, and Gangster Dreams* (New York: Simon & Schuster, 1998), 18.

[51] Riv-Ellen Prell, "Triumph, Accommodation, and Resistance: American Jewish Life from the End of World War II to the Six-Day War," in *The Columbia History of Jews and Judaism in America*, ed. Marc Lee Raphael (New York: Columbia University Press, 2010), 114–41.

[52] Paul Buhle and Robin D. G. Kelley, "Allies of a Different Sort: Jews and Blacks in the American Left," in *Struggles in the Promised Land: Toward a History of Black-Jewish Relations in the United States*, ed. Jack Salzman and Cornel West (New York: Oxford University Press, 1997), 197–229.

[53] This was the title of the first chapter in Betty Friedan's, *The Feminine Mystique* (New York: Norton, 1963).

[54] See Daniel Horowitz, *Betty Friedan and the Making of The Feminine Mystique: The American Left, the Cold War, and Modern Feminism* (Amherst: University of Massachusetts Press, 1998).

[55] Emily Taitz, "Rosalyn Yalow," in *Jewish Women in America: An Historical Encyclopedia*, ed. Paula S. Hyman and Deborah Dash Moore (New York: Routledge, 1997).

[56] On the Soviet Jewry movement see Gal Beckerman, *When Whey Come for Us, We'll be Gone: The Epic Struggle to Save Soviet Jewry* (New York: Houghton Mifflin Harcourt, 2010).

[57] Steven J. Gold, "Soviet Jews in the United States," *American Jewish Year Book* 94 (1994): 3–56.

[58] See Harriet Hartman and Moshe Hartman, *Gender and American Jews: Patterns in Work, Education and Family in Contemporary Life* (Waltham, MA: Brandeis University Press, 2009).

Greek immigrant George Christopher (shown here at age fourteen) sold newspapers and delivered messages as a young boy—long before he became mayor of San Francisco.

GREEK AMERICANS

By Alexander Kitroeff

WHEN JOHN MASSOURIDES PLANNED an evening out with seventeen-year-old Lillian Breese in February 1909, he could never have anticipated the disastrous outcome. The local residents of South Omaha had certainly resented the interest shown by Greek immigrant newcomers in the town's young women—most of whom were the daughters of well-established families of British or Irish heritage. Lillian Breese, however, was one of those who did not mind the newcomers. She had worked as an English tutor to many Greeks and other immigrants to help them adjust and integrate into the small Nebraska meatpacking town. In this, she was probably the exception to the rule. Resentment against new immigrants, and especially the largest group in South Omaha, the Greeks, had grown to ominous proportions in recent years.

Nativist sentiment was widespread in the western states during the turn-of-the-century period, motivated by an anxiety that the latest immigrants from southeastern Europe posed a threat to the livelihoods of those already settled there.[1] The newcomers appeared willing to take low-paying jobs and they were steeped in completely different cultural values. Also, because the southeastern Europeans were still present in smaller numbers in the West as compared to the East and the Midwest, they were more easily identified as outsiders.

All of these stigmas applied to the Greeks, who began arriving in the United States in large numbers in the 1890s from rural regions of Greece, the Ottoman Empire, and Cyprus. A small number of Greeks had already settled in America before this period, primarily a few wealthy merchants and orphans rescued by American missionaries during the Greek revolution of 1821. But mass migration did not begin in earnest until the late nineteenth century. Starting in the 1890s and continuing until the early 1920s, about 400,000 Greeks immigrated to the United States, fleeing poor economic conditions or, for those living in the Ottoman Empire, the growing persecution of ethnic minorities. During the winter of 1909, the Greek presence in the greater Omaha area had swelled to

2,000—many of whom were seeking employment after widespread railroad layoffs had put them out of work.

These Greek immigrants shared many of the general characteristics of the other southeastern Europeans arriving in the United States during this period: they came from rural areas, spoke little or no English, and had only rudimentary education. Initially attracted by the prospect of making quick money and returning to their homeland, they took up lower-rung common labor jobs in industries such as mining, textiles, and railroad construction. Often, they were recruited as strikebreakers. Because they lacked capital and planned to stay only on a temporary basis, the Greeks preferred the quick returns available in service industry jobs.

Initially, Greeks settled mostly in the large urban centers. Chicago had the largest concentration of Greek immigrants, followed by New York. Chicago was the destination of many Greeks from the southern region of Peloponnesus, and they soon established a vibrant network of ethnic institutions there.[2] It was not until the post-World War II period that Chicago finally lost its place as the "Greek American capital" to New York City.

Greek immigrants also settled in the mill towns of New England and the mid-Atlantic industrial regions of Pennsylvania and Virginia. The Greeks of New England, following the Irish and the French Canadians, represented the third major wave of ethnic laborers in that region. Through 1920, the roughly 10,000 Greeks of Lowell, Massachusetts, made it the American town with the third largest Greek population.[3] Greeks remained in Lowell and other New England towns even after the textile industry began moving south, with most workers moving gradually into self-employment or other jobs in the service industry.

The search for employment led many of them to spread out far beyond the original regions of Greek settlement. Using Chicago as a stepping-stone, thousands of Greek immigrants spread through the Great Plains, the Rocky Mountain West, and eventually to the West Coast. During the first decade of the twentieth century, the Greek population of the West rose to more than 20,000, almost a quarter of the over 100,000 Greeks in the country recorded in the 1910 census. It was this westward spread that propelled individuals like John Massourides into a region undergoing a rising swell of xenophobia against newcomers.[4]

The sentiment against Greeks ran especially high in South Omaha because of their role as strikebreakers. In 1904, Greek and Japanese immigrants had helped break a strike in the meatpacking industry. In 1907, the *Omaha Examiner* pointed out that while California's Japanese problem was well known, the people of Omaha had better review the growing Italian, Greek, Bulgarian, and Serbian problem in their own backyard. The Irish and other town residents looked upon the growing number of young Greek men as clannish, immoral, and generally "un-American." Another meatpacking strike in early 1909, during which Greeks once again were enlisted as strikebreakers, led to a renewal of hostilities. A local newspaper joined the fray in describing the Greeks as an unsanitary menace.

This was the context in February 1909 when an Irish American policeman, Edward Lowery, approached Massourides and Breese on the street and determined to arrest the Greek under suspicion of consorting with a prostitute. What happened next is less clear. By some accounts, Massourides tried to escape and pulled a gun. Others claimed that Lowery drew his weapon first, prompting the Greek to use his own in self-defense, or that Massourides had shot the officer accidentally in a scuffle. In any case, Lowery was shot dead and the police arrested Massourides and charged him with murder.[5]

Within two days, a crowd of angry residents gathered and attacked the Greek neighborhood. A South Omaha community leader, Joseph Murphy, circulated a petition calling upon local residents to attend a meeting on how the town could rid itself of the "filthy" Greeks. A day later, a crowd estimated at three thousand assembled near the Greek quarter. The meeting passed several resolutions calling on the meatpacking industry to bar Greeks from employment. The resolutions claimed that the Greeks were dirty, immoral, unhygienic, afflicted with diseases like syphilis, and unsuitable for handling meats. Successive speeches whipped up the crowd's emotions until a group broke off and moved toward the houses, beating the residents and destroying property.

The riot continued through the night with the burning of several buildings and little intervention by the police. There were twenty-five arrests on the evening of the riots but not one person was ever convicted. A report later commissioned by the Greek Consulate in Washington, DC, cast doubts on Officer Lowery's actions during the initial arrest and established that Lillian Breese was not a prostitute, as had been alleged.

Nonetheless, the riot marked the end of the Greek presence in South Omaha. Of the city's 1,300 Greeks, 200 fled immediately to nearby Omaha. Within weeks, the Greeks had disappeared almost entirely from the local meatpacking plants and the Greek neighborhood of South Omaha stood abandoned. The initial assessments of the damages caused by the rioters ranged from $35,000 to over $280,000, the equivalent of about one to seven million dollars in 2010.

News of the riot spread across the country, especially among Greeks. There had been earlier anti-Greek riots, as for example in Roanoke, Virginia in 1907, but the damage then was less extensive and the consequences less widely felt. Several months after the 1909 South Omaha riot, similar but smaller-scale events shook the Greek communities of Montana and Idaho.[6] Anti-Greek discrimination lingered on in the following years, especially in the West and the South.

Reactions to the Nebraska riot were mixed elsewhere in the country, where "old stock" Americans were still reacting to the southeastern European influx and its implications. The *New York Times* detailed the destruction wrought by the mob, but also blamed the riot on the self-imposed isolation of the Greeks and urged foreigners to avoid creating separate "colonies."[7] There were also clear signs of support for the newcomers. One of the most thoughtful was put forward by the social worker Grace Abbot, a Nebraskan, who applied sociological theories and statistics in her work on child welfare and other social issues including the needs of recent immigrants. Abbot worked in Hull House, the urban center that focused on female and immigrant welfare issues in Chicago, one of the largest population centers of Greek immigrants in the country. In an article published in November of 1909, Abbott sought to explain the alleged propensity of Greeks to commit crimes as the result of language misunderstandings, unfamiliarity with American rules and regulations, and disproportionate exposure to policing because so many operated pushcarts and other businesses in public spaces.[8]

The view that the Greeks tended towards criminality was only one piece of a larger set of prejudices confronting them. Greek immigrants were also accused of being degenerate, uncivilized versions of their ancestors, the classical Greeks. As was also true of other southeastern European immigrants, questions were often raised about Greek racial purity or "whiteness." The Dillingham Commission formed by the US Congress produced a well-known report in 1911 that supposedly proved the intellectual backwardness and racial inferiority of this new wave of southeastern European immigrants. The sociologist (and later eugenicist) Henry Pratt Fairchild echoed many of these negative stereotypes in his first book, *Greek Immigration to the United States*, also published in 1911. "One of the most pronounced features of the Greek character," Fairchild wrote, "is a factiousness, a sectionalism, a clannishness, an inability to take the point of view of one's neighbor."[9]

The leaders of established Greek communities throughout the United States were already engaged in a debate over the status of Greek immigrants. After the 1909 riots, their task became more urgent. Ethnic associations were a means of both educating and offering assistance to Greek immigrants, and by the time of the incident in South Omaha a great deal had been achieved through the establishment of churches, community organizations, fraternal associations, and newspapers. The Greek American philanthropists who underwrote these efforts included Michael Anagnos (head of the Perkins Institute for the Blind in Boston), Aristides Phoutrides (a professor at Harvard), the Rodocanaki family (cotton merchants), the Stephano brothers (owners of a cigarette manufacturing plant in Philadelphia), and the Vlasto brothers (import-export merchants in New York).

Whatever particular cause the ethnic associations adopted, they all called upon their compatriots to maintain high standards of behavior so as not to besmirch the standing of the Greek American community and, by extension, Greek culture or Greece itself. The major Greek newspaper in Chicago, the *Greek Star*, urged the entire Greek community to adopt the manners and customs of the host country and launched a broadside against "delinquents" in its midst. Similar appeals issued from the two Greek newspapers of New York, the *Atlantis* and the *Ethnikos Kyrix* (National Herald). An important aspect of the way the Greeks proclaimed their ties with America was to assert the parallels between classical Greek democracy and the ideals of the American Revolution.

For the most part, the community leaders left it to sympathetic outsiders to confront the accusations against Greeks more directly. Most notably, the Reverend Thomas Burgess, secretary of the Episcopal Church's Bureau of Immigration, published a book in 1913 aimed at familiarizing the American public with the background and cultural attributes of Greek immigrants in the United States. His purpose was to demonstrate that Greeks were not as backward as some people believed.[10]

The most effective rebuttal to anti-Greek prejudices turned to be the very evolution of the immigrant community itself, which by the second decade of the twentieth century had begun to carve out a measure of permanence in its adopted country. One of the earliest signs came when the Greeks began joining unions, abandoning the ranks of strikebreakers, and even participating in labor mobilizations and strikes. Greeks went on strike at the Utah copper mines in 1912 and in the following year in the coalfields of Colorado. The strike leader at Ludlow, Colorado, where one of the largest tent colonies of striking coal miners was located, was a Greek immigrant named Louis Tikas; he was shot dead when the National Guard violently put down the strike in 1914. Greek immigrants, along with eastern European Jews, also became involved in the activities of the International Fur and Leatherworkers Union, which fought to improve working conditions in the 1920s and 1930s.

The size of the Greek presence continued to grow in the second decade of the twentieth century as more immigrants began to settle permanently. Those ethnic Greeks who came from the Ottoman Empire were always unlikely to return to what was becoming an increasingly hostile environment. But those from mainland Greece, as well, were beginning to think of themselves as permanent residents in the United States. Significantly, the numbers of Greek immigrant women began to rise, furnishing proof that the Greeks were creating family units and putting down new roots in the New World.

Perhaps most importantly, immigrant Greeks who had found jobs as street peddlers, store employees, or small business owners began to enjoy the beginnings of economic prosperity. Many opened their own businesses, mostly modest eateries, inaugurating what would become a long tradition of Greek American involvement in the restaurant and confectionary businesses. The Greek diner or candy shop—with its eagle-eyed and parsimonious proprietor—became a fixture of cities and small towns throughout the United States.

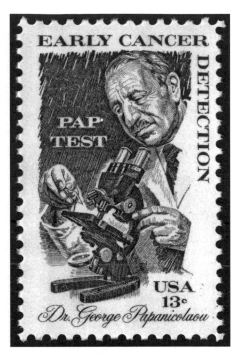

Georgios Papanikolaou, who immigrated in 1913, was a pioneer in cancer detection and the inventor of the "Pap smear."

These were family businesses, an environment in which wives and daughters were also employed. Although some Greek women did work outside the home and even in factories in New England, the traditional male-privileged culture the Greeks brought with them meant that most women spent their time raising children and tending to the home. Working in a family-owned business was a compromise between the domestic ideal and the need to earn income, and it afforded a degree of financial protection for the females. Stable, family-oriented communities, strengthened by ethnic associations and parishes of the Greek Orthodox Church, began to emerge. Across the board, Greek immigrants were moving toward middle-class respectability.

A few Greek immigrants were already middle class on arrival. In addition to the large numbers of peasants fleeing dire economic conditions in Greece, the influx in the early twentieth century also included a small group of skilled and trained white-collar professionals who came to America with the hope of advancing their careers. The doctor and pathologist Georgios Papanikolaou was an exemplary member of this group. After studying medicine in Athens and in Germany, Papanikolaou emigrated in 1913 to continue research at New York Hospital-Cornell Medical Center. He would go on to become a pioneer in cytology and cancer detection as well as the inventor of the "Pap smear."

The prejudice the Greeks experienced in America served to sharpen the debate within the community about how to balance between maintaining ties to the homeland and demonstrating loyalty to the host society. At this time, Greece was making explicit claims on its immigrant communities abroad as it entered what was to be the final phase of the "Great Idea": the vision of a greater Greece that would extend its frontiers to include historically Greek lands and peoples that remained under Ottoman rule. The outbreak of the Balkan Wars of 1912–13, which resulted in Greek territorial gains, brought about 25,000 Greek American immigrants back across the Atlantic as volunteers in response to Greece's pleas for help and an enthusiastic and noisy recruitment campaign across the United States. The volunteers were received warmly in their homeland, but the majority returned to the United States when the wars were over.[11]

The outbreak of World War I and the suspension of most maritime travel prevented Greek Americans from returning as volunteers but offered them an opportunity to demonstrate loyalty to their adopted country. Domestic political divisions delayed the entry of both Greece and the United States into the war effort. By 1917, however, with the two countries both fighting on the side of the Entente Powers, large numbers of American Greeks enlisted in the US Army, purchased liberty bonds, and voted for public resolutions supporting the war effort and affirming loyalty to the United States. Greek American leaders during this time repeatedly pointed to parallels between American and classical Greek democratic values and claimed that volunteering for the American army was tantamount to volunteering for the Greek one. There are no accurate figures revealing how many Greeks volunteered, but an informed estimate places the figure at about 60,000.[12]

In the aftermath of the First World War, nativist sentiment raged in many parts of the United States and many Greek Americans were obliged to publicly demonstrate their intention to fully integrate into American society. They could do nothing in the early 1920s to prevent Congress from using clearly xenophobic criteria to curtail the quotas of immigrants from southeastern Europe. After 1924, therefore, the number of incoming Greeks was reduced to a trickle, leaving the total number of Greeks in the United States to remain at around 300,000 during the period between the two world wars. The Census of 1940 recorded the presence of 326,672 persons either born in Greece or of Greek parentage. The Greeks from the Ottoman Empire were counted as part of the total of 95,839 coming from "Turkey in Asia."[13] Meanwhile, the "Great Idea" had ended in 1922 with Greece's defeat in a war against Turkey that sent almost a million Ottoman Greek refugees to Greece, creating difficult social conditions that discouraged much return migration from the United States in the following two decades.

The interwar period witnessed the consolidation of several Greek ethnic institutions in the United States. The most important of these was the Greek Orthodox Church, which during the early twentieth century had an especially strong presence in the rural areas of Greece from which most immigrants originally came. Following two decades of decentralized and disorganized religious life in the New World, the Greek Orthodox Church acquired a central organization in 1922, the Greek Orthodox Archdiocese of North and South America. For many Greeks, the Church symbolized a line of continuity between life in America and life in the ancestral homeland, where it represented the religion of over ninety percent of the population. The Archdiocese established Greek language schools and also encouraged the participation of women in civic life through the Ladies Philoptochos Society, a women's-only charity organization with local parish

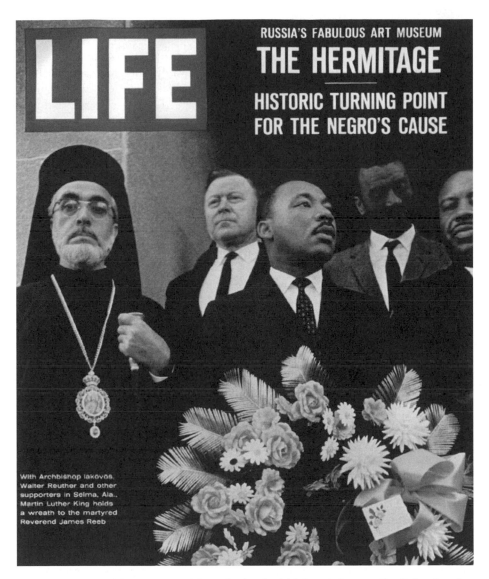

RUSSIA'S FABULOUS ART MUSEUM

THE HERMITAGE

HISTORIC TURNING POINT FOR THE NEGRO'S CAUSE

With Archbishop Iakovos, Walter Reuther and other supporters in Selma, Ala., Martin Luther King holds a wreath to the martyred Reverend James Reeb

chapters governed by a national board that reported to the Archbishop.

Some organizations, like the Greek Orthodox Church and certain fraternal associations, sought to strengthen the ties between immigrants and their communities back in Greece. Others aimed to help the newcomers assimilate into American society. This latter movement was in some ways a rejoinder to the nativism of the postwar years. Especially in the South, where "100 percent Americans" were boycotting immigrant business or joining a newly revived Ku Klux Klan, the whole project of assimilation took on a new sense of urgency.

Archbishop Iakovos, the Primate of the Greek Orthodox Archdiocese of North and South America, marched with the Reverend Martin Luther King, Jr. in Selma, Alabama.

The American Hellenic Progressive Association (AHEPA) was the main vehicle for Greek Americans' strategy for Americanization. A group of Greek American businessmen in Georgia founded the organization in 1922, and within a decade it had established branches throughout the country and counted over twenty thousand members. AHEPA's founding charter vowed to advance "pure and undefiled Americanism among the Greeks of the United States" and to instill in them "the deepest loyalty and allegiance" for their adopted country.[14]

From the organization's earliest years, the members of AHEPA engaged in vigorous internal debates over the proper role of the Greek language and Greek culture in American society, at a time when foreign language publications and foreign languages themselves were under siege. Compared to some of the other Greek ethnic organizations, AHEPA seemed initially overeager to comply with the general mood of hyperpatriotism. Ultimately AHEPA decided to include some Greek in its publications and not to force the issue of language. It had an easier time over Greek culture. AHEPA embraced the idea that classical Greek and American democratic values were identical. This stance attenuated what some members saw as its excessive Americanism on other issues.

Greeks widely heeded AHEPA's call to Americanize, most directly by acquiring US citizenship in large numbers. The naturalization rates for Greeks throughout the 1920s correspond to the overall figures for other immigrant groups, but the Greeks appear to have gotten a later start and caught up toward the end of the decade.[15] AHEPA also reflected the Greek American community's move toward the mainstream in the 1920s by relocating its offices to Washington, DC, organizing annual congressional banquets, and setting up annual visits to the White House.[16]

Dean Alfange (Constantinos Alfantzis) was the veritable embodiment of the AHEPA's goal of assimilation. He had arrived in the United States with his parents as an infant in 1898. A lawyer by training, Alfange championed the Americanization of his fellow Greeks and served as the national president of AHEPA from 1927 to 1929. Throughout his six-decade long political career, Alfange was a strong backer of liberal causes and the New Deal; he was nominated and appointed to various posts by Democrats, Republicans, the American Labor Party, and New York's Liberal Party, which he helped to found in 1944. Alfange is perhaps best known for his composition of "My Creed," a stirring ode to self-reliance and Americanism.

AHEPA's success in the 1920s would have been unlikely without the rising Greek American business class that financed its initiatives. During this period, a few Greek American entrepreneurs managed to achieve something greater than local prominence, yet they too faced discrimination. A good example is Alexander Pantages, who arrived in Seattle via Canada as a young man. By 1920, he owned more than thirty vaudeville theatres in both the United States and Canada and controlled perhaps sixty more through management contracts. The theaters Pantages constructed in several cities in Canada and the American West Coast remain cultural landmarks, the most famous of which is the one located on Hollywood Boulevard. Pantages's career came to an abrupt end when competitors apparently framed him for rape and tabloid depictions of his "otherness" helped to convict him. A successful appeal in the 1930s overturned the conviction, but by that time he was ruined.[17]

There would be happier success stories among the earliest Greek immigrants. The hotel business afforded several Greeks the opportunity to make good, especially during

the Roaring Twenties, when leisure and luxury became middle class commodities. S. Gregory Taylor (Soterios Gregoriou Tavoularis), who like many of his fellow immigrants Anglicized his name upon arrival to the United States, rose from

In 1905, John Cocoris brought advanced sponge fishing techniques from Greece to Tarpon Springs, Florida.

bellhop to manager and partial owner of some New York City's finest hotels. Among these was the St. Moritz on Central Park (later to become the Plaza Hotel), which Taylor managed with considerable flair, giving it a pronounced European ambiance. Jean (Ioannis) G. Venetos's life was another Greek success story in the hospitality industry. After working as a cook upon his arrival in 1901, he managed and eventually purchased a hotel in Brooklyn, which became the first of several hotel acquisitions in New York City and Connecticut.[18]

A unique entrepreneurial project was meanwhile unfolding on the Gulf Coast. In 1905, a Greek immigrant named John Cocoris "imported" the more advanced techniques of sponge fishing already used in several Aegean islands and persuaded many of the inhabitants of those islands, especially Kalymnos, to settle in Tarpon Springs, Florida. Within a few years, the small fishing town became the center of a flourishing sponge industry. Its prosperity continued through the late 1940s, when a marine algae bloom wiped out the sponge fields in the Gulf of Mexico. Most of the sponge boats and divers switched to shrimp fishing and the city ultimately became a resort destination.[19]

By the 1930s, the Greeks had made considerable advances. In contrast to earlier times, the popular media began to offer the group a measure of respect and even praise. An article in the *Brooklyn Daily Eagle* published in 1932, for example, described the

Greeks of Brooklyn as "thousands of sturdy, industrious men and women, who have done their full share in helping to make the borough one of the leading communities in the world."[20] Greek organizational life suffered along with the rest of American civil society in the early years of the Great Depression, but by the late 1930s many ethnic associations were being revitalized. This was true above all of the Greek Orthodox Church, which soon became the community's organizational backbone and moral compass.

If Pantages's entrepreneurship was representative of the emergence of a Greek American business class in the 1920s, the popularity of wrestler Jim Londos, also known as the "Golden Greek" or the "Greek God," embodied the new positive image being ascribed to Greeks. Londos, born Christophoros Theofilou in Greece, worked a series of odd jobs in the United States before taking up wrestling. His muscular physique and good looks helped make him a showman in the ring, and he won several titles in bouts that drew large audiences throughout the 1930s. Londos remained widely popular until his retirement in 1946.

The Second World War, which put Greece and the United States on the same side of the largest international conflict in history, provided the context in which Greek immigrants and their children gained full acceptance in the United States. In late 1940, the Greek army overcame long odds to push Mussolini's invading forces back into Albania, earning paeans to Greek heroics on the front pages of many American newspapers and magazines. Ordinary Greek Americans joined the US Armed Forces in large numbers while more prominent citizens formed the Greek War Relief Association to raise funds for the Greek resistance. In cooperation with the US Treasury Department, AHEPA launched a drive that eventually produced half a billion dollars-worth of US war bonds. Finally, the status of the Greeks appears to have benefited from the migration of southern blacks to the large urban centers of the Northeast and the Midwest in search of work in the flourishing war industries. The consequent redefining of racial boundaries meant that Greeks were now considered indisputably "white."

The campaign to support the Greek resistance and the sale of US war bonds brought national prominence to several Greek American business leaders who were already on the rise. These included the film executive Spyros Skouras, who spearheaded the Greek War Relief Association. Skouras had originally arrived in the United States in 1910 with his brothers and settled in St. Louis, where they acquired a series of theaters that they sold to Warner Brothers. After several years rising through the ranks of the film industry, Skouras and his brothers took over the management of the Fox West Coast Theater chain. Skouras served as the company's president and presided over its merger with Twentieth Century Pictures in 1942. As the head of Twentieth Century Fox studios, Skouras produced such classics as *The King and I* and *Gentlemen Prefer Blondes*; he was instrumental in launching the careers of several young actors and actresses, including Marilyn Monroe.

Coming out of the Second World War, the Greek community in the United States made even more important strides. In the 1950s, those who had arrived as children between the 1890s and the 1930s reached adulthood. More so than their parents, these immigrants largely spoke English and experienced little xenophobia when entering the labor market (although many still Anglicized their names). Those who had served in the military during World War II were greeted upon their return with an unfamiliar deference from fellow citizens and with generous educational or borrowing opportunities from the recently signed GI bill.

Some Greeks, such as Tom Carvel (Karavelas), became innovators in the food industry. In the 1930s, Carvel had manned an ice cream truck in Hartsdale, New York. During the war years, he served as a refrigeration consultant and concessionaire in the army and used the skills he acquired to improve his ice cream freezer and develop a new, patented brand of liquid ice cream. By the early 1950s, he had opened twenty-five stores and began marketing his equipment to franchisees around the country. A trendsetter in advertising as well as in ice cream, Carvel put his own voice and face on radio and television, paving the way for other corporate chiefs to make their own direct pitches to consumers. Carvel eventually sold the business in 1989 for eighty million dollars.[21]

A few Greek immigrants pursued careers in politics and public service in the postwar era. Their election to office was yet another sign of the growing acceptance of Greeks in American society. Although Greek Americans are generally identified with the Democratic Party, the first generation Greeks who went into professional politics tended to be Republicans. They include one of the few politically active women in Greek American life, Adeline Geo-Karis. Brought to the United States by her parents when she was a small child, Geo-Karis attended law school and won election to the Illinois House of Representatives in 1973. Six years later she was elected to the Illinois Senate, where she served for twenty-five years, earning a reputation as a no-nonsense politician with a knack for crossing party lines.[22]

George Christopher (Christopheles) is perhaps the most celebrated elected official among Greek immigrants. Like Geo-Karis, Christopher was a highly regarded Republican centrist. He got his start as a copy boy at the *San Francisco Examiner*, later became an accountant, and eventually bought out one of his client businesses, a small dairy he renamed "Christopher Dairy Farms" and turned into a multi-million-dollar concern. A growing involvement in politics led to his election as Mayor of San Francisco. In the eight years of his mayoralty (1956–64), Christopher undertook municipal reforms and major urban renewal projects that revived what had been an ailing city. He stood firm on issues of racial equality and gay rights and left office to great acclaim. His obituary in the *San Francisco Chronicle* described him as "one of the last of the old-time political leaders—an immigrant who made a fortune through hard work, rose to become chief executive of his adopted city, and died full of years and honors."[23] Christopher stood for governor of California in 1966, but lost to Ronald Reagan in the Republican primary.

The arts and entertainment field is not one automatically associated with foreign-born immigrants, but first-generation Greeks made their presence felt there as well. The landscape painter Aristodimos Kaldis and the sculptor Polygnotos Vagis both made significant careers in the New York art scene, but the biggest name among this generation of Greek American artists was the stage director and filmmaker Elia Kazan (Elias Kazantzoglou). The son of Greeks who fled the Ottoman Empire in 1913 when he was but four years old, Kazan introduced new methods of acting to the American stage and promoted the careers a number of aspiring actors, including Marlon Brando and James Dean. Among his directing credits were *A Streetcar Named Desire*; *East of Eden*; and *America, America*; which paid tribute to his family's escape from oppression and its journey to the United States.

Although Greek immigration never recovered to its heights before the Immigration Act of 1924, several prominent individuals—often with prior training or connections of

d—did successfully immigrate and naturalize in the interwar years, and saw
ers blossom after the war. Gregory Vlastos, for many years considered the pre-
scholar of Socrates and Plato, earned his PhD at Harvard in the late 1920s and
ost of his distinguished career as a professor of philosophy at Princeton.[24] The
orchestral conductor Dimitri Mitropoulos had already achieved a measure of European
fame when he made his American debut in 1936, at the age of forty. Shortly thereafter, Mitropoulos became an American citizen and began conducting for the New York
Philharmonic, where he was a mentor to the young Leonard Bernstein.

Equally impressive to the successes of those actually born in Greece was the rise of
second-generation Greek Americans during this period. After the Second World War,
the American-born offspring of the immigrants were beginning to outnumber the immigrants themselves. In 1950 they made up fifty five percent of all those reporting Greek
ethnicity in the United States. These children of immigrants benefited from the high
value their parents placed on education: while native Greek immigrants had an average
of about seven and a half years of schooling, second-generation Greek Americans could
claim over eleven years.[25] By 1970, a survey showed that half of the second generation
Greeks had some college education and, even more strikingly, almost one in three had
gone on to graduate studies.[26] The numerous and divergent opportunities secured by
so much education signaled the end of a definable occupation pattern among Greek
Americans. Inevitably, some took over their family businesses (especially restaurants),
but many others sought out new avenues for professional development.

In the same way as the Greek-born immigrants had made a name for themselves
as restaurateurs or small retail businessmen, many of the second generation sought to
pursue careers as entrepreneurs and surpass the relatively modest successes of their parents. Peter G. Peterson, for example, an investment banker and commerce secretary
under President Nixon, was the son of a Nebraska diner owner. Alex Gus (Alexandros
Konstantinou) Spanos, a real estate tycoon and the current owner of the San Diego
Chargers, is the son of a California baker. These "self-made men" of the second generation were helped by their knowledge of English, their superior education, and their
understanding of the American culture in which they had been raised. In many cases,
the rising second generation displayed the types of behavior we associate with successful
businessmen: extraordinary motivation, a willingness to take risks, conservative politics, and occasionally a measure of ruthlessness.

The early success stories of the second generation include the Pappas brothers,
Thomas and John, who turned their father's grocery in Massachusetts into a major food
importing business that became the springboard for lucrative international projects in
real estate development, petrochemicals, and steel manufacturing. John, the younger
brother, served as a judge and funded several philanthropic projects in the Boston area.
Thomas, the older sibling, parlayed his business activities into a prominent position in
the Republican Party and friendships with presidents Eisenhower and Nixon.[27] William
P. Tavoulareas, the president and chief operating officer of Mobile Oil from 1969 to 1984,
was another successful businessman who exhibited a single-minded and uncompromis-
ing drive toward success. Starting off as an accountant, he slowly rose through the ranks
at Mobile Oil, despite being told that his background would be a handicap. In addition
to his ethnic impediment, he also lacked the Ivy League education that many believed
to be a prerequisite for success in a major American corporation. After reaching the

Greek-born Tom Carvel (Karavelas) developed and patented a new brand of liquid ice cream that he fran chised around the country.

pinnacle of corporate success at Mobile Oil, Tavoulareas proved to be an aggressive and accomplished leader who forged close ties with Saudi Arabia. He was also known for his outspoken opposition to conservation efforts.[28]

George P. Mitchell was another risk-taking oil and gas giant. Mitchell was born in 1919 to Greek immigrant parents in Galveston, Texas. The Mitchell family acquired its Anglicized handle when a railroad timekeeper who couldn't pronounce Savva Paraskevopoulos decided to call George's father "Mike Mitchell." Young George studied geology in college, served in the army during the Second World War, and upon his return purchased land in an area of north Texas known as a "wildcatter's graveyard." Mitchell found oil, however, and within a few years established his own firm, Mitchell Energy and Development Corporation. The company became Texas's top independent gas producer and the country's third-ranked independent interstate gas marketer. Mitchell's firm survived the downturns of the market in the late 1970s and early 1980s and developed new horizontal drilling technology to facilitate the extraction of natural gas from shale rock—the controversial process known as hydraulic fracturing, or "fracking." In the 1960s, Mitchell envisioned a massive real estate project on the outskirts of the booming Houston area—a complete new town. The Woodlands opened in late 1974 and touted a population of 48,000 when Mitchell sold it in 1997.[29]

The American pharmaceutical industry (which expanded dramatically during the 1950s and 1960s) was also buoyed by several rising second-generation Greek American careers. These included Michael Jaharis of Kos Pharmaceuticals, Pindaros Roy Vagelos of Merck & Company, and George Behrakis of Dooner Laboratories and Muro Pharmaceutical. All three men rose from modest backgrounds to become major philanthropists late in life. Of the three, Vagelos probably achieved the most prominence. The son of a diner owner in Rahway, New Jersey, Vagelos began a promising career as a doctor and medical researcher before taking charge of basic research at Merck in 1975 and rising through the ranks to serve as the company's CEO and chairman of the board in the late 1980s and early 1990s. Vagelos made substantial donations to the University of Pennsylvania, his undergraduate alma mater, and Columbia University, where he attended medical school.

Philanthropic giving to the Greek Orthodox Church was (and is) an activity shared by many wealthy second-generation Greek American businessmen and their spouses. Often the sons and daughters of deeply-religious immigrants, they entered the business world at a time of rising prominence, visibility, and respectability for the Greek Orthodox Archdiocese of North and South America. The Archdiocese had made serious efforts to establish Greek Orthodoxy as a major faith in the United States, and a number of public gestures affirmed its mainstream status in the postwar era. In 1956, President Eisenhower participated in the dedicatory ceremonies of the Church's cathedral in Washington, DC. In 1961, Archbishop Iakovos delivered the opening prayer at President John F. Kennedy's inauguration, and in 1965 he marched alongside the Reverend Martin Luther King, Jr., at Selma, Alabama. Bolstering the Church through generous donations affirmed the heritage of the business class and helped to consolidate Greek Orthodoxy's public profile.

Several among the second generation achieved national prominence as academics. A small group specialized in subjects related to their own cultural heritage, such as Byzantine studies, classical Greek thought, modern Greece, and Greek American studies. Deno John Geanakoplos became a renowned scholar of Byzantine and Italian Renaissance history, spending most of his career at Yale and building a reputation as one of the foremost scholars of Byzantine history in the world. Speros Vryonis, another preeminent Byzantinist, taught at UCLA, the University of Athens, and New York University. Theodore Saloutos and Charles Moskos are among the best known chroniclers of the Greek American experience. Salutos was an authority on American agrarian history while Moskos, a sociologist of the American military when he was not writing on Greek America, helped formulate military policy on social issues like the acceptance of homosexual service members.

Among artists and entertainers, the expressionist painter Theodore Stamos, ceramic sculptor Peter Voulkos, rhythm and blues pianist Johnny Otis, and fashion designer James Galanos (Nancy Reagan's favorite) were all second-generation Greek Americans born in the 1920s.[30] The soprano opera singer and diva *par excellence* Maria Callas attained perhaps the greatest international fame of all Greek Americans. Born in New York City in 1923, Callas was taken by her parents to Greece, where she studied voice for several years before making her official debut at Milan's La Scala in 1951. That prestigious theatre became her artistic home throughout the 1950s, when she became one of the most famous opera singers of the twentieth century. She made her American debut in Chicago in 1954 and her New York Metropolitan Opera debut in 1956. That year, Callas became the first Greek American ever to appear on the cover of *Time* magazine.

One of the unintended outcomes of the Civil Rights movement and its accompanying cultural trend toward validating roots was the emergence of a growing sense of identity among white ethnics, especially those whose ancestors originated from eastern and southern Europe. In general, these ethnic revivals were not so much vehicles for social demands (as with underprivileged groups like African Americans) as subjective choices to embrace and project cultural backgrounds. It became permissible, even fashionable, to publicize one's ethnic identity. At the time, films and television did a great deal to promote images of white ethnicity. In the case of the Greeks, the best example of this phenomenon is the character of Greek American detective Theo Kojak in the television series that aired between 1973 and 1978. The show featured the Greek American actor Aristotelis "Telly" Savalas and included many references to Greek heritage.

In contrast with other white ethnic groups, however, the Greek revival had implications beyond the merely cultural sphere; it was supported by real demographic change. As American immigration law began to gradually liberalize in the postwar years, the Greek American community was being replenished by new arrivals from Greece. The 1965 Immigration Act, which repealed the restrictive quotas that had been in place since the 1920s, allowed an entire new cohort of Greeks to immigrate in the following decade, bringing the total number of post-WWII immigrants to about 125,000. One in five of the one million Greek Americans was Greek-born, giving the community a decidedly "ethnic" image compared to other groups.

The "Greektown" neighborhood in the Astoria section of Queens in New York City came to symbolize this status, and the new blood helped to preserve ethnic identity at a time when intermarriage with non-Greeks was on the rise and use of the Greek language on the wane. Moreover, many of the new arrivals were highly educated or skilled laborers as well as students and professionals seeking to complete their training or develop their careers. Some pursued the well-trodden path of business entrepreneurship and a few achieved remarkable success, such as California real estate broker Angelo Tsakopoulos and New York City grocery store magnate John Catsimatidis (who has also been successful in several other industries).

The other development that shaped Greek ethnicity in the 1970s was the emergence of a self-consciously Greek presence in American politics. Second-generation Greeks were of course not new to the postwar political scene. The 1959 election of Representative John Brademas, an Indiana Democrat who had a long career as an education policy reformer and majority whip, paved the way for other members of the Greek second generation, including Nick Galifianakis (a North Carolina Democrat), Gus Yatron (a Pennsylvania Republican), and Paul Sarbanes (a Maryland Democrat). In 1968, Maryland Governor Spiro Agnew was elected to the vice presidency on Richard Nixon's Republican ticket, although he would resign in disgrace just ten months before his boss did the same. Before the 1970s, the Greek American community's involvement in Greece's politics was limited although the majority was positively inclined toward the military dictatorship established in Greece in 1967. It was a sign of the growing conservatism of Greek Americans as well as their lack of understanding of the sociopolitical dynamics in their ancestral homeland. Agnew, in fact, openly supported the dictatorship, as did businessman Tom Pappas, who became Washington's unofficial go-between with the military junta.

Turkey's 1974 invasion and occupation of northern Cyprus, an independent country with a large Greek ethnic majority, was a turning point in Greek American political life. The Turkish invasion, and the concomitant collapse of the dictatorship in Athens, triggered a communitywide mobilization led by Brademas, Sarbanes, and several Greek American lobbying organizations in Washington, DC. The campaign succeeded in both the short and the long term, resulting in an American arms embargo on Turkey that lasted through 1978 and a more lasting period of Greek American political engagement. In the years after the Turkish invasion, more and more Greeks were elected to the House and Senate with the active support of the Greek community. These rising politicos included Democrats like Paul Tsongas of Massachusetts and Republicans like Olympia Snowe of Maine. Meanwhile, the Greek American lobby became a permanent fixture in Washington, DC.

This mainstreaming process reached its symbolic apogee in 1988, when Michael Dukakis won the Democratic Party's nomination for president. Dukakis, who had served two terms as Massachusetts governor, was the son of white-collar Greek immigrants in the early twentieth century, both of whom settled in Massachusetts mill towns and attended college or graduate school. His father, Panos, trained at Harvard Medical School and became the first American-trained Greek-speaking doctor in New England.

A less well-recognized symbolic moment occurred in 1975, when another second-generation Greek, Helen Boosalis, was elected mayor of Lincoln, Nebraska. Few noted the significance at the time, but the city lay just sixty miles southwest of Omaha City, which since the 1909 anti-Greek riot had incorporated its southern neighbor of South Omaha. In the intervening years, the Greek Americans had achieved levels of respectability and upward mobility that would have been unthinkable to their ancestors driven from South Omaha.

When sociologist Charles Moskos published his landmark study of Greek Americans in 1980, he adopted the subtitle, "struggle and success." We should take that phrase with a pinch of salt. Not all Greek Americans have achieved success, but the once-stigmatized Greek Americans have unquestionably joined the American mainstream. The community no longer worries about how it can prove its Americanization. Rather, it focuses on retaining its ethnic heritage, which is being eroded over time.

Endnotes

[1] John Higham, *Strangers in the Land: Patterns of American Nativism, 1860–1925*, 2nd ed. (New Brunswick, NJ: Rutgers University Press, 1992), 68–105.

[2] Andrew Kopan, "Greek Survival in Chicago: The Role of Ethnic Education 1890–1980" in *Ethnic Chicago*, ed. Peter d' A. Jones and Melvin Holli (Grand Rapids, MI: W.B. Eerdmans Publishing, 1981), 80–139.

[3] Charles C. Moskos, *Greek Americans: Struggle and Success* (New Brunswick, NJ: Transaction, 1980), 18.

[4] Theodore Saloutos, "Cultural Persistence and Change: Greeks in the Great Plains and Rocky Mountain West, 1890–1970," *Pacific Historical Review* 49, no. 1 (1980): 77–103.

[5] John G. Bitzes, "The Anti-Greek Riots of 1909-South Omaha," *Nebraska History* 51 (1970): 201–203.

[6] Alice Scourby, *The Greek Americans* (Boston: Twayne, 1984), 34–35.

[7] Topics of the Times, "Colonies Not Aliens Are Persecuted," *The New York Times* February 24, 1909.

[8] Grace Abbot, "A Study of the Greeks in Chicago," *American Journal of Sociology* 15, no. 3 (1909): 379–93.

[9] Henry Pratt Fairchild, *Greek Immigration to the United States* (New Haven: Yale University Press, 1911), 10.

[10] Thomas Burgess, *Greeks in America: An Account of Their Coming, Progress, Customs and Aspirations* (Boston: Sherman French, 1913).

[11] Theodore Saloutos, *The Greeks in the United States* (Cambridge: Harvard University Press, 1964), 109–15.

[12] Ibid., 167–68.

[13] US Bureau of the Census, *1940 Census of the Population, Table 5: Nativity and Parentage of the Foreign White Stock*, 42.

[14] "The Charter of the Order of AHEPA, September 25, 1922 State of Georgia," as cited in George J. Leber, *The History of the Order of AHEPA 1922-1972* (Washington, DC: AHEPA, 1972).

[15] Dorothee Schneider, "Naturalization and United States Citizenship in Two Periods of Mass Migration: 1894–1930, 1965–2000," *Journal of American Ethnic History* 21, no. 31 (2001): 50–82.

[16] Leber, *History of the Order of AHEPA*, 289–301.

[17] Taso Lagos, "Poor Greek to 'Scandalous' Hollywood Mogul: Alexander Pantages and the Anti-Immigrant Narratives of William Randolph Hearst's Los Angeles Examiner," *Journal of Modern Greek Studies* 30, no. 1 (May 2012): 45–74.

[18] Babis Malafouris, *Hellenes tes Amerikes 1528-1948* ("Hellenes of America, 1528–1948") (New York, 1948), 377.

[19] Edwin Clarence Buxbaum, *The Greek American Group of Tarpon Springs, Florida: A Study of Ethnic Identification and Acculturation* (New York: Arno Press, 1980); George Th. Frantzis, *Strangers at Ithaca. The Story of the Spongers at Tarpon Springs* (St. Petersburg, FL: Great Outdoors Publishing, 1962).

[20] Maurice McLoughlin, "Story of Greeks Who Have Settled in Brooklyn Is One of Commendable Thrift and Industry," *Brooklyn Daily Eagle*, May 8, 1932.

[21] Glen Fowler, "Tom Carvel, 84, Gravelly Voice of Soft Ice Cream Chain, is Dead" *New York Times*, Oct. 22, 1990.

[22] Elaine Thomopoulos, *Greek American Pioneer Women of Illinois* (Chicago: Arcadia, 2000), 113–26.

[23] Carl Nolte, "George Christopher 1907–2000: Big-Thinking S.F. Mayor of '50s and '60s is Dead," *San Francisco Chronicle*, September 15, 2000.

[24] Bruce Lambert, "Gregory Vlastos, 84, Philosopher Who Analyzed Classical Works," *New York Times* October 14, 1991.

[25] Charles Hirschman and Ellen Percy Kraly, "Racial and Ethnic Inequality in the United States, 1940 and 1950: The Impact of Geographic Location and Human Capital," *International Migration Review* 24, no. 1 (1990): 4–33.

[26] US Bureau of the Census, *Census of the Population 1970, Subject Reports, National Origin and Language, Final Report PC(2)-1A*; see also Moskos, *Struggle and Success*, 111–13.

[27] "John Pappas Dies; Industrialist, 66," *New York Times*, December 4, 1972; "Entrepreneurs: the Greek for Go-Between," *Time Magazine*, February 14, 1969; "T.A. Pappas, 89, Dies; Was Envoy to Greece," *New York Times*, January 17, 1988.

[28] Agis Salpukas, "William P. Tavoulareas, 75, Former Mobil President, Dies," *New York Times*, January 16, 1996.

[29] Joseph W. Kutchin, *How Mitchell Energy & Development Corp. Got Its Start and How It Grew: An Oral History and Narrative Overview* (Universal Publishers, 2001), 363–442.

[30] Suzy Kalter, "If Nancy Reagan Makes It to the White House, So Will Designer James Galanos," *People Magazine*, June 1980.

The SS *St. Louis* was filled with Jewish refugees, some released from concentration camps. In 1939, the passengers were not permitted to disembark in Cuba or at any port in the United States but were returned to Europe, where many of them died in the Holocaust.

CHAPTER | 8

REFUGEES

By David W. Haines

IN AUGUST 1755, CAPTAIN JOHN WINSLOW and his troops landed in Grand Pre, on the Bay of Fundy in what is now Nova Scotia, Canada. The purpose of his visit was unknown to the local inhabitants, heirs of the former French colony of Acadia, a possession that had fallen under British control nearly a half-century earlier. Two weeks later, on September 5, having called all the village men to the church, Winslow read aloud a proclamation: their lands were to be seized in the name of the King of England, and they were "to be removed from this his Province." The men were then imprisoned in the church until they and their families could be forced on board ships a month later. Their farms were burned to the ground. Almost a century later, Henry Wadsworth Longfellow commemorated the experience of the Acadians in his epic poem *Evangeline*: "Waste are those pleasant farms, and the farmers forever departed. Scattered like dust and leaves . . . far o'er the ocean."

Winslow's action was but one of many in a concerted British effort to expel French Catholics from the region, to make their lands available for settlement by English Protestant colonists, and to outmaneuver the French in the imperial rivalry for control of what is now Canada. The "Great Upheaval" would send about half of the Acadian population into exile and the other half into increasingly desperate hiding in the hills and along the rivers on both sides of the St. Lawrence. Ultimately, roughly half of the Acadians perished from a multitude of causes: exposure (whether in Canada or the Caribbean); famine; war; and diseases acquired on shipboard, on Caribbean plantations, and while imprisoned in England. The Acadians, like most refugees, were a people caught in the middle of a crisis not of their own making. Their expulsion came despite a decades-long agreement of neutrality that was only upended by a combination of British strategic war interests against the French and the financial interests of certain British merchants and colonists in New England.[1]

There was—as again is true for most refugees—no safe and durable haven for the Acadians. To the north, some found their way to the two small islands of St. Pierre and Miquelon, just off Newfoundland, the last outposts of French control in the region.

The Acadians there believed they had found a permanent home, although one that was hardly ideal in its climate or soil. Yet their hopes were dashed when British forces twice temporarily occupied the islands, again expelling the Acadians and destroying the settlements they had so laboriously constructed. The fate of those transported south to the other British colonies was no better. The largest contingents were sent to Massachusetts and Virginia. Those who arrived safely (and many died in transit) faced two rather different fates. In Massachusetts, they were dispersed across the countryside, with few resources, limited job opportunities, no freedom of movement, and the constant threat of indenture for their children if they failed to meet their own expenses. In Virginia, the refugees were not even accepted. A plea from the governor to the British government allowed the refugees to land temporarily in the fall, but they were sent on their way again in the spring. In Governor Dinwiddie's view, the Acadians had "occasioned a general discontent among the people, as we had no Roman Catholics here before, and they are very great Bigots." They were transported to England and imprisoned there under conditions that may have cost the lives of a third, perhaps half, of their number. Once there was peace between England and France in 1763, most of these refugees moved on, either back to France or on to Louisiana, where new political arrangements between the French and the Spanish made them valuable as a buffer.[2]

Two centuries later, another set of refugees was in sight of America's Atlantic Coast. It was 1939, and these refugees were on board the St. Louis, a German cruise liner bearing 937 passengers, almost all of them Jews fleeing the rising tide of anti-Semitism in Nazi Germany. They ranged from well-heeled professionals to those released from the concentration camps on the condition that they leave Germany immediately. The original destination of the St. Louis had been Havana, where most of the refugees planned to wait until United States immigration slots became available. But only twenty-eight of the passengers were allowed to disembark in Cuba. The remaining refugees, anchored in the harbor and holding what turned out to be worthless Cuban visas, could only wave at the family members, supporters, and reporters whose boats bobbed among the police patrols around the ship. Ultimately, the St. Louis was expelled from the harbor as negotiations with the Cuban government bogged down in a mix of anti-Semitic propaganda and haggling over the amounts of money that had to be deposited in order to gain legal entry of the passengers into Cuba.[3]

As the St. Louis steamed along the east coast of the United States, exhausting its food and fuel resources, pleas to the American government fell largely on deaf ears. The Goebbels-directed Nazi propaganda machine went into high gear to exploit the incident: here were Jews that the Nazi's had allowed to leave but the world did not seem interested in them. If no one wanted these Jews, then the Germans could claim they must find their own "solution." The situation on the St. Louis deteriorated as the United States, and then Canada, ignored all pleas. There were suicide patrols, harassment of passengers by the Nazi Party members among the crew, and an abortive attempt to take over the vessel. The ship's captain did his best, even planning a desperation grounding of the ship in English waters rather than returning the refugees to Hamburg, almost certain imprisonment, and death. The story of the St. Louis seemed to reach a favorable resolution when it was granted the right to land in Antwerp, Belgium instead of Hamburg. The governments of England, France, Belgium, and the Netherlands had agreed to each take some of the 908 remaining refugees. But that seemingly happy ending darkened

as war broke out in the fall of 1939 and the refugees on the continent found themselves once again under German control. A painstaking effort to track down the fate of the *St. Louis* passengers indicates that over forty percent of those who were returned to the continent did not survive the war, and the majority of those died in the extermination camps.[4]

At the end of the twentieth century, there were again boats laden with refugees making for America's coast.

The Coast Guard policy of interdicting refugee-filled vessels in the Caribbean was publicly portrayed as a humanitarian life-saving measure. It also constituted a legalistic refusal to consider asylum claims unless the passengers somehow managed to physically set foot on American soil.

This time they were small vessels and rafts attempting to land refugees from Cuba and Haiti. In 1980, a large seaborne exodus from Cuba brought some 125,000 people to the United States; another 25,000 arrived on boats from Haiti. As a result of public anxiety about the scale of this operation, President Ronald Reagan signed an executive order in 1981 calling for Haitian boats to be interdicted on the high seas, thus preventing them from landing on US soil, where the refugees would have access to American courts. The directive did not formally deny the right of the passengers to seek asylum, but it did require that they make a claim when their boat was intercepted. Yet that glimmer of hope for asylum rarely yielded any haven in the United States. The Lawyers Committee for Human Rights found that, from 1981 to 1990, only six of the 21,461 Haitians who were intercepted were allowed to enter the United States and apply for asylum.[5]

This system of keeping Cuban and Haitian refugees at a distance, but not technically refusing them an opportunity for asylum, remained in effect for another decade. Under President George H.W. Bush (in 1992) and then Bill Clinton (in 1993), a new rule evolved: refugees intercepted at sea could be returned to their home country without the opportunity for consideration of their asylum claims. The new interdiction regime was impressive in its practical scope and also in its ideological implications. President

Clinton, for example, at one point called these aspirants "illegal refugees." That phrase suggested a new kind of standard, implying that refugees did not have the right to flee unless they did so in an officially sanctioned manner. Perversely, their bid for "legal" refugee status would be recognized if they somehow managed to physically set foot on American soil.

In 1994, the number of people on boats interdicted by the US Coast Guard exceeded 63,000. Coast Guard reports inevitably stressed the way the interdiction campaign saved lives as people on barely seaworthy boats were "rescued." But in practice the result was a sort of humanitarian rejection, saving the biological lives of refugees yet returning them to the persecution from which they had fled. For the Cubans there was to be at least a special immigration program to which they could apply before leaving Cuba. For Haitians, however, there would be little in the way of alternatives, even when conditions became severe.

The most damaging act toward refugees is often this very basic refusal to provide them safe haven. That act reverberates throughout American history: from the colonial period with its rejection of the Acadians, through the Second World War and the rejection of Jewish refugees, to this more recent and continuing rejection of those fleeing from Cuba and Haiti. It is most graphically visible in cases like these, in which boats are physically kept away from American shores. But the refusal also manifests itself in the "paper walls" erected against refugees at various points in American history.[6] Particularly glaring examples include the limitation in visas during the World War II period, often because of blatant anti-Semitism among State Department staff; the slow development of refugee legislation after the war (also often ascribed to anti-Semitism); and the overwhelming rejection of asylum seekers from the Caribbean and Central America during the last decades of the twentieth century.

Yet the United States has also long stood as a beacon of possibility to refugees around the world, the "asylum for mankind" in a "world overrun with oppression" that Thomas Paine evoked in *Common Sense*. Indeed, since World War II the United States has accepted over four million refugees for permanent settlement. That openness in the decades since World War II grew directly out of the earlier refusal of refuge to the Jews of Europe, and the retrospective discomfort it caused. But the postwar acceptance of refugees also grew out of the need to validate America's role as the major guarantor of the post-war peace, including a fair share contribution to refugee issues. The result was a different kind of policy for this newly defined kind of immigrant: someone who, as codified in the 1951 UN Convention relating to the Status of Refugees was forced to flee due to a fear of persecution, whether because of race, religion, nationality, political opinion, or membership in a particular social group. Despite a few lapses and limitations, America assumed this new responsibility by making refugees a significant component of overall immigration policy, and thereby also making the United States the most important permanent destination for refugees unable to return to their home countries.

The American relationship with refugees, then, is a story both of refusal and of acceptance. The dynamic interplay between the two has been acted out on many stages: in domestic and foreign policy; in the complex interactions between state and federal agencies over who is responsible for managing refugee programs; among the many religious and secular organizations committed to giving succor to refugees; in the media; in the arts; and in the lives of individual Americans, many of whom trace their heritage back not merely to immigrants, but to the refugee experience of flight from oppression to freedom. Many Americans understand very well that their country has been both a land of opportunity and land of refuge.[7]

The initial postwar beginnings of this new American responsibility for the world's refugees were limited but auspicious. On December 22, 1945, President Harry Truman issued a directive to immediately make existing immigration slots available for displaced persons from Europe. The wording of Truman's directive invoked both the humanitarian and the international commitments of the United States. Americans should, he said, "consider that common decency and the fundamental comradeship of all human beings require us to do what lies within our power . . . in order to reduce human suffering." He also noted, "it is essential that we do this ourselves to show our good faith in requesting other nations to open their doors." Many of these slots were for Jews, but also for other Europeans caught up in the maelstrom of postwar and Cold War chaos and political maneuvering. One particular fear was that displaced persons would be repatriated back to countries then under Soviet control. This was a point on which President Truman and Eleanor Roosevelt, longtime refugee advocate and widow of the former president, strongly agreed. The last round of letters in their long correspondence reflected her concern about such forced repatriation and Truman's assurance that most displaced persons had been saved from that fate.[8]

The US Congress was slower to respond, but in 1948 passed the Displaced Persons Act providing for the entry of 280,000 "DPs." That number was later increased to 415,000, and the Refugee Relief Act of 1953 would provide 214,000 additional slots for refugees. At a time when American immigration remained quite limited, this attention to refugees was proportionately far greater than it is today. The legislation did not pass unopposed. Anti-Semitism remained strong in the United States and it took the lobbying of voluntary agencies on behalf of Christian DPs to make the bill acceptable. One argument that was persuasive for some legislators was that these refugees, although in need, would do well as immigrants in the United States. The reason for their admission might well be humanitarian, but the net effect would be a positive one for America—new workers and new families producing beneficial growth. In addition, the voluntary agencies would be responsible for the resettlement programs and the refugees would thus impose no specific financial obligations on the US government.[9]

Much of the support for displaced persons reflected the growing Cold War rivalry between the US and the Soviet Union. In 1956, that conflict produced a new kind of refugee situation after the failed uprising against Communist authority in Hungary. As refugees streamed across the border into Austria, President Eisenhower acted quickly to furnish an American sanctuary for some of the Hungarian exiles in an initiative dubbed, "Operation Mercy." Like Truman before him, Eisenhower highlighted America's humanitarian goals and its desire to aid its allies, noting, "providing asylum to these Hungarian refugees would give practical effect to the American people's intense desire to help" and would also "assist the Government of Austria, which has responded so generously to the refugees' needs." Eventually some 38,000 Hungarians were resettled in the United States. The federal government assumed a larger role than before, including the establishment of a reception center at Camp Kilmer, New Jersey. Yet most resettlement responsibilities still lay with voluntary agencies. Overall, the Hungarian case was a positive one and proved a model for similar efforts in years to come. The numbers were

In the aftermath of the 1956 uprising, 200,000 Hungarians fled their country. By executive order, President Eisenhower admitted 38,000 to the United States.

small, and the Hungarian refugees had relevant economic skills as well as solid political credentials as "freedom fighters." Once again, humanitarian efforts on behalf of refugees yielded individuals well positioned for economic success in the United States.[10]

When Cubans began to flee from the rise of Fidel Castro a few years later, the stage was set for stronger US government involvement. In the fall of 1960, President Eisenhower authorized an emergency center in Miami, an action supported immediately by his successor John F. Kennedy. President Kennedy's statement of January 27, 1961 emphasized "the tradition of the United States as a humanitarian sanctuary" and the frequency with which America had "extended its hand and material help." Here again humanitarian concerns for the refugees overlapped with the need to embarrass a Communist satellite with which the United States had a particularly bitter relationship. The result was a willingness to accept some 650,000 refugees from Cuba over the next fifteen years.

The Cold War continued to play a dominant role in American refugee policy over the succeeding decades. By the time Cuban refugee and resettlement efforts were winding down in the mid-1970s, the American-supported governments in Indochina were collapsing and another refugee crisis was set into motion. As the Republic of Vietnam fell

IMMIGRANT STRUGGLES, IMMIGRANT GIFTS

to communist forces in the spring of 1975, President Gerald Ford acted to provide support for the evacuation of refugees from the region either directly to the United States or through temporary camps in the Pacific region. While voluntary agencies retained a central role in resettlement, costs were now greater and borne more heavily by the federal government. Ultimately the refugees from Southeast Asia would outnumber the Cubans and define American resettlement efforts for the rest of the twentieth century.[11]

At the end of the 1970s, American refugee resettlement efforts were in very good shape by many measures. The resettlement of 125,000 Vietnamese refugees in 1975 showed how effective the US military could be in relief efforts, how well the government and private sector could complement each other in resettling refugees, and how welcoming the American people could be to refugees, whether or not they had supported the American military effort in Vietnam. Furthermore, these humanitarian efforts had yielded refugees who seemed to be thriving in their new American environment. Based on survey data from the late 1970s, for example, the labor force participation rate for the early Vietnamese refugees exceeded that for the American population at large. Like the Cubans before them, the Vietnamese were also very vocal about the benefits of political freedom and the need for hard work to achieve economic success. Vietnamese streamed into the educational system. That the Soviet Jewish refugees arriving at the same time were also well educated helped to fuel a vision of refugees as success stories in their home lives, their work lives, and their educational aspirations and achievements.[12]

The situation, however, was neither as simple nor as stable as it seemed. The events transpiring around the pivotal year of 1980 attest to the complexity and difficulties that continued to attend American refugee and resettlement policy. There were four main factors.

First, despite the emphasis on the Vietnamese, the refugees coming out of Southeast Asia were becoming increasingly diverse. There were many indigenous ethnic minorities arriving from camps in Thailand and Laos, such as the montagnard tribesmen of the central highlands. The most numerous of these were the Hmong, a group recruited by the Central Intelligence Agency to fight what has come to be known as the "Secret War" in Laos. Although the Hmong were a population with very strong social and cultural resources, including impressively resilient family and clan ties, they were nevertheless unprepared for life in a largely urban America. Also among the ranks of refugees were increasing numbers of survivors of the Cambodian genocide. Many of these were rural peasants with limited education, and thus also at risk in adapting to life in the United States. The simplistic notion that humanitarian admissions would automatically yield ideal candidates for life in America no longer seemed tenable; choices would have to be made between those in need and those who were best positioned to succeed in America. The survey research that had yielded such consistent portraits of success now revealed more ambiguous findings.

Second, the early 1980s saw a harsh recession, sending unemployment rates over ten percent. As job prospects for all Americans fell, newcomers experienced an even sharper decline. As with other immigrants, it was now increasingly apparent that the adaptation and success of refugees hinged not simply on the capabilities and desire of the people themselves, but also on the status of the American economy and the nature and availability of jobs in particular localities. For the refugee program this unvarnished truth posed particular dilemmas since the refugees, unlike typical immigrants, were part of a formal resettlement program that attempted to match them with localities that provide a good mix of economic opportunities, ethnic support networks, and effective social services. What if a "good" resettlement location suddenly had low employment opportunities? The recession thus challenged refugees' ability to advance economically as well as the underlying logic of the refugee resettlement program.

Third, 1980 saw the passage of new legislation, the Refugee Act. In opening hearings on the bill, Senator Edward Kennedy echoed the importance of refugees to the American past, noting how "our national policy of welcome to the homeless has served our country and our traditions well." The resulting legislation made fundamental changes to refugee resettlement. The Refugee Act required more coordinated planning of the number of refugees allowed into the United States each year and formally allocated the resettlement responsibilities among federal agencies, among federal, state, and local governments, and between the public and private sectors. Furthermore, the definition of refugee was formalized to follow that of the 1951 UN Refugee Convention and a dual-track system for obtaining refugee status was instituted. Those screened overseas would be considered "refugees," while those screened after arrival in the United States would be "asylees." There was also a strong programmatic emphasis on refugee self-sufficiency and an expansion of research efforts to assess how refugees were progressing toward self-sufficiency.

There were, however, also problems with the Refugee Act. The emphasis on self-sufficiency led almost immediately to concerns about refugee "dependency." Indeed, the refugee program itself publicized a new "dependency ratio" that, given the increased diversity of the refugee population and declining employment prospects during the recession, turned out to be quite high. Instead of demonstrating how refugees were advancing in their new lives, the federal refugee program wrestled with explaining why refugees were not advancing more quickly. The bureaucratic answer to this "dependency" problem turned out to be the reduction of transitional assistance to refugees—if there was no assistance (or less of it) then by definition, refugees would be less "dependent" on it. The decline in assistance to refugees throughout the 1980s was precipitous. The availability of special cash assistance for newly arrived refugees declined from thirty-six months in 1980 to eighteen months in 1982, and eight months by 1991; reimbursement to states for their cash assistance to refugees under regular programs declined from thirty-six months in 1980 to twenty-four months in 1988, and to zero by 1990.[13]

Fourth, and finally, 1980 once again saw ships loaded with refugees off the coast of the United States. Only a month after the signing of the Refugee Act, Fidel Castro made a blanket pledge to allow any Cuban to leave for the United States through the Cuban port of Mariel. The immediate result was a flotilla of boats from Florida seeking to bring relatives and others to safety in the United States. It was a massive undertaking that yielded some 125,000 refugees by the end of the year. During that same period, 25,000 Haitians also sought a haven in the United States. President Carter initially assumed a welcoming posture, but the public reaction turned sour as stories circulated of criminals, mental patients, and other undesirables among the Cuban and Haitian refugees. Whatever the extent of such undesirables (and the numbers were small) the sheer size of this arriving population, its chaotic processing, and its coexistence with over 200,000 other refugee arrivals that year, made for both logistical and political problems. The policy solution was to grant these arrivals a new legal status of "Cuban-Haitian Entrant" and then provide assistance and legalization options to them by special legislation.

The single year of 1980 thus produced a grand shift, partly planned and partly unanticipated, in American refugee resettlement efforts. Before that year, refugee resettlement had consisted of ad hoc programs largely directed at particular refugee groups whose reasons for being in the United States were clear: Cubans had fled the Castro regime, Vietnamese feared another repressive communist government, and Soviet Jews were escaping from political and religious persecution. After 1980, the refugee program became simultaneously more formally organized and more complex, involving many different countries and refugees less clearly connected to American foreign policy aims. The refugee program's burgeoning diversity resulted in numerous logistical difficulties for its administration and much confusion in the public mind. The new refugees were not well

The admission of Southeast Asian "boat people" to the United States is an example of American refugee policy being driven by both geopolitical and humanitarian concerns.

known and their reasons for immigrating were sometimes more obscure. For example, recent "Burmese" refugees are not ethnic Burmese; rather, they were highland minorities who opposed the Burmese-dominated government. Similarly, "Bhutanese" refugees from Nepal are in historic terms actually Nepalese. To add to the confusion, the formal legal status of certain refugees is often complicated. Cuban-Haitian "entrants" might appear to be refugees in broad terms, but they never obtained that specific legal status.

And what of the refugees themselves? How are they faring in their new American lives? As might be expected from the major shifts in American policy, the varied social and cultural backgrounds of refugees, and changing economic conditions in the United

States, the answer is not a simple one. For refugees, there are also the continuing effects of the horrors from which they have fled, the traumas of their journeys, and their relative lack of preparation for life in the United States, sometimes including lengthy gaps in education. Furthermore, the welcome refugees find in America is often ambivalent. Many American organizations and individuals act steadfastly on their behalf, yet others react negatively to them whether because they are different or because of the sheer confusion in the cultural, religious, political, and legal definitions of what constitutes a "refugee."

For refugees, then, the aftereffects of their experience are stacked on top of the basic challenges common to all American immigrants. Some refugees face much higher hurdles than others, either in terms of their socioeconomic background or the psychological reverberations of their experiences. Most Cambodian refugees, for example, survived the "Killing Fields" of the Khmer Rouge, and even their children must inevitably face the unimaginable horror of that genocidal nightmare. Primitive farmers from the highlands of Southeast Asia experienced paralyzing culture shock when trying to assimilate into the industrialized American society. The "Lost Boys of Sudan" had to recover from the physical and emotional damage of years of trekking to and between refugee camps in East Africa.

Refugees have also suffered from a volatile mix of ethnic prejudice and misconceptions about refugee status and benefits in the United States. Like other immigrants, they are often discriminated against because of their race or nationality. Vietnamese Americans have been physically attacked or insulted as "chinks." while Iranian exiles were sometimes the victims of assaults in 1980 because of an Iranian revolution that they themselves opposed. Refugees are thus victims not only of prejudice, but also of confusion and ignorance. That bewilderment is often aggravated by political attacks on the asylum system, especially ill-founded charges of "bogus" or "illegal" refugees.

Despite all those problems, the success and contributions of refugees after arrival in America have often been impressive. A short list of notables from a post-WWII report (1947) reads like a Who's Who of Nobel laureates: Albert Einstein, Enrico Fermi, James Frank, Victor Hess, Wolfgang Pauli, and Otto Stern.[14] Many refugees have indeed done very well in their new lives and made substantial contributions to America, whether in science, business, or the arts. Many others forged more modest new lives, contributing to the commonweal through their work and taxes, and bequeathing a brighter future to their children, who will in turn do their part to help build a stronger nation.

The experience of different groups varies, but the available data on Cubans and Vietnamese demonstrate the socioeconomic achievement of these two largest of refugee groups in the United States. Research on early Cuban refugees reveals a population with strong economic skills and the kinds of family and community resources enabling them to prosper by both engaging with and adapting to American society. Cubans Americans logged high marriage rates and, because of a willingness of both spouses to work, solid household incomes even when individual salaries were modest. Business links within the Cuban community and concentration within South Florida also permitted a more autonomous economic environment, a kind of in-between economy that helped to buffer Cuban immigrants from the secondary, low-wage economy to which many immigrants are relegated.[15] This Cuban success story, and the related renaissance of Miami, was somewhat tempered by the 1980 influx of Mariel Cubans who generally lacked the very skills that had made the prior Cuban arrivals so successful. By the end of the twentieth century, however, census data still showed Cubans to be the most economically successful large Hispanic group in the United States.

The Vietnamese provide certain parallels. Although their resettlement patterns have been more widely dispersed than those of the Cubans, the Vietnamese American population's attention to hard work, tight-knit families, and strong ethnic community structures have also created a portrait of considerable success. As with the Cubans, the original arrivals had a particularly sterling early record. They pursued a wide variety of jobs, from computer assembly to meatpacking, to sustain themselves, but they also used those jobs as launching pads toward better careers. Despite their language handicap, many attended community colleges, acquiring skills that they parlayed into good technical jobs, or as a stepping-stone to baccalaureate degrees. But the Vietnamese who arrived later faced greater problems. American commitments to Amerasian children and to the elderly brought people with special difficulties. Yet the census data at the end of the twentieth century still showed a relatively successful population. While their individual incomes lagged behind the high standards set by other Asian groups (such as the Chinese and Indians), the overall numbers were positive. Vietnamese had a greater pro portion of workers in high-skill jobs than the native-born population and, because of their extended family relationships, higher household income than the Asian American average. Compared to other non-Asian minorities, they also had higher percentages with college degrees, both undergraduate and graduate.

These two cases of refugee success and there are many others echo the hopes of many after the Second World War that refugees not only deserved a safe haven but would in fact become successful contributors to the American economy and society generally. The aforementioned post-war report suggested that despite initial difficulties in adjusting, refugees would likely experience a "more rapid assimilation" by starting off with "an advantage over their predecessors." In hindsight, that comment seems overly optimistic.[16] As the origins of refugees have expanded, and as American refugee admissions have become more inclusive of people from different walks of life, the certainty of that very high degree of success has faded. After all, since 1980 the United States has accepted over 10,000 refugees each from Afghanistan, Bhutan, Burma, Cambodia, Cuba, Ethiopia, Iran, Iraq, Laos, Liberia, Poland, Romania, Somalia, the former Soviet republics, Sudan, Vietnam, and the countries comprising the former Yugoslavia, along with lesser numbers from various other nations. Furthermore, many countries have been the source of very distinct refugee flows—the many Baha'i, Christian, Jewish, and Muslim refugees from Iran, for example. With diversity has come uncertainty about the best course of adjustment to American culture, and even greater strain on the significantly reduced federal government support of resettlement. A brief consideration of three groups who have faced particular difficulties—Cambodians, Hmong, and Sudanese—will help illuminate the diverse adjustment experiences of refugees.

Approximately 150,000 Cambodian refugees came to the United States. Their socioeconomic origins are disparate, from well-educated professionals to illiterate farmers, from intact families to isolated individuals. Such a mosaic combined with the high degree of trauma involved poses considerable difficulties in adjustment, and the overall economic profile of Cambodians in America is indeed less impressive than that for the Cubans or Vietnamese. Succeeding generations in America have faced additional problems. Cambodian kinship structures tend to be fairly narrow, lacking the potential of both the Cubans and Vietnamese to actively use family ties as a compensatory support mechanism in resettlement, and the Cambodian tendency to allow a child's character to develop on its own does not work well when a new American environment, especially in low-income neighborhoods, does not provide very positive role models.[18]

As a new generation of Cambodian Americans comes of age in America, it must also begin to confront the legacy of genocide. Jonathan Lee, a religious studies professor at San Francisco State University, describes the convoluted process by which he came to understand his own origins in Cambodia. The most poignant scene in his story involves his visit to the infamous Tuol Sleng prison in Cambodia and how he processed the horror by taking pictures of the victims on the wall: "I insulated myself . . . by viewing them through the lens of my camera. . . . The sound of my camera clicking, of my film automatically advancing, assured me that I was safe, and that they were just faces on a wall." The Cambodian American experience, then, is not one characterized by a simple, lineal process of "adaptation" to the United States; rather, it involves a continuing, agonizing effort to create a new kind of life in America that acknowledges the pain of the past, the struggles of the present, and the hope for a better future.[19]

The situation of the Hmong provides a different kind of example. The roughly 100,000 Hmong who have come to the United States since 1975 are a highland people, traditionally practicing "slash and burn" agriculture along the borders of Vietnam, Laos, and China. They are notable for very extensive and well-organized family structures that bind the people together in a migratory lifestyle quite different from that of other ethnic groups, such as the Lao, Khmer, and Vietnamese who lived in the valleys below. They became involved in the Vietnam War because the areas they inhabited, once quite peripheral to the governments on the plains below, became crucial to controlling the flow of troops and military supplies through the jungles by communist forces along the famous "Ho Chi Minh trail." As participants in the CIA's clandestine operations in Laos, they were at great risk when communist forces won the war in 1975. Many fled to Thailand and often lived there in camps for many years before coming to the United States.[20]

The Hmong were particularly unprepared for life in the United States. A combination of high fertility rates, early marriages, very large families, limited education, few connections to urban jobs, and frequent illiteracy did not augur well for economic success in the United States. Yet most observers of the Hmong have been impressed by their resilience and strong commitments to family and community. Chia Youyee Vang, a Hmong American and historian at the University of Wisconsin points out how quickly the Hmong worked to recreate community structures in the United States, whether they were traditional kinship groups or newer Christian congregations. The story of the Hmong is an impressive one of reconciling the past with the present, and aiming for a future that incorporates both. As Hmong American artist and writer Kou Vang notes, "We have the capacity to travel back and forth between the generations—adapting, fostering, repairing, and modifying."[21]

The Sudanese provide another example of the extraordinary diversity in the refugee experience. The United States has accepted some 30,000 Sudanese refugees. Among these, the group that has probably received the most public attention is the "Lost Boys of Sudan," orphaned youngsters who fled from spreading violence in what is now the

independent state of South Sudan. Most of them initially made their way to refugee camps in Ethiopia, but were expelled from that country and had to cross Sudan again before reaching the Kakuma refugee camp in Kenya.

The Mariel boatlift of 1980 brought 125,000 Cuban refugees to South Florida.

From there, many came to the United States, where they rapidly gained public attention due in part to their incredible journey, but also to their profound commitment to education and self-improvement. Perhaps it was their flexibility and herculean efforts in adapting to their new home that has garnered so much respect. Without the conventional resources of family to depend on, they have instead banded together in a new kind of refugee household based on mutual support and pooled resources. [22]

Their concerns are not limited to their own new lives in the United States. They also seek to employ their own experience in the development of a new and better Sudan. John Bul Dau is particularly eloquent about that commitment in his autobiography, *God Grew Tired of Us*. In addressing the totality of his American and Sudanese experiences and relationships, he issues a clarion call for "one people, sharing one circle of hope," a dream rendered possible by his being the "latest in a long line of immigrants, in this magnificent land of second chances." Dau's comments also reveal how refugee resettlement enriches both the newcomers and the host country alike. "Without even pausing to think," he definitively concludes, " I can tell you America's greatest strength is its enormous spirit, manifest in its generosity."[23]

Refugee resettlement and community sponsorship depend on a sense of moral responsibility to newcomers based on traditional values and webs of religious and civic ties. In some cases, refugees have been the locus of even stronger moral commitments. During the Sanctuary Movement of the 1980s, over 500 religious congregations comprising a variety of denominations declared themselves "sanctuaries" for Central

American refugees seeking asylum. In offering shelter and even legal advice to these "illegal immigrants," the aid workers set themselves at defiance of federal immigration law. A number of activists were arrested, indicted, and brought to trial, and while eight were eventually convicted, they received suspended sentences due to the public outcry. As a result of pressure brought to bear by these activists, a bill was drafted in 1990 granting Central American refugees Temporary Protected Status; the adoption of the Nicaraguan Adjustment and Central American Relief Act seven years later finally allowed these refugees to apply for permanent residence.

Refugees serve as a profound reminder of the importance of freedom of speech and assembly to all Americans. During a return visit to his native country, a Vietnamese refugee remarked to a student who had asked him what was most important to him, "I told him, for me it was political freedom and access to information and that, once you had them, you would not want to live in any country where they were lacking."[24] Yet another benefit America derives from refugees is the diversity they add to an already diverse country. In this respect, too, refugees link America outward to the full range of the global human experience. They may sometimes be a challenge to the communities in which they settle, but refugees are an invigorating challenge that demonstrates America's commitment to the rest of the world and may benefit American interests in the increasingly integrated global economy of the twenty-first century.

America's relationship with refugees has been a stormy but productive one. Some of the benefits are intangible and hard to quantify; others are clearer and easier to document. Perhaps most important are the many children of refugees who not only contribute to America's demographic growth but also to its socioeconomic development. One major indicator has been the relative success of refugee children in the educational system. For the two major refugee groups—Cubans and Vietnamese—the data are quite convincing. One of the most comprehensive studies of the early refugees from Indochina found that these refugees and their children were progressing more quickly than expected. The reasons lay with the importance of cultural and familial factors, and the high premium placed on education by refugee parents. A similar positive portrait of both Vietnamese and Cuban youth appears in a longitudinal study in which being Vietnamese was a significant predictor of educational success even when all other factors (age, sex, parental economic status) were taken into account. The situation of Cuban youth was more complicated, but when parents put their children into private schools, being Cuban was a strong predictor of success. It may be impossible to fully unravel how much of this success has to do with cultural background and how much has to do with refugee status, but it is hard to avoid thinking that refugees would be particularly committed to seizing new opportunities, both for themselves and for their children.[25]

There is much cause for hope for the fate of refugees and their children in the United States. But what is the future fate of refuge itself? Here the answer is less clear. On the negative side lies the decline in admissions in the decade since 2000. From 1975 to 1999, refugee admissions averaged nearly 100,000 per year. The events of 9/11, however, brought refugee processing to a halt for many months, with the result being that admissions were cut to about 25,000 in fiscal years 2002 and 2003. By the end of the decade, the numbers had crept back up to 73,000, with an average of barely over 50,000 per year—half of what it had been.

The more recent arrivals are a particularly diverse set of newcomers with distinct needs. One of the ongoing debates between liberals and conservatives over refugees has involved the question of whether to admit higher numbers or to more effectively resettle a smaller group. Either way, it cannot be denied that while the refugees' long-term contributions are a net benefit to the United States, some transitional assistance is essential. This includes addressing the aftereffects of traumatic events and providing the necessary tools for effectively navigating American society, including language fundamentals.

There are now other mechanisms that facilitate temporary and permanent safe haven in America. The asylum application provisions of the Refugee Act of 1980 offer a legal immigration avenue for a significant number of people. Still, asylum approvals were very low throughout the 1980s. In recent years, however, approval rates have increased, with the total number averaging nearly 30,000 persons per year in the first decade of this century. If one adds these "asylees" to the number of people admitted as regular "refugees" (based on overseas screening), then the total number begins to approach the 1975 to 2000 period average of 100,000. Alternatives for temporary asylum in the United States have also expanded, particularly Temporary Protected Status, a presidential determination that citizens of certain foreign countries can legally remain in the United States until conditions in their home countries improve.[26]

The United States now possesses a broader array of policy options to deal with humanitarian crises reaching beyond the confines of the traditional refugee resettlement program. This array of options may cause confusion, particularly between the general idea of what constitutes a "refugee" and the various legal statuses and processing procedures that apply to different categories of refugees. Whether the United States can continue to apply this policy array in a useful and flexible way remains to be seen. But the needs of refugees are clear and their historical contribution to American society, and to the American economy, are equally so. While America is often characterized as an "immigration country," it is also very much a "refugee country." Refugees remind us that America is indeed both a land of opportunity and a land of refuge. It is a powerful combination.

Endnotes

[1] This sketch of the Acadian experience is drawn from Carl A. Brasseaux, "Scattered to the Wind": Dispersal and Wanderings of the Acadians, 1755–1809 (Lafayette, LA: Center for Louisiana Studies, University of Southwestern Louisiana, 1991) and John Mack Faragher, A Great and Noble Scheme: The Tragic Story of the Expulsion of the French Acadians from Their North American Homeland (New York: W.W. Norton, 2005). Some comparative information is found in Ronnie-Gilles LeBlanc, ed. Du Grand Derangement a la Deportation: Nouvelles Perspectives Historiques (Universite de Moncton, Chaire d'Etudes Acadiennes, 2005). The journals of John Winslow are available on line at the Nova Scotia government web site: http://www.gov.ns.ca/nsarm/virtual/deportation/

[2] Official Records of Robert Dinwiddie, Lieutenant-Governor of the Colony of Virginia, 1751–1758 (Virginia Historical Society, 1933); Elliot Dow Healy, "Acadian Exiles in Virginia," The French Review 22, no. 3 (1949): 233–40; Clifford Millard, "The Acadians in Virginia," The Virginia Magazine of History and Biography 40, no. 3 (1932): 241–58. Partial transcripts of colonial council meetings provided in "The Acadians in Virginia," The Virginia Magazine of History and Biography 6, no. 4 (1899): 386–89.

³ This discussion of the *St. Louis* is drawn from a variety of sources, particularly David Wyman, *Paper Walls: America and the Refugee Crisis, 1938–1941* (New York: Pantheon Books, 1985) and *The Abandonment of the Jews: America and the Holocaust, 1941–1945* (New York: The New Press, 1998). For a more charitable view of President's Roosevelt's position see Robert N. Rosen, *Saving the Jews: Franklin D. Roosevelt and the Holocaust* (New York: Thunder's Mouth Press, 2006); and for a more popularized account of the voyage see Gordon Thomas and Max Morgan-Witts, *Voyage of the Damned: A Shocking True Story of Hope, Betrayal, and Nazi Terror* (New York: Stein and Day, 1974), from which the movie of the same name was derived (though the film version takes considerable liberties with the facts).

⁴ A careful accounting of the fates of the ship's passengers is provided in Sarah A. Ogilvie and Scott Miller, *Refuge Denied: The St. Louis Passengers and the Holocaust* (Madison: The University of Wisconsin Press, 2006).

⁵ See Ruth Ellen Wasem "U.S. Immigration Policy on Haitian Migrants," order code RS21349 (Washington, DC: Congressional Research Service, January 15, 2010); Ruth Ellen Wasem, "Cuban Migration to the United States: Policy and Trends," order code R40566 (Washington, DC: Congressional Research Service, June 2, 2009); and the US Coast Guard's review of its interdiction efforts at http://www.uscg.mil/hq/cg5/cg531/AMIO/amio.asp. For a review of the legal issues, see Stephen Legomsky, "The USA and the Caribbean Interdiction Program," *International Journal of Refugee Law* 18 (2006): 677–95; Bill Frelick, "Abundantly Clear: Refoulement," *Georgetown Immigration Law Journal* 19, no. 1 (2005); and Lawyers Committee for Human Rights, *Refugee Refoulement: The Forced Return of Haitians under the US-Haitian Interdiction Agreement* (New York, 1990).

⁶ The term is David Wyman's; see *Paper Walls*.

⁷ Two recent reviews of the history of refugees in the United States are Carl Bon Tempo, *Americans at the Gate: The United States and Refugees during the Cold War* (Princeton, NJ: Princeton University Press, 2008); and David Haines, *Safe Haven? A History of Refugees in America* (Sterling, VA: Kumarian Press, 2010). Earlier works include Gil Loescher, *Beyond Charity: International Cooperation and the Global Refugee Crisis* (New York: Oxford University Press, 1993); Gil Loescher and John Scanlan, *Calculated Kindness: Refugees and America's Half Open Door* (New York: Macmillan, 1986); Norman L. and Naomi F. Zucker, *The Guarded Gate: The Reality of American Refugee Policy* (San Diego: Harcourt Brace Jovanovich, 1987), and *Desperate Crossings: Seeking Refuge in America* (New York: M.E. Sharpe, 1997).

⁸ Key sources for the discussion of "displaced persons" are Leonard Dinnerstein, *America and the Survivors of the Holocaust* (New York: Columbia University Press, 1982); Robert A. Divine, *American Immigration Policy, 1924–1952* (New Haven, Connecticut: Yale University Press, 1957); Mark Wyman, *DPs: Europe's Displaced Persons, 1945–1951* (Ithaca: Cornell University Press, 1989); and Roger Daniels (Ed.), *Immigration and the Legacy of Harry S. Truman* (Kirksville, Missouri: Truman State University Press, 2010).

⁹ For a careful review of these admissions, and their complicated interaction with other immigration quotas, see Congressional Research Service, *U.S. Immigration Law and Policy: 1952–1979* (Report prepared for the Committee on the Judiciary, US Senate, May 1979) and *Review of U.S. Refugee Resettlement Programs and Policies* (Report prepared for the Committee on the Judiciary, US Senate, July 1979).

¹⁰ A particularly useful review of the Hungarian case is provided in Bon Tempo, *Americans at the Gate*, 60–85.

¹¹ In the Southeast Asian case, the response to ships at sea was quite different from the cases discussed earlier in this chapter. Here American ships not only saved refugees from death at sea in their often unseaworthy craft, but also saved them from the despair of refugee camps in Southeast Asia and the threat of forced return by providing resettlement in the United States.

¹² For detailed reviews of these refugees and their adjustment, see David Haines, ed., *Refugees as Immigrants: Cambodians, Laotians, and Vietnamese in America* (Totowa, NJ: Rowman & Littlefield, 1989); Gail P. Kelly, *From Vietnam to America: A Chronicle of the Vietnamese Immigration to the United States* (Boulder, Colorado: Westview Press, 1977); Andres R. Hernandez, ed., *The Cuban Minority in the U.S.* (Washington, DC: Cuban National Planning Council, 1974); Richard Fagen, Richard A. Brody, and Thomas J. O'Leary, *Cubans in Exile: Disaffection and the Revolution* (Stanford: Stanford University Press, 1968); María Cristina Garcia, *Havana USA: Cuban Exiles and Cuban Americans in South Florida, 1959–1994* (Berkeley: University of California Press, 1996), and the nicely succinct summary by Guillermo J. Grenier and Lisandro Pérez, *The Legacy of Exile: Cubans in the United States* (Boston: Allyn & Bacon, 2003).

¹³ David Haines, "Synchronizing Domestic and Foreign Policy Concerns: The Case of the 1980 Refugee Act," *Federal History* 4 (2012): 12–27.

¹⁴ Maurice R. Davie, *Refugees in America: Report of the Committee for the Study of Recent Immigration from Europe*, (New York: Harper & Brothers, 1947).

[15] This has been a particularly influential line of research in sociology, laid out in detail in Alejandro Portes and Robert Bach, *Latin Journey: Cuban and Mexican Immigrants in the United States* (Berkeley: University of California Press, 1985).

[16] Davie, *Refugees in America*, 46.

[17] "Former Yugoslavia patches itself together: Entering the Yugosphere." *The Economist*, 20 August 2009, http://www.economist.com/node/14258861

[18] In particular, see Carol Mortland, "Tacoma, Washington: Cambodian Adaptation and Community Response," in *Manifest Destinies: Americanizing Immigrants and Internationalizing Americans*, ed. David Haines and Carol Mortland (Westport, CT: Praeger, 2001), 71–88; Aihwa Ong, *Buddha is Hiding: Refugees, Immigrants, the New America* (Berkeley: University of California Press, 2003); Nancy Smith Hefner, *Khmer American: Identity and Moral Education in a Diasporic Community* (Berkeley: University of California Press, 1999).

[19] Jonathan Lee, *Cambodian American Experiences: Histories, Communities, Cultures, and Identities* (Dubuque, IA: Kendall Hunt, 2010), 347.

[20] Useful sources on the Hmong are Sucheng Chang, *Hmong Means Free: Life in Laos and America* (Philadelphia: Temple University Press, 1994); Nancy Donnelly, *Changing Lives of Refugee Hmong Women* (Seattle: University of Washington Press, 1997); Anne Fadiman, *The Spirit Catches You and You Fall Down* (New York: Noonday Press, 1997); Dwight Conquergood, "Life in Big Red: Struggles and Accommodation in a Chicago Polyethnic Tenement," in *Structuring Diversity: Ethnographic Perspectives on the New Immigration*, ed. Louise Lamphere (Chicago: University of Chicago Press, 1992), 95–144; and Chia Youyee Vang, *Hmong in Minnesota* (Minneapolis: Minnesota Historical Society Press, 2008).

[21] Kou Vang, "Making the Invisible Visible," in *Hmong and American*, ed. Vincent K. Her and Mary Louise Buley-Meissner (St. Paul: Minnesota Historical Society Press, 2012), 222.

[22] Mark Bixler, *The Lost Boys of Sudan: An American Story of the Refugee Experience* (Athens: University of Georgia Press, 2006); Joan Hecht, *The Journey of the Lost Boys* (Jacksonville, FL: Allswell Press, 2005); Benson Deng, Alephonsion Deng, and Benjamin Ajak (with Judy A. Bernstein), *They Poured Fire on Us from the Sky: The True Story of Three Lost Boys from Sudan* (New York: Public Affairs, 2005). There were actually a number of "lost girls" as well, but since they tended to be absorbed into other families, they have been less visible as a separate group. See Laura DeLuca, "Transnational Migration, the Lost Girls of Sudan, and Global 'Care Work,'" *Anthropology of Work Review* 30, no. 1 (2009). 13–15.

[23] John Bul Dau (with Michael S. Sweeney), *God Grew Tired of Us* (Washington, DC: National Geographic, 2007), 277, 281.

[24] Nguyen Manh Hung, "Leaving and Returning," in *Diversity at Mason: The Fullbright Experience*, ed. Sandarshi Gunawardena and Karen Rosenblum (Fairfax, VA: George Mason University, 2008), 5.

[25] Nathan Caplan, Marcella H. Choy, and John K. Whitmore, *Children of the Boat People: A Study of Educational Success* (Ann Arbor: University of Michigan Press, 1991), vi, 174; Alejandro Portes and Rubén G. Rumbaut, *Legacies: The Story of the Immigrant Second Generation* (Berkeley: University of California Press, 2001).

[26] Numbers concerning refugees should always be treated with caution. The number of people included in the category varies even between different federal agencies. This chapter generally reflects Department of State (DOS) figures for overall admissions, but Office of Refugee Resettlement (ORR) for numbers from specific countries of origin over the last three decades.

These women arrived at Ellis Island from Guadeloupe, French West Indies, on the SS *Korona*, 1911.

9

BLACK WEST INDIAN AMERICANS

By Nancy Foner

O N THE NIGHT OF DECEMBER 20, 1986, Michael Griffith, a twenty-three-year-old Trinidadian immigrant, was riding in a car with three other black men in the borough of Queens when their 1976 Buick broke down and the men found themselves in an unfamiliar part of New York City. Griffith and two of the others walked several miles north to find the subway in Howard Beach, at the time a virtually all-white, mostly Italian American working-class community.

Entering Howard Beach at around midnight, they were accosted by some white passersby who yelled racial slurs and warned them to leave the neighborhood. Hungry and tired, the men decided to eat at a local pizza parlor. When they left the restaurant, a mob of about a dozen white youths was waiting for them in the parking lot with baseball bats, tire irons, and tree limbs, yelling, "Niggers, get out of the neighborhood; you don't belong here!" When one of the white teens lashed a bat across the thighs of Cedric Sandiford, a Guyanese-born construction worker, the three black men began to run. One of them, Timothy Grimes, made his getaway through a hole in a nearby fence, but Griffith and Sandiford were caught by the mob and seriously beaten. Again fleeing from their attackers, Griffith and Sandiford split up; Sandiford managed to hide, but Griffith kept running until he reached the nearby Belt Parkway. As the panic-stricken man darted across the busy six-lane expressway, he was hit by a car and instantly killed.

In protests that followed, more than a thousand demonstrators marched through the streets of Howard Beach, holding signs denouncing the attacks and comparing the community to apartheid South Africa. One sign read, "I don't need a passport to walk through Howard Beach. This is 1986!"[1] New York City mayor Ed Koch condemned the attack, likening the incident to lynchings in the Deep South.[2] In the trial that followed, three of the men involved in the beatings were convicted of first-degree assault and second-degree manslaughter; a fourth defendant was acquitted.[3]

The Howard Beach incident is of course an unusual case; explicitly anti-black violence is mercifully rare in contemporary New York City, as well as the rest of the country.

Yet the event underscores, tragically and dramatically, some essential features of the West Indian immigrant experience in the United States, in particular the complicated and painful role of race.

"My son's death," Michael Griffith's mother told the *Trinidad Express*, "opened the eyes of the public. Racism was something we read about in the Deep South. Maybe it was there all along in New York."[4] That racism was "there all along in New York" is a fact most West Indians in the United States know all too well. Race is the master status for foreign-born blacks in the United States; it shapes where they live, work, and go to school, how they enter the political system, and how they are perceived by others as well as how they see themselves.

As immigrants, black West Indians are often invisible to other New Yorkers. The mainstream media's coverage of the Howard Beach affair focused on the victims' blackness; most Americans never knew, or cared, that they were also West Indian. The Howard Beach residents who hurled racial slurs and cudgels at Michael Griffith and Cedric Sandiford probably did not know they came from the Caribbean. When one of the assailants said to his companions, "There's some niggers at the pizza parlor, and we should go back and kill them," he plainly meant they should be killed because they were black.[5]

As the Howard Beach incident demonstrates, many Americans are only dimly or intermittently aware of the West Indian presence in the United States. Even less well known is its history, which extends back at least to the nineteenth century. Voluntary West Indian immigration began almost as soon as the international slave trade was abolished. At that time, the numbers were comparatively small. According to one estimate, the foreign-born black population (nearly all of Caribbean origin) was about 4,000 in 1850 and 20,000 in 1900. It included a significant number of skilled craftsmen, preachers, lawyers, and students as well as a few prominent abolitionists and politicians. Among these immigrants were John Brown Russwurm of Jamaica, co-founder of the first black newspaper published in the United States, and Barbadian-born David Augustus Straker, a distinguished lawyer and fighter for civil rights during the Reconstruction period.[6]

Yet it was not until the early twentieth century that West Indians began to arrive in the United States in large numbers. The first major wave lasted a little more than two decades, beginning around 1900 and ending by the mid-1920s. In the peak years, from 1913 to 1924, some 5,000 to 12,000 black immigrants (nearly all West Indian) were admitted to the United States annually. By 1930, the foreign-born black population in the country had grown to almost 100,000, the overwhelming majority from the Caribbean. More than half of the West Indians arriving in that era headed for New York City. In 1930, 55,000 foreign-born blacks made up nearly a fifth of the city's black population. Almost a quarter of black Harlem, at the very time of the Harlem Renaissance, was of Caribbean origin.[7] It is no coincidence that some of that movement's most eminent writers and intellectuals, such as Claude McKay and Eric Walrond, came from the West Indies.[8]

West Indian migration had been fueled, and to a certain extent remains so, by a variety of push factors that have operated in the Caribbean since the end of slavery in the British colonies in 1838. Then, as now, West Indians utilized emigration as a strategy for survival and advancement whenever they were free to do so. The roots of migration in the English-speaking Caribbean run deep: they are traceable to the legacy of slavery, the distorting effects of colonial rule, and the centuries-long domination of the islands' economies by plantation agriculture. Scarce resources, overpopulation, high unemployment, and limited opportunities for advancement have long spurred West Indians to look abroad for better job prospects and improved living standards. Emigration, in short, has been a way of life in West Indian societies for centuries.

In the early twentieth century, West Indian migration to the United States was facilitated by the United Fruit Company's development of the banana industry, which brought the banana boat to the Caribbean and the beginning of regular steamship travel to the Atlantic ports of the United States.[9] Immigrants wrote letters home encouraging friends and relatives to join them and often sent back funds for the voyage. In a pattern that persists today, family members pooled resources to enable one of their own to emigrate. Many tickets were paid for with remittances sent by family members already in the United States. [10]

Barbadian-born David Augustus Straker was a prominent lawyer and civil rights advocate during the Reconstruction period.

Early twentieth-century Caribbean immigrants to the United States were a select group, disproportionately from the upper occupational tiers of West Indian societies, but they still faced severe barriers upon their arrival. Given the virulent racism of the 1910s and 1920s, West Indian women were mainly confined to work as domestics or similar personal service jobs, while men pursued the few urban jobs available to them in transportation, personal service, and a limited number of other lower skilled professions.[11] It was a struggle to move from menial jobs to respectability in an era when newspaper advertisements in the classified sections of major newspapers like the *Boston Globe* routinely called for "Colored man needed to work in tailor store as porter" (1910), "Supervisor needed, white man only" (1918), and "Colored women wanted for shining shoes" (1918).[12]

From the time of their earliest arrivals, West Indians left large and distinctive marks on black American political life, especially in the radical tradition. Perhaps the most famous West Indian political leader was Marcus Garvey, the Jamaican born black nationalist, who came to the United States in 1916. Through his Harlem-based organization, the United Negro Improvement Association, and newspaper, *The Negro World*, Garvey attracted hundreds of thousands of blacks in the late 1910s and early 1920s to a movement emphasizing black pride, black economic empowerment, and links between people of African ancestry in America and Africa. Garvey has been an inspirational figure for subsequent generations of black activists, including civil rights leader Malcolm X, whose mother was born in Grenada.

Immigration to the United States fell off sharply in the mid-1920s as a result of restrictive US legislation. The Great Depression and World War II kept the numbers low in the 1930s and 1940s, as did the McCarren-Walter Act of 1952, which set an annual quota of one hundred for each colony in the Western Hemisphere. At the same time, many thousands of West Indians went to Britain (the "mother country") in the 1950s, which was then welcoming immigrants to meet postwar manpower needs. Altogether, between 1924 and 1968 about 84,000 West Indians from the Anglophone Caribbean were admitted to the United States, most arriving after 1945 and a third after 1961 in what has been called the second wave of West Indian migration. Most were joining family members who had immigrated earlier in the century, but some were young professionals entering on student visas.[13]

One of the better-known Caribbean immigrants in American entertainment came into the country during this period. The actor Sidney Poitier, who in 1963 would become the first black person to win an Academy Award for best actor, originally emigrated from the Bahamas in 1943. In his memoir, he recounted an anecdote from shortly after he arrived in the United States. In search of a birth certificate, the fifteen-year-old Poitier visited a Miami police station:

I walked into the police station, and the desk sergeant—a big, burly, rough-looking guy—says, "Take off that cap, nigger." I turned around to see who was behind me and then suddenly realized that he was talking to me. So I said, "Are you talking to me?" He said, "Yes, I'm talking to you." I said, "Are you crazy?" He said, "What?" I said, "Are you crazy?" He said, "What did you say, boy?" I say, "My name is Sidney Poitier, you calling me names? Do you know who you're talking to?" The room is full of lots and lots of cops, and at this point they're falling down on the floor with laughter. Never in their lives have they seen such a nutty little black boy—he's got to be insane, or somebody's paid him fifty cents to come in and play this little charade. The guy behind the desk is looking at me—his mouth is wide open—and he says, "What did you say your name is, boy?" I say, "My name is Sidney Poitier—it's not 'boy.'" He says, "Okay, Mr. Poitier, would you mind telling us what it is you want?" I said, "I've come here because I want you to give me a pass to go across the Bureau of Vital Statistics to see about my birth certificate." He said, "All right, sir," having decided he would go along with the joke, whatever it was. And then he said to me, "Where are you from?" I said, "I'm from the Bahamas." And he said, "Oh, I see." At which point they realized that I just didn't know what was going on; that I just wasn't familiar with the established behavior pattern, the reflex conditioning, that would activate automatically if I stayed on in Miami much longer.[14]

This rough introduction to the American racial landscape and Poitier's sense of astonishment and incomprehension at American racial mores presaged the experiences of many more modern Caribbean immigrants.

A number of second-generation West Indian Americans have become prominent public officials. Clockwise from top left: Congresswoman Shirley Chisholm, Congresswoman Yvette Clarke, Attorney General Eric Holder, and Secretary of State Colin Powell.

Some of the first blacks to hold important political positions in the United States were West Indian immigrants (or their children) who arrived in the early twentieth century. In keeping with racial realities in America, they were usually known as "black firsts" and their West Indian origins were rarely noticed. In the mid-twentieth century, West Indians in New York City were the first black Democratic district leader, the first black borough president of Manhattan, the first black leader of Tammany Hall, and the first black state senator from Brooklyn.[15] Shirley Chisholm, the first black woman elected to the House of Representatives (1968) and the first black House member from Brooklyn, was born in Brooklyn to West Indian immigrant parents and spent much of her childhood with her maternal grandmother in Barbados. Constance Baker Motley, born in New Haven, Connecticut, to immigrant parents from Nevis, was the first African American woman elected to the New York State Senate (1964), as a New York City borough president (1965), and to be appointed as a federal court judge (1966).

We are currently in the midst of a massive and unprecedented influx, the third wave of West Indian migration, which began after passage of the Hart-Celler Immigration Act of 1965. Just as Britain was shutting out West Indians with restrictive immigration legislation in 1962, the United States opened its doors. In the ten years after the 1965 immigration reforms went into effect, West Indian immigration exceeded that of the previous seventy years; the numbers continued to grow in the 1980s and have remained at very high levels ever since. Figures on migration patterns from Jamaica demonstrate Hart-Celler's impact. In the decade leading up to 1965, about 1,500 Jamaicans per year migrated to the United States. From 1966 to 1975, Jamaican immigration averaged 12,400 annually. Between 1976 and 1985 it was up to about 18,000 a year, in large part a result of the political unrest, high crime rates, and economic recession in Jamaica during that period.[16]

By 2005, a remarkable 1.7 million black Caribbean immigrants were living in the United States, about two-thirds from Jamaica, Haiti, and Trinidad and Tobago. Black Caribbean immigrants represented two-thirds of all foreign-born blacks in the United States, with the other third coming from Africa. Altogether, foreign-born blacks totaled 2.8 million in 2005, a more than twentyfold increase since 1960 and more than triple the number in 1980.[17]

In the past few decades, economic crises, inflation, and unemployment have continued to fuel emigration from the Caribbean. West Indian small-island economies cannot deliver the kinds of jobs and lifestyles that people at all levels of society want or expect. And those expectations have only mounted as improved communications, the expansion of education, and reports and visits from migrant family members have raised awareness of the opportunities available in America. A national opinion survey in Jamaica in the late 1970s found that sixty percent of the population would move to the United States if given the chance.

Politics has also been a motivator. Jamaican Prime Minister Michael Manley's socialist reforms in the 1970s and early 1980s caused both political turmoil and the exodus of many highly skilled professionals from Jamaica. During the same period, many thousands fled the repressive Haitian regimes of Francois "Papa Doc" Duvalier and Jean Claude "Baby Doc" Duvalier in the 1960s, '70s, and '80s. As in the past, family networks have helped to perpetuate the flows to the United States, lowering the costs and reducing the risks of moving. By allocating immigrant visas along family lines, current US immigration law reinforces and formalizes the operation of family migrant networks. Recently, most West Indians have been legally admitted as immediate relatives of United States citizens or under family-based preferences.

Since 1965, West Indian migrants have come from virtually every sector of Caribbean society, including well-educated members of the urban elite seeking to protect their wealth in volatile economies, children of the middle class searching for broader opportunities, and large numbers of poor people looking for a better standard of living.[18] United States government statistics for 2005 show that as many well-educated as poorly-educated Caribbean-born blacks have come to America. Among those twenty-five and older, a fifth had a bachelor's degree or higher while another fifth had not graduated from high school.[19]

New York City remains the most popular destination, in part because of previous migration patterns. The very presence of an established (though aging) West Indian community from the earlier era drew immigrants there once the 1965 law made mass migration possible again. Networks of friends and relatives have continued to channel West Indians to the city, serving as financial safety nets for the new arrivals and sources of information about life in the United States. New York City also appeals because of its vibrant West Indian neighborhoods and glamorous, international reputation.

Of course, much has changed since West Indian immigrants first started arriving en masse in the early 1900s. Immigrants now come by plane, not steamship. The number of

West Indians in the United States, and in cities such as New York, is substantially larger. New York is still the dominant locale for these immigrants, but South Florida is becoming an important destination in its own right. In 2005, forty-two percent of foreign-born Caribbean blacks lived in the New York City metropolitan area, twenty percent were in Miami-Fort Lauderdale, and another ten percent collectively lived in the Washington, DC, Boston, or Atlanta metropolitan areas.[20]

Today's immigrants come from a different Caribbean than their predecessors a century ago. Anglophone West Indian societies are no longer British colonies but independent nations with black- and brown-skinned elites and government leaders. Jamaica and Trinidad, the two largest sending countries, became independent in 1962. British political, economic, and cultural influence has waned, while American influence has grown. Increased tourism and modern technology—especially television, cell phones, the internet, and jet travel—afford people in the most remote West Indian villages an up-close view of American life before they even get here. Once they have arrived and settled, the migrants can maintain intensive and extensive ties to their home societies in ways that were not possible in the early twentieth century. Whereas West Indian migration shrank to small numbers in the lull between the mid-1920s and mid-1960s, today's enormous influx has already lasted longer than the first large wave and is still going strong. Barring restrictive changes to American immigration law, a sizable flow is likely to continue for years to come.

One thread of continuity across all West Indian migration to America, then and now, is the painful significance of race. To be sure, West Indian immigrants today face much less overt prejudice and discrimination than did their predecessors of a century ago. One reason hardly any of the earlier cohort moved to Florida and other southern states was because legal segregation was still in force in the South. In the aftermath of the civil rights movement of the 1950s and 1960s, many American whites have become more racially tolerant. A series of laws and court decisions have attempted to ban racial discrimination, and new government agencies and systems are in place to enforce them. In the post-civil rights era, West Indians (especially the better-educated) have access to a much wider array of jobs and higher-education opportunities. Nonetheless, racial stereotypes, prejudice, and discrimination against blacks have a tenacious hold and persist in a variety of insidious forms.

At one extreme, blatant interpersonal racism—physical threats or attacks, denial of housing or employment, and harassment by the police—is still distressingly common in American life. The Howard Beach incident took place some twenty-five years ago, but it is not inconceivable that something similar could happen in New York today. Less dramatic but no less painful, many West Indians report an accumulation of racial slurs, insults, and slights, and a sense that some whites do not want to socialize or associate with them. Young black men seem to have an especially difficult time; it is not unusual for whites to cross the street or clutch their handbags when they see a young black man approach, and they do not stop to wonder whether the man is West Indian or African American. "In Manhattan, you'll walk into a store," a young Jamaican computer programmer explained, "you'll find that people will be following you around. Things like that you have never been accustomed to. To me, what has been a shocker here is to walk on the train and for women to clutch their handbags. ... That has been, to me, my worst problem to overcome since I have been here."[21]

Girls, too, feel targeted because of their skin color. "Because when you go to the stores," said one fourteen-year-old, "people follow you around, you go on the bus and people hold their pocketbooks. They don't discrimination against you because you're West Indian. They are discriminating against you because you are black."[22]

Race is a primary factor in determining where West Indians live. Choice, of course, also plays a role. Like other newcomers, West Indians gravitate to neighborhoods with kinfolk and friends, where they find comfort and security in an environment of familiar institutions. Yet racial discrimination and prejudice also contribute to the high rates of segregation among black West Indians. In New York, where the dynamics of segregation have been studied in the greatest depth, real estate agents often steer West Indians to black neighborhoods or withhold information on housing availability elsewhere. West Indians themselves often prefer communities where they can avoid racism and rejection, creating a self-perpetuating cycle of racial concentration. "Some neighborhoods," one West Indian New Yorker said, "are not yet ready for black people. And I don't want to be a hero."[23]

Those who during the 1980s and 1990s braved open hostility and branched out from West Indian areas of Brooklyn and Queens into adjacent white communities invariably found their new neighborhoods becoming increasingly black. Anti-black prejudice tended to fuel a process of racial turnover characterized as "white flight." The result is a pattern of segregation in which West Indian residential enclaves are located in largely black areas of the city and its suburbs. Although West Indians in New York City are largely segregated from whites, they are less segregated from African Americans than from any other ethnic or racial group.[24]

Residential segregation limits the informal contacts between West Indian immigrants and whites, and confines most immigrants to areas with inferior schools, relatively high crime rates, and poor government services. Whether at home or on the job, most West Indian immigrants find themselves moving in all black or mostly black social worlds. This trend seems to hold true for their American-born children, as well. A study of second-generation young adult New Yorkers found that most West Indians (as well as native blacks) worked in predominantly black work sites.[25]

The sting of racial prejudice in the United States is especially painful for immigrants because West Indians come from societies with different racial hierarchies and conceptions of race. "I wasn't aware of my color until I got here, honestly," said a Jamaican man in New York City. To be sure, when he lived in Jamaica he knew he had very dark skin. He was also aware of American racism before he immigrated: like most other aspiring immigrants, he had been exposed to American racial inequalities through reports in newspapers, on the radio and television, and from friends and relatives living in the United States—he had even seen it firsthand on a previous visit himself. But it is one thing to hear about racial prejudice or even to experience it briefly, and quite another to live with it as a part of one's daily existence.[26]

Of course, black immigrants were not leaving behind racial paradises back home. The long history of West Indian plantation slavery and colonial social arrangements left a white bias in its wake that lingers on today; dark skin often continues to be associated with poverty and whiteness still stands for wealth, power, and privilege. But blackness does not carry the same stigma as in the United States, and blackness is not in itself a barrier to social acceptance or upward mobility. Whites and European residents are very

IMMIGRANT STRUGGLES, IMMIGRANT GIFTS

few in West Indian societies, and people of African ancestry constitute the overwhelming majority; the exceptions are Trinidad and Guyana, where East Indian descendants of indentured laborers make up about forty percent of the population.

West Indian societies, moreover, never had a "one drop rule" in which the slightest trace of African ancestry rendered individuals categorically "black." Whereas in the United States the category "black" includes those who range from very dark skinned to very light skinned, in the West Indies there is a keen consciousness of shade: the lighter, the better. The mixed race, middle-class segment of West Indian societies has always been accepted as distinct from either blacks or whites. This dates back to the days of slavery when free people of color, often the product of unions between white men and slave women, enjoyed economic and other privileges denied to slaves. After emancipation in the British territories in 1838, whites generally monopolized the highest-ranking positions, blacks, the lowest positions, and the colored (mixed-race) individuals the stratum of prestigious and decently paid occupations in between. This pattern persisted for more than a century, partly out of prejudice and partly because the mixed race had access to education.[27]

The days of white rule are gone, and middle-class West Indians are now less likely to be light skinned than a century ago. For the last fifty years, black as well as colored individuals (and in Trinidad and Guyana, East Indians) have dominated public affairs and routinely filled prestigious and professional positions. West Indians, consequently, do not generally associate race with achievement, since they are daily presented with a full palette of high achievers and social failures, who are different shades of black and brown. In this context, race recedes behind other social markers. As one Jamaican immigrant said, "In Jamaica we didn't have color prejudice, we had class prejudice." What matters above all is having a high level of education, wealth, a "respectable" standard of living, and well-placed associates. No wonder then, that when West Indians come to live in the United States, they are often unprepared for and astonished by the outsize role that race plays in their lives.

One of the few integrative effects of this heightened race consciousness is the sense of solidarity and identification many West Indians sometimes feel with African Americans. Not only do West Indians and African Americans tend to live in the same neighborhoods and sometimes work together, but they also experience similar episodes of racial discrimination in public and tend to perceive important social institutions as being biased against blacks. For example, the group of black men whose drive through Queens ultimately led to the Howard Beach incident included two West Indians and two African Americans—all from the same section of Brooklyn. Cultural affinities also bind the two groups: black American popular and religious music, for instance, and admiration for American heroes of the civil rights struggle such as Martin Luther King, Jr.

Even as their racial environment binds West Indians to African Americans, it also encourages the immigrants to distance themselves from their black American neighbors. Distancing generally involves a stress on ethnic identity, either as natives of a particular Caribbean island or as West Indians as a group. In part, this ethnic awareness is nurtured by their immersion in immigrant neighborhoods and social networks and ongoing contacts with friends and relatives in the home society.

Something else is at play here as well. Ethnic self-consciousness is a response to the experience of racism in America, what social scientists refer to as "reactive ethnicity": a way to avoid the stigma associated with poor American blacks. According to one West Indian journalist, his countrymen have come to New York to get on, and although there are "no guarantees that identification with the white ruling class assures upward mobility, it is certain, they feel, that affiliation with the black underclass does not."[28]

West Indians assert an ethnic identity in order to make a case that they are culturally different from—and superior to—black Americans, emphasizing their strong work ethic, the value they place on education, and their lack of antisocial behaviors. Jamaican immigrants in New York City often claim that they are more ambitious and harder working than African Americans and place more value on education and discipline, despite the unfairness of such gross generalizations.[29]

Accents also enter into the picture. For many other immigrant groups, foreign accents are a stigma and newcomers work hard to eliminate them. But for West Indians from the Anglophone Caribbean, their accent is a clear marker of identity and plays a large role in ensuring that they are seen as distinct from black Americans. Until they speak, the only thing other people usually notice about West Indians is the color of their skin.[30] Many Jamaican immigrant New Yorkers report that they are viewed and treated more favorably when whites find out they are Jamaican and not African American. "Once you say something," one man said, "and they recognize you're not from this country, they treat you a little different." To what extent this is actually the case is hard to say.[31] What is clear is that many West Indian New Yorkers believe it to be true, and the belief itself further bolsters their sense of ethnic pride a feeling of superiority to African Americans.

West Indian identities also have implications in the political arena, and here too both race and ethnicity play a role. On the one hand, the shared experience of being black in America provides a basis for coalition building between West Indians and African Americans. The voting patterns of the two groups parallel each other; both are by and large loyal Democrats and supporters of a strong social safety net. In 1989 in New York City, West Indians voted in large numbers for David Dinkins, the first black man to be elected as the city's mayor.[32] Not surprisingly, West Indians enthusiastically backed Barack Obama in his successful presidential campaign and were one of the highest turnout groups in New York City in the 2008 presidential election.[33]

On the other hand, West Indians have increasingly practiced ethnic politics. This trend is especially noticeable in New York City, where West Indian immigrants today constitute more than a quarter of the black population and together with their children over a third. In the first half of the twentieth century, West Indian politicians in New York City deliberately downplayed their ethnic distinctiveness. Entering America at the height of racial segregation and when their numbers were much smaller, West Indians immersed themselves in the broader African American community. Prior to the 1970s, said one former New York state senator, "There were persons of Caribbean background, myself included, who were elected officials with a one hundred percent identification of themselves as American black politicians. ... Most of them went out of their way to overcompensate and deny their Caribbean heritage. They did not speak publicly on any Caribbean issues—national, international, or local."[34]

This is no longer the case. Successful ethnic politics is possible because New York City's West Indian community is now, after nearly half a century of massive immigration, more than ten times the size it was in the early twentieth century. Blacks of immigrant ancestry now make up about forty-four percent of the black electorate in New

York City.[35] West Indians' residential concentration has provided a political base in large, densely populated neighborhoods. Dominant political interests have also helped this process along, as

The West Indian Day Parade in Brooklyn attracts one to two million people every Labor Day.

political figures of all stripes actively court West Indian leaders and make use of West Indian symbolism to garner votes. Under the provisions of the federal Voting Rights Act of 1965, two Brooklyn districts were explicitly drawn in 1991 to give West Indians an effective plurality, and these districts have subsequently elected West Indian members to the New York City Council.

West Indian politicians in New York City and in many southern Florida communities increasingly play the "ethnic card" to appeal to the growing West Indian electorate. In addition to stressing their own Caribbean background, they often take positions to differentiate themselves from African American politicians and attract West Indian support, showing, for example, greater concern for immigration legislation and economic development in the Caribbean and adopting more conservative positions on law and order issues. In New York, some local elections have been fought quite explicitly between native-born and Caribbean blacks. It is in fact when one of their own is competing with an African American that West Indians and African Americans have most noticeably parted ways.[36] One example was the bitter contest between Major Owens (African American) and Una Clarke (Jamaican) in 2000 in a Brooklyn Democratic primary for a seat in the US Congress. Owens, the incumbent, won that race, but the seat is now held by Clarke's daughter, Yvette.

On a national scale, West Indian political involvement is much more ethnically muted. In recent decades, several individuals of West Indian ancestry—mostly the children of early twentieth-century immigrants—have ascended to national recognition and responsibility. Colin Powell, born in Harlem and raised in the Bronx by Jamaican immigrant parents, was the first black four-star general in the US Army (1989) as well as the first black American to chair the Joint Chiefs of Staff (1989–93) and serve as Secretary of State (2001–05). In 2009, Eric Holder (whose father and maternal grandparents were immigrants from Barbados) became the nation's first black attorney general.

Although only a few first- and second-generation West Indians have reached impressive political heights, many others have made significant contributions to American society. Their impact has been especially pronounced in the areas where they have settled in large numbers, primarily the New York City and Miami-Fort Lauderdale metropolitan areas, but also in other cities such as Boston, Atlanta, Hartford, and Washington, DC. West Indian immigrants stand out for their high rates of labor force participation and for living in households where many members are working.

The question of why black immigrants do much better in the economy than African Americans frequently bedevils social scientists. In fact, one of the consequences of the American racial hierarchy is to distort notions of West Indian achievement. West Indian immigrants are seen as a success story precisely because they are compared to African Americans, rather than to other immigrant groups.[37] Nonetheless, the evidence on West Indian success relative to African Americans is clear. Studies show that West Indian immigrants fare better than African Americans in terms of labor force participation, employment, and occupational prestige.

It has been persuasively argued that immigrant self-selectivity is the key factor explaining the difference. West Indians who migrate are, as a rule, the best and brightest. Those who leave their home societies for new lives abroad are economically motivated migrants who generally have more ability, education, and drive than those who remain.[38] Once settled in the United States, moreover, they evaluate jobs by an "immigrant metric," comparing wages to what they could earn in the Caribbean and tolerating jobs that natives, black and white, reject. Many see their stays as temporary, aiming to save money with the intent of improving their status upon return.

A sizable number of West Indian immigrants are in management and professional jobs, but most are found in the service sector. In the New York area, West Indian immigrant women are highly concentrated in the health care industry as nurses and aides, and many men are in skilled trades or transportation.[39] Despite a common stereotype that West Indian immigrants have a genius for business, they actually show extremely low rates of self-employment in New York City.[40] Still, there are a few large ethnic businesses that mainly serve the West Indian community, as do some smaller enterprises such as bakeries, travel agencies, and record stores. West Indian New Yorkers have created a jitney van industry, the idea of which was brought over from the Caribbean. The vans that ply the streets of Brooklyn and Queens are less expensive than public buses and subways and more convenient because they pick up and drop off customers anywhere along a route.

West Indians have added to the flavors of America's cities with their Jamaican patties and Trinidadian *roti* (a kind of curry wrap). West Indian Carnival has been transplanted from Trinidad to become a pan-West Indian event, enriching street life in many cities. The West Indian Day Parade held on Brooklyn's Eastern Parkway is by far the largest, attracting between one and two million people every Labor Day; it is now a mandatory campaign stop for politicians seeking citywide office. Other cities, including Miami, Atlanta, and Washington, DC, have adopted West Indian Carnivals as well.[41]

West Indian immigrants have had an outsize impact on American popular music. Hip-hop is usually considered an African American form, but in its developmental years in New York City it was as much a creation of Afro-Caribbean (and Latino) youth. Several famous hip-hop artists, including Busta Rhymes and Biggie Smalls (later Notorious B.I.G.) were American-born sons of Jamaican immigrants; Haitian-born Wyclef Jean first became well known as a member of the Fugees. More recently, a new generation of West Indians has yielded many popular music figures, such as Sean Paul and Damian Marley (Jamaican ancestry), Nicki Minaj (Trinidadian ancestry), and Rhianna (Barbadian ancestry).

As with most immigrant groups, West Indians' largest contributions to the United States are their children. A large second generation—the American-born sons and daughters of post-1965 immigrants—is coming of age and entering adulthood. Overall, the offspring of West Indian immigrants are doing better than their parents in terms of education and occupation, and also better than African Americans. While some of the second generation have moved well up the occupational ladder, obtaining highly paid and valued professional positions, many are working members of the lower middle-class service economy, employed as white collar clerical or service workers in retail or financial services.[42] The West Indian second generation has made significant progress because, like most second-generation immigrants, it comprises a highly selected group. They are the children of exceptional and ambitious parents who have uprooted themselves to come to a new society and are strongly motivated to improve their own socio-economic lot as well as that of their children.

The issue that will no doubt shape the second generation's future prospects most decisively is whether, and how thoroughly, it will become African American. Some degree of assimilation into black America (including into the growing African American middle class) seems inevitable for the children of Afro Caribbean immigrants. As it has been for their foreign-born parents, West Indian heritage can also be a powerful tool to mitigate (if not entirely escape) the stigma of being black in America.

Class also complicates matters. Virtually all the children of black immigrants identify as black, but middle-class adolescents and young adults are much likelier to emphasize their ethnicity than less-successful members of the second generation.[43] Much depends on the situation. Some may feel pressure to conform to black American culture at school, for example, but be "West Indian at night" when they are at home with their parents.[44]

However they identify themselves, it remains uncertain how others will view them. Will they be recognized as Afro Caribbean or West Indian? As black ethnics? Or as black American? At present, second-generation West Indians have difficulty marshaling their West Indian background in a society with a powerful tendency to homogenize blacks with little regard to ethnicity.[45] Whether this will continue depends largely on the future of the "color line" in America. The image of blacks as poor, unworthy, and dangerous remains tenaciously potent, despite the success of many black Americans and the growth of a sizable black middle class.[46] Without an accent or other clues to immediately telegraph their ethnic status to others, the American-born children of black immigrants are likely to "fade to black."[47]

At the same time, it may be that the presence of large numbers of black immigrants will lead Americans in cities like New York to gradually become more sensitive to ethnic distinctions within the black community, particularly if continued immigration sustains and increases the proportion of Caribbeans (and Africans) in the black population. It may be that West Indians are helping to challenge notions that blackness is incompatible with socioeconomic success in the United States and that ethnic and racial identities are mutually exclusive. In the long run, perhaps the greatest contribution of black West Indian immigrants will be to broaden and help transform American understandings of race.[48]

Endnotes

[1] Charles Hynes and Bob Drury, *Incident at Howard Beach: The Case for Murder* (New York: G.P. Putnam's Sons, 1990), 4.

[2] Ibid., 35.

[3] For reports on the Howard Beach incident see Hynes and Drury, *Incident at Howard Beach*; Reed Albergotti, Thomas Zambito, Marsha Schrager, and John Rofe, "Racism Comes Home: The Howard Beach Case," *Queens Tribune* (2003), http://www.queenstribune.com /anniversary2003/howardbeach.htm; and Mark Dwayne, "Howard Beach Incident (1986), *An Online Reference Guide to African American History*, http://www. blackpast.org?q=aah/howard-beach-incident-1986.

[4] Quoted in Philip Kasinitz, *Caribbean New York: Black Immigrants and the Politics of Race* (Ithaca: Cornell University Press, 1992), 247.

[5] Hynes and Drury, *Incident*, 20.

[6] Winston James, *Holding Aloft the Banner of Ethiopia* (London: Verso, 1998), 9–12.

[7] Ibid.; Kasinitz, Caribbean New York, 24–25, 41; Irma Watkins Owens, *Blood Relations: Caribbean Immigrants and the Harlem Community, 1900–1930* (Bloomington: Indiana University Press, 1996).

[8] Watkins-Owens, *Blood Relations*.

[9] Ransford Palmer, *Pilgrims of the Sun: West Indian Migration to America* (New York: Twayne, 1995), 6.

[10] Violet Shower Johnson, *The Other Black Bostonians: West Indians in Boston, 1900–1950* (Bloomington: Indians University Press, 2006), 21.

[11] See Suzanne Model, *West Indian Immigrants: A Black Success Story?* (New York: Russell Sage Foundation, 2008); Suzanne Model, "Where New York's West Indians Work," in *Islands in the City: West Indian Migration to New York*, ed. Nancy Foner (Berkeley: University of California Press, 2001); and Irma Watkins-Owens, "Early Twentieth Century Caribbean Women: Migration and Social Networks in New York City," in *Islands in the City*.

[12] Johnson, *The Other Black Bostonians*, 28.

[13] Kasinitz, Caribbean New York, 26; Model, *West Indian Immigrants*, 21–22.

[14] Quoted in James, *Holding Aloft the Banner of Ethiopia*, 85–86.

[15] Calvin Holder, "West Indies," in *The New Americans: A Guide to Immigration Since 1965*, ed. Mary C. Waters and Reed Ueda (Cambridge: Harvard University Press, 2007), 681–82.

[16] Milton Vickerman, "Jamaicans: Balancing Race and Ethnicity" in *New Immigrants in New York*, ed. Nancy Foner (New York: Columbia University Press, 2001), 203.

[17] Mary Mederios Kent, "Immigration and America's Black Population," *Population Bulletin*, 62, no. 4 (2007). These figures include Haitians. Black immigrants from the former British territories in the Caribbean, including Guyana and Belize, totaled about 1.2 million.

[18] Kasinitz, *Caribbean New York*, 27–28.

[19] Kent, "Immigration and America's Black Population."

[20] Ibid.

[21] Milton Vickerman, "Tweaking a Monolith: The West Indian Immigrant Encounter with 'Blackness,'" in *Islands in the City*, 245.

[22] Vilna Bashi, "We Don't Have That Back Home: Race, Racism, and the Social Networks of West Indian Immigrants," paper presented at the annual meeting of the American Sociological Association, August, 1996.

[23] Quoted in Nancy Foner, *From Ellis Island to JFK: New York's Two Great Waves of Immigration* (New Haven: Yale University Press, 2000), 152.

[24] Crowder and Tedrow, "West Indians and the Residential Landscape of New York," in *Islands in the City*, 81–114.

[25] Philip Kasinitz, John Mollenkopf, Mary C. Waters, and Jennifer Holdaway, *Inheriting the City: The Second Generation Comes of Age* (New York: Russell Sage Foundation, 2008), 198.

[26] Mary C. Waters, *Black Identities: West Indian Immigrant Dreams and American Realities* (Cambridge: Harvard University Press, 1999), 171.

[27] Nancy Foner, *Status and Power in Rural Jamaica: A Study of Educational and Political Change* (New York: Teachers College Press, 1973).

[28] Cited in Nancy Foner, *From Ellis Island to JFK*, 154–55.

[29] Waters, *Black Identities*, 67.

[30] Ibid., 78.

[31] For a more in-depth discussion of this issue, see Waters, *Black Identities*.

[32] Milton Vickerman, "Jamaica," in *The New Americans*, 486–87.

[33] John Mollenkopf, "The Rise of Immigrant Influence in New York City Politics," in *Immigrants and the New Urban Landscape: New York and Amsterdam*, ed. Nancy Foner, Jan Rath, Jan Willem Duyvendak, and Rogier van Reekum (forthcoming).

[34] Kasinitz, *Caribbean New York*, 207–208.

[35] Mollenkopf, "The Rise of Immigrant Influence in New York City Politics."

[36] Reuel Rogers cited in Mollenkopf, "The Rise of Immigrant Influence in New York City Politics."

[37] Philip Kasinitz, "Invisible No More: West Indian Americans in the Social Scientific Imagination," in *Islands in the City*, 257–75.

[38] Model, *West Indian Immigrants*.

[39] See Ibid.; Vickerman, "Jamaica," 480–81.

[40] Model, *West Indian Immigrants*, 19.

[41] Holder, "West Indies," 675–77.

[42] Kasinitz et al, *Inheriting the City*, 348.

[43] Mary Waters, "Growing Up West Indian and African American," in *Islands in the City*, 193–215.

[44] Sherri Ann Butterfield, "'We're Just Black': Racial and Ethnic Identities of Second Generation West Indians in New York," in *Becoming New Yorkers: Ethnographies of the New Second Generation*, ed. Philip Kasinitz, John Mollenkopf, and Mary Waters (New York: Russell Sage Foundation, 2004).

[45] Vilna Bashi Bobb and Averil Clarke, "Experiencing Success: Structuring the Perception of Opportunities for West Indians," in *Islands in the City*, 233; Vickerman, "Tweaking a Monolith," 254.

[46] Waters, "Growing Up," 213.

[47] Kasinitz, Battle, and Miyares, "Fade to Black? The Children of West Indian Immigrants in South Florida," in *Ethnicities: Children of Immigrants in America*, ed. Ruben Rumbaut and Alejandro Portes (Berkeley: University of California Press, 2001), 267–300.

[48] Vickerman, "Tweaking a Monolith," 255.

A Mexican worker arriving in the United States, 1942. The Bracero Program helped meet labor shortages in the United States during World War II.

CHAPTER 10

MEXICAN AMERICANS

By Wayne A. Cornelius

O n November 8, 1994, California voters ushered in the modern era of anti-Mexican nativism. By a healthy eighteen-point margin (fifty-nine to forty-one percent), they approved Proposition 187 (also known as the "Save Our State" initiative), a ballot measure barring undocumented immigrants from public elementary and secondary education, all forms of tax supported health care, and other public social services. School districts were required to verify the legal status of all children enrolled, as well as their parents. Other public service providers were required to report any applicant for benefits they suspected of being in the country illegally. Similarly, police who stopped a person suspected of being underdocumented were required to refer the detainee to immigration authorities.

California Governor Pete Wilson had made the movement to pass the referendum the centerpiece of his reelection campaign. His most effective commercial showed grainy, black-and-white footage of menacing waves of Mexicans rushing into the United States at the San Ysidro port of entry, overwhelming border guards, as an off-camera announcer gravely intoned, "They just keep coming. ..." While Wilson's authority as a state governor to regulate immigration was questionable, he succeeded in convincing a majority of Californians that by voting for him they could send a message of protest to the federal government in Washington against uncontrolled Mexican immigration.

Ironically, during his previous US Senate career, Wilson was considered a moderate Republican; he had even co-sponsored legislation to permit an ample supply of Mexican labor for California agribusiness. With his unflinching support of a crackdown on "illegal aliens," Wilson handily won his reelection bid. Before boarding the "Yes on 187" bandwagon, he had been trailing his Democratic opponent in opinion polls by more than twenty percentage points. In addition to calling attention to the federal government's failure to secure the border, Wilson stirred up anti-immigrant sentiment within California by rhetorically dividing the state's population into two categories: "tax payers" and "tax users." Undocumented immigrants were lumped into the latter category, ignoring the fact that the majority of such immigrants actually pay taxes to the state and federal governments. Harkening back to the arguments deployed against Mexican migrant workers during the 1920s and 1930s, Wilson characterized the undocumented immigrants as freeloaders who were likely to become welfare abusers.

Exit polls showed that most "yes" voters on Proposition 187 did not expect it to be implemented. Theirs was a purely symbolic protest about undocumented immigration, primarily from Mexico.[1] In fact, Proposition 187 was struck down three years later by a federal court that found the measure to be an unconstitutional infringement on the federal government's exclusive jurisdiction over immigration policy.

Proposition 187 had long-term, national political consequences. Its passage sent shock waves through the entire American political establishment. The successful campaign to pass 187 framed the immigration debate in Congress from 1996, when legislation was passed to limit the access of even legal permanent immigrants to federal benefits, through the acrimonious debates over comprehensive immigration reform bills in 2006 and 2007.

In anticipation of the 1996 reelection campaign, President Clinton's advisers took steps to insulate him from intensifying anti-immigration sentiment. The Clinton Administration embraced a strategy of "concentrated border enforcement operations," pioneered by a Border Patrol district director in El Paso, Texas.[2] The strategy focused Border Patrol resources on a few, heavily transited corridors of illegal entry: San Diego, El Paso, and central Arizona. The Clinton Administration also backed a sharp increase in spending on border enforcement. The political insulation tactic worked; illegal immigration did not become a major issue in the 1996 presidential election. The new border enforcement strategy failed; it merely redistributed clandestine entries, shifting them away from the newly fortified border sectors into more remote areas.

Proposition 187 was the ancestor of the raft of anti-immigrant measures pushed through state legislatures and city councils throughout the United States in the first decade of the twenty-first century.[3] Like Proposition 187, the vast majority of these measures have been struck down by the courts, but they continue to be advanced, especially in states with rapidly growing Mexican immigrant populations. Anti-immigrant policy activism at the state and local levels mushroomed after Congress failed in 2006–2007 to pass comprehensive immigration reform legislation. State and local politicians saw this inaction as an opening, an opportunity to claim credit for dealing aggressively with a major public problem that the federal government had failed to resolve and one that had paralyzed the US Congress since the 1990s. That most of these measures could not possibly have affected the volume or destinations of undocumented immigrants arriving in specific states or localities was lost in the angry, emotional debate over how to "stem the tide of illegal aliens." While these laws and ordinances were not targeted explicitly at Mexicans, most were introduced in states and cities where Mexicans constituted the overwhelming majority of immigrants.

Many Americans believe that Mexicans, acting entirely on their own interests and initiative, began "sneaking into" the United States in large numbers sometime in the 1980s, circumventing overwhelmed Border Patrol assets. The real story is quite different. Large-scale labor migration from Mexico began a century earlier, and it was American employers who instigated the first major wave of migrants—sometimes with the direct involvement of federal officials. They did not "sneak in," they were recruited from their home communities and helped to relocate with the assistance of the American

government. The United States wanted their labor, and the Mexicans needed jobs. Political upheavals in Mexico, such as the Mexican Revolution of 1910 and the Cristero Rebellion of 1926–1928, also played a role in sending emigrants north of the border, but the main impetus for

Pro- and anti-Proposition 187 activists separated by a police line in 1996 Los Angeles. The ballot measure provoked emotional responses from both sides and its passage was a catalyst for anti-immigrant legislation nationally.

most early Mexican American immigration came from within the United States.

Mexican migrants flowed freely across an unfortified, unpatrolled southwestern border from the 1880s to 1924, when the US Border Patrol was created. Hundreds of thousands of Mexicans entered the United States during this period; they worked in mines and on the railroads and farms—anywhere cheap manual labor was required. American companies in these industries sent labor recruiters deep into the Mexican interior, promising generous wages and free transportation to the border and beyond. The labor shortage of the First World War led to the first US government-sponsored "guest worker" program aimed at Mexican nationals. World War I also marked the onset of an "opening and closing door" policy, in which the door was closed to Mexican immigration during periods of economic contraction and associated nativist anxiety, but re-opened when American economic growth or war-related labor shortages generated strong employer demand for Mexican workers. The Great Depression temporarily dried up the American demand for Mexican labor. Mexican migration into the United States all but ceased during this period, and American officials organized campaigns to repatriate hundreds of thousands of Mexicans, including many naturalized American citizens of Mexican descent, during the 1929–35 period.[4]

The long-term pattern of Mexican migration to the United States by multiple genera-tions within the same families and from the same home communities was set by another temporary worker program, popularly known as the Bracero Program, which operated in various forms from 1942 to 1964. This program was much larger than the World War I program, at its peak bringing more than half a million Mexican workers into the United States each year for short-term agricultural labor. An elaborate system of labor contracting, again reaching deep into the Mexican interior, was created to manage this massive movement of workers. Individuals, families, and communities that had never before engaged in migration to the United States were drawn into the flow. The conse-quences of the Bracero Program have been remarkably durable and widely distributed throughout Mexico; many first-time Mexican migrants today are likely to be related to men—fathers, grandfathers—who were recruited as Braceros.

The termination of the Bracero Program (due to rising anti-immigrant sentiment in Congress and among American labor unions) had little effect on the northbound migration of Mexican laborers. Because Mexicans had come to depend on income earned in the United States and western farmers continued to need the labor, such migration continued illegally. A robust smuggling industry sprang up in Mexico in the 1970s, with so-called "coyotes" charging hundreds and eventually thousands of dol-lars to assist clandestine entries. Today, an estimated nine out of ten undocumented Mexican migrants hire coyotes to facilitate their border crossing, often using money borrowed from American-based relatives.

In 1965, the year after the Bracero Program was allowed to expire, the US Congress passed the Immigration and Nationality Act. While the law expanded opportunities for many overseas immigrants, it imposed a cap on Western Hemisphere migration for the first time. Later (in 1976), the Western Hemisphere countries including Mexico were absorbed under the preference system for the 1965 Act and its per-country visa caps. The upshot of these legal changes is that since the late 1960s, Mexican migration to the United States has been largely undocumented. Since 1965, Mexico has become the single most important source of legal immigrants to the United States, but it is the enormous illegal component of Mexican immigration that drives nativist agitation and restric-tive legislation in Congress. According to estimates by the Pew Hispanic Center, about fifty-five percent of all Mexicans living in the United States today are undocumented, and fifty-nine percent of undocumented immigrants, of all nationalities, are Mexican.[5]

The initial waves of post-Bracero migrants consisted almost entirely of unaccom-panied men, both single and married. As these pioneer migrants consolidated their position in the American labor market, the era of large-scale Mexican migration for family reunification began. Trans-border social networks based in migrants' communi-ties of origin and destination took shape, greatly increasing the information available to prospective migrants about conditions in America and expanding their contacts for finding housing and employment in the United States. Relatives based in the United States became the most important source of loans to finance a trip, including the cost of hiring a coyote to assist the crossings of those without papers. The location of friends and relatives also became the key factor in choosing an American destination.[6] Today, the vast majority of Mexican migration is "network-mediated." Mexicans with access to an extended kinship network on the US side of the border are more likely to migrate to the United States, put down roots, and encourage the immigration of their own friends and relatives.

The Immigration Reform and Control Act (IRCA), enacted by Congress in 1986 was another important development in the promotion of a more demographically diverse and stable population of Mexican immigrants. Among other provisions, IRCA created two legalization programs, a general program for longtime residents of the United States and a special program for people who had been working in seasonal agriculture. About 2.7 million undocumented migrants took advantage of these two programs to gain permanent legal residency in the United States; four out of five were Mexicans.[7] Undocumented family heads who already had an economic foothold in the United States legalized themselves and called for their Mexico-based families to join them.

Cyclical, temporary migration by Mexican workers continued to fall into eclipse during the 1990s. One factor was a change in the American labor market, where employers began offering more year-round jobs, even in agriculture. But it was the border enforcement buildup launched by the Clinton administration in 1994 that essentially ended short-term Mexican migration by making it more costly and risky for migrants lacking visas to come and go. Their average length of stay increased steadily, as did the likelihood of their settling permanently in the United States. Probabilities of returning to Mexico have dropped to record lows. An estimated two million Mexicans now live in the United States, as de facto permanent residents, who probably would not have come and stayed absent tougher immigration enforcement since 1994. Majorities or pluralities of would-be migrants to the United States, interviewed in their hometown, routinely tell researchers that they would prefer short-term employment in the United States over permanent settlement, but the current US immigration system promotes the latter. New temporary worker programs went down to defeat in Congress almost every year from the mid-1990s through 2007, despite the pleas of American agribusiness and its congressional allies.

The contributions of Mexican immigrants to the growth and functioning of the American economy have been large and diverse. As a consistent source of inexpensive labor, Mexican immigrants have been unequaled by any other immigrant group throughout American history. The building of much of the United States' basic physical infrastructure in the late nineteenth and early twentieth centuries, including the transcontinental railroad, would not have been possible without Mexican (as well as Chinese and Irish) immigrant labor. The rapid growth of American agribusiness, beginning in the 1890s and continuing for several decades thereafter, was also made possible by an abundant supply of Mexican labor. Clearly, the ability of the United States to feed its populace and its troops in two world wars would have been severely constrained without large-scale access to Mexican workers.

Similarly, the growth of labor-intensive industries in non-agricultural areas of the American economy—construction, manufacturing, and various parts of the service industry—has also depended on employers' ability to tap a relatively low-cost Mexican labor supply. Expansion of these industries created jobs for millions of American-born workers and significantly boosted tax revenues to local, state, and federal governments. In the case of some "footloose" manufacturing activities, access to Mexican labor encouraged business owners to keep their operations within the United States rather than exporting them to Third World countries, which would have caused major collateral job losses for US citizens.[8] Entrepreneurial Mexican immigrants have established hundreds of thousands of businesses—from restaurants and other retail operations to car washes and construction firms—that helped reinvigorate inner-city neighborhoods, generate new employment for immigrants and natives alike, and increase the flow of tax revenues to governments at all levels.

Many Mexican immigrants pay taxes, based on their income, regardless of their legal status. National surveys as well as micro-studies have found that at least half of undocumented immigrants pay federal and state income taxes, which typically are withheld from their wages. In recognition of this reality, the US Treasury regularly issues taxpayer identification numbers to undocumented immigrants who work for themselves or are paid in cash and wish to file income tax returns. Many undocumented immigrants file tax returns because they believe that having a record of tax payments will be necessary to adjust their legal status at some point in the future; indeed, all recent congressional proposals for a legalization program have included a requirement that applicants be fully paid up on their taxes.

The Institute for Taxation and Economic Policy (ITEP) has estimated that households headed by undocumented immigrants of all nationalities paid $11.2 billion in state and local taxes in 2010.[9] The state of California alone received $2.7 billion in tax revenues from such households. Mexican immigrants also stimulate tax revenues through their behavior as consumers, paying state and local sales taxes on their purchases. In addition, undocumented Mexican immigrants are believed to account for the vast bulk of the federal Social Security system's unclaimed funds account, representing Social Security contributions that have been credited to fictitious Social Security numbers and thus are not paid out as benefits. Undocumented workers are estimated to be providing the Social Security system with a subsidy of up to $7 billion per year.[10]

Opinion polls reveal the widespread public belief that Mexican immigrants disproportionately make use of tax-supported social services, thus draining the government's coffers and crowding out other potential recipients of welfare dollars. Available, credible data show that this is not true. Based on their age and income level, Mexican immigrant families, including those headed by undocumented persons, actually underutilize many services. Far from receiving preferential treatment from government agencies, undocumented immigrants are barred by state and federal laws from receiving cash assistance benefits of any kind, including general welfare benefits, unemployment compensation, and payments from health care programs such as Medicaid. Most agencies dispensing social welfare benefits have instituted effective screening procedures, and prospective applicants for benefits know that they will be interrogated about their immigration status. Legal permanent resident Mexican immigrants and naturalized citizens do have access to social services, including tax-supported health care programs; but, of course, they help to pay for these programs through state and federal income taxes. Since Congress enacted a restrictive immigration law and welfare reform measures in 1996, even legal immigrants have been required to wait five years before they can access such benefits.

Most attempts by economists to estimate the national fiscal impact of Mexican immigrants have shown a very mixed picture. States and localities with large Mexican immigrant populations pay more to provide human services to them, but they also reap disproportionate benefits in the form of higher rates of economic growth, immigrant

entrepreneurship, and revenues generated by consumption taxes, rents, licenses, and other fees. Critics of Mexican immigrants brandish frightening statistics on the fiscal effects of

Immigrant workers, mostly Mexican, reportedly fill eighty percent of the jobs in Nebraska's meatpacking industry.

immigration that systematically underestimate the immigrants' contributions to public finances and overstate negative fiscal impacts by relying on approximations of service utilization rates provided by public agencies. Such guesstimates, however, have no defensible methodology for separating out general costs from those specifically imposed by immigrants.[11]

As for Mexican immigrants' impact on economic output, most rigorous studies show that it is positive but relatively modest.[12] Using a model developed by the National Research Council in 1996, immigrants of all nationalities contributed up to $15 billion to the US gross domestic product in 2010 (in a $15 trillion economy).[13] Some economic theory predicts that if immigrants are adding to the labor supply they will depress average wages for native-born workers. However, studies of wage trends in specific cities with large Mexican immigrant populations, compared with cities where they have less of a presence in local labor markets, have not found evidence of wage depression attributable to immigration. Immigrants—even the undocumented—actually improve wages for American-born workers when they are complements rather than competitors in the labor market, improving the natives' productivity. Most Mexican immigrants appear to play this complementary role.

Mexican immigrants are distinguished by a remarkably strong work ethic. Restrictionists tend to downplay this attribute, even turning it against the immigrants, accusing them of competing unfairly against US citizens for jobs because employers have a preference for Mexicans who "work hard and scared," in the oft-quoted words of former US Labor Secretary Ray Marshall.[14] According to this argument, immigrants—especially the undocumented—accept low wages, few or no fringe benefits, and poor working conditions, making them highly attractive to unscrupulous employers.

Ironically, many of the same Americans who believe Mexican immigrants are "all on welfare" also claim that such immigrants are "taking our jobs."

The reality is that US citizens are rarely in direct competition for jobs with Mexican immigrants, especially the undocumented. Natives and immigrants, native-born Latinos and recent arrivals, African American workers, and first-generation Mexican Americans all tend to be channeled into different segments of the labor market. Much of this channeling results from social networks that deliver workers to specific employers with histories of hiring immigrant workers. Even more important than employer preference is the fact that Mexican immigrants mostly take jobs that native-born Americans do not want, due to the offensive or physical nature of the work as well as the inadequate compensation. Mexican immigrants are usually the only people who apply for such jobs, and in most immigrant-dominated occupations that has been the case for several decades or longer.

Immigration critics respond that native workers would line up to take these jobs if employers would only raise wages and improve benefits. Because the vast majority of jobs now held by Mexican immigrants, including the undocumented, pay at least the legal minimum wage, employers would have to pay the "prevailing wage" or higher to attract native-born applicants. But even if the primarily small businesses where "Mexican jobs" reside could provide dramatically better compensation, the nature of the work would not change. It would still be dirty, physically demanding, often dangerous work, with little job security and few prospects for promotion, often performed on inconvenient schedules (night shifts, weekends, etc.) or isolated job sites. For Mexican immigrants who work hard at them, such undesirable jobs can be a springboard to better, more remunerative jobs, perhaps in other sectors of the economy. But in the foreseeable future, entry-level work in these occupations is likely to remain unattractive to native-born workers, including the offspring of Mexican immigrants themselves.

Nevertheless, the "need" for Mexican immigrants to meet labor demand in the US economy is hotly debated among advocates and some academics. Mexican immigrants fill numerous occupational niches in the US economy today. They include manual labor in agriculture and horticulture, landscape and building maintenance, gardening, dishwashing in restaurants, car washing, horse grooming, meatpacking, roofing and other construction trades, housecleaning, hotel room cleaning, and many other low-skilled service jobs. Critics of Mexican immigration make much of national statistics showing that the majority of workers in these occupations are not Mexicans. Such statistics supposedly disprove the "need" for Mexican immigrants to fill low-skilled and physically demanding jobs in our economy. But national statistics may be almost meaningless for this purpose, because the key arbiter is actually supply and demand in local and regional labor markets. When one examines employment patterns in, say, California agriculture, or Arizona roofing, or Georgia carpet manufacturing, one finds that Mexican immigrants constitute a large majority of the labor force.

Anti-immigration activists and some academics have argued that, if the jobs currently filled by Mexicans cannot be "upgraded" sufficiently to attract native-born workers, those jobs should be eliminated, perhaps shipped overseas or eliminated through mechanization. But most service jobs must be performed *in situ*, and most labor-intensive industries in the United States have already reached the limits of substituting machines for workers, or else they produce goods that require extensive hand labor to satisfy consumers. The classic example is the tomato industry in northern states, where employers mechanized rapidly after the demise of the Bracero Program. The result was leathery tomatoes suitable for making ketchup but not for fresh salads. Agricultural employers in states like California depend on large amounts of manual labor, provided by Mexican immigrants, to harvest delicate crops like table grapes and tomatoes for high-end restaurants and supermarkets. In these cases, consumer tastes drive the demand for Mexican labor. In other industries, from many construction trades to horticulture to the breeding of racehorses, native-born workers often lack the willingness and expertise needed to do the jobs now performed by Mexican immigrants.

In macroeconomic and demographic terms, the need for Mexican immigrants to help replenish the US labor force and to finance social services to current and future retirees is clear. Because the United States population is aging and barely reproducing itself, the rate of labor force growth already has dropped sharply and is expected to decline further in coming decades. The nation's birth rate would be below replacement level if not for the higher than average fertility rates of today's immigrants. Mexican immigrants arriving today are also filling holes in the US labor force created by Americans not born in the 1990s. Future financing of public health care and retirement systems in the United States will depend increasingly on tax contributions from young immigrant workers.

For some native-born Americans, the fundamental issue posed by mass immigration from Mexico is not economic but rather, the increased ethnic, linguistic, and cultural diversity that this wave of immigration has introduced into the United States. These natives may not see Mexican immigrants as a threat to their personal economic interests, but they do fear the prospect of becoming an ethnic or cultural minority within their own city, state, or country. Persistent Spanish language use by Mexican immigrants is a particular lightning rod. Will native-born Americans someday have to speak Spanish to communicate with merchants, or postal clerks, or public school teachers? What happens if they do not buy into the "culture of multiculturalism"? Will natives' votes, their influence on the political process, be diluted as they become "minoritized"? Will today's Mexican immigrants resist assimilation into American society, perhaps paving the way to political separatism? Do their continued use of Spanish and other cultural behaviors signal a failure of assimilation? Perhaps, as nativists of the 1920s feared, the new immigrants are simply "inassimilable."

These concerns have gained much currency in mainstream public discourse over the last ten years, fueled by the writings of public intellectuals like the late Samuel P. Huntington of Harvard University, whose strongly anti-Mexican immigrant book, *Who Are We?*, became a national bestseller.[15] In Huntington's telling, the present, heavily Mexican wave of immigration presents a new and unprecedented threat to America's national identity. Unlike the Italian and other European communities of yesteryear, they argue, today's Mexican immigrant communities will never assimilate because their native language and cultural traditions are constantly being reinforced by new arrivals.

It is true that the United States is in the midst of demographic change, though not as dramatic as some restrictionists suggest. By 2050, non-Hispanic whites are projected to comprise fifty-two percent of the US population, while Hispanics will be twenty-nine percent (the rest consisting of blacks, Asians, and other ethnicities).[16] But there is no evidence that today's Mexican immigrants are resisting cultural assimilation. If anything, the evidence runs in the opposition direction. Spanish language use remains strong in

Mexicans often risk hardship and death to enter the United States.

the first generation but declines rapidly in the second and third generations. All but a small minority of second-generation Mexican Americans are English-dominant. First-generation Mexican immigrants continue speaking Spanish years after arriving in the United States mostly because they have not had the time and opportunity to master English. English as a Second Language classes are routinely oversubscribed in major American cities, and the strong demand for such instruction belies a lack of motivation on the part of immigrants themselves.

Despite their willingness to learn English, it is undeniable that Mexican immigrants have helped to diversify American cultural life, cuisine, and sports. But this diversity might as easily be celebrated as feared. For example, Mexican immigrants and their families have played a large role in the development of soccer in the United States. From youth soccer to adult amateur leagues to the professional game, Mexicans immigrants have been involved at all levels. Often made up of teams consisting of players from specific hometowns in Mexico, local soccer leagues bring together immigrants and their families on a weekly basis. Mexican immigrants have also made a strong impact on professional soccer in the United States. The Mexican national team has also recognized the importance of the American market, and often plays "home" games in the United States that draw tens of thousands of soccer fans.

Mexican immigrants can also be credited with helping to strengthen family life in the United States. Mexicans hold some of the strongest "family values" commitments in the country, a point usually overlooked by immigration critics who tend to focus on gang activity, drug-trafficking, and other forms of criminal behavior in communities with Mexican American majorities. In most cases, Mexican immigrant residents are even more incensed by crime in their communities than the nativists. First-generation Mexican immigrants also tend to have higher religiosity than the general population, and their participation has saved countless declining urban churches from oblivion.

One of the most frequent complaints of Americans who oppose Mexican immigration is that tolerating such immigration simply rewards Mexican elites for bad behavior. They ask, "If Mexico refuses to care for its own people, why should we?"[17] Mexican migrants themselves would be the first to criticize the performance of their home country government in creating jobs and educating its population to first-world standards. Indeed, by going to *el Norte* they have voted with their feet against the deficiencies of their home country's governance and economy. Moreover, it is clear from the survey data that poor economic conditions and lack of opportunity in Mexico have been the strongest motivations for heading north. This was particularly true during the economic recessions that gripped Mexico in 1975–1976, 1982–1988, and 2005–2006.

Still, surveys have consistently found that four out of five Mexican migrants cite economic opportunities in United States (pull factors) rather than economic and social conditions in Mexico (push factors) as most important in their decision to immigrate. The lure of the American Dream looms even larger when the presence of relatives based in the United States is included among the key reasons for migration. Political corruption remains endemic in many parts of Mexico and undoubtedly constrains local development in many ways. But if all the corrupt politicians, police, and businesses in Mexico were somehow to vanish, there would still be powerful economic and family incentives to migrate to the United States, as has been true for well over a century.

How are current US immigration policies affecting the Mexican immigrant community? The most evident consequences of tougher border enforcement since 1994 have been unintended. Millions of migrants who would otherwise return to Mexico have decided to settle permanently in the United States. American policy since 1994 has also created the most dangerous land border in the world. Unless they pay smugglers to take them through legal ports of entry, clandestine entrants are now exposed to extreme, life-threatening climate conditions in the deserts and mountains of the Southwest. The undocumented regularly succumb to dehydration, heat stroke, hypothermia, and drowning in irrigation canals and rivers that run along the US–Mexico border. Border crossing fatalities since 2000 now total nearly 7,000, in some years reaching 800 to 900.[18] And these statistics reflect only known deaths; unknown numbers of additional bodies likely lie undiscovered in remote areas. County coroners are sometimes forced to rent refrigerated trucks to supplement their limited storage facilities to handle the surplus of corpses discovered during summer months when triple-digit temperatures prevail.

People-smugglers, for their part, are now reportedly charging, on average, five times more than at the outset of the border enforcement buildup in 1994. Today, the going rate is reportedly $3,000 for a crossing through remote desert or mountainous areas, $5,000 for passing through a legal port of entry concealed in a vehicle or using false papers, and a similar amount for being smuggled by sea from Baja California fishing villages to the beaches of southern California. The "coyotes" have profited handsomely from the concentrated border enforcement operations introduced from 1994 to 2005 and continually reinforced by new infusions of money, personnel, and surveillance technology.[19]

With the failure of border enforcement to create a potent deterrent, pressure has mounted to develop new approaches. One result has been the "Enhanced Consequences Delivery" strategy, which has been implemented in various forms in several Border Patrol sectors beginning in 2006. The logic of this approach is to raise the legal penalties for illegal entry, especially repeat entries. Apprehended migrants are no longer automatically given the option of "voluntary departure" whereby they waive their right to an immigration hearing and board a bus back to Mexico within hours of apprehension. Rather, the immigrants must experience "consequences": they are incarcerated for at least a fortnight (and up to 180 days), put into federal judicial proceedings, and hauled before immigration judges, whose black robes and intimidating surroundings are supposed to strike fear into the hearts of undocumented immigrants. By this method, migrants guilty of clandestine entry—a civil offense, not a crime, under federal law— will leave the country with a record. Authorities then can escalate charges and jail time if a migrant is caught again. As a further deterrent, if a migrant is formally removed, he or she is barred from legal reentry for at least five years.

The efficacy of this approach remains unproven. It has not been fully implemented because of bottlenecks in the judicial system, especially lack of bed space for immigrant detainees and a lack of capacity in the court system. Even in heavily transited Border Patrol sectors like Tucson, only about one third of detained migrants were being processed through the criminal justice system as of spring 2011. Prospective migrants in Mexico are largely unaware of the new strategy, so it has had little deterrent effect on new migration. Nevertheless, immigration authorities seem convinced that they are building a better mousetrap with a greater potential to deter immigration, so implementation is likely to continue.

Identifying, rounding up and deporting undocumented immigrants in the American interior has long been advocated by anti-immigration organizations and certain members of Congress but until recently has been given short shrift in the allocation of federal enforcement resources, with the lion's share flowing into border enforcement. The balance is now shifting gradually toward interior enforcement. Beginning with the George W. Bush administration and accelerating under President Obama, immigration enforcement in the interior of the country—work-site raids and audits, traffic stops, surveillance of public transport and popular gathering places for migrants, mass deportations—has broken up tens of thousands of immigrant families. Under President Obama deportations reached record levels of nearly 400,000 per year, at a cost of nearly $5 billion to the federal government in the 2010 fiscal year alone—$12,500 for each deported immigrant.

Thus far, the main consequences of the shift toward interior enforcement have been to generate fear in the Mexican immigrant population, to discourage even legal immigrants from seeking needed medical care, and to chase migrants from one state or locality to another, from one employer or industry to another. For example, audits of employers' hiring records—the "silent raids" that quadrupled from 2009 to 2011[20]—have not removed a single undocumented migrant from the country. Undocumented workers summoned to interviews to account for anomalies in their Social Security numbers simply fail to show up. There is no evidence that those affected have left the country, or even the same locality where they had been working. If anything, federal and state worksite enforcement activity pushes undocumented migrants deeper into the underground

IMMIGRANT STRUGGLES, IMMIGRANT GIFTS

economy, into the hands of more exploitative employers who pay them in cash and do not withhold federal and state taxes.[21]

Traffic stops—supposedly conducted to detain drunk or unlicensed drivers but sometimes used as immigration enforcement—have become routine in many southwestern American cities. Local police have thus been recruited, sometimes unwillingly, into the business of detaining immigrants and turning them over to federal authorities. At best, detained immigrants who cannot show papers have their vehicles confiscated and pay a hefty fine. At worst, being stopped for a broken taillight puts them on the path to deportation.

"Attrition through enforcement" has become the mantra of today's anti-immigration groups. The logic of this approach to immigration control is that by making migrants' lives in the United States as miserable as possible they will be induced to give up and go home, to "self deport," the term first popularized by Governor Pete Wilson and revived in the Republican presidential primaries of 2012. This goal is to be accomplished by passing laws or ordinances that reduce undocumented immigrants' access to jobs, rental housing, medical care, health insurance, and public education for their children. An added benefit of this strategy, according to its proponents, is that potential new migrants will think twice before heading north.

There is, however, no evidence that the "immiseration" approach is working, in states and localities that have passed anti-immigrant laws and where federal immigration law is most strictly enforced. Mexican migrants are not "self deporting" in appreciable numbers, at least as a consequence of what is being done by governments to make their lives more difficult. According to estimates by the Pew Hispanic Center, the number of undocumented Mexicans living in the United States has been remarkably stable since 2007.[22] The Great Recession beginning in that year appears to have done more to shrink the number of Mexican immigrants and to discourage new migration from Mexico than anything that governments at all levels have done in the post-1994 era of immigration control.

The single most important step that could be taken to reduce stress on the Mexican immigrant community, to increase their income-earning (and thus their tax-paying) potential, and to develop their human capital would be a broad legalization program. Critics of such a program argue that it would function as a magnet for people who would not otherwise have migrated. The evidence from the IRCA legalization programs of the late 1980s shows a major spike in emigration from Mexican communities with a history of heavy American-bound migration, with new migration reaching a peak in 1988. There is no question that IRCA added a new impetus to female migration by encouraging wives to join their legalizing spouses in the United States. But the strictly IRCA-related migration surge lasted less than two years, and it is difficult to separate that pull from the push of Mexico's severe economic crisis of the 1980s.

The massive federal government investment in border enforcement since 1994—now approaching $40 billion—has yet to achieve its stated goal of keeping undocumented migrants out of the country or out of American labor markets. Evidence from more than 6,000 interviews with Mexican migrants conducted by the Mexican Migration Field Research Program at the University of California, San Diego since 2005 indicates that fewer than two out of five first attempts at illegal entry have resulted in apprehension, and among migrants caught on their first attempt, between ninety-two and ninety-eight percent succeeded in entering on the second or third try.

American policymakers and independent researchers debate the causes of the sharp drop in border apprehensions since 2007, falling to levels not seen since the 1960s. What explanatory weight should be assigned to tougher border enforcement as against depressed US labor market conditions during the Great Recession? Disentangling enforcement and macroeconomic effects is a major analytic challenge that has rarely been attempted, at least in rigorous empirical work.[23] But there is widespread consensus among academic researchers that the sharply downward trend in both border apprehensions and new migration flows from Mexico since 2007 is not just an "enforcement story."

A recently published study of immigration enforcement by the National Research Council concluded that rising levels of border enforcement have had little deterrent effect on undocumented migration from Mexico.[24] There are several reasons for this failure. One is that tougher enforcement on some segments of the border simply displaces the illegal entries, causing migrants to cross elsewhere. Another factor, even more important, is economic: earnings gains from migration still far outweigh border crossing costs. Field interview data show that border enforcement is more likely to discourage potential migrants when they also face lack of jobs in the United States. Deterrence results from the interaction of border enforcement and a weak American job market. The Great Recession that began in 2007 changed the calculus of expected returns to migration, causing some would-be migrants to postpone going north. If correct, this view suggests that as American job creation rebounds, border enforcement will have an even weaker effect on the probability of migration.

Despite the recession and despite unprecedented levels of border enforcement, new migration from Mexico has not ceased entirely, and it is premature to conclude that the era of mass undocumented migration has effectively ended. Future migration flows may never approximate those seen in the early 2000s, when immigration from Mexico to the United States was at its zenith. But absent the complete collapse of the US economy and an unimaginable development boom in Mexico that wipes out tremendous US–Mexico differentials in real wages and employment opportunities, there will continue to be strong incentives for migration. About eighty-five percent of Mexicans living in high-emigration towns today, and close to forty percent of Mexico's total population, have US-based relatives. This dynamic suggests a large potential for future family reunification migration. One way or another, this migration is likely to occur.

The current generation of Mexican immigrants, including the undocumented, is better positioned than any previous wave of Mexican migrants to succeed in the United States. Its members are significantly better educated, healthier, and speak more English than their predecessors. They are predominantly young and will spend the most productive years of their lives in the United States. There is no evidence that today's Mexican immigrants are on a fundamentally different path concerning economic incorporation and mobility than was followed by European immigrants from earlier generations.[25] Gaps persist between them and the native-born population in terms of educational attainment, occupational status, and income, but those disparities narrow over time.

If there is a serious cloud on the horizon, it is high secondary school dropout rates among Mexico-origin students—up to fifty percent in some urban school districts.

This trend reflects poor quality schools, barriers to employment that discourage students from staying in school, and the undocumented status of students or their parents. Even high school valedictorians who happen to be undocumented have no legal right to be employed in the United States once they graduate. Research shows that having an undocumented parent also drags down educational attainment among second-generation Mexican Americans.[26] Here, as well, a legalization program could significantly reduce the unacceptably high dropout rate in this population, both by raising family incomes and by providing incentives for legalized students to stay in school.

It is a vast human tragedy that an estimated 6.7 million undocumented Mexicans must continue to lead lives in the shadows, fearful of going to work, to the supermarket, to community clinics, and even to churches because of the risk of detection and deportation. These men and women want to be fully contributing members of American society. Those who would deny them that opportunity, by putting most of the United States' energy and resources into police measures to intimidate or "immiserate" undocumented immigrants, are sacrificing not only the economic contribution that these first generation immigrants could make, but the manifold, unimagined contributions of their children.

Endnotes

[1] See Kent A. Ono and John M. Sloop, *Shifting Borders: Rhetoric, Immigration, and California's Proposition 187.* (Philadelphia: Temple University Press, 2002).

[2] Timothy J. Dunn, *Blockading the Border and Human Rights: The El Paso Operation that Remade Immigration Enforcement* (Austin: University of Texas Press, 2010) offers an excellent history of the El Paso operation.

[3] For an overview of what has been happening in immigration policy at the state and local levels, see Monica Varsanyi, ed., *Taking Local Control: Immigration Policy Activism in U.S. Cities and States* (Stanford: Stanford University Press, 2010).

[4] See Abraham Hoffman, *Unwanted Mexican Americans in the Great Depression: Repatriation Pressures, 1929–1939* (Tucson: University of Arizona Press, 1974).

[5] Jeffrey Passel and D'Vera Cohn, "A Portrait of Unauthorized Immigrants in the United States," Pew Hispanic Center, Washington, DC, April 14, 2009, http://www.pewhispanic.org/2009/04/14/a-portrait-of-unauthorized-immigrants-in-the-united-states.

[6] This remains the case, but in the last ten years Mexican immigrants have begun to fan out across the country, working and settling in cities in the Midwest, Southeast, and Northeast that had not previously hosted substantial Mexican communities. This increased geographic dispersion reflects higher rates of job growth in these non-traditional destinations, relative to long-standing gateway cities like Los Angeles and Chicago. Migrant networks are developing in these "new destination" cities, attracting migrants directly from Mexico. See Robert C. Smith, *Mexican New York* (Berkeley: University of California Press, 2005), and Douglas S. Massey, ed., New Faces in *New Places: The Changing Geography of American Immigration* (New York: Russell Sage Foundation, 2010).

[7] Nancy Rytina, "IRCA Legalization Effects: Lawful Permanent Residence and Naturalization through 2001," paper presented at the conference on "The Effects of Immigrant Legalization Programs on the United States," National Institutes of Health Main Campus, October 25, 2002, http://www.dhs.gov/xlibrary/assets/statistics/publications/irca0114int.pdf.

[8] Gianmarco I.P. Ottaviano, Giovanni Peri, and Greg C. Wright, "Immigration, Offshoring, and American Jobs," National Bureau of Economic Research Working Paper No. 16439, 2010, accessed June 15, 2012, http://www.nber.org/papers/w16439.

[9] Immigration Policy Center, "Unauthorized Immigrants Pay Taxes, Too," IPC Policy Brief, April 18, 2011, http://www.immigrationpolicy.org/sites/default/files/docs/Tax_Contributions_by_Unauthorized_Immigrants_041811.pdf.

[10] Eduardo Porter, "Illegal Immigrants Are Bolstering Social Security with Billions," *The New York Times*, April 5, 2005.

[11] Tracy Vericker, Karina Fortuny, Kenneth Finegold, and Sevgi Bayram Ozdemir, *Effects of Immigration on WIC and NSLP Caseloads* (Washington, DC: The Urban Institute, Research Report, August 2010).

[12] See Gordon H. Hanson, *The Economic Logic of Illegal Immigration* (New York: Council on Foreign Relations, Council Special Report No. 26, April 2007).

[13] Philip Martin and Elizabeth Midgley, "Immigration in America 2010," *Population Bulletin Update*, Population Research Bureau, June 2010, 2.

[14] Quoted in Jonathan Tilove, "Strange Bedfellows: Unintended Consequences and the Curious Contours of the Immigration Debate," in Carol Miller Swain, ed., *Debating Immigration* (New York and Cambridge: Cambridge University Press, 2007), 215.

[15] Samuel P. Huntington, *Who Are We?—The Challenges to America's National Identity* (New York: Simon & Schuster, 2005).

[16] Martin and Midgley, "Immigration in America 2010," 3, figure 2.

[17] Personal communication to the author from a reader of *The Los Angeles Times*.

[18] Wayne A. Cornelius, "Controlling 'Unwanted' Immigration: Lessons from the United States, 1993–2004," *Journal of Ethnic and Migration Studies*, 31, no. 4 (2005): 775–94; US General Accountability Office, "Illegal Immigration: Border-Crossing Deaths Have Doubled Since 1995," Report #GAO-06-770, August 2006, http://www.gao.gov/new.items/d06770.pdf; and Maria Jiménez, "Humanitarian Crisis: Migrant Deaths at the US-Mexico Border," Mexican National Commission of Human Rights and American Civil Liberties Union of San Diego and Imperial Counties, October 1, 2009, http://www.aclu.org/files/pdfs/immigrants/humanitari-ancrisisreport.pdf.

[19] For a detailed case study of the people-smuggling industry and how it has become embedded in the social fabric of Mexican migration to the United States, see David Spener, *Clandestine Crossings: Migrants and Coyotes on the Texas-Mexico Border* (Ithaca, NY: Cornell University Press, 2009).

[20] Mirian Jordan, "More 'Silent Raids' Over Immigration," *The Wall Street Journal*, June 16, 2011.

[21] See Magnus Lofstrom, Sarah Bohn, and Steven Raphael, "Lessons from the 2007 Legal Arizona Workers Act," Public Policy Institute of California, San Francisco, CA, March 2011, http://www.ppic.org/content/pubs/report/R_311MLR.pdf.

[22] Jeffrey S. Passel and D'Vera Cohn, "Unauthorized Immigrant Population: National and State Trends, 2010," Pew Hispanic Center, Washington, DC, February 1, 2011, http://www.pewhispanic.org/files/reports/133.pdf.

[23] For an exception, see Scott Borger and Leah Muse-Orlinoff, "Economic Crisis vs. Border Enforcement: What Matters Most to Prospective Migrants?" in Wayne A. Cornelius, et al., ed., *Mexican Migration and the U.S. Economic Crisis: A Transnational Perspective* (La Jolla, CA and Boulder, CO: UCSD Center for Comparative Immigration Studies and Lynne Rienner Publishers, 2010), 95–103.

[24] National Research Council of the National Academies of Science, *Budgeting for Immigration Enforcement* (Washington, D.C.: The National Academies Press, 2011), 33–36.

[25] See, for example, Joel Perlmann, *Italians Then, Mexicans Now: Immigrant Origins and Second-generation Progress, 1890 to 2000* (New York: Russell Sage Foundation, 2005).

[26] Frank D. Bean, "Unauthorized Mexican Migration: Effects on Second-Generation Educational Attainment," paper presented at the Third Annual University of California International Migration Conference, Center for Comparative Immigration Studies, University of California-San Diego, February 10, 2012.

A group of Muslim immigrants who arrived at Ellis Island from the Turkish Empire in the early part of the twentieth century.

CHAPTER | 11

MUSLIM AMERICANS

By David M. Reimers

In 2010, what was meant as a gesture of religious toleration by a group of American Muslims drew some of the most visible and vehement anti-Muslim rhetoric in recent American history. The controversy started with what should have been an innocuous idea: the construction of an Islamic community center in lower Manhattan modeled after the famous Ninety-second Street YMHA (better known as 92Y), a highly regarded Jewish organization. Conceived by a group of Muslim developers and the Sufi imam Feisal Abdul Rauf, the project was intended to promote interfaith dialogue and was initially dubbed "Cordoba House," after the Andalusian city that formed a rare oasis of religious intermingling in an otherwise intolerant medieval Spain. The center was later rebranded "Park 51," a reference to its street address on Park Place.

The project's opponents were especially rankled by the location of the proposed center, two blocks from the site of the destruction of the World Trade Center by terrorists on September 11, 2001. In fact, wreckage from the plane that struck the South Tower also badly damaged the building where Imam Feisal proposed to build Park 51. He and the other planners had picked the location in part as a reminder of the several hundred Muslims killed in the attacks and as a rejoinder to those who imagined 9/11 had been staged by the religion of Islam itself, rather than by radical Islamic extremists. A memorial to 9/11 and its victims was included in the center's plans. The idea of the center, Imam Feisal told the *New York Times* in 2009, "sends the opposite statement to what happened on 9/11. We want to push back against the extremists."[1]

This message proved too subtle for many. Although early planning for the project passed largely without comment, New Yorkers protested vehemently as the developers steered the project over legal and zoning hurdles. In May 2010, a Manhattan community board meeting featured four hours of raucous debate over the project's application in which a hundred people spoke, some of them carrying signs reading, "Show respect for 9/11. No mosque." A mosque, in fact, was only one component of the planned thirteen-story complex, which was also to include a food court, a gym, a theater, and a swimming pool.

Still, the widespread identification between the September 11 attacks and the religion of Islam made the center's location seem like a deliberate provocation to many, a sort of triumphal victory monument by the terrorist perpetrators of the attack. "The pain never goes away," said one attendee at the community board meeting, whose son had been killed on September 11. "When I look over there and I see a mosque, it's going to hurt. Build it someplace else."[2] Nevertheless, the board approved the application by a vote of twenty-nine to one, with ten abstentions.

Despite the stirrings of a popular outcry against the project, it retained the support of important political figures like Manhattan borough president Scott Stringer and Mayor Michael Bloomberg. By July, both the city council and the Landmarks Preservation Commission had approved the construction of Park 51. Mayor Bloomberg was particularly outspoken in defense of the proposed center. He claimed that the opposition reminded him of the anti-Semitism he had encountered as a youth growing up outside of Boston. Of those who lost their lives in the World Trade Center, he said, "We do not honor their lives by denying the very constitutional rights they died protecting. We honor their lives by defending those rights and freedoms that the terrorists attacked."[3]

The battle over Park 51 escalated in street demonstrations and in the courts. Marchers in the annual Muslim Day Parade seemed particularly supportive of the center, while "anti-mosque" demonstrators thronged the area around Ground Zero. The Fire Fighters Union, which lost many members on 9/11, joined the chorus of voices criticizing the proposal and planned to hire lawyers to fight the building's approval. One individual fire fighter sued on his own to kill the project, arguing that the city Landmarks Preservation Commission had been unfairly pressured by the mayor to grant approval.

The uproar was by no means limited to residents of New York City. At the state level, former governor George Pataki criticized the location of the planned center while Congressman Peter King and gubernatorial candidate Rick Lazio both called for an investigation into its finances. Several months later, King held hearings in his capacity as chairman of the House Homeland Security Committee to examine an alleged connection between American Muslims and terrorism. Even before the Park 51 controversy, the Long Island Republican had been one of the loudest voices in Congress proclaiming the threat posed by radicalization within the Muslim American community. His remarks and hearings came under sharp attack by Muslims and non-Muslims alike and drew little support from fellow Republicans.[4]

Nationally, the story of the "Ground Zero mosque" caught the attention of bloggers, Tea Party activists, and conservative politicians. Numerous high-profile officials assailed the "insensitivity" and "provocation" of the proposed center. Republican presidential aspirant and former speaker of the house Newt Gingrich compared the center's location to "putting a Nazi sign next to the Holocaust Museum" and even appeared in a TV ad to further proclaim his disapproval.[5] Former vice-presidential candidate Sarah Palin also joined the fray with a now-famous twitter message: "Ground Zero Mosque supporters: doesn't it stab you in the heart, as it does ours throughout the heartland? Peaceful Muslims, pls refudiate."[6] The opposition of the Anti-Defamation League, a Jewish advocacy group and longtime defender of religious freedom, was particularly upsetting to many of the project's supporters.

The signs in the photograph read:

"NO MOSQUE IN THE GROUND ZERO AREA! PRESERVE THE DIGNITY OF OUR LOVED ONES KILLED HERE ON 9/11!"

"WHAT WOULD MAKE TERRORIST #1 OSAMA BIN LADEN MORE HAPPY, THAN A MOSQUE DOMINATING OVER THE ASHES OF HIS VICTIMS— OUR FALLEN AMERICANS?"

Others, locally and nationally, came to the center's defense. To the charge that Imam Feisal was using Park 51 to advance an extremist agenda, the project's backers held up the cleric's moder-

Protesters against the Park 51 project equated the religion of Islam with 9/11 terrorists.

ate credentials and his numerous goodwill tours to the Middle East on behalf of the State Department. When President Barack Obama weighed in on the subject, he defended the center's right to religious freedom and emphasized the distinction between terrorism and Islam. The president made his remarks at the White House's *Iftar* celebration, breaking the annual Ramadan fast. Later, Obama softened his support of the project, arguing that the plan may have been legal and constitutional, but not advisable or wise.

A poll revealed that most New Yorkers disapproved of Park 51, even though a majority agreed there were no valid legal grounds to stop it. Even a number of New York City Muslims expressed reservations.[7] Across the Hudson River, a New Jersey transit worker was so upset about Park 51 that he joined with other opponents in a demonstration to burn the Koran. When the New Jersey Transit Authority fired him, however, the American Civil Liberties Union took up his cause and thus came to sit on both sides of the controversy. The man's defenders pointed out that he did not wear any symbols of the Transit Authority while burning the Koran and was exercising his First Amendment right to free speech. In April 2011, the court agreed and the worker was restored to his job.

The building's last legal obstacle was cleared in July 2011 when a judge denied standing to the former 9/11 fire fighter who had tried to sue the city. But at the time of this book's publication the center's prospects remained in doubt, and the building may yet founder on financial rather than legal or religious shoals: in March 2011 the planners announced that some backers had withdrawn their financial support and that "no management staff has been hired, no members have been named to the project's [formal] board, and no money has been raised."[8]

While Park 51 monopolized the headlines because of its proximity to the site of the World Trade Center, other Muslims seeking to build mosques also encountered suspicion, obstruction, or worse. In the borough of Staten Island at about the same time, a group attempting to convert an unused Roman Catholic convent into a mosque met with stiff and unexpected opposition. During a hearing on the proposal, one woman asked, "Wouldn't you agree that every terrorist, past and present, has come out of a mosque?" When Ayhman Hammous, president of the Staten Island branch of the Muslim American Society, responded that he did not, his answer was drowned out by catcalls and boos from the crowd of a packed gymnasium. The Catholic Church and the American Muslim Society were ultimately forced to drop the project.[9]

Similar controversies have derailed or disrupted plans for mosques in Tennessee, Ohio, Wisconsin, and California. In Temecula, California, opponents brought dogs to a hearing on the expansion of a mosque because some Muslims hold dogs to be unclean. In another hearing over the same project, one woman spoke of her anxieties concerning Islam itself:

> As a mother and a grandmother, I worry. I learned that in twenty years with the rate of birth population, we will be overtaken by Islam, and their goal is to get people in Congress and the Supreme Court to see that Shariah [Islamic law] is implemented. My children and grandchildren will have to live under that.

In 2010, Muslims made up less than two percent of the nation's more than 300 million persons. For the woman's grandchildren to live in an Islamic state would require a widespread conversion of Americans to Islam, a tremendous and unprecedented influx of Muslim immigrants, or astronomical changes in the Muslim birth rate.

Her understanding of Islam also left something to be desired. "I do believe everybody has a right to freedom of religion," the woman went on. "But Islam is not about religion. It's a political government, and it's a hundred percent against our Constitution."[10] While eccentric, this view is far from rare. To some, Islam represents a foundational threat to American political liberty. A Brooklyn-based lawyer named David Yerushalmi has been organizing a grass roots campaign to lobby states to bar the inclusion of any aspect of Shariah in American laws—this despite the lack of any visible organized efforts to do so. Yerushalmi attracted many followers and got several states to enact his proposals.

In northeastern Illinois, yet another controversy flared when the pastor of the Reformed Church of Palos Heights put his church up for sale. The Chicago-based Al Salam Mosque Foundation wanted to purchase the building, but resistance quickly surfaced in public hearings held by the city council of this overwhelming white and Christian community. The city council offered to pay the foundation to walk away from their bid and the foundation accepted the offer, a move that many local Muslims found craven. The mayor of Palos Heights, in turn, vetoed the buyout. In an environment of universally bruised feelings, the foundation responded by suing the town for religious discrimination. Remarked the lawyer for Al Salam, "There was a cloud hanging over us in terms of not being welcomed by the city. And then the buyout offer was made and vetoed. We were really left with no choice."[11]

How did mosques come to play such a heated and divisive role in American life in the early twenty-first century? Until recently, the presence of Muslims—and mosques—was scarcely visible in the United States at all. One obvious reason for the change has been the general backlash against Islam in the wake of the September 11 attacks. But the past decades have also seen a very real rise in the number of immigrants from Africa, the Middle East, South Asia, and other parts of the world where Islam claims many of its adherents. While talk of an impending Muslim "takeover" is wildly overblown, it is true that the Muslim presence in America is larger than it has ever been before in the country's history.

Islam probably first appeared in the United States in the crews of European sailors and explorers. While the ships sailed under the flags of individual nations, their crews were often men of varied origins and homelands, including areas such as North Africa or Eastern Europe where Islam flourished. Yet these explorers did not leave any significant religious mark on American society. They were largely paid hands, who came to seek the riches of the New World.

The first Muslims to settle permanently came from Africa as enslaved people. There is no record of how many of the approximately 450,000 slaves transported from Africa to the United States were Muslims—and they themselves left no written record on this subject—but the forced immigrants hailed from parts of West Africa where Islam was strong. References can be found in newspaper advertisements for runaway slaves and in the notes of slaveholders indicating that at least some of them must have been followers of Islam. A few African Muslims, such as Bilali Muhammad or Salih Bilali, appear to have been slave drivers. Muslim slaves were often called "Moors," a common European word of the day referring to North Africans.

In any event, no slaves organized mosques and few left accounts of their religious beginnings. What most white Americans knew of Islam during the late eighteenth and early nineteenth centuries came from contacts and intermittent wars with the Barbary pirates off the coast of North Africa. Among the African American slaves, those few who maintained vestiges of Islamic culture did so largely on their own. In the course of the eighteenth and nineteenth centuries, evangelical Protestantism came to dominate African American communities. The World's Parliament of Religions, held in conjunction with the Columbian Exposition in Chicago in 1893, featured nearly 200 speakers from a wide variety of religions, yet there were only two representing Islam and neither was African American.

With the exception of the unknown numbers of Muslims among the slave population, there were very few Muslim immigrants of any description until the age of mass migration in the late nineteenth century. In that period, an unlikely group of people—American Protestant missionaries—became the unwitting agents of Muslim immigration from the Middle East. The missionaries did not win many Muslim converts to Christianity and as a general rule did not even try, focusing their efforts instead on Eastern Orthodox Christian Arabs. Yet by promoting the United States in the Middle East, the missionaries did manage to instigate a general wave of immigration from that region. The missionaries established hospitals, schools, and colleges (the most notable being the American University of Beirut) and persuaded a number of their converts to seek a better life and education in America. Beginning in the 1870s, the general interest in immigration caught on among Muslims as well, often men from the Syrian province of the Ottoman Empire (today's Syria, Lebanon, Jordan, and Palestine).

In the years before the First World War, immigration from Turkey ran to nearly 25,000 and was probably the main source of Muslims in the United States. As economic conditions deteriorated, thousands more from outside Turkey left for America in the years before World War I. Exactly how many is difficult to determine because the federal government did not (and still does not) record religion in immigration statistics. Estimates range from several thousand to a dubious figure of 60,000. They were recorded as coming from "Turkey in Asia" and eventually as "Syrians."[12]

Once in the United States, many Middle Eastern immigrants Anglicized their names: from Muhammad to Mo, from Rashid to Dick. One such immigrant was A. Joseph Hawar, a Muslim who arrived from Palestine via India and England in 1903:

> My true name is Mohammed Asa Abu-Howah. But people I met on the boat told me I'd better change my name. They said it labeled me as a Muslim, and no immigration officer would allow a Muslim to enter the United States. I had two cousins who'd become American citizens. One had taken the name of Abraham and the other Joseph. So I took both those names, and since the British had pronounced Howah as if it were Howar, I made my American name A. Joseph Howar. That's how I was naturalized in 1908.

Some Arabs had to go to court to be recognized as white, for only "white persons" and persons of "African descent" were permitted to naturalize. Middle Easterners ultimately won their cases and were widely allowed to naturalize as whites.

In addition to racism and religious intolerance, many Muslim immigrants also confronted a basic unfamiliarity with the norms and culture of the United States. A. Joseph Howar continued his immigration story thus:

> When I reached New York, one of the immigration officers asked me where I was going. I didn't know. So I asked him, "Where does your king live?" He laughed at me. "We don't have a king in America," he said; "we have a President, and Washington, D.C." "Then I'll go to Washington, D.C.," I told him; "if it's good enough for the President, it's good enough for me."[13]

Once in Washington, DC, Howar's experience mirrored that of many early Arab Muslims in America. He found work in a variety of jobs—as a kitchen hand, as a peddler of women's clothing, as shop proprietor, and finally as a successful building contractor. Most of the Arab Muslims were laborers or peddlers, and later some opened grocery stores and other ethnic shops catering to their fellow nationals.

The Middle East was not the only source of Muslim immigrants during this period. A few also came from Eastern Europe and were sometimes labeled "Russian Tartar Moslems." Some were Albanians fleeing the mayhem of the Balkan Wars just before World War I. Others were Bosnian Muslims whose aim, like many from southern and eastern Europe during this time, was to find temporary work in America and return home with savings. A few Muslims probably also came from India, for that region included the future Islamic nations of Pakistan and Bangladesh.

The turn-of-the-century wave of Muslims was cut short by the legal restrictions on American immigration enacted in the wake of the First World War. Due to their relatively small numbers, Muslims were scarcely mentioned in the wartime and interwar debates over who was desirable (and who was not), but the effect of the legislation was nevertheless to stem immigration from many Muslim countries. In 1917, Congress created an "Asiatic Barred Zone" that banned immigration from large regions of Asia, including India and much of the Middle East. In 1924, the lawmakers designed a new system that reaffirmed the ban on East Asian immigration and allocated extremely small quotas to Middle Eastern countries. Turks, for example, had a quota of only one hundred. During the lean economic times of the Great Depression, the bans were tightly enforced; only 700,000 immigrants of any kind were recorded during the 1930s and World War II.[14]

The small Muslim community in America did build a few mosques and purchased land for burial grounds during these years. One key figure was Satti Majid, known as the "Sheikh of Islam in North America." Under his leadership, the Detroit Muslim community established a Muslim cemetery and mosque at the cost of $55,000 in the early 1920s.[15] Other mosques sprung up in southern Maine, New York, Chicago, and Iowa. In typical immigrant fashion, Muslim Americans also founded societies for community improvement and maintained some contact with the lands of their birth.

Even as restrictive legislation kept out Muslims from abroad, the Muslim American community changed and expanded greatly from within during this time, a development that would shape the experience of future generations of Muslim immigrants. The new Muslims in the United States were not themselves immigrants but African Americans. The first of the black Muslim converts in the twentieth century were led by Timothy Drew, who called himself Noble Drew Ali and founded the Moorish Science Temple in the 1920s. Ali had visions of an eclectic "Islamism" in the United States and preached a return to Africa for black Americans. Whether Muslim immigrants influenced his ideology is unknown, but neither the Muslim immigrant community nor the Near Eastern community recognized him. In the end, the Moorish Science Temple drew few followers.

Of more lasting significance was the Nation of Islam. The group was established in Detroit in 1930, and some accounts identify the mysterious figure of Wallace D. Fard as the movement's founder. He was a peddler and almost certainly an immigrant, either from Afghanistan or Saudi Arabia. Fard urged African Americans to reject white culture, prepare for an apocalyptic race war, and recover their true roots in Islam. His successor, Elijah Muhammad, perpetuated Fard's teachings and built up a vast network of schools, businesses, real estate holdings, and mosques from his headquarters in Chicago. The charismatic civil rights leader Malcolm X became the Nation of Islam's public face during the 1950s. He later suffered a falling out with Elijah Muhammad and formed his own organization, which he led until his assassination in 1965. Immigrant Muslims, for their part, did not immediately embrace the Nation of Islam's black Muslims, even though both groups largely embraced the orthodox precepts of the Sunni sect. Gradually, many black Muslims moved closer to traditional Islam, especially after the rise in 1975 of Elijah Muhammad's more moderate successor (and son) Warith Dean Muhammad.

Following World War II, American policy changed to make the immigration of large numbers of Muslims possible once again. Restrictions were lifted on Asians who had been barred and new Middle Eastern nations received moderate quotas. When Congress overhauled the country's immigration laws in 1965, the old quotas favoring Western Europeans were abolished and the gates were thrown open to newcomers from Asia and the Middle East. Under the new system, all Eastern Hemisphere countries were given quotas of 20,000. So for example, when Bangladesh broke off from Pakistan in 1971, it received 20,000 new slots.

Equal quotas did not immediately guarantee major migrations. In the mid-1960s, few Muslim countries had significant family ties or migration networks in place to facilitate the flow of people to the United States. Indonesia, which became independent in 1949, is the largest Muslim nation in the world, but Indonesian migration to the United States has been relatively small. Pakistan has the world's second-largest Islamic population, but until the last few years Pakistanis have tended to migrate to Great Britain rather than to America. Much the same was true for Bangladesh, which only began sending large numbers of immigrants to America in the last two decades. India also has a large Muslim population, but most Indian immigrants to America—even since the 1960s—have been Hindus or Sikhs.[16]

Among countries with large Muslim populations, the Arab and other Islamic nations of the Middle East were the main beneficiaries of the revised quotas. At first, Christians and Jews were dominant in these countries' immigrant streams. But Muslims increasingly showed up as well, especially after sustained bouts of political violence and a series of wars between Israel and its neighbors during the 1960s and 1970s. But not all of the new Muslim immigrants were Arabs. Turkey, an overwhelmingly Islamic nation, sent growing numbers to the United States. In addition, roughly 300,000 Iranians settled in America after the Islamic revolution of 1979.[17] Smaller numbers of Muslim refugees also came in the wake of American-led wars in Iraq in 1991, Afghanistan in 2001, and again in Iraq in 2003.[18]

Around the end of the twentieth century, the American Muslim community swelled with a new group of blacks. These were not African Americans, as during the 1950s, but rather first-generation immigrants from Africa, the population of which is about half Muslim. The largest group of Africans came as government-sponsored refugees from war-torn Somalia. Because of the active role of Minnesota refugee organizations, the biggest Somali community was in Minneapolis, but some Somalis also found their way to Atlanta.[19] From West Africa, the biggest group was Senegalese, many of whom settled in New York City (sometimes on expired tourist visas). As a group the Senegalese were highly educated (like African immigrants generally), but many of the newcomers nevertheless had to scramble for menial labor jobs or peddle goods on the streets of Brooklyn or Queens.

Exactly how many of these new immigrants after the 1970s were Muslims cannot be ascertained with any accuracy. A few religious organizations have claimed the number of Muslims in the United States to be as high as eleven million; scholars have suggested seven million would be a more reasonable figure.[20] The newcomers settled throughout the United States, and especially in cities such as New York, Los Angeles, and Detroit. This broad pattern of dispersal has called the attention of many Americans to Islam as a growing force in American society.

The Islamic Center of America, Dearborn, Michigan. The Detroit metropolitan area, especially around Dearborn, has one of the largest concentrations of Muslim immigrants in the country.

Whatever their numbers and wherever their homes, Muslims in America are a remarkably diverse group; indeed, the American Islamic population is the most diverse of any country in the world. Perhaps one-third is African American, with the rest divided among Asians, Middle Easterners, and smaller numbers of Africans. This diversity reflects the general demographic shift in the United States' over the past forty years. At the end of World War II, about eighty-eight percent of the American population was European in origin. By 2010, that group represented roughly two-thirds of the population, with the rest divided among African Americans and growing numbers of Asians, Latinos, and foreign-born blacks. In this sense, American Muslims are a mirror of the changing demography that is making the United States a "world nation," representing peoples from all parts of the globe.

In the last four decades, the new Muslim immigration has met an ambivalent response. Exactly because Islam is such a diverse phenomenon in the United States, presenting a thousand different faces of varied origins and colors, its adherents have sometimes avoided being targeted (or even recognized) as Muslims. Stereotypes do exist, however. Sometimes they are based on international news events rather than contact with actual American Muslims. Beginning with the oil crises in the 1970s, the media has widely portrayed Arabs and Middle Easterners as greedy profiteers. Against the backdrop of the Israeli-Palestinian conflict and other violence in the Middle East, Muslims have also been cast as terrorist fanatics. The bombing of the World Trade Center in 1993, attacks on American military personnel in Muslim countries overseas, and the shocking events of September 11, 2001 reinforced this view.

In the aftermath of 9/11, the denunciation of Muslims in America was fierce and wide-ranging. "In its long history of immigration," wrote the Middle East scholar Daniel Pipes, "the United States has never encountered so violent-prone and radicalized a community as the Muslims who have arrived since 1965."[21] The conservative columnist Ann Coulter, also writing after 9/11, went further:

> This is no time to be punctilious about locating the exact individuals directly involved in this particular terrorist attack. Those responsible include anyone anywhere in the world who smiled in response to the annihilation of patriots. ... The nation has been invaded by a fanatical, murderous cult. ... We should invade their countries, kill their leaders, and convert them to Christianity. We weren't punctilious about locating and punishing only Hitler and his top officers. We carpet-bombed German cities; we killed civilians. That's war. And this is war."[22]

This apocalyptic language may have been unusual in extremity, but not in kind.

The onslaught was not merely rhetorical: American Muslims, religious organizations, and government agencies reported a pattern of intimidation and discrimination after 9/11. A number of women who chose to wear a *hijab* (head scarf) reported being harassed or asked to leave their jobs. One such woman in Delaware, who had been fired from a shoe store, took her case to the Equal Opportunity Employment Commission. The company offered her job back but she declined. "I normally have tough skin," she later said, "but I'm very sensitive when it comes to my religion. The whole thing was very embarrassing. This is America, not a third-world country."[23]

The federal government responded to 9/11 by seeking out Arabs who might be connected in any way with 9/11 or terrorism generally. Immigration policy began to focus on terrorism prevention rather than economic opportunity or family reunification. The federal government rounded up thousands of Arabs for questioning and held some of them for weeks without access to a lawyer. Despite these draconian measures, the government found no direct ties between the American Muslim community and al-Qaeda, the organization behind the attacks. The main effect of these proceedings was the deportation of several thousand Arab Americans. In addition, the authorities tightened rules for immigrants entering from predominately Islamic nations, mainly in the Middle East.

These popular and government reactions created an environment of fear, confusion, and trauma among American Muslims, especially Arabs. Many Muslims reported that they were afraid to go outside or to show any outward signs of their religion, such as wearing a headscarf. One Yemeni-born man recounted his anguish to an interviewer:

> I really did go through a depression. I had no goals. I thought there is nothing worth going for. ... I thought I might have to go drop out of school. ... I might have to move back to the Middle East. ... We were afraid. People on the radio were saying we were all going to be deported—every Arab, every Muslim shipped away.[24]

The New York City Police responded to 9/11 with its own program to seek out terrorists or potentially dangerous Muslims in the city's midst. With the cooperation of the FBI, the police force set up an intelligence division to observe mosques, college campuses, and student organizations. Many faculty members and students—as well as members of the New York City Council—were outraged when these activities became public. One incident involved the investigators infiltrating Muslim student groups that participated in recreational paintball outings; the agents were convinced that the paintball sessions were in fact paramilitary instruction for radicals-in-training. A member of a Muslim student organization at Brooklyn College reacted to the idea with scorn: "You could say the same thing about football. You know, football's violent. They could say 'They're trying to teach Muslims how to hit.'"[25]

Other parts of the American government fortunately refrained from such suspicions. President George W. Bush even went out of his way to reassure the nation that the vast majority of Muslims in the country were loyal Americans. When the president met with Islamic leaders in the White House only two months after 9/11, he extended warm greetings to Muslims throughout the United States and around the world during Ramadan.[26] Secretary of State Colin Powell also hosted prominent American Muslim leaders for an *Iftar* dinner at the State Department. It was within this context of outreach to Muslims around the world that the State Department initially enlisted the imam Feisal Abdul Rauf for international goodwill tours. President Barrack Obama followed in the footsteps of the Bush administration in trying to reassure American Muslims that they were welcome in the United States.

For its part, the Muslim community issued repeated assurances that Islam was not a terrorist religion and offered an outpouring of statements condemning the attacks. Clerics were particularly vocal in drawing the line between terrorist violence and their religion. A number of American Muslims also supported—and in some cases have actually fought in—the ensuing war in Afghanistan against al-Qaeda and its Taliban protectors. James Yee, a Chinese American Muslim convert and Muslim chaplain for the US Army, expressed the views of many Muslims in the armed services when he said, "An act of terrorism, the taking of innocent civilian lives, is prohibited by Islam, and whoever has done this needs to be brought to justice, whether he is Muslim or not."[27]

The growing presence of Muslims in the armed forces was a trend already well underway before 9/11. The United States military installed its first Muslim chaplain in 1993, at a time when some 2,500 service members identified themselves as Muslim. By 2001, the number of Muslim chaplains had risen to fourteen and the number of Muslims in uniform to about 4,000. In fact, the latter figure is likely to be much higher, since many Muslims elect not to reveal their religion on their enlistment papers. Still, the culture of the military has changed markedly in the past twenty years. "Muslims can now feel themselves becoming a little more mainstream," said Abdul-Rasheed Muhammad, the army's first Muslim chaplain.[28]

Outside the military, in American society at large, this has also been true. A 2007 Pew Research Center poll among American Muslims indicated that most still believed America was the land of opportunity and their communities were excellent places to thrive if they worked hard.[29] A Gallup poll also revealed that most Muslim Americans considered themselves to be economically well off and politically moderate.[30] In this, the United States forms a sharp contrast with some Western European countries, where the reception accorded to Muslim immigrants has been notably chillier and where Muslim neighborhoods have been the site of intense rioting. Compared to their American counterparts, Western European Muslims are economically impoverished, socially constrained, and politically alienated.

It is true that since 9/11 there have been several attacks or attempted attacks by American Muslims connected to Islamist extremism or al-Qaeda. The most notorious of these incidents came in 2009, when a US Army major shot and killed twelve of his fellow soldiers at Fort Hood, Texas. The following year, an American-born man of Pakistani descent unsuccessfully tried to explode a car bomb in Times Square in the heart of New York City. In general, however, American Muslims have been responsible for a very small fraction of all domestic terrorism incidents in the United States. Moreover, Muslim communities have assisted law enforcement agencies in identifying al-Qaeda operatives and thwarting as many as a half of that organization's plots against the United States in the last several years.[31]

The events of 9/11 made many American Muslim leaders realize the necessity of political organization and alliances with other minorities, especially in areas of foreign policy, civil liberties, and hate crimes. One such alliance has sprung up between Muslims and Indian Sikhs. Even more so than the Muslim community, Sikhs in the United States were targeted in the aftermath of 9/11 due to their dark skin, long beards, and religiously mandated turbans. In response, Muslims and Sikhs began to hold discussions on how to deal with the violence. "It would be antithetical to our faith to have materials saying, 'We are not Muslims,'" said one Sikh in Boston. "It's understandable that people now are worried about being mistaken for Muslims, but we have to be very careful not to do that."[32]

Using politics to secure their rights and advance their interests, Muslims faced two problems: relatively small numbers and high proportions of unnaturalized or unregistered immigrants among those numbers. In 2006, voters in Minneapolis elected Keith Ellison, a black Democrat, as the first Muslim to Congress. A convert to Islam at age nineteen, Ellison was a defense attorney and state representative who hailed from an African American family in Detroit. He downplayed his faith during the campaign, but was certainly buoyed by the large Somali Muslim community in Minneapolis. Two years later, the voters of central Indiana elected another Muslim, André Carson, to the House of Representatives. Carson—also an African American convert to Islam—served with an anti-terrorism unit in the Indiana Department of Homeland Security.

Many persons from Islamic nations are registered to vote, and naturalization rates for immigrants from those countries are higher than Latinos but below that of most South and East Asians. Dispersal around the country, however, complicates efforts to forge a concentrated political bloc.

Despite their lack of political organization and their vulnerability to the long arm of the state, Muslims are still drawn to the United States and still consider it to be a land of opportunity. The years immediately following 9/11 saw immigration from Islamic nations fall by as much as a third, due mostly to the heightened security measures, but the numbers rebounded as bureaucratic and other pressures eased. Immigrants from Bangladesh, Turkey, Algeria, and other Muslim nations rose by twenty percent beginning in 2004.

The newcomers arrive with wildly diverse, and even divergent, aspirations. Two young Turkish women, for example, came to New York City in part so they could wear the *hijab* then banned by the secular Turkish state. Meanwhile, a twenty-five-year-old Pakistani woman, who had worn a headscarf since the age of ten, removed her *hijab* very shortly after her arrival in Brooklyn. "I got freedom in this country," the Pakistani woman told the *New York Times*. "Freedom of everything. Freedom of thought. ... I came to the United States because I want to improve myself. This is a second birth for me."[33]

While some came for religious or political freedom, others of course came for better job prospects. Unlike the mostly unskilled and poorly paid Muslims who arrived around the turn of the twentieth century, today's Muslim immigrants are on average better paid and better educated than their native-born counterparts. A survey conducted by Queens College in New York City during the late 1990s found that contrary to the stereotype of Muslims becoming taxi drivers, the most common occupation among Muslims was business owner or manager.[34] Another recent survey confirmed that the post-1965 émigrés from the Middle East were extremely well educated and twice as likely as Americans to run their own businesses.[35] As such, Muslim Americans have rapidly moved into the middle class and assimilated into American life in the early twenty-first century.

One difficulty for this growing Muslim middle class is buying a home when the Koran seems to forbid paying or receiving interest. Most *halal* Islamic financing occurs on the basis of partnerships or lease-to-buy arrangements, although even Islamic scholars differ on exactly what kinds of transactions should be permitted. Several companies and bank divisions have sprung up to provide services tailored to Islamic religious law. One banker, the head of global Islamic finance at HSBC Bank USA, said his program was aimed at the American Muslim "who believes in his religious values but at the same time is proud to be an American and wants the American dream of owning a car and a home."[36]

For traditional American Muslims who believe American society is too permissive and secular, the mosque is the center of religious life. The country's largest mosque was built in 2005 in Dearborn, Michigan, and caters to that city's predominantly Shia Muslim population. Most mosques in the United States are Sunni and occupy much smaller quarters, often buildings formerly used as houses, offices, or churches. About 2,000 imams minister to the American devout, and they represent a considerable diversity of theological and political views. Some imams, like religious leaders in other faiths, are critical of American foreign policy. The vast majority preaches a moderate, flexible theology and a conciliatory political line. Some mosques cater to one specific ethnic group while others host a more ecumenical membership. As much as eighty percent of the American Muslim population is not associated with any mosque.[37]

Muslims have also created a variety of organizations devoted to Islamic values, some of which are self-consciously moderate. In Pennsylvania, a group of Muslims founded an Islamic day camp to nurture adults as well as children. Its slogan was: "No to terrorism, yes to moderation."[38] Other organizations range from local study groups to college Muslim student organizations to national charities. The two most visible political organizations are the Council on American-Muslim Relations (CAIR), a civil liberties advocacy group, and the Arab-American Anti-Discrimination Committee, a civil rights organization.

In concentrated Muslim communities such as Dearborn—commonly considered the heart of Arab America—a variety of businesses and community groups serve the local population. Entire city blocks are filled with shops and storefronts covered in Arabic signage. At Fordson High School, where enrollment is ninety-percent Muslim, the football

Iqbal Quadir, founder and director of the Legatum Center for Development and Entrepreneurship at the Massachusetts Institute of Technology, has launched several successful businesses.

team holds its practices in the dead of night during Ramadan to allow the student athletes to eat a meal before going on the field and then hydrate during practice. One player expressed his approval by saying that practice without the modified schedule would be impossible. "No way," he said, "You'd dehydrate or faint. It's not happening without water."[39]

Women's status has been a major challenge for American Muslims. Muslim women in the United States appear to be more highly educated than women in every other ethnic group except perhaps Jews and Asian Indians. A good number also work paying jobs, something that is not common among the women of their homelands. Some Muslim women who enjoyed few rights in their home societies have begun to reject the notion of arranged marriages and to insist upon more democratic decision-making in the household. Others have opened their own businesses and become involved in Islamic organizational life. Among the most notable women's organizations are Muslim Women Lawyers for Human Rights, Muslim Women's Services, and the North American Council for Muslim Women. In 2006, Ingrid Mattson, a professor at Hartford Seminary in Hartford, Connecticut, was elected as the first woman president of the Islamic Society of North America, the largest umbrella Islamic organization in the United States and Canada. Some men reportedly did not approve.

Muslims can be found working in jobs across the income scale. Somalis, for example, who often lack English-language skills and educational accomplishments, labor alongside Latinos in the meat and chicken processing plants of the Upper Midwest. Some Arab American Muslims work white-collar jobs while others operate grocery stores and other small businesses. Because Muslims are better educated than most immigrants and many Americans, the highly educated are notable for their contributions to American society.

The contributions of elite Muslims are outstanding, especially in view of the hostility they often face for their religion. South Asia has been a particularly rich source of well-educated Muslim immigrants who thrive in America. These include the Bengali-born architect Fazlur Khan (who designed some of America's most famous skyscrapers), the Afghan-born diplomat Zalmay Khalilzad (who served as ambassador to Iraq, Afghanistan, and the United Nations during the second administration of George W. Bush), and the Indian-born journalist Fareed Zakariya (who currently serves as an editor for *Time* magazine).

Born in Bangladesh in 1958, Iqbal Quadir has been one of the most notable economic contributors to his home country as well as the United States. Quadir conceived what would later become his multibillion-dollar business idea while he was still a teenager living in Bangladesh. After spending an entire day attempting to track down medicine for his sick brother, Quadir became convinced of the necessity and efficiency of an advanced telecommunications network for rural villagers in Bangladesh. After coming to America in 1976, he received two advanced degrees and in the 1990s founded Grameenphone, the largest telecommunications operator in Bangladesh today. Quadir's goal was to enable the rural poor to contact medical professionals, but also to seek employment opportunities. In Bangladesh over a hundred-million persons eventually gained access to the network. Quadir was also active in several global microfinance ventures and is also the founder and director of the Legatum Center for Development and Entrepreneurship at the Massachusetts Institute of Technology.

Quadir's desire to aid his native land is not atypical; immigrant remittances have developed into an important source of funds for emerging nations. For example, Bangladesh received 10.8 billion dollars in remittances in 2010, and was one of the top receivers of such funds. Some twenty-five billion dollars in remittances were recorded in the Middle East in that year.[40] Because remittances are so vital to Middle Eastern and South Asian economies, some countries have encouraged American immigration despite the fact that it siphons off much of their top talent.

Doctors are a key occupational subgroup in the elite Muslim diaspora, many of whom are Pakistani Americans. Foreign-born doctors are extremely important to the American medical community, with about 100,000 practicing in the United States. Many of these physicians set up practices in rural or small-town locations that would otherwise go without a medical professional. Asian Indians are by far the largest group of the foreign physicians, but Pakistanis have been numerous enough to form their own organization, the Association of Physicians of Pakistani Descent of North America (APPNA). By 2010, the group counted more than 12,000 members and ran free medical clinics in more than half of the states. At the opening of one such clinic in Florida, Pakistani doctor Husam Zarad drew the connection between medical service and religion: "Charity and doing good make up the Third Pillar of Islam," he said. "And after talking about this for so long, we decided to make it really happen. I'm losing sleep just to think of the benefits this will bring for the community."[41]

South Asia was not the only region to produce highly skilled or highly educated Muslim immigrants. Thousands who fled from Iran to escape the religious revolution in 1979 were among the elite of that society. Fully one-half of immigrants from Iran held bachelor's degrees and nearly half were estimated to be Muslims. Among this group were physicians—about 8,000 strong in 2010. Also included were many scientists and professors who secured faculty posts in American universities.

Perhaps the best-known Muslim scientist from the Middle East is Ahmed Zewail, who was born on the banks of the Nile River in Egypt in 1946. After attending college at the University of Alexandria, Zewail came to America to receive his PhD at the

University of Pennsylvania and a postdoctoral fellowship at the University of California in Berkeley. He eventually took up a professorship at Cal Tech, naturalized in 1982, and pursued his research interests in *femtochemistry*—the study of very fast chemical reactions as they occur. In 1999, Zewail was honored with a Nobel Prize in Chemistry. When President Barack Obama announced a new program to promote better relations between the United States and Muslims worldwide, he appointed Zewail to become the first US science envoy to the Islamic world.

Because much of the post-1965 immigration from Muslim countries is so recent—and because the Muslim American second generation is only just now coming of age—its impact on American society is not yet quantifiable. One thing, however, is clear: in a world where nearly a quarter of the total population is Muslim, there is a vast reservoir of talent, potential, ideas, and know-how residing in the Islamic nations around the globe. Despite the outpouring of popular Islamophobia and the heavy-handed government response in the wake of 9/11, many of these promising and upcoming Muslims still want to come to America. It would be both foolish and tragic if the United States allows fears of terrorism to keep this talent abroad.

Endnotes

[1] Ralph Blumenthal, "Muslim Prayers and Renewal Near Ground Zero," *New York Times*, December 8, 2009.

[2] Javier C. Hernandez, "Vote Endorses Muslim Center Near Ground Zero," *New York Times*, May 26, 2010.

[3] Michael Barbaro, "Mosque Plan Clears Hurdle in New York," *New York Times*, August 3, 2010.

[4] Gail Russell Chadock, "Peter King Hearings: Are American Muslims the Problem or the Solution," *Christian Science Monitor*, March 10, 2011.

[5] Edward Wyatt, "3 Republicans Criticize Obama's Endorsement of Mosque," *New York Times*, August 14, 2010.

[6] Nick Bilton, "A Twitter Flub Becomes a 'Word of the Year,'" *New York Times*, November 15, 2010.

[7] Editorial, "Mistrust and the Mosque," *New York Times*, September 3, 2010.

[8] Paul Vitello, "Planners of Mosque Considering New Project," *New York Times*, March 29, 2010.

[9] Paul Vitello, "Heated Opposition to a New Mosque," *New York Times*, June 10, 2010.

[10] Laurie Goodstein, "Across Nation, Mosque Projects Meet Opposition," *New York Times*, August 7, 2010.

[11] Pam Belluck, "Intolerance and an Attempt to Make Amends Unsettle a Chicago Suburb's Muslims," *New York Times*, August 10, 2010.

[12] United States Department of Homeland Security, *Statistical Yearbook* (Washington, DC, 2008), 6. Immigration authorities recorded only a few persons other than "Turkey in Asia."

[13] Quoted in Kambiz Ghanea Bassiri, *A History of Islam in America* (New York: Cambridge University Press, 2010), 141.

[14] DHS, *Statistical Yearbook*, 2008. 8. Only a few thousand of these immigrants hailed from the Middle East and practically no Asians.

[15] Bassiri, *Islam in America*, 173.

[16] United States Department of Homeland Security, *Statistical Yearbook* (Washington, DC, 2009), 12–13. From 2000–2009, Bangladesh averaged fewer than 10,000 entrants annually and Pakistan about 16,000. Indonesia accounted for fewer than 3,000 annually in that period.

[17] For Iranian American immigrants, see Shirin Hakimzadeh and David Dixon, "Spotlight on the Iranian Foreign Born," (Migration Information Source, June 1, 2006), 1–6. Most immigrants from Iran came as regular immigrants, not as refugees.

[18] DHS, *Statistical Yearbook* (2008), 40; DHS, "Refugees and Asylees," 2010. Afghan refugees numbered less than a thousand annually and the numbers dropped after 9/11. Under pressure, the federal government did admit an increasing number of Iraqi refugees, who numbered 18,000 in 2008. Many more entered as regular immigrants.

[19] DHS, *Statistical Yearbook* (2008), 49. Somali refugees averaged 9,000 between 2000 and 2008.

[20] Yvonne Yazbeck Haddad, "The Shaping of American and Muslim Identity in the United States," in *Immigration and Religion in America*, ed. Richard Alba, Albert J. Raboteau, and Josh DeWind (New York: New York University Press, 2009), 248.

[21] Daniel Pipes and Khalid Duran, "Muslim Immigrants in the United States" (Center for Immigration Studies, August 2002), 6.

[22] Quoted in Lori Peek, *Behind the Backlash: Muslim Americans After 9/11* (Philadelphia: Temple University Press, 2011), 117.

[23] Sam Wood, "Muslim Fired for Wearing Headscarf is Reinstated," *Philadelphia Enquirer*, October 20, 2010.

[24] Quoted in Peek, *Beyond the Backlash*, 118.

[25] Chris Hawley and Matt Apuzzo, "NYPD Infiltration of Colleges Raises Privacy Fears," Associated Press, October 11, 2011.

[26] United States Department of State, International Information Programs, "President Bush Honors Islam Holy Month," December 7, 2001.

[27] Laurie Goodstein, "Military Clerics Balance Arms and Allah," *New York Times*, October 7, 2001.

[28] "Muslim Chaplain Sees Historic Role in Army," *New York Times*, Dec. 25, 1993; Goodstein, "Military Clerics."

[29] Pew Research Center Publications, "Muslims Americans: Middle Class and Mostly Mainstream," May 22, 2007.

[30] Laurie Goodstein, "Poll Finds U.S. Muslims Thriving, but Not Content," *New York Times*, March 2, 2009.

[31] Alejandro Beutel, "Data on Post 9/11 Terrorism in the United States" (Muslim Public Affairs Council: January 2012), 2–3.

[32] Laurie Goodstein and Tamar Lewin, "Victims of Mistaken Identity, Sikhs Pay a Price for Turbans," *New York Times*, September 19, 2001.

[33] Andrea Elliott, "More Muslims Arrive in U.S., After 9/11 Dip," *New York Times*, September 10, 2006.

[34] Dylan Loeb McClain, "Immigrant Muslim Workers: Few Drive Taxis, Many Are Managers," *New York Times*, November 14, 2001.

[35] See Aaron Terragas, "Middle Eastern and North African Immigration to the United States" (Migration Information Source, March 2011); Steven A. Camarota, "Immigrations from the Middle East: A Profile of the Foreign-born Population from Pakistan to Morocco" (Center for Immigration Studies, August 2002).

[36] Susan Sachs, "Muslims in U.S. Seek Financing; Pursuing the American Dream While Following the Koran," *New York Times*, July 5, 2001.

[37] Yvonne Yazbeck Haddad, *Becoming American: The Forging of Arab and Muslim Identity in Pluralist America* (Waco, Texas: Baylor University Press, 2011), 30.

[38] Neil MacFarquar, "At a Muslim Camp, Studies Before Sports," *New York Times*, August 26, 1995.

[39] Jeré Longman, "All-Nighters Keep Football Team Competitive During Ramadan," *New York Times*, August 10, 2011.

[40] Global Remittances Guide: Migration Policy Institute Data Hub (2010).

[41] Chandra Broadwater, "Muslim Doctors to Open Clinic in Brooksville," *St. Petersburg Times*, June 11, 2008.

Naturalization ceremonies in 1917 (top) and 2011 (bottom). The faces of America's immigrants look different, but their courage, determination, and ability to contribute to American society remain unchanged.

IMMIGRANT STRUGGLES, IMMIGRANT GIFTS

IMMIGRANT GIFTS

By Charlie Riggs

I n 1906, a New York Baptist minister named Howard B. Grosse expressed an anxiety as characteristic of our own time as of his. Near the beginning of his treatise on immigration and religious reform entitled, *The Incoming Millions,* Grosse described a recent visit to the United States Immigration Station at Ellis Island, where ships carrying immigrants to New York City landed and the newcomers disembarked. Grosse was given a tour of the facilities and told that on the day before his tour, some twelve thousand people had been processed at Ellis Island. In the past year, the number had approached one million.

In the main hallway, Grosse observed a cadre of bureaucrats and doctors standing by to issue paperwork and to check the new arrivals for infectious diseases. Trailing away from this huddle down the entrance stairway, Grosse beheld a great, snaking line of humanity. This great line, he rhapsodized, was

> the main current of that great stream of peoples constantly moving westward from the crowded and downtrodden quarters of the globe to the freer lands and the breathing spaces where life promises brighter possibilities. The stream is forced onward for the most part, by the hope of better things which centuries of dreary poverty, spiritless toil, and unending oppression have failed to crush. . . . When our visitor [Grosse] at last boards the ferry which will carry him back to New York, he still sees in imagination that swarming immigrant stream which is so potent for good or ill to the nation he loves. He finds himself wondering as to the future of the throngs who daily pass through the Gateway of the Republic, and wondering as to the future of the nation which admits them.[1]

Grosse was generally sympathetic to the immigrants' struggles, and the rest of his book registers a plea to religious leaders to establish settlement houses and religious outreach programs to help the immigrants assimilate into American life. In the above passage and elsewhere, however, his ruminations on the "immigrant flood," or "invading army" as he also called it, betrayed a deep anxiety that the numbers were simply too large for the United States to properly absorb. "In 1905," he wrote nervously, "it overtopped the million mark by 26,499 (1,026,499), and in the year ending June 30, 1906, it reached the highest recorded point, with a total of 1,100,735. There is no reason to suppose that this enormous rate will diminish, so long as our prosperity continues to invite."[2]

The history and continued prosperity of the United States since 1906 dramatically demonstrates that Howard Grosse worried mostly for naught. The essays included in *Immigrant Struggles, Immigrant Gifts* were assembled to allay the fears of the Howard Grosses of our own time. They are not addressed to outright xenophobes or bigots, who are mostly unpersuadable. Rather, they are aimed at the skeptics who feel naturally sympathetic toward immigrants but anxious about the meaning and consequences of their arrival on so large a scale.

Contemporary opponents of immigration like to claim that the United States is today being buffeted by a wave of immigrants both massive and unprecedented. Massive? Unquestionably. But unprecedented? How do our own "incoming millions" compare to Howard Grosse's back at the beginning of the twentieth century?

It is true that the number of arrivals in recent decades has been staggering. In recent years a little over a million legal immigrants arrive annually to the United States, far more than to any other country on the planet. Another 400,000 or so enter the country without documentation, although that number has fallen off dramatically in the past two years. In the almost five decades since the passage of the landmark 1965 immigration law, the foreign-born population of the United States has more than trebled to 37 million in 2010, twelve percent of the total population.

Impressive as the numbers are, however, they mask important continuities with our nation's past. Throughout its history the United States has enjoyed several periods of great immigration that rival the present, seemingly unique, era of influx. The 1840s and 1850s saw the arrival of mostly German and Irish immigrants on a scale, relative to the total population, that has gone unmatched before or since. In the four decades surrounding the turn of the twentieth century, nearly twenty-five million people came into the United States. Almost 1.3 million arrived in 1907 alone, making the year after Howard Grosse toured Ellis Island the peak year of legal immigration in all American history. Although the immigration of the past two decades has been more sustained than its earlier counterparts, the arrivals from those earlier times constituted a significantly larger portion of the overall population than they do today.

In short, we have been here before. The "new" immigrants of the post-1965 period may not, and almost certainly will not, repeat the history of their immigrant predecessors in every particular. But even a cursory glance at that earlier history reveals some illuminating parallels between past and present. To any observer of the contemporary scene, the foregoing chapters of this book will have suggested several continuities.

The starkest and most obvious of these are between the various, damaging things that have been said, then and now, about this country's immigrants. Over the past one hundred and fifty years, the character of American nativism has been in equal parts tenacious and tedious. Over and over again, nativists in the United States have deployed the same, tired arguments against wave after wave of immigration, mostly regardless of time and circumstance. Immigrants, according to their critics, are freeloaders, job stealers, criminals, bearers of disease, and peddlers of dangerous, foreign, subversive political doctrines. These recurring slanders have been expressed by different people, in different contexts, and in different rhetorical garb, but they all belong to the same vicious and boring ideological refrain.

Economic anxiety has always been one of the most important notes in this refrain. It is no coincidence that some of the worst periods of nativist agitation in American history have been simultaneous with economic downturns. The 1890s, an era of economic depression the likes of which would not be seen again until the 1930s, saw a great and feverish surge in anti-immigrant sentiment and some of the ugliest episodes of intolerance against immigrants in the country's history. Two of these, the New Orleans lynchings of 1891 and the Lattimer Massacre of 1897, were profiled in the pages of this book.

In times of economic upheaval, many native-born Americans have turned their ire on the foreigners in their midst, who they imagine have stolen their rightful jobs and opportunities. During the 1870s, Chinese workers on the West Coast were maligned as "coolie" contract laborers, whom greedy capitalists were said to have shipped in from abroad and exploited for their willingness to accept subhuman wages. Similar prejudices later targeted Greek immigrants in the meatpacking plants of the Midwest, east European Slavs in the coal fields of Pennsylvania, and more recently, Mexican immigrants in numerous industries all over the country today.

Like most prejudices springing from economic distress, these sentiments have not been notable for their logic or consistency. In the initial stages of a group's introduction to the American workforce, its constituents have frequently been pictured as "coolies," "scabs," or the docile and malleable playthings of oligarchs, too servile and degraded to demand an honest wage. But then when the immigrants have begun to press for better wages, often by joining organized labor movements, the nativists have tarred them with the brush of socialism or radicalism.

Indeed, some of the worst slings against immigrants have been for their supposed allegiance to radical doctrines from overseas. German immigrants who came to the United States in the wake of the failed 1848 revolutions were seen by many as the carriers of a dangerous breed of liberalism foreign to American life. Later, Germans gained a reputation in some quarters as anarchists and socialists, especially after the notorious Haymarket riots of 1886. In the early 1920s, the specter of Bolshevism hovered over Jewish and east European immigrants. During the 1970s, fears of Islamic radicalism dogged some Iranian exiles who were in fact the victims of the Iranian Revolution rather than its partisans.

The fear of foreign religions, as much as of foreign politics, has exercised American nativists, both then and now. In the pre-Civil War period, a deep tradition of anti-Catholicism culminated in a succession of bloody riots and the briefly prominent Know Nothing political movement of the 1850s. Anti-Catholicism lived on after the Civil War, too, in the American Protective Association during the 1890s, in the Ku Klux Klan during the 1920s, and in the campaign of denunciation against Al Smith's presidential bid in 1928.

These venerable prejudices have their modern-day counterparts. Like Catholicism in the nineteenth century, Islam today has raised fears about the conflicting loyalties of its adherents. Now as then, this religion has been maligned as incompatible with American traditions of political liberty. Now as then, these arguments shed more light on their advocates than they do on Muslims or Catholics or American political liberty.

Wars and conflicts abroad have been other perennial stirrers of the nativist pot. German immigrants enjoyed a relatively easy transition into American life compared to other groups, until the First World War put them on the wrong side of a massive geopolitical conflict mobilizing the whole of American society. Similarly, few Americans took much notice of the country's growing population of immigrants from the Middle East and other parts of the Muslim world until the attacks of September 11, 2001. In both cases, a widespread fear of an "enemy within" produced a noxious atmosphere of bigotry and intolerance.

Immigrants, in the nativist mind, have been infected with physical contagions as well as ideological and religious ones. Over and over again, hysteria has gripped the American public surrounding the germs and maladies immigrants supposedly carry with them from their home countries. When Lou Dobbs maintains that illegal immigrants to the United States have been the cause of a leprosy epidemic—the very existence of which is a farce—he belongs to a long and storied tradition of such claims in American life. In the eighteenth century it was scarlet fever, also known as "Palatine fever," after the German immigrants who allegedly bore it. In the antebellum era, it was cholera, thought to be especially prevalent among the Irish. In the early twentieth century, it was tuberculosis, or the "Jewish disease." More recently, Haitian immigrants have found themselves burdened with the stigma of AIDS.[3]

Crime, like disease, is a mark of degeneracy that nativists have been all too eager to link with immigration. Today, the widespread fear of immigrant criminality is bizarre, given that crime rates are lower among immigrants than among the native born.[4] In their own time, Irish, Chinese, and Italian communities in America were blamed for bringing vice to American shores. The stigma of crime has particularly, and quite unjustly, followed Italians. The Italian "dago" and *Mafioso* were congenitally criminal types in the popular mind: the "dago" a violent, hot-tempered vagrant, and the *Mafioso* a member of an all-powerful underworld crime syndicate. The New Orleans episode of 1891 did more than perhaps any other incident to cement these reputations in the popular imagination.

Language about "dirty," "criminal," and "dusky" immigrants inevitably had, and continues to have, a racial edge. Even in the nineteenth century, when most immigrants were what would today be considered "white," many native-born Americans saw newcomers from Ireland, Italy, and eastern Europe as belonging to inferior racial stock. These prejudices arguably grew even worse in the early twentieth century, as pseudoscientific theories of race proliferated among intellectual elites. Even if these European immigrants did not face the same level of prejudice as African Americans, they occupied an "in between" status, aspiring to but falling short of whiteness.

Those immigrants with even less of a claim to whiteness, like the West Coast Chinese, obviously fared worse than Europeans in this racially charged atmosphere. In the nineteenth-century nativist mind, the Chinese immigrant was filthy, androgynous, and criminal by birth. He belonged to a race of "heathens" and "barbarians" that if allowed would overrun the whole of "White civilization." This racist discourse played no small part in the recurrent incidents of violence directed against Chinese immigrants in the late nineteenth century and the pattern of legal discrimination culminating in the Chinese Exclusion Act of 1882.

Contemporary America may be a good deal more enlightened in these matters than it once was, but we are still haunted by the specter of racial bigotry. Black immigrants find themselves lumped together with African Americans on one side of the color line. Present-day immigrants from China and other parts of East Asia encounter many of the old canards directed against their immigrant forerunners. Many of the same racist stereotypes that have historically dogged the Chinese are now employed to describe different, newer groups. Mexican immigrants, in particular, encounter language about "hoards" and "invasions" from the dusky regions south of the border.

The stubborn way these tropes reprise and repeat themselves over the decades is indeed one of the central ironies and tragedies of American immigration history. For today's nativists are yesterday's immigrants. This is true in the obvious sense that all inhabitants of the United States, with the arguable exception of Native Americans, are either descended from immigrants or are themselves immigrants. Those who press the anti-immigrant case most tirelessly give voice to arguments that in another time (sometimes quite recently) would have been used to bar the entry of their own parents or grandparents to the country.

In some cases, the forgetting process has been almost instantaneous. Irish laborers initiated the anti-Chinese agitations on the West Coast as they saw the Chinese as competing for the same jobs they were after. Their leader, the firebrand populist Denis Kearney, was himself an immigrant from Ireland. Earlier, the shock troops of anti-Irish nativism in the 1840s and 1850s were not only immigrants, but *Irish* immigrants: Ulster Protestants, or "Scotch Irish," whose deep anti-Catholicism trumped any solidarity they may have felt with fellow immigrants or fellow Irishmen.

More often, it has taken a generation or two of upward social mobility for amnesia to fully set in. As soon as groups have achieved some modicum of social standing or respectability, they have repeated the pattern of finding a new group to scorn, of climbing upwards while kicking downwards. Italians, Greeks, east European Slavs, and other groups have all used their racial status as nominal "whites" to contrast themselves favorably with other groups, such as Asians or African Americans. Even within ethnic or religious groups this dynamic has been at work: established German Jews, for example, were frequently contemptuous of their immigrant coreligionists from Russia and the Ukraine.

Perhaps Grover Cleveland illustrated the dynamic best in 1898 when he vetoed a proposed literacy test requirement for new arrivals that would have restricted immigration from eastern and southern Europe. In those days, this was what was known as the "new immigration" or the "recent immigration," as contrasted with the "old immigration" of Germans, Irish, and Scandinavians from the mid-nineteenth century. "It is said that the quality of recent immigration is undesirable," Cleveland wrote. "The time is quite within recent memory when the same thing was said of immigrants who, with their descendants, are now numbered among our best citizens."[5]

The nativist will respond to this argument that the comparison between then and now is flawed, that the new immigrants are less capable of advancement or assimilation than their forerunners, that "this time, it's different." But, as Cleveland's words suggest, the claim of novelty is itself an old saw, as tired as any other in the nativist arsenal.

Of course, "this time" is always different, in one way or another. Concerning immigrants, however, the story has been the same often enough to cast serious doubt on the alarmist claims of novelty put forward by restrictionists. Especially since many of the supposedly new and disturbing features they detect in contemporary immigration also belonged to that of earlier periods, to groups whose status in American life is now considered uncontroversial. In the long view, many of the supposed "defects" in today's immigration—poverty, urban overcrowding, return migration—begin to appear as mere growing pains, inevitable and temporary, accompanying the introduction of new citizens into a society in any age.

By historical standards, these problems are all mild today. Throughout American history, immigrants have tended to be poor upon their arrival. In this respect, the turn-of-the-century critics of immigration may have had a more legitimate gripe than those of today. Historically, the overwhelming majority of immigrants started near the very bottom rung of the American socioeconomic ladder—as miners, construction workers, sweatshop hands, domestic servants, and the like—and slowly, painfully worked their way up. By contrast, contemporary immigrants include not only the traditional low-wage earners but also a much larger stratum of well-educated and well-trained professionals: Indian software programmers, Chinese businessmen, Iranian doctors, Filipino nurses, and so on.

There are, of course, large numbers of unskilled workers among today's new arrivals, mostly from Latin America. And like their immigrant forbears, these highly motivated migrants, toiling away in agriculture or the service industry, display encouraging signs of upward mobility in their levels of income and educational attainment. The small lag experienced in these areas by Mexican and other Latin American immigrants, compared to their turn-of-the-century predecessors from eastern and southern Europe, reflects structural economic trends of widening inequality in our post-industrial economy. In any case, the direction of low-wage immigrants is clearly up.[6]

The repeating pattern of upward mobility in subsequent generations is one of the reasons why it is narrow and foolish to insist that immigrants must contribute immediately to validate their presence in the United States. It is all well and good that many of today's immigrants possess graduate degrees and high levels of technical training, but even a brief look at the history of American immigration supports the importance of the long view, in which more modest immigrants also make significant contributions; and if they do not achieve great heights themselves, they produce children who will.

Crowded ethnic neighborhoods are another inevitable byproduct of mass immigration that existed as surely in the past as they do in the present. Many old ethnic enclaves in big cities, formerly the exclusive provinces of Irish or Italians or Jews, now host large communities of West Indians or East Asians or West Africans. Some striking examples of this phenomenon in New York City include the Flatbush section of Brooklyn, Little Italy in lower Manhattan, and parts of the South Bronx.

Malden, Massachusetts, just outside of Boston (and home to The Immigrant Learning Center) was a largely working-class Italian and Jewish city for the better part of the twentieth century, but in the past twenty years Malden has experienced a dramatic demographic turnover led by Haitian, North African, Salvadoran, Chinese, and Vietnamese immigrants—many of them sharing extremely tight quarters. Whether this state of affairs represents a disorderly, urban scrum or a vibrant, diverse mélange of ethnic groups depends on one's point of view. In either case, it is worth noting that contemporary immigration is much more evenly dispersed throughout the country than it was in the past, thus limiting the overcrowding effects in any one city or neighborhood.

Restrictionists allege that the close proximity of the countries nowadays sending the most immigrants to America sharply sets off today's immigration from its predecessors. However, as one of the final chapters in this book attests, emigration from Mexico to the United States has a long pedigree, going back at least to the 1880s and continuing, on and off, with varying degrees of encouragement and resistance, throughout the twentieth century. The supposedly "new" Mexican immigration is hardly that new.

It is also false that the contemporary immigrants from south of the border differ so much from the Irish or Italians or Poles of yesteryear that we cannot draw pertinent lessons from the experiences of these earlier groups. The relative transience of Mexican immigrants is imagined to mark them as permanently mobile and inassimilable. Even acknowledging the high rates of return migration among Mexicans, it is equally true that earlier generations of American immigrants did exactly the same thing. Millions of temporary migrants from Italy, Greece, and eastern Europe came to the United States with every intention of working for a few years, saving money, and returning to their home countries.

In 1909, when the anti-immigrant Dillingham Commission issued its report, the commissioners wrote:

> The old immigration movement was essentially one of permanence. The new immigration is very largely one of individuals, a considerable proportion of whom apparently have no intention of changing their residence, their only purpose in coming to America being to temporarily take advantage of the greater wages paid for industrial laboring in this country.

History has shown that in time the Slavic and Italian worker migrants settled down permanently, to such a degree in fact, that in the minds of many nativists the "new immigration" thought to be so transitory in 1909 now forms a favorable contrast to the "*new* new immigration" of Mexicans, Central Americans, West Indians, and others.

As is true today, the immigrants of yesteryear maintained strong ties with the politics and culture of their home counties—Greek Americans nurtured the "Great Idea" of pan-Greek unification, while east European Slavs read foreign language newspapers that kept them connected to political and cultural debates back home. Refugees, from all periods of American history, have been authoritative witnesses and compelling advocates for the plight of those left behind. Irish American nationalists were frequently more militant and anti-British than their counterparts in Ireland. In this context, it seems more than a bit silly to feel threatened by Mexican flags or Spanish-language television.

None of this is to deny that there are no costs or downsides to immigration, either then or now. It is not the purpose of this book to anachronistically "rebut" the claims of yesterday's nativists or to suggest that no immigrant ever performed a criminal act, or bore an infectious disease, or contributed to native unemployment by his or her presence. Instead, it is to show that in the long run we should be thankful for the impressive record of the immigrant heritage in America. A more balanced appraisal reveals that in historical hindsight, the claims of the restrictionists are distinctly overwrought and overblown; the contributions of immigrants serve as a massive and persuasive rejoinder to those who assert similar claims today.

The contributions of immigrants are legion. So much of what we take for granted today stems from the sweat and toil of the foreign born, from the building of our transportation infrastructure to such great engineering feats as the Brooklyn Bridge to innovations as disparate as the washing machine, Levi's blue jeans, and alternating electrical current. In every area of American life—politics, culture, academics, science, medicine, the military, and every aspect of the American economy—immigrants and the children of immigrants have added their invaluable talents, creativity, energy, and work.

Over the years, low-wage immigrant workers have dedicated their labor to the many unglamorous but necessary tasks of laying rail, mining coal, and milling steel that made America's industrialization and sustained economic growth possible. Immigrants have also started businesses large and small. The countless mom-and-pop Greek restaurants, Italian fruit stands, and Chinese laundries were as important in this respect as larger and more famous concerns such as Pfizer (founded by a German immigrant) or Bank of America (founded by an Italian immigrant).

Once again, the similarities between past and present stand out. The later chapters in this book address many of the concrete ways in which immigrants contribute to the contemporary economy: Mexicans in landscaping, the construction trades, and agriculture; Pakistani doctors; Somali meatpackers; Arab grocers. This is but a sampling of the immigrant presence in the contemporary American workforce. A growing body of economic research confirms in the aggregate what these examples suggest anecdotally: immigration is a great asset for the American economy.

Whatever other blessings or costs they may bring, the foreign born add to the nation's income by something in the vicinity of thirteen percent annually—slightly greater than their share of the population. This means that America's gross domestic product is over an eighth bigger—about 1.8 trillion dollars these days—than it would be without our large population of immigrants in the workforce. Most of this income accrues to the immigrants themselves, but natives benefit from the presence of the foreign born in other ways.[7]

Many Americans assume that if an immigrant takes a job, it must mean that some luckless, native-born citizen is out of one. For a variety of reasons, the labor market rarely works this way. To begin with, immigrant workers are also consumers. They may vie for jobs, but they also create demand for goods and services, thus minting new growth, new businesses, and new job opportunities in the process. If the job market automatically tightened every time it added new workers, we would all have cause to rue the graduation of every college senior. Obviously, we do not, because those newly employed graduates buy groceries and drive cars and purchase real estate and engage in the multifarious forms of consumption that make our economy tick. The same is true of immigrants.

If there is any cause for anxiety over the economic effects of immigration, it concerns only the employment and wages of high school dropouts—those at the very bottom of the socioeconomic ladder—rather than the economy generally. To say this is not to dismiss such anxieties, which are founded upon a very real stagnation in wages for America's poorest workers in the past fifteen years. But it is worth remembering that most legitimate disputes about immigration and economics occur only over this relatively narrow question. On immigration's more general beneficent effects, most economists are in broad agreement.

Even on the score of low-income workers, there is good reason to side with those who doubt that immigration makes much of a difference to their plight at all. Numerous studies comparing different local labor markets around the country have found almost no correlation between immigrant settlement and low wages or unemployment. On the contrary, many of America's most flourishing and prosperous cities, such as New York, Boston, and Chicago, are also hubs for immigrants.

Of course, immigrants are naturally attracted to cities where the job situation is already favorable, and the influx of new workers could theoretically be causing an exodus by others. The most pessimistic interpretations of American immigration peg its negative effect on the wages of high school dropouts at around five percent over the 1980s and 1990s. The same models also show a relatively modest gain for other workers. According to this "revisionist" view, the main effect of immigration over the past thirty years has been to help redistribute income away from the poor and toward the wealthy. If true, the revisionist position would form a meaningful argument for selecting for higher- (rather than lower-) wage immigrants.[8]

The problem with these conclusions and the logic that undergirds them is that they assume native and immigrant workers to be more or less interchangeable, or "perfect substitutes" in economics jargon. Research and experience suggest otherwise. Immigrants fill niches in the economy, both at the high and the low end of the income scale. In fact, immigrants are frequently what economists call "complementary" to native labor, meaning that their presence actually adds jobs and grows incomes among those already working. More Indian doctors may mean more jobs for native-born nurses or hospital administrators. More Mexican construction workers may equate to promotions for those already working on construction crews.[9]

One vivid example of "complementarity" in the American economy concerns companies planning to relocate overseas. In recent years the phenomenon of "offshoring" has received a tremendous amount of national attention. What rarely registers in this debate is that low skilled immigrants can and do alleviate the problem by furnishing relatively cheap labor here in the United States. In a globalized economy, immigrants are thus competing with foreign rather than native-born American workers. And by keeping plants and factories open in America, they preserve the associated jobs of foremen, managers, repairmen, and a whole suite of other workers in a company's supply chain.[10]

These are the kinds of indirect and positive sum phenomena that characterize so many aspects of immigration and its economic effects. Other examples abound. Some studies suggest that the recent growing availability of immigrant nannies and housekeepers has liberated native-born women to enter the labor force in greater numbers. The willingness of low-wage immigrants to relocate to other parts of the country has alleviated temporary labor shortages. Immigrants' international contacts and social networks, meanwhile, have helped American businesses to sell their products in new and emerging markets overseas.

The gains from immigration are even more obvious for highly skilled immigrants. Among native-born Americans there is an unmistakable shortage of doctors, nurses, scientists, computer programmers, engineers, and numerous other highly skilled professionals. By filling these niche roles, immigrants not only create jobs in ancillary fields but also provide socially important and necessary services. Many rural areas and small towns, for example, would lack medical care without the recent immigration of doctors from India and Pakistan. And highly educated immigrants publish patents at about twice the rate of their native-born counterparts.[11]

Immigrants are also entrepreneurs. Because they are so well represented in the science and technology fields, the foreign born have established a disproportionate number of the high-tech startups that are so important to the twenty-first century American economy. A 2005 study found that a quarter of all technology and engineering companies started in the previous decade had at least one immigrant among the founders. Unsurprisingly, many of the biggest names in American tech—Google's Sergey Brin (from Russia), Intel's Andy Grove (from Hungary), and Yahoo!'s Jerry Yang (from Taiwan)—are immigrants.

In addition to the high-profile success stories of Silicon Valley, a host of smaller shops and businesses thrive under the immigrant banner, just as they have done in the past. Visit any large American city nowadays and you are likely to find Vietnamese nail salons, Korean groceries, Mexican bodegas, Chinese restaurants, and many more such establishments. What their proprietors may lack in specialized skills or education they make up for with sheer energy and hard work. At first, these businesses often cater to their respective ethnic communities, but in time they expand to a broader clientele. They also help to revitalize struggling neighborhoods by encouraging local commerce and improving the physical appearance of the buildings they occupy.[12]

It should not be surprising that immigrants succeed as entrepreneurs, for immigration itself is an entrepreneurial act. To uproot oneself from native familiarity, to travel thousands of miles, to make a new life in trying and sometimes hostile circumstances, requires a tremendous reservoir of personal ambition and an impressive capacity for risk taking. These qualities naturally lead to individual achievement in business and other fields.

An important alchemy seems to occur when immigrants arrive in the United States. In a society without economic mobility or opportunity, talented people may be discouraged from work or may toil and innovate for naught. But on the dynamic American scene they have the chance to realize their dreams. Anyone who has spent substantial time with immigrants recognizes the peculiar immigrant energy, the drive, the special sense of restlessness and striving that emerges out of a life of emotional and physical upheaval.

In the end, however, some immigrants can only rise so far. Which is why the richest and most enduring gifts they bestow upon America are not necessarily themselves but their children. The only consolation for those who work backbreaking jobs or punishing hours with little prospect of improvement during their own lives is the hope of a better lot for their offspring. "My children are everything. The work, the difficulty, everything—it is all about improving things for my children," said one Algerian woman in Boston. The sentiment is near-universal among American immigrants.

Many immigrants speak of their children as the primary reason for coming to America. And more often than not, the children of immigrants seem to inherit their parents' restless drive. Two Salvadoran immigrants who illegally breached the Mexican border during the 1980s worked for years as vendors at a flea market in Los Angeles. Without much formal education of their own, they nevertheless nourished high hopes for their American-born son. "Never give up," they told him, "and finish the journey that we have struggled to begin." He later earned an advanced degree from MIT.[13]

In today's second generation, we are seeing a variation on an old story. While the pages of this book attest to the extraordinary accomplishments of immigrants themselves, it has only been in subsequent generations that America has fully reaped its immigration harvest. In time, the children of immigrants pay back with ample interest whatever costs their parents may have imposed when they arrived. In time, each group overcomes prejudice, produces leaders and innovators, and assimilates so well as to make the complaints of yesterday's restrictionists seem almost quaint. Except that they persist.

These people are not here to ruin society or to take away jobs. They are gifts to America. We should accept them gratefully and graciously.

Endnotes

[1] Howard Benjamin Grosse, *The Incoming Millions* (New York: Fleming H. Revel, 1906), 12–13.

[2] Ibid., 14.

[3] See Alan Kraut, *Silent Travelers: Germs, Genes, and the "Immigrant Menace"* (Baltimore: Johns Hopkins University Press, 1994).

[4] Kristen F. Butcher and Ann Morrison Piehl, "Why are Immigrants' Incarceration Rates so Low? Evidence on Selective Immigration, Deterrence, and Deportation," National Bureau of Economic Research Working Paper No. 13229, 2007, accessed June 15, 2012, http://www.nber.org/papers/w13229.

[5] Grover Cleveland, "Presidents Cleveland, Taft, and Wilson Veto Literacy Test Legislation," in Immigration Issues, ed. Henry Bischoff (Westport, CT: Greenwood Press, 2002), 167.

[6] Joel Perlmann, *Italians Then, Mexicans Now: Immigrant Origins and Second-generation Progress, 1890 to 2000* (New York: Russell Sage Foundation, 2005), 116–25.

[7] Neeraj Kaushal, Cordelia W. Reimers, and David M. Reimers, "Immigrants and the Economy," in *The New Americans: A Guide to Immigration Since 1965*, ed. Reed Ueda and Mary Waters (Cambridge: Harvard University Press, 2007), 180–81.

[8] George Borjas, "The Labor Demand Curve Is Downward Sloping: Reexamining the Impact of Immigration on the Labor Market," National Bureau of Economic Research Working Paper No. 9755, 2003, accessed June 15, 2012, http://www.nber.org/papers/w9755.

[9] Giovanni Peri and Chad Sparber, "Task Specialization, Immigration, and Wages." *American Economic Journal: Applied Economics* 1(2009): 135–69.

[10] Gianmarco I.P. Ottaviano, Giovanni Peri, and Greg C. Wright, "Immigration, Offshoring, and American Jobs," National Bureau of Economic Research Working Paper No. 16439, 2010, accessed June 15, 2012, http://www.nber.org/papers/w16439.

[11] Pia Orrenius and Madeleine Zavodny, *From Brawn to Brains: How Immigration Works for America* (Dallas: Federal Reserve Bank of Dallas, 2010), 11.

[12] Michael Liu and Paul Watanabe, *Immigrant Entrepreneurs and Neighborhood Revitalization* (Malden, MA: Immigrant Learning Center, 2005).

[13] Nga-Wing Anjela Wong, Paul Y. Watanabe, and Michael Liu, *Adult Children of Immigrant Entrepreneurs: Memories and Influences* (Malden, MA: Immigrant Learning Center, 2011), 31.

BIOGRAPHIES

CONTRIBUTORS

WAYNE A. CORNELIUS IS CO-DIRECTOR FOR EDUCATION PROGRAMS for the University of California Global Health Institute, Associate Director for the UC Center for Expertise on Migration and Health, and a Core Faculty Member of UC San Diego's Division of Global Public Health. At UCSD he is also the Theodore Gildred Distinguished Professor of Political Science and US-Mexican Relations, Emeritus, and founding Director of the Center for Comparative Immigration Studies and the Center for US-Mexican Studies. He is past President of the Latin American Studies Association, the world's largest interdisciplinary professional organization of Latin America specialists. Wayne is one of the nation's leading experts on Mexican migration to the United States and the author of 280 publications on this and related topics.

ANNA GRESSEL-BACHARAN IS AN HISTORIAN OF THE UNITED STATES, Ireland, and the United Kingdom. Her research focuses on the relationships between these three countries and their respective domestic politics. One particular area of interest for Anna has been American and Irish-American involvement in the conflicts in Northern Ireland. She studied history and political science at the Sorbonne, Sciences Po, and Georgetown. She has taught at Georgetown, the University of Cergy, the University of Versailles, and Harvard University.

NANCY FONER IS DISTINGUISHED PROFESSOR OF SOCIOLOGY at Hunter College and the Graduate Center, City University of New York. Her main area of interest is immigration. She has studied Jamaicans in their home country as well as in New York and London and has written widely on immigration to New York City. She is the author or editor of fifteen books including *From Ellis Island to JFK: New York's Two Great Waves of Immigration* (Yale University Press, 2000); *In a New Land: A Comparative View of Immigration* (New York University Press, 2005); and *Islands in the City: West Indian Migration to New York* (University of California Press, 2001). Her forthcoming book,

One Out of Three: Immigrant New York in the Twenty-First Century (Columbia University Press, 2013), is a collection of original essays that provides an in-depth and up-to-date look at immigrant New York after nearly half a century.

DAVID W. HAINES is Professor of Anthropology at George Mason University. Prior to coming to George Mason in 1997, he had worked for the federal government's refugee resettlement program. His publications include several edited volumes on refugees and immigrants, an alternative introductory anthropology text, an historical monograph on Vietnamese kinship, and various journal articles on migration, kinship, and governance. His most recent books are *Safe Haven? A History of Refugees in America* and *Wind over Water: Migration in an East Asian Context* (co-edited with Kaeiko Yamanaka and Shinji Yamashita). He is a two time Fulbright scholar (Korea and Western Europe) and past president of the Society for Urban, National, and Transnational/Global Anthropology. He was a recipient of GMU's Teaching Excellence Award in 2003.

LUCIANO J. IORIZZO is Professor of History, Emeritus, at SUNY Oswego, where he taught for 30 years. Born and raised in New York City, he earned a doctorate in American History at the Maxwell School, Syracuse University. A founding member and past president of the American Italian Historical Association, he has written two books and coauthored four others in addition to publishing scores of scholarly and popular articles and lecturing extensively on Italian immigration to the United States. His latest effort was co-editing *Italian Americans: Bridges to Italy, Bonds to America* (2010). A former chair of the Public Justice Department, he is also a recognized authority on the history of organized crime. His biography of Al Capone has been widely read and reviewed in the United States as well as abroad in China and Korea.

ALEXANDER KITROEFF is Associate Professor of History at Haverford College. He is a social historian specializing in Greek identity in the diaspora. He was born in Athens and studied in the United Kingdom where he received his D.Phil. from Oxford University in 1984. His publications include two books on the Greek diaspora: *The Greeks in Egypt, 1919–1937* and *Griegos en America, 1492–1992*. He has also written numerous chapters in other books and articles on the history of Greek Americans. He is a member of the editorial board of the *Journal of the Hellenic Diaspora*. Most recently, he served as an historical consultant for a Piraeus Bank Cultural Foundation project on the role of the Greeks in the cotton industry in Modern Egypt and for a 2007 film documentary entitled "The Journey: the Greek Dream in America."

ERIKA LEE is an American historian and Director of the Immigration History Research Center at the University of Minnesota. She is the author or co-author of the award winning books *Angel Island: Immigrant Gateway to America* (with Judy Yung, Oxford University Press, 2010) and *At America's Gates: Chinese Immigration During the Exclusion Era, 1882–1943* (University of North Carolina Press, 2003). She has given invited lectures at numerous universities, media outlets, and community organizations throughout the United States and Canada. She is currently working on *Asian Americas*, a global history of Asians in the Americas.

DEBORAH DASH MOORE IS THE FREDERICK C.L. HEUTWELL PROFESSOR of History at the University of Michigan and Director of the Jean and Samuel Frankel Center for Judaic Studies. She specializes in twentieth century American Jewish history. Her books include *At Home in America: Second Generation New York Jews; To the Golden Cities: Pursuing the American Jewish Dream in Miami and L.A.; B'nai B'rith and the Challenge of Ethnic Leadership*; the award winning two volume *Jewish Women in America: An Historical Encyclopedia*, co-edited with Paula Hyman; *G.I. Jews: How World War II Changed a Generation*; and *Gender and Jewish History*, co-edited with Marion Kaplan.

DAVID M. REIMERS IS PROFESSOR EMERITUS AT NEW YORK UNIVERSITY where he taught American history for 30 years. He is the co-author of *Ethnic Americans* (now in its fifth edition) with Leonard Dinnerstein; *Natives and Strangers* (also in its fifth edition) with Leonard Dinnerstein and Roger Nichols; and *All the Nations under Heaven: a Racial and Ethnic History of New York City* with Fred Binder. He is also the author of *Still the Golden Door: the Third World Comes to America; Unwanted Strangers: American Identity and the Turn Against Immigration*; and *Other Immigrants: The Global Origins of the American People*. He is currently writing a short history of immigration to the United States since 1945 called *New Laws, New People: Immigration and American Society since 1945* (to be published by Oxford University Press).

WILLIAM G. ROSS IS A PROFESSOR AT THE CUMBERLAND SCHOOL OF LAW in Birmingham, Alabama, where he has taught since 1988. His courses include constitutional history, constitutional law, legal ethics and civil procedure. A graduate of Stanford University and Harvard Law School, he practiced law in New York City from 1979 to 1988. He is the author of three books on American constitutional history: *A Muted Fury: Populists, Progressives and Labor Unions Confront the Courts, 1890–1937; Forging New Freedoms: Nativism, Education, and the Constitution 1917–1927*; and *The Chief Justiceship of Charles Evans Hughes, 1930–1941*. His various publications on legal ethics include a book, *The Honest Hour: The Ethics of Time-Based Billing by Attorneys*.

ROBERT M. ZECKER TEACHES US HISTORY AT SAINT FRANCIS XAVIER UNIVERSITY in Nova Scotia, with a focus on immigration, race, and ethnicity. He is the author of three books: *Streetcar Parishes: Slovak Immigrants Build their Nonlocal Communities, 1890–1945; Metropolis: The American City in Popular Culture*; and *Race and America's Immigrant Press*. He has had numerous articles published in journals such as *Ethnic Forum, American Studies, The Journal of Social History, The Oral History Review, The Journal of Popular Culture*, and *The Journal of American Ethnic History*.

EDITORS

DIANE PORTNOY IS A GRADUATE OF BOSTON UNIVERSITY and has a master's degree from Cornell University. Diane first became interested in teaching English as a second language while living in Italy during the 1970s. She then spent twenty years teaching English to immigrants and adult basic education in the Boston area. After the fall of communism, the United States saw a new influx of Eastern European immigration as well as continued immigration from Vietnam. Diane determined to establish The Immigrant Learning Center, Inc. (ILC) to provide intensive English instruction to these new arrivals in Malden, Massachusetts, where she and her parents had settled when they immigrated to the United States after World War II. As immigration became a hot political topic after 9/11, Diane expanded the mission of The ILC to promote immigrants as assets to the country through various programs, including research projects that show the positive impact immigrants continue to have on our nation's economy. Diane is an expert in the areas of adult education and immigrant issues, and she has received numerous awards in recognition for her work on behalf of immigrants, including the Ellis Island Medal of Honor.

BARRY PORTNOY IS A GRADUATE OF HARVARD COLLEGE and Cornell Law School. He was a law clerk at the US Ninth Circuit Court of Appeals and a research fellow at the Faculty of Jurisprudence at the University of Florence, Italy. Barry practiced law for twenty-five years and became chairman of a medium-sized law firm with offices in Boston, New York City, and Washington, DC. In the mid-1980s, while still working as a lawyer, he founded Reit Management and Research LLC ("RMR"). Today, Barry serves as full-time chairman of RMR, which manages eight publicly owned companies and various private businesses doing about $12 billion per year in sales and employing about 45,000. Barry is an avid reader of American history and biographies. He was recruited for this book project by his wife, Diane, who founded The Immigrant Learning Center, Inc. and who directs its operations.

CHARLIE RIGGS IS A PhD CANDIDATE IN HISTORY at Rutgers University, specializing in the cultural and intellectual history of the United States. He graduated in 2010 from Harvard College, where his senior thesis, "The Life of an Irish Libel: William Drennan's 'Address to the Volunteers of Ireland,' 1792–94" won a Hoopes Prize. He has previously worked as an editor for Morgan Reynolds Publishing and for the budget travel guide *Let's Go*. Charlie was recruited by Barry and Diane Portnoy to help develop and edit this book and has devoted almost two years to making it a reality.

PHOTOGRAPH AND ILLUSTRATION CREDITS

Front Cover

Elaine Lan Chao. US Government photo.

Felix Frankfurter. Library of Congress.

Chang-Lin Tien. John Blaustein, photographer. University of California, Berkeley.

Claude McKay. The New York Public Library.

Ahmed Zewail. Best Free Photos.

Rosario Marin. US Government photo.

John William MacKay. Wikipedia Commons.

Nicola Tesla. Library of Congress.

Francesca S. "Mother" Cabrini. Wikipedia Commons.

Dean Alfange. Wikipedia Commons.

Enrico Fermi. *World-Telegram* photo. Library of Congress.

Henry Kissinger. *U.S. News & World Report* photograph. Library of Congress.

Madeleine Albright. US Government photo.

Fazlur Khan. Wikipedia Commons.

Introduction

Page xii. Immigrants viewing the Statue of Liberty from Ellis Island. Library of Congress.

Page 7. California "Cornucopia of the World" poster. The Granger Collection. Nebraska Lands advertisement. Nebraska State Historical Society.

Chapter 1

Page 14. William Boeing. AVSIM Online.

Page 19. *New York Herald* Karl Muck editorial cartoon, 1917. W.A. Rogers, illustrator.

Page 22. Friedrich Wilhelm von Steuben postage stamp. National Postal Museum Collection, Smithsonian Institution.

Page 27. German American musicians at a picnic, 1897. Annie Sievers Schildhauer, photographer. Wisconsin Historical Society.

Page 34. Margarethe Meyer-Schurz in her Watertown, Wisconsin classroom. xtimeline. com.

Chapter 2

Page 36. Andrew Jackson. Painting by D.M. Carter, engraved by A.H. Ritchie, c. 1860. Library of Congress. John F. Kennedy, 1962. New York *World-Telegram* and the *Sun* Newspaper Photograph Collection, Library of Congress.

Page 41. *The Awful Disclosures of Maria Monk*. Publication cover.

Page 49. Irish miners in Butte, Montana, 1908. Collection of John Taylor, Bloomington, Illinois.

Page 51. Thomas Murray with Thomas Edison, 1908. Smithsonian Institution.

Chapter 3

Page 54. Mulberry Street, Little Italy, New York City, c. early 1920s. Library of Congress.

Page 57. 1891 New Orleans Italians lynching. Illustration, *History of the United States* by E. Benjamin Andrews, 1912.

Page 62, Italian American band, Pueblo, Colorado. LatinAmericanStudies.org.

Page 67, Planters Nut and Chocolate Company scene. Courtesy of Obici Healthcare Foundation.

Page 71, Amadeo P. Giannini. *The Daily Bail*.

Chapter 4

Page 74, Group of Angel Island photos. Library of Congress and National Park Service Collection.

Page 81. Lue Gim Gong. Wikipedia Commons.

Page 84. Mary Tape and family. Smithsonian Institution.

Page 89. Chang-Lin Tien. Peg Skorpinski, photographer. University of California, Berkeley.

Chapter 5

Page 96. Slovak American girl with the American flag. Courtesy of Robert M. Zecker.

Page 100. East European mine workers outside Lattimer, Pennsylvania, 1897. Pennsylvania State Archives.

Page 107. Garfield, New Jersey, Belmont Hilltops, 1919 Baseball Champs. Courtesy of Robert M. Zecker.

Page 112. Michael Pupin. Wikipedia Commons.

Chapter 6

Page 116. Irving Berlin aboard the USS *Arkansas*, 1944. US Government photo.

Page 119. *The Dearborn Independent* cover, May 22, 1920. Wikipedia Commons.

Page 124. Levi Strauss. Wikipedia Commons.

Page 127. Joseph Seligman. Wikipedia Commons.

Page 132. Carl Laemmle. Library of Congress.

Chapter 7

Page 140. George Christopher with bicycle, 1910. Lewis Wickes Hine, photographer. Library of Congress.

Page 146. Georgios Papanikolaou postage stamp. National Postal Museum Collection, Smithsonian Institution.

Page 147. Cover of *Life* magazine with Archbishop Iakovos and the Reverend Martin Luther King, Jr. © Time Life.

Page 149. Greek American sponge fishermen in Tarpon Springs, Florida, c. 1944. Library of Congress.

Page 153. Tom Carvel. ©1990, *New York Daily News* collection, Getty Images.

Chapter 8

Page 158. The SS *St. Louis* with Jewish refugees aboard, 1939. National Archives and Records Administration.

Page 161. Haitian refugees aboard vessel. 1998, Duke University Libraries, US Coast Guard photo.

Page 164. Hungarian refugees boarding a train, c. 1956. BBC News.

Page 167. Southeast Asian "boat people." US Navy photo.

Page 171. Mariel boatlift, 1980. © *Miami Herald*, Tim Chapman, photographer.

Chapter 9

Page 176. Women from Guadeloupe, French West Indies, on Ellis Island, 1911. Augustus F. Sherman, photographer. Manuscripts and Archives Division; The New York Public Library; Astor, Lenox, and Tilden Foundations.

Page 179. David Augustus Straker, 1902. General Research & Reference Division; Schomburg Center for Research in Black Culture; The New York Public Library; Astor, Lenox, and Tilden Foundations.

Page 181. Congresswoman Shirley Chisholm. Library of Congress. Congresswoman Yvette Clarke, Secretary of State Colin Powell, and Attorney General Eric Holder. US Government photos.

Page 187. West Indian Day Parade, Brooklyn. © *New York Daily News* collection, Getty Images. Todd Maisel, photographer.

Chapter 10

Page 192. Mexican worker during the Bracero Program, 1942. Dorothea Lange, photographer. Lange Collection, Oakland Museum of California.

Page 195. Pro- and anti-Proposition 187 activists, Los Angeles, 1996. © AP photo/Frank Wiese.

Page 199. Immigrant meatpacking workers. © *Lincoln Journal Star*.

Page 202. Border death. Courtesy of Peggie Peattie, photographer.

Chapter 11

Page 210. Turkish Muslim immigrants, Ellis Island, c. 1902–1913. Photography Collection; Miriam and Ira D. Wallach Division of Art, Prints, and Photographs; The New York Public Library; Astor, Lenox, and Tilden Foundations.

Page 213. Park 51 project protestors, 2010. © David Shankbone, photographer. Wikipedia Commons. Used with permission.

Page 219. The Islamic Center of America, Dearborn, Michigan. © Dane Hillard, photographer.

Page 224. Iqbal Quadir. © Siragr, photographer. Wikipedia Commons. Used with permission.

Conclusion
Page 228. Naturalization ceremony, 1917. National Park Service Collection. Naturalization ceremony, 2011. Courtesy of The Immigrant Learning Center, Inc.

Back Cover
Albert Einstein. *World-Telegram* photo. Library of Congress.
John Shalikashvili. US Government photo.
Elia Kazan. Wikipedia Commons.
Margarethe Meyer-Schurz. Wisconsin Historical Society.
George Christopher. Wikipedia Commons.
Oscar Mayer. Find A Grave.
An Wang. © Bettmann/Corbis.
Constantino Brumidi. National Archives and Records Administration.
Mary Harris "Mother" Jones. Library of Congress.
Charles Pfizer. Courtesy of Pfizer.
Thomas E. Murray. Wikipedia Commons.
Sergey Brin. Wikipedia Commons.
Sidney Poitier. National Archives and Records Administration.
Pierre Omidyar. American Academy of Achievement.

INDEX

IMMIGRANT STRUGGLES, IMMIGRANT GIFTS

IMMIGRANT STRUGGLES, IMMIGRANT GIFTS